# COMPENSATING ASBESTOS VICTIMS

*To the memory of Papà Carlo*

# Compensating Asbestos Victims
## Law and the Dark Side of Industrialization

ANDREA BOGGIO
*Bryant University, USA*

Routledge
Taylor & Francis Group

LONDON AND NEW YORK

First published 2013 by Ashgate Publishing

2 Park Square, Milton Park, Abingdon, Oxfordshire OX14 4RN
52 Vanderbilt Avenue, New York, NY 10017

*Routledge is an imprint of the Taylor & Francis Group, an informa business*

First issued in paperback 2020

**British Library Cataloguing in Publication Data**
A catalogue record for this book is available from the British Library

**The Library of Congress has cataloged the printed edition as follows:**
Boggio, Andrea.
 Compensating asbestos victims : law and the dark side of industrialization / By Andrea
 Boggio.
   pages  cm
 Includes bibliographical references and index.
 ISBN 978-1-4094-1907-5 (hardback)
1. Asbestos—Law and legislation. 2. Compensation (Law) 3. Products liability—
Asbestos. 4. Asbestosis. 5. Toxic torts. I. Title.
 K954.A83B64 2013
 346.03'8—dc23

                                                                        2013002728

ISBN 978-1-4094-1907-5 (hbk)
ISBN 978-0-367-60129-4 (pbk)

# Contents

# List of Figures

# List of Tables

# List of Acts

*Code Civile [Civil Code].* March 21, 1804 (as amended on April 6, 2012) (Belgium).

*Code d'instruction criminelle [Code of Criminal Procedure].* November 19, 1808 (as amended on November 30, 2011) (Belgium).

*Constitution.* 1831 (as amended in 1994) (Belgium).

*Legge [Law]* March 17, 1898, n. 80 (Italy).

*Asbestos Industry (Asbestosis) Scheme of 1931* (England).

*Supreme Court Act 1981* (England).

*The Social Security (Industrial Injuries) (Prescribed Diseases) Regulations 1985 as amended by the Social Security (Industrial Injuries) (Miscellaneous Amendments) Regulations 1997* (England).

*Regio Decreto [Royal Decree], Regolamento per l'applicazione del testo unico sulla legge per il lavoro delle donne e dei fanciulli [Regulations implementing the framework law on working conditions of women and minors].* June 14, 1909, n. 442 (Italy).

*Loi [Law] relative à la réparation des dommages causés par les maladies professionnelles [concerning compensation for injuries caused by occupational diseases].* July 24, 1927, in Moniteur Belge, August 12, 1927 (Belgium).

*Regio Decreto [Royal Decree], Assicurazione obbligatoria contro malattie professionali [Mandatory insurance for occupational diseases].* May 13, 1929, n. 928 (Italy).

*Codice di Procedura Penale [Code of Criminal Procedure].* 1929 (Italy).

*Codice Penale [Criminal Code].* 1930 (Italy).

*Legge [Law], Unificazione degli istituti per l'assicurazione obbligatoria contro gli infortuni degli operai sul lavoro [Merger of worker's compensation administrations].* June 22, 1933, n. 860 (Italy).

*Regio Decreto [Royal Decree], Disposizioni per l'assicurazione obbligatoria degli infortuni sul lavoro e delle malattie professionali [Regulations pertaining to mandatory insurance of occupations injuries and diseases].* August 17, 1935, n. 1765 (Italy).

*Codice Civile [Civil Code].* 1942 (Italy).

*Legge [Law], Estensione dell'assicurazione obbligatoria contro le malattie professionali alla silicosi ed all'asbestosi [Worker's compensation extension to silicosis and asbestosis].* Aprile 12, 1943, n. 455 (Italy).

*Law Reform (Personal Injuries) Act 1948* (England).

*Decreto Presidenziale [Presidential Decree], Testo unico delle disposizioni per l'assicurazione obbligatoria contro gli infortuni sul lavoro e le malattie professionali [Consolidated law pertaining to mandatory insurance of occupational injuries and diseases].* June 30, 1965, n. 1124 (Italy).

*Restatement (Second) of Torts (1965)* (USA).

*Asbestos Regulations (1969).* Statutory Instrument 1969 No. 690 (England).

*Lois [Laws] relatives à la prévention des maladies professionnelles et à la réparation des dommages résultant de celles-ci, coordonnées le 3 juin 1970 [concerning the prevention of occupational disease and the compensation of damages caused by the disease, coordinated on June 3, 1970].* June 3, 1970, in Moniteur Belge, August 27, 1970 (Belgium).

*Health and Safety at Work etc Act 1974* (England).

House of Representatives. *The Asbestos Health Hazards Compensation Act of 1977.* H.R. 8689 (USA).

*The Pneumoconiosis Etc. (Workers' Compensation) Act 1979* (England).

*Limitation Act 1980* (England).

*The Courts and Legal Services Act 1990* (England).

*Loi [Law] portant des dispositions sociales [regulating social security and other matters].* December 29, 1990, in Moniteur Belge, January 9, 1991 (Belgium).

*Decreto Legislativo [Legislative Decree], Attuazione delle direttive n. 80/1107/ CEE, n. 82/605/CEE, n. 83/477/CEE, n. 86/188/CEE e n. 88/642/CEE [Enacting Directives n. 80/1107/CEE, n. 82/605/CEE, n. 83/477/CEE, n. 86/188/CEE e n. 88/642/CEE].* August 15, 1991, n. 277 (Italy).

*Council Directive 91/382/EEC of 25 June 1991 amending Directive 83/477/EEC on the protection of workers from the risks related to exposure to asbestos at work (second individual Directive within the meaning of Article 8 of Directive 80/1107/EEC).* March 27, 1992 (EU).

*Legge [Law], Norme relative alla cessazione dell'impiego dell'amianto [Regulations pertaining to the ban of asbestos use]* March 27, 1992, n. 257 (Italy).

*Legge [Law], Regolamento recante le nuove tabelle delle malattie professionali nell'industria e nell'agricoltura [New charts regulating occupational diseases in the manufacturing and agricultural sectors].* April 13, 1994, n. 336 (Italy).

*Decreto Ministeriale [Ministerial Decree], Normative e metodologie tecniche di applicazione dell'art. 6, comma 3, e dell'art. 12, comma 2, della legge 27 marzo 1992, n. 257, relativa alla cessazione dell'impiego dell'amianto [Rules and regulations pertaining to art. 6, sec. 3, and art. 12 , sec. 2, of Law March 27, 1992, n. 257, banning asbestos uses].* September 6, 1994 (Italy).

*Civil Procedure Rules.* 1998 (England).

*Access to Justice Act 1999 (*England).

*Decreto Legislativo [Legislative Decree], Disposizioni in materia di assicurazione contro gli infortuni sul lavoro e le malattie professionali, a norma dell'articolo 55, comma 1, della legge 17 maggio 1999, n. 144 [Regulations pertaining to mandatory insurance for occupational injuries and diseases].* February 23, 2000, n. 38 (Italy).

Ministero del Lavoro e delle Politiche Sociali [Department of Labor and Social Policy]. *Decreto Ministeriale [Ministerial Decree], Approvazione di "Tabella delle menomazioni," "Tabella indennizzo danno biologico," "Tabella dei coefficienti," relative al danno biologico ai fini della tutela dell'assicurazione contro gli infortuni e le malattie professionali [Adoption of "Injury Chart," "Awards Chart for 'Danno Biologico'," "Coefficient," pertaining to "danno biologico" in relation to occupational injuries and diseases].* July 12, 2000, in Gazzetta Ufficiale July 25, 2000, n. 172 (Italy).

Sénat de Belgique. *Proposition de loi modifiant l'article 51 des lois coordonnées du 3 juin 1970 relative à la réparation des dommages résultant des maladies professionnelles pour y intégrer la faute inexcusable en cas d'exposition des travailleurs à l'amiante* [Bill to amend article 51 of the coordinated laws of June 3, 1970, allowing the compensation of asbestos workers in the event of faute inexcusable]. July 3, 2003, n. 3-22/1 (Belgium).

Senate Committee on the Judiciary. *Rep. No, 108-118, The Fairness In Asbestos Injury Resolution Act of 2003, S.1125 (108th Congress).* Washington, DC, July 30 2003 (USA).

*Decreto Legge [Law Decree], Disposizioni urgenti per favorire lo sviluppo e per la correzione dell'andamento dei conti pubblici [Urgent rules to promote development and to address public finances' issues].* September 30, 2003, n. 269 (Italy).

Sénat de Belgique. *Proposition de loi visant à créer un Fonds pour les victimes de l'amiante* [Bill aiming to create a Fund to compensate asbestos victims]. June 28, 2004, n. 3-788/1 (Belgium).

Ministero del Lavoro e delle Politiche Sociali [Department of Labor and Social Policy]. *Decreto Ministeriale [Ministerial Decree], Benefici previdenziali per i lavoratori esposti all'amianto [Asbestos workers' benefits].* October 27, 2004, in Gazzetta Ufficiale December 17, 2004, n. 295 (Italy).

*James Hardie (Investigations and Proceedings) Bill 2004* (Australia).

Conseil National du Travail. *Faute inexcusable en cas d'exposition des travailleurs à l'amiante—Proposition de loi ["Faute inexcusable" and asbestos workers' risk—Bill],* Avis 1.517, June 16, 2005 (Belgium).

Conseil National du Travail. *Faute inexcusable en cas d'exposition des travailleurs à l'amiante—Proposition de loi ["Faute inexcusable" and asbestos workers' risk—Bill],* Avis 1.518, June 16, 2005 (Belgium).

*Legge [Law], Legge finanziaria del 2006 [2006 Annual Budget Act].* December 23, 2005, n. 266. (Italy).

*Legge [Law], Modifiche al codice di procedura penale, in materia di inappellabilità delle sentenze di proscioglimento [Amendments to the code of criminal procedure, with regard to appellability of acquittals].* February 20, 2006, n. 46 (Italy).

Senato della Repubblica Italiana. *Proposta di legge [Bill], Estensione delle prestazioni previste per gli infortuni sul lavoro e le malattie professionali ai soggetti danneggiati dall' esposizione all' amianto [Extension of benefit entitlements for occupational injuries and diseases to individuals exposed to asbestos].* October 17, 2006, n. 23 (Italy).

*Loi-programme (I) du 27 décembre 2006 portant création d'un Fonds d'indemnisation des victimes de l'amiante [Law (I) December 27, 2006 creating the Asbestos Compensation Fund].* December 27, 2006, in Moniteur Belge, December 28, 2006 (Belgium).

*Arrêté royal [Royal Decree] portant exécution du chapitre VI, du titre IV, de la loi-programme (I) du 27 décembre 2006 portant création d'un Fonds d'indemnisation des victimes de l'amiante [for the implementation of the Asbestos Victims Compensation Fund].* December 27, 2006, *in* Moniteur Belge, May 11, 2007. (Belgium).

*Compensation Act of 2006* (England).

*The Social Security (Industrial Injuries) (Prescribed Diseases) Amendment Regulations 2006* (England).

*Legge [Law], Misure in tema di tutela della salute e della sicurezza sul lavoro e delega al Governo per il riassetto e la riforma della normativa in materia [Regulations pertaining to workplace health and safety and assignment of power to the Executive to reorganize regulation in this matter].* August 3, 2007, n. 123. (Italy).

*Legge [Law], Legge finanziaria del 2008 [2008 Annual Budget Act].* December 24, 2007, n. 244 (Italy).

*The Pneumoconiosis etc. (Workers' Compensation) (Payment of Claims) (Amendment) Regulations 2007* (England).

Ministero del Lavoro e delle Politiche Sociali [Department of Labor and Social Policy]. *Decreto Ministeriale [Ministerial Decree], Nuove tabelle delle malattie professionali nell'industria e nell'agricoltura [New occupational disease charts for the manufacturing and agricultural sectors].* April 9, 2008, in Gazzetta Ufficiale, July 21, 2008, n. 169 (Italy).

Sénat de Belgique. *Proposition de loi modifiant l'article 51 des lois coordonnées du 3 juin 1970 relative à la réparation des dommages résultant des maladies professionnelles pour y intégrer la faute inexcusable en cas d'exposition des travailleurs à l'amiante [Bill to amend article 51 of the coordinated laws of June 3, 1970, allowing the compensation of asbestos workers in the event of "faute inexcusable"].* October 1, 2008, n. 4-934/1 (Belgium).

*The Mesothelioma Lump Sum Payments (Conditions and Amounts) Regulations 2008* (England).

*The Damages (Asbestos-related Conditions) Act of 2009* (Northern Ireland).

*The Damages (Asbestos-related Conditions) Act of 2009* (Scotland).

*Third Parties (Rights against Insurers) Act 2010* (England).

Ministero del Lavoro e delle Politiche Sociali [Department of Labor and Social Policy]. *Regolamento concernente il Fondo per le vittime dell'amianto [Guidelines for the Asbestos Victims' Fund].* January 1, 2011, n. 30, in Gazzetta Ufficiale, March 29, 2011, n. 72 (Italy).

Conseil d'État. *Proposition de loi complétant l'arrêté royal du 11 mai 2007 portant exécution du chapitre VI, du titre IV, de la loi-programme (I) du 27 décembre 2006 portant création d'un Fonds d'indemnisation des victimes de l'amiante, en vue d'augmenter la cotisation à payer par les employeurs dont la responsabilité a été retenue dans le cadre du Fonds amiante [Bill supplementing the Royal Decree of May 11, 2007 on the implementation of Chapter VI of Title IV of Law (I) of December 27, 2006 establishing a compensation fund for asbestos victims, to increase the contribution payable by employers whose responsibility has been found in the context of the Asbestos Fund]*, Avis 51.636/1, July 26, 2012 (Belgium).

Conseil National du Travail. *Problématique en lien avec l'amiante et les produits de substitution à l'amiante—Propositions de loi [Issues relating to asbestos and its substitutes—Bills]*, Avis 1.826, November 27, 2012 (Belgium).

*Legal Aid, Sentencing and Punishment of Offenders Act 2012* (England).

*The Pneumoconiosis etc. (Workers' compensation) (Payment of Claims) (Amendment) Regulations 2012* (England).

*House of Representatives. Furthering Asbestos Claim Transparency (FACT) Act of 2013.* H.R. 982 (USA).

# List of Cases

*Sentenza [Opinion] n. 1197/06*, Società Anonima The British Asbestos Company Limited v Avvocato Carlo Pich (Tribunale [District Court], Torino, 1906) (Italy).

*MacPherson v Buick Motor Co.*, 271 N.Y. 382 (N.Y. 1916) (USA).

*Jacque v Locke Insulator Corp.*, 70 F.2d 680 (2nd Cir. 1934) (USA).

*Borel v Fibreboard Paper Prods Corp.*, 493 F.2d 1076 (5th Cir. 1973), cert. denied, 419 U.S. 869 (1974) (USA).

*Cunningham v Harrison* [1973] 1 QB 942 (England).

*George v Pinnock* [1973] 1 WLR 118 (England).

*Daly v General Steam Navigation Co Ltd (The "Dragon")* [1979] 1 Lloyd's Rep 257 (England).

*Lim Poh Choo v Camden and Islington Area HA* [1980] AC 174 (England).

*Beshada v Johns-Manville Products Corp.*, 442 A.2d 539 (D.N.J. 1982) (USA).

*O'Brien v Muskin Corp.*, 463 A.2d 298 (N.J. 1983) (USA).

*Church v Ministry of Defence* [1984] 134 NLJ 623 (England).

*Feldman v Lederle Laboratories*, 479 A.2d 374 (N.J. 1984) (USA).

*Margereson and Hancock v J.W. Roberts* [1986] PIQR 358 (England).

*Matter of Johns-Manville Corp.*, 68 BR 618 (Bankr. S.D.N.Y. 1986) (USA).

*Sentenza [Opinion]. July 14, 1986, n. 184* (Corte Costituzionale [Constitutional Court]) (Italy).

*Patterson v Ministry of Defence* [1987] CLY 1194 (England).

*Sentenza [Opinion]. February 18, 1988, n. 179* (Corte Costituzionale [Constitutional Court]) (Italy).

*Adams v Cape Industries plc* [1991] 1 All ER 929 (England).

*In re Asbestos Prodcs Liab. Litig. (No. VI)*, 771 F. Supp. 415 (J.P.M.L. 1991) (USA).

*Chase Manhattan Bank, NA v Turner & Newall, PLC*, 964 F.2d 159 (2nd Cir. 1992) (USA).

*Sentenza [Opinion]*, Virga (Pretura [District Court], Pordenone, July 7, 1992) (Italy).

*Hunt v Severs* [1994] 2AC 350 (England).

*In re Joint E. & S. Dist. Asbestos Litig.*, 878 F. Supp. 473 (S.D.N.Y. 1995) (USA).

*Sentenza [Opinion]*, Barbotto Beraud et al. (Pretura [District Court], Torino, February 2, 1995) (Italy).

*Amchem Products, Inc. v Windsor*, 521 U.S. 591 (1997) (USA).

*Metro-North Commuter R. Co. v Buckley*, 521 U.S. 424 (1997) (USA).

*Jugement définitif [Final order]*, n. 96/7741/A (Tribunal de Première Instance [District Court], Bruxelles, October 1, 1997) (Belgium).

*Sentenza [Opinion] n. 3101/98*, Giannitrapani (Corte d'Appello [Court of Appeals], Torino, September 17, 1998) (Italy).

*Sentenza [Opinion] n. 10722/98*, INPDAI v Vianco (Corte di Cassazione [Highest Court], October 27, 1998) (Italy).

*Arrêt [Order]*, n. 1998/4253 (Cour d'Appel [Court of Appeals], Brussels, 4th Chamber, November 2, 1998) (Belgium).

*Ortiz v Fibreboard Corp*, 527 U.S. 815 (1999) (USA).

*Holtby v Brigham & Cowan (Hull) Ltd* [2000] 3 All ER 421 (England).

*Sentenza [Opinion] n. 5/00* (Corte Costituzionale [Constitutional Court], January 12, 2000) (Italy).

*Sentenza [Opinion] n. 660/00*, Santullo et al. (Corte d'Appello [Court of Appeals], Torino, February 10, 2000) (Italy).

*Sentenza [Opinion] n. 1522/00*, Humbert (Corte d'Appello [Court of Appeals], Torino, March 14, 2000) (Italy).

*Sentenza [Opinion] n. 5037/00*, Camposano (Corte di Cassazione [Highest Court], March 30, 2000) (Italy).

*Ballantine v Newalls Insulation Co Ltd* [2001] ICR 25 (England).

*Cherry Tree Machine Co Ltd and Shell Tankers UK Ltd v Dawson, Shell Tankers UK Ltd v Jeromson* [2001] EWCA Civ 101 (England).

*Arrêt [Order]* n. 2001/31 (Cours d'Arbitrage [Highest Court], March 1, 2001) (Belgium).

*Sentenza [Opinion] n. 127/02* (Corte Costituzionale [Constitutional Court], April 11, 2002) (Italy).

*Gunderson v A.W. Chesterton Co.*, Case n. 406207, Verdict (Cal. Super., San Francisco Co. December 12, 2002) (USA).

*Norfolk & Western R. Co. v Ayers*, 538 U.S. 135 (2003) (USA).

*In re Combustion Eng'g, Inc.*, 391 F.3d 190 (3rd Cir. 2004) (USA).

*Adams v Bracknell Forest BC* [2005] 1 AC 76 (England).

*Baron & Budd, P.C. v Unsecured Asbestos Claimant Comm.*, 321 B.R. 147 (D.N.J. 2005) (USA).

*Maguire v Harland & Wolff plc and Another* [2005] EWCA Civ 01 (England).

*Sentenza [Opinion] n. 7362/05* (Corte di Cassazione [Highest Court], Civile, April 11, 2005) (Italy).

*Johnston v NEI International Combustion Ltd* [2007] UKHL 39 (England).

*Sentenza [Opinion] n. 19342/07*, Rubiero et al. (Corte di Cassazione [Highest Court], February 20, 2007) (Italy).

*Simonetta v Viad Corp.*, 197 P.3d 127 (Wash. 2008) (USA).

*Sentenza [Opinion] n. 2729/08*, M.V. v Croce Rossa Italiana (Corte di Cassazione [Highest Court], Lavoro, February 5, 2008) (Italy).

*Sentenza [Opinion] n. 317/08*, Cozzini et al. (Corte d'Appello [Court of Appeals], Trento, June 10, 2008) (Italy).

*Richiesta di Rinvio a Giudizio [Indictment], Case 24265/04, Schmidheiny and De Cartier De Marchienne*, (Procura della Repubblica [Office of the Prosecutor], Torino, October 10, 2008) (Italy).

*Taylor v Elliott Turbomachinery Co. Inc*, 90 Cal. Rptr. 3d 414 (Ct. App. 2009) (USA).

*Willmore v Knowsley Metropolitan BC* [2009] EWCA Civ 1211 (England).

*Sentenza [Opinion]*, Stringa (Tribunale [District Court], Bari, June 16, 2009) (Italy).

*In re Asbestos Products Liability Litigation (No. VI)*, MDL No. 875, Amended Administrative Order No. 12 (As Amended Effectively August 27, 2009) (E.D. Pa., September 3, 2009) (USA).

*Evans v A.W. Chesterton Co., et al.*, Case n. 418867, Verdict (Cal. Super., Los Angeles Co. April 29, 2010) (USA).

*Shepherd v Pneumo-Abex, LLC*, 2010 WL 3431663, Memorandum and Order (E.D. Pa. August 30, 2010) (USA).

*In re Global Indus. Technologies, Inc.*, 645 F.3d 201 (3rd Cir. 2011) (USA).

*In re Pittsburgh Corning Corp.*, 453 BR 570 (Bankr. W.D. Pa. June 16, 2011) (USA).

*Ferguson v Lorillard Tobacco Co.*, 2011 WL 5903453, Memorandum and Order (E.D. Pa. November 22, 2011) (USA).

*In re Asbestos Prodcs Liab. Litig. (No. VI)*, MDL No. 875, Order Adopting Suggestion To The Panel Concerning Future Tag-Along Transfers (E.D. Pa., December 13, 2011) (USA).

*Durham v BAI (Run Off) Ltd (in Scheme of Arrangement)* [2012] UKSC 14 (England).

*Motor Vehicle Cas. Co. v Thorpe Insulation Co. (In re Thorpe Insulation Co.)*, 671 F.3d 980 (9th Cir. 2012) (USA).

*In re Asbestos Prodcs Liab. Litig. (No. VI)*, MDL No. 875, Order Regarding Bankruptcy Claims (MARDOC cases) (E.D. Pa. January 27, 2012) (USA).

*Sentenza [Judgment] n. 5219/09*, Schmidheiny and De Cartier De Marchienne, (Tribunale [Trial Court], Torino, February 13, 2012) (Italy).

*Campbell v Ford Motor Co.*, 206 Cal. App. 4th 15 (Ct. App. May 21, 2012) (USA).

*Garner v Salford City & Anor* [2013] EWHC 1573 (QB) (England).

*Sentenza [Judgment] n. 5621/12*, Schmidheiny and De Cartier De Marchienne, (Corte d'Appello [Court of Appeals], Torino, June 3, 2013) (Italy).

# Preface

This book should never have been written. However, it has been. It should never have been written because it is a book about preventable disease and death. Unfortunately, disease and death that affected thousands of asbestos victims have not been prevented. This book explains how law contributed to the rise of asbestos disease and was used as a set of responses to the asbestos epidemic. The initial idea of the project was to look at how legal systems used scientific evidence in adjudicating toxic tort claims. It soon became apparent to me that in-depth analysis that could lead to meaningful insights as to the comparative operation of legal systems needed to go beyond the mere analysis of the use of scientific evidence in litigation. The first major comparative difference that I observed was that toxic tort claims were adjudicated by civil courts in the United States and criminal courts in Italy. This initial observation triggered an inquiry that led me to explore the causes of the different treatment of these claims in the two legal systems. Initial answers were not satisfying, and therefore the inquiry progressively unfolded as I was searching for the causes of the cause … of the causes. This book is the result of this inquiry: in the end, I found that, in the tradition of sociolegal scholarship, the most compelling explanation is a cultural one—one that is based on an analysis of the values, beliefs, and schemas that social actors have referred to in giving legal meaning to the asbestos epidemic.

The idea of working on asbestos originated from my biography. As a young scholar I was looking for a context in which I could conduct meaningful comparative analysis. Early on, I realized that the comparative literature on asbestos compensation was very limited. I also realized that the largest asbestos mine in Europe, one of the largest asbestos-cement plants in the world, and the prosecutor's office that was more active in prosecuting asbestos defendants law were all located in Piemonte, the region of Northern Italy where I grew up. My biography thus became an invitation to focus my comparative inquiry on asbestos. The resulting experience was a long and complex journey during which I saw my transformation from a practicing attorney into a tenured academic. It was an important journey, one that was possible because of the help and support of friends and colleagues. I want to acknowledge my gratitude to all those who took part in this journey, bearing in mind that I will certainly forget some.

I want to thank Deborah Hensler, who helped me begin this journey and become a social scientist. She believed in my potential, she nourished it through advising and teaching, and most of all by inspiring me through her example of a scholar with integrity and clarity. I also thank all the people that agreed to sit and talk to me throughout the past years. This is especially true for those who agreed to be interviewed by an unknown young scholar from Stanford University asking for their time, their stories, and sometimes for sensitive information. I promised and granted confidentiality. Nonetheless, as I dug deeper into the practices of the asbestos industry, its secrecy and its power, I have become even more appreciative of the respondents' willingness to agree to talk to me. Some decided not to: I understand and fully respect their decision. Many scholars also shared their insights and encouragement with me. Lawrence Friedman and Bob Rabin read early drafts of this work. Bob Kagan and Sanja Kutnjak Ivkovic both encouraged me to turn my research into a book. David Nelken and Susan Silbey contributed by nudging my theoretical framework in the right direction. Anna Zimdars patiently read and provide thorough comments to early drafts of each chapter. I also benefitted from conversations with Dale Jamieson, with several colleagues at Bryant (including Alex Perullo, Rich Holtzman, John Dietrich, Mike Bryant, Jay Reedy, Gregg Carter, and Marsha Peipstein Posusney) as well as many other colleagues at conferences, at dinner tables, and other venues (I have fond memories of an insightful conversation with John Harrington while having breakfast in his Liverpool home). I also want to thank the librarians at Stanford and Bryant as well as Joseph Robertson for his research assistance.

I would like to thank Alison Kirk at Ashgate, for immediately believing in the project and for being extremely patient as I kept asking for deadline extensions, as well as her colleagues (Sadie Copley-May, Carolyn Court, Sarah Horsley, and Albert Stewart) who have worked on the production of the book with dedication and care. I want to thank the anonymous reviewers of the manuscript for the constructive criticism, which I hope is reflected in the final product, as well as the reviewers of the papers that were published in academic journals and whose comments have somehow found their ways into this manuscript.

On a personal level, I must thank my parents Paola and Carlo for encouraging me and supporting my choice to move to the United States to pursue a graduate degree, which eventually changed the course of my life. Their support is part of a much longer, caring relationship for which I am both mindful and grateful. I want to thank Yoko for her support. She met me when I was already working on this book. At some point, although she stopped asking me whether the book was done, she never stopped believing in my ability to complete it in a satisfactory way. Finally, I want to thank my friends (as well as my brother Luca and his family) who tolerated various social hiatuses as I was working on the book manuscript.

To me, these two pages are the most important of the book, and it was a pleasure to write them.

Andrea Boggio

# Chapter 1
# Asbestos disease and compensation

L'amianto era una cosa veramente subdola perché comunque sia non la si vede, magari non la si sente, però esiste, e adesso ultimamente una o due persone alla settimana muoiono tra i cittadini, tra gli ex-lavoratori. [Asbestos is a very sneaky thing: you can never see it, you can sometimes smell it, but it exists. Lately, one or two people have died every week among the residents of this town, among those who once worked with asbestos.] (Romana Blasotti)[1]

I grabbed his face and put it between my hands and said, "Honey, honey, honey!" I was screaming bloody murder, "Oh my God, he's gone. He's gone." (Karen McQueen)[2]

Death in old age is inevitable, but death before old age is not. (Richard Doll)[3]

… toute la structure sociale est présente au coeur de l'interaction, sous la forme des schèmes de perception et d'appréciation inscrits dans le corps des agents en interaction. [The whole social structure is present at the heart of the interaction, in the form of schemes of perception and appreciation inscribed in bodies of the interacting agents.] (Pierre Bourdieu)[4]

Our problem is to work out a social organization which shall be efficient as possible without offending our notions of a satisfactory way of life. (John Maynard Keynes)[5]

---

1    Redazione di Reality, "Casale Monferrato: Una Chernobyl italiana [Casale Monferrato: An Italian Chernobyl]," La7, http://www.la7.it/approfondimento/dettaglio.asp?prop=reality&video=5478.

2    Dionne Searcey, "For One Asbestos Victim, Justice is a Moving Target," *Wall Street Journal*, June 17, 2013, A1 (quoting Karen McQueen giving an account of her realization that her husband had succumbed to mesothelioma).

3    Words attributed to Sir Richard Doll and posted on Sir Richard Peto's door and written on a plaque inside the Richard Doll Building on Oxford. See Siddhartha Mukherjee, *The emperor of all maladies: a biography of cancer*, 1st ed. (New York: Scribner, 2010), 462.

4    Pierre Bourdieu, *La domination masculine* [Masculine domination](Paris: Seuil, 1998), 70.

5    John Maynard Keynes, *Laissez-faire and communism* (New York: New Republic, 1926), 53.

… sans considérer que c'est toujours le mauvais côté, qui finit par l'emporter sur le côté beau. C'est le mauvais côté qui produit le mouvement qui fait l'histoire, en constituant la lute. [… irrespective of the fact that it is always the bad side that in the end triumphs over the good side. It is the bad side that produces the movement which makes history, by providing a struggle] (Karl Marx)[6]

## Law and the dark side of industrialization

The poignant words of Romana Blasotti, a soft spoken 83-year-old woman and longtime resident of Casale Monferrato, a peaceful blue collar town in Piemonte in Northern Italy, set the stage for this book: the story of how victims of asbestos exposure have been compensated for injuries caused by this invisible killer. Ms. Blasotti lost her husband, her sister, her daughter, a nephew, and a cousin to asbestos.[7] While Ms. Blasotti represents one of the most tragic accounts of how asbestos has killed throughout the years, her story is far from being unique. Victims throughout the world have been heard screaming "bloody murder" just like Karen McQueen did in San Antonio, Texas, after realizing that her beloved husband and father of two had just been killed by asbestos.[8] Asbestos use has caused a global epidemic in which its deadly effects affected hundreds of communities, thousands of families, and tens of thousands of men and women throughout the world. Data on 82 countries published by the World Health Organization indicate that, from 1994 to 2010, 128,015 persons died of mesothelioma.[9] An estimated 20,000 asbestos-related lung cancers and 10,000 cases of mesothelioma, an invariably deadly form of cancer, occur annually across the population of Western Europe, Scandinavia, North America, Japan, and Australia. The asbestos epidemic kills one person every two hours in the United States, one every four hours in the United Kingdom, three every day in

---

6   Karl Marx, *Misère de la philosophie (réponse à "La Philosophie de la Misère" of M. Proudhon)* [The poverty of philosophy (a reply to "La philosophie de la misère" of M. Proudhon)] (Paris: V. Giard & E. Brière, 1896), 168.

7   "La testimonianza di Romana Blasotti Pavesi: 'Un solo malato di mesotelioma non vale un conto in banca spropositato' [Romana Blasotti Pavesi's testimony: 'a single mesothelioma victim is not worth a huge bank account']" *Casalenews.* Published electronically June 28, 2010. http://www.casalenews.it/notizia/cronaca/2010/06/28/la-testimonianza-di-romana-blasotti-pavesi-un-solo-malato-di-mesotelioma-non-vale-un-conto-in-banca-spropositato/amianto-eternit/f02d2208965df21b1577b1930ef2926d.

8   Dionne Searcey, "For One Asbestos Victim, Justice is a Moving Target."

9   Rachmania Diandini, Ken Takahashi, Eun-Kee Park, Ying Jiang, Mehrnoosh Movahed, Giang Vinh Le, Lukas Jyuhn-Hsiarn Lee, Vanya Delgermaa, and Rokho Kim, "Potential years of life lost (PYLL) caused by asbestos-related diseases in the world," *American Journal of Industrial Medicine.* Published online electronically June 12, 2013.

Italy and Germany, two every day in France, Japan, and Australia, and one a day in the Netherlands.[10]

All these deaths were premature and certainly evitable, as Sir Richard Doll's words suggest. Even worse: they were man-made because they were the result of the decision to use asbestos extensively in the course of the industrialization process that led to Fordist production of the twentieth century. Asbestos disease is a man-made epidemic and thus a social event, as Pierre Bourdieu argued, as it can be construed as an "inscription" of the social structure on human bodies. Indeed, the social structures that are involved in the making of this epidemic are primarily economic. It is capitalism with its inherent tension between profit and equity. Asbestos disease thus offers an opportunity to investigate the capitalist tension between profits and equity and resulting social struggle between victims and corporate powers. I am particularly interested in the mediating role of institutions and law. In fact, the rise of the asbestos epidemics has led to the emergence of an array of institutional mechanisms aimed at compensating the victims of the asbestos epidemic. While industrialized nations with experience of asbestos use have developed some form of asbestos compensation, norms, institutions, and procedures of asbestos compensation vary greatly across nations and across time.

This book presents a comparative study of the emergence and transformations of asbestos compensation in the past century in Belgium, England, Italy, and the United States. While grounded on an analysis of formal law, I construe and analyze these mechanisms as cultural responses to the rise of the asbestos epidemic. Legal redress for asbestos disease is seen as a social event, and more specifically a cultural practice that emerges from the cultural fabric of our societies and it contributes to its constitution. Engel and McCann defined a cultural approach to the study of law as emphasizing "the ways that legal practice is embedded within the larger framework of cultural norms, routines, and institutional relations."[11] This assumes that law is a cultural phenomenon. Throughout the book, asbestos compensation is thus understood as a set of cultural responses to the broader challenges of addressing risks generated by industrialization, its dark side, and assignments of responsibility, compensation, and obligation related to injury caused by exposure to asbestos. Framing asbestos compensation as a cultural phenomenon allows me to investigate and expose the deeper social tensions that compensation practices address, and in particular the tension between individual profits and social costs that is inherent to capitalism. Asbestos compensation emerged and developed as cultural response aiming to address this tension between efficiency and equity, or in Keynes's words, as "a social organization" aimed to make our societies as "efficient as possible without offending our notions of a satisfactory way of life." This book unfortunately

---

10   Bruce W.S. Robinson and Richard A. Lake, "Advances in Malignant Mesothelioma," *New England Journal of Medicine* 353, no. 15 (2005).

11   David M. Engel and Michael W. McCann, eds, *Fault lines: tort law as cultural practice* (Stanford: Stanford Law Books, 2009), 6-7.

shows that asbestos compensation failed to satisfactorily address the fundamental capitalist tension: compensation was bitterly contested, came too late, and did not include all victims of the asbestos epidemic. Furthermore, the individuals and organizations that significantly contributed to the emergence of the asbestos epidemic have for the most part escaped accountability. Asbestos disease is a dark side of industrialization that the laws of compensation failed to fully redress.

## Asbestos use and industrialization

Asbestos is a naturally occurring mineral with such extraordinary insulating properties that, since the early days of its modern use, it was labeled as the "magical fiber."[12] Its remarkable insulating properties, as well as its abundant, relatively cheap availability and its adaptability, made this product an almost indispensable ingredient of industrialization. As a result of industrialists' interest in the mineral, towards the end of nineteenth century, many asbestos mines were opened. A consortium of capitalists opened the Balangero mine in Northern Italy. Others looked at Québec and its vast reserves of chrysotile asbestos. In a matter of a few years, asbestos became available in large quantities and at a very reasonable cost. Other entrepreneurs processed asbestos fiber and created a brand new form of cement that was easy to install and allegedly indestructible when applied as a covering to boilers, steam pipes, hot blast furnaces, and stills. Others started traveling around the world, some to Russia and South Africa to purchase land that offered promising prospects of containing asbestos, and to Australia to set up pipe manufacturing plants. Even cities named after asbestos appeared on the map: Asbestos—a 7,000 resident town of Southeastern Québec, developed around the Jeffrey Mine, the world's largest asbestos mine in the world (in 2005, Canada contributed 40 percent of the worldwide production of asbestos).[13] Another example is Asbest City—a mining town in the Ural Mountains with a population of 71,000. The city continues to be the source of 25 percent of the chrysotile asbestos that is used worldwide.[14]

In a matter of a few decades, hundreds of applications were introduced, which propelled a flourishing industry.[15] Asbestos truly became the "magical mineral"

---

12    Geoffrey Tweedale, *Magic mineral to killer dust: Turner & Newall and the asbestos hazard* (Oxford: Oxford University Press, 2000).

13    Hervé Kempf, "Asbestos, la ville maudite de l'amiante," [Asbestos, the damned asbestos city] *Le Monde*, December 28, 2005.

14    Marie Jégo, "Dans l'Oural, la mine d'amiante à ciel ouvert pollue toujours la ville d'Asbest," [In the Ural, an asbestos mine pullutes the city of Asbestos daily], ibid., November 10, 2009.

15    For a list of asbestos containing products marketed in the United States, see LLC Products Research, "Welcome to Asbestos Catalogs. At a glance: manufacturers with asbestos based products," http://www.asbestoscatalogs.com/.

and contributed to the development of the industries that defined the economic growth that took industrial nations from the Second Industrial Revolution into the twentieth century. During these times, the remarkable insulating properties of asbestos were an essential ingredient of the widespread availability of electric power, internal combustion engines, and assembly lines. Insulating properties, versatility, and cheapness made asbestos a highly successful product, used in countless applications in countless industries: from shipbuilding to cars, from roofing to cigarette filters.

With all these products on the market, asbestos soon became a permanent presence, often an invisible presence, in the lives of people throughout the industrialized world. Commercial building, private homes, offices, schools, hospitals, post offices, as well as boats, airplanes and most of the other means of transportation were filled with asbestos. The asbestos miracle led people to mix asbestos fibers with flour and other ingredients to make muffins, to add it to the soil as a garden fertilizer for homegrown vegetables, and to insert its fibers in cigarette filters to protect smokers' fingers. People ate and smoked asbestos.

Unfortunately, the story of asbestos is not simply a tale of success: it is also a tragic story of death and suffering. In fact, it is now clear that asbestos is a highly toxic substance: exposure to asbestos fibers may cause various respiratory problems, eventually leading to death. A well-established body of medical evidence shows that asbestos may cause respiratory conditions, lung cancer, and mesothelioma—a rare and incurable form of cancer of the pleura and from which patients often die within a few months of diagnosis.[16] Typically mesothelioma is diagnosed in victims who worked in asbestos mining but also in jobs in industries such as textiles, railroads, shipbuilding, car manufacturing, and construction. However, in recent years, victims are increasingly counted among "end-users often exposed when installing asbestos products or handling asbestos materials still in place (construction workers, electricians, plumbers, heating workers, etc.)."[17] While pleural mesothelioma is a signature disease, the causes of lung cancer are various. Smoking in particular is responsible for a large proportion of cancers of the lung, and unfortunately many asbestos victims smoked during their lives. Attributing lung cancer to asbestos exposure is thus harder than in the case of mesothelioma.[18]

---

16 The median survival of untreated cases is six to nine months with less than 5 percent of asbestos victims surviving for more than five years from diagnosis. See Jan P. van Meerbeeck et al., "Malignant pleural mesothelioma: the standard of care and challenges for future management," *Critical Reviews in Oncology/Hematology* 78, no. 2 (2011).

17 Ibid.

18 Furthermore, evidence that exposure to asbestos causes lung cancer has a complex history. See Barry I. Castleman, *Asbestos: medical and legal aspects*, 5th ed. (New York: Aspen Publishers, 2005); Geoffrey Tweedale, "Science or public relations? The inside story of the Asbestosis Research Council, 1957-1990," *American Journal of Industrial Medicine* 38, no. 6 (2000): 730-731; ibid.

Besides the two forms of cancer discussed above, exposure to asbestos is also linked with other diseases of the lung. Among them, asbestosis occupies an important place. This chronic inflammatory and fibrotic medical condition affecting the tissue that surrounds the lungs is caused by the inhalation and retention of asbestos fibers and is dose dependent: the greater the cumulative dose, the higher the incidences of asbestosis. Asbestosis is a condition that causes impairment and presents significant symptoms. It is usually associated "with dyspnea, bibasilar rales, and changes in pulmonary function: a restrictive pattern, mixed restrictive–obstructive pattern, and/or decreased diffusing capacity."[19] Epidemiologists agree that asbestosis in nonsmokers may increase by six times the risk of developing lung cancer.[20] A review of 15,557 deaths occurring to workers listed on the Great Britain Asbestosis or Mesothelioma Registers between 1971 and 2005 shows that "[t]he majority of asbestosis cases (76%) did not have asbestosis as the underlying cause of death. Lung cancer was the underlying cause of death in over 40% of the asbestosis cases."[21] Because of its responsiveness to the dose exposure, asbestosis cases were much more frequent in the past when asbestos was more frequently used and when workers were exposed to higher quantities.

Finally, asbestos exposure may finally cause calcified and noncalcified pleural plaques, diffuse pleural thickening, and rounded atelectasis. They are mostly non-fatal, and descriptions in the literature are less prominent than asbestosis and asbestos cancers. Indeed, labeling them as diseases is controversial. From a medical point of view, pleural plaques are the most common and earliest manifestation of asbestos exposure. "These plaques develop slowly over time, with a previously reported average latency of twenty to thirty years from first exposure before they become detectable on chest radiographs."[22] Pleural plaques consists thus in evidence of pleural and parenchymal consequences of asbestos exposure. They often cause difficulties in breathing because of a restrictive ventilation pattern, especially in cases where the plaques are calcified.[23] Diffuse pleural thickening makes breathing difficult, painful, and overall harder. In some patients, pleural plaques develop in a fibrosis of the visceral pleura that is fused to the parietal

---

19   American Thoracic Society, "Diagnosis and Initial Management of Nonmalignant Diseases Related to Asbestos," *American Journal of Respiratory and Critical Care Medicine* 170, no. 6 (2004).

20   Janet M. Hughes and Hans Weill, "Asbestosis as a precursor of asbestos related lung cancer: results of a prospective mortality study," *British Journal of Industrial Medicine* 48 (1991).

21   Anne-Helen Harding, "The Great Britain Asbestos Survey 1971-2005. Mortality of workers listed on the Great Britain Asbestosis or Mesothelioma Registers" (London: Health and Safety Executive, 2010).

22   E. Brigitte Gottschall, "Taking a retrospective look at asbestos-related thoracic disease produces interesting results," *Radiology* 255, no. 3 (2010).

23   A.M. Preisser, D. Wilken, and X. Baur, "Changes in Lung Function Due to Asbestosis and Asbestos-Related Pleural Plaques," *American Journal of Respiratory and Critical Care Medicine* 179, no. 1 (Meeting Abstracts) (2009).

pleura, often covering a wide area of the lungs. Clinical practice defines as diffuse pleural thickening.[24] Symptoms of diffuse pleural thickening are more severe than pleural plaques, and include localized chest pain, significant restrictive ventilatory impairment, and a diminished vital capacity and total capacity of the lungs.[25] Finally, some asbestos sufferers develop rounded atelectasis, a unique form of pleural thickening that causes the collapse of part or all of a lung. It is caused by the inflammation and subsequent fibrosis in the most superficial layer of the visceral pleura. As the fibrous tissue matures, the pleura buckles into the lung and causes the collapse of part or all of a lung. It is often asymptomatic, but occasionally it may cause chest pain, cough, and difficulty in breathing.[26]

This book focuses on asbestos use in four countries: Belgium, England, Italy, and the United States. All these countries have made great use of asbestos and experienced the asbestos epidemic to a considerable degree. Data on mesothelioma incidence show that Belgium and Great Britain have very high incidence of mesothelioma cases. In Belgium, "about 300 mesothelioma cases are yearly diagnosed" with a corresponding "crude incidence rate of 29 cases per million."[27] The crude incidence rate for Great Britain is "about 30 cases per million." Italy belongs to a "second group of countries [with] annual crude incidence rates of mesothelioma … comprised between 11 and 20 cases per million."[28] The United States belongs to a "group of countries whose annual crude incidence rates of mesothelioma are below 11 cases per million."[29] However, since "mesothelioma case distribution exactly reflects the location of using asbestos industries,"[30] some regions in the United States have incidence of mesothelioma similar to Great Britain and Belgium.

Belgium imported and consumed high volumes of asbestos. A former imperial power, Belgium's industrialization took place in the twentieth century during the golden years of the magical mineral. With no domestic mines, asbestos was primarily imported in Belgium and then used to manufacture products that will be sold on the domestic market and abroad. Cyprus and South Africa were the main source countries. An efficient system of ports and transportations supported asbestos imports (it also exposed many transportation workers and neighboring communities to asbestos dust as the magical mineral killer was transferred from the port of entry to the manufacturing sites). The production of asbestos took

---

24 Albert Solomon, "Radiological features of asbestos-related visceral pleural changes," *American Journal of Industrial Medicine* 19, no. 3 (1991).

25 Laurent Greillier and Philippe Astoul, "Mesothelioma and Asbestos-Related Pleural Diseases," *Respiration* 76, no. 1 (2008).

26 Ibid.

27 Claudio Bianchi and Tommaso Bianchi, "Malignant mesothelioma: global incidence and relationship with asbestos," *Industrial Health* 45, no. 3 (2007): 380.

28 Ibid.

29 Ibid., 382.

30 Ibid.

place primarily at Eternit's plant in Kapelle-op-den Bos, a small town with a railroad and canals, which also hosted smaller asbestos manufacturers. Eternity's significance however goes beyond Belgium: during the golden years of asbestos production, the firm became the world's second largest seller of the magical mineral, with significant market shares in Europe and Asia. It was connected to a network of asbestos-cement producers in Europe and exported its asbestos production to Brazil and India. Asbestos was also used by those traditional industries in which it had become commonplace. Shipbuilding in particular played an important role in industrial development of this rather small country. Despite the history of asbestos use, very few epidemiological data are available. As Bianchi and Bianchi put it in their 2007 review of the global incidence of mesothelioma, "[s]carce data are available for Belgium."[31] In part, this is due to the fact that Belgian authorities do not release individual information from death certificates and that no mesothelioma registry has ever been established, contrary to the common practice of other European countries including Italy and England. Nonetheless, there is evidence of asbestos disease cases. In 1980, Lacquet and colleagues studied the annual chest radiographs, work history and mortality of 1,973 workers in an asbestos-cement factory. They reported one death due to pleural mesothelioma and 29 cases of asbestosis.[32] More clear data come from the Belgian Fund for Occupational Diseases: between 2000 and 2004 the Fund attributed 203 deaths to asbestos exposure. Based on this data, Nawrot and colleagues estimated an asbestos mortality of about eight per million men per year,[33] which is a figure higher than in any of the 33 country studies by Lin and colleagues.[34] In 2013, after fieldwork conducted as part of litigation, the Belgian victims' association reported that, in the two major asbestos towns (Mons and Kapelle-op-den-Bos), 381 individuals were deceased due to asbestos exposure.[35]

England also has a long and intense history of asbestos use. The country was a heavy importer of asbestos and producers of products incorporating the "magic mineral." Although no asbestos mine was opened on the British Islands, two of the largest asbestos firms around the world flourished in England: Turner & Newall and Cape. Founded in 1871, the leading asbestos manufacturer Turner & Newall grew to be one of the largest asbestos companies in the world. The

---

31    Ibid., 379-387.

32    L.M. Lacquet, L. van der Linden, and J. Lepoutre, "Roentgenographic lung changes, asbestosis and mortality in a Belgian asbestos-cement factory," *IARC Scientific Publications*, no. 30 (1980): 783-793.

33    Tim S. Nawrot et al., "Belgium: historical champion in asbestos consumption," *The Lancet* 369, no. 9574 (2007): 1692.

34    Ro-Ting Lin et al., "Ecological association between asbestos-related diseases and historical asbestos consumption: an international analysis," ibid., no. 9564: 844-849.

35    Franchimont, Benoit, "L'amiante a tué 171 fois autour de Harmignies! [Asbestos has killed 171 times around Harmignies!]." *Soirmag.lesoir.be.* Published electronically May 14, 2013. http://soirmag.lesoir.be/l%E2%80%99amiante-tu%C3%A9-171-fois-autour-harmignies-2013-05-14-29758.

firm became involved with asbestos in 1879 when it became the first business in the United Kingdom to weave asbestos cloth with power-driven machinery. Over time, the company expanded its asbestos business. For over seven decades Turner & Newall was synonymous of an industrial group which owned asbestos mines, operated foreign subsidiaries with asbestos interests, and sold asbestos products or franchises overseas. Overall, the group owned and operated fourteen plants in Great Britain and owned 16 businesses overseas, including asbestos mines at Havelock in Bulembu in the Kingdom of Swaziland, Southern Africa. By 1939, the firm controlled 20 percent of the asbestos trade in the United Kingdom. However, Turner & Newall experienced tremendous business success after WWII as its share in asbestos trade peaked to 60 percent of the market in 1965. Now owned by the US multinational Federal-Mogul, the firm faced significant hurdles in dealing with its asbestos liabilities. The firm was the largest British employer in the asbestos industry and therefore the number of asbestos victims that could link their diseases to exposure to asbestos dust at Turner & Newall is very robust. On October 1, 2001, Federal Mogul filed for voluntary Chapter 11 reorganization in the US and administration under the UK Insolvency Act of 1986, and Turner & Newall ceased paying asbestos claims. Cape was the second major asbestos firm. Incorporated in England in 1893 under the name Cape Asbestos Company Limited, the firm's main business was to mine and process asbestos as well as selling products containing asbestos. The London-based holding company controlled interests that extended from South African mines of blue and brown asbestos as well as various manufacturing plants located in various regions of the world including South Africa, England, the United States, France, Germany, and Italy. Over time Cape conquered the slice of the English asbestos market that was not under the control of Turner & Newall. As manufacturing and sales expansion reached its peak after World War II, thousands of asbestos workers were exposed daily to the killer dust. Exposure caused disease and ultimately legal liabilities that have engaged Cape for many years. Later in this book, I will discuss Turner & Newall's and Cape's records of asbestos litigation and compensation in detail. The legacy of the presence of these two firms in England is tragic. England has one of the highest rates of asbestos diseases among industrialized nations. The number of annual cases of mesothelioma is high and on the rise. Since 1968, the year in which the British Mesothelioma Register was established, mesothelioma deaths have risen rapidly, with deaths in 2001 12 times higher than in 1968.[36] A person dies every five minutes due to mesothelioma. By 2050, there will have been approximately 90,000 deaths from mesothelioma in Great Britain, 65,000 occurring after 2001.[37] Asbestos disease is distributed in many parts of the country, in urban and coastal communities, in blue collar and white collar workers, in England as well as in all other regions of the United Kingdom.

------

36   J.T. Hodgson et al., "The expected burden of mesothelioma mortality in Great Britain from 2002 to 2050," *British Journal of Cancer* 92, no. 3 (2005).
37   Ibid.

Italy's history is also intertwined with asbestos. Its relationship with the magical mineral is longstanding. For most of the twentieth century, Italy was the second largest producer of asbestos in Europe, behind Russia. The Balangero mine was the most important mine in Europe. Chrysotile asbestos was mined there from 1918 and 1990, date of closure of the mine. Italy had an active asbestos manufacturing industry and exported less than half of its asbestos production. The key asbestos production was asbestos-cement applications, which was produced in various plants, the largest being located not far from Balangero and owned by Eternit Switzerland. Furthermore, the naval industry prospered in part by heavily relying on the magical mineral: 811 mesothelioma cases were diagnosed between 1968 and 2008 in the Northeast of Italy, along a narrow coastal strip with a strong presence of the shipbuilding industry in the Trieste and Monfalcone districts.[38] Data on asbestos deaths have been collected for many years, thanks to a first rate group of epidemiologists to recording committed to studying occupational diseases and unraveling on the asbestos epidemic. Data show that 8,868 cases of mesothelioma were entered into the National Mesothelioma Registry between 1993 and 2004 (exposure to asbestos was validated for 6,603 of them).[39] Roughly 10 percent of the cases occurred because of environmental or household exposure to asbestos dust.[40] Epidemiologists predict that, at the peak of the epidemic, approximately 800 individuals will die from mesothelioma annually.[41]

Asbestos has been used in the United States since the middle of the nineteenth century. "The manufacture of asbestos products in the US began just before the Civil War with simple versions of asbestos paper, textiles, and packing being made in small workshops."[42] Slowly its use grew as American businesses invested in asbestos mines in Québec. One of them, Johns-Manville, with its large plant located in Manville, NJ, soon became one of the world's leading building materials and insulating companies. The other major asbestos firm in the early use of asbestos was US Steel. Together they "were major suppliers to the building,

---

38   Claudio Bianchi and Tommaso Bianchi, "Malignant pleural mesothelioma in Italy," *Indian Journal of Occupational and Environmental Medicine* 13, no. 2 (2009): 80-83.

39   Alessandro Marinaccio et al., "Pleural malignant mesothelioma epidemic: incidence, modalities of asbestos exposure and occupations involved from the Italian National Register," *International Journal of Cancer. Journal International du Cancer* 130, no. 9 (2012): 2146-2154.

40   Daniela Ferrante et al., "Cancer Mortality and Incidence of Mesothelioma in a Cohort of Wives of Asbestos Workers in Casale Monferrato, Italy," *Environmental Health Perspectives* 115, no. 10 (2007): 1401.

41   Alessandro Marinaccio et al., "Predictions of mortality from pleural mesothelioma in Italy: a model based on asbestos consumption figures supports results from age-period-cohort models," *International Journal of Cancer. Journal International du Cancer* 115, no. 1 (2005): 142-147.

42   Jock McCulloch and Geoffrey Tweedale, *Defending the indefensible: The global asbestos industry and its fight for survival* (Oxford: Oxford University Press, 2008), 20.

automobile, and railroad industries and both sold most of their products to buyer specifications" and had a close relationship with J.P. Morgan.[43] As America developed its industrial force, these two companies amassed large profits. The use of asbestos grew from 20,000 metric tons per year in 1900 to 170,550 in the 1930s and 672,900 in the 1950s.[44] Asbestos use peaked in 1973, up to 803,000 metric tons per year.[45] Asbestos was extensively mined in the United States. One of the chrysotile asbestos mines was located near Coalinga, California, USA (now a US EPA Superfund reclamation area). The world's largest vermiculite mine was located near the town of Libby, Montana.[46] The mine opened in 1923, and was owned and operated by the W.R. Grace & Company from 1963 until it closed in 1990. Finally, the Great Valley of California hosted at least 26 asbestos mines or asbestos prospects.[47]

### The making of the asbestos epidemic

Although some evidence that asbestos was dangerous had been documented in pre-modern times, its toxicity was established only decades after the modern rise of the material. Asbestos toxicity became known gradually. In 1899, "government factory inspectors in Britain singled out asbestos because of its 'easily demonstrated danger' to the workers' health."[48] Asbestos deaths were first noted in 1906 when "medical experts fully described the ill effects of breathing asbestos particles."[49] The first medical paper on asbestosis was in fact published in the British Medical Journal in 1924.[50]

Evidence of a causal link between asbestos exposure and lung cancer become public only decades after in 1955. Evidence of the link slowly grew in the 1930s and 1940s. Cases of lung cancer among asbestos workers were reported in the 1930s in England among Turner & Newall's employees. Turner & Newall's internal

---

43   Ibid., 22.

44   Jeb Barnes, *Dust-up: asbestos litigation and the failure of common sense policy reform* (Washington, DC: Georgetown University Press, 2011), 16-17.

45   Ibid., 17.

46   For an account of the asbestos industry in the United States, see Paul Brodeur, *Outrageous misconduct: the asbestos industry on trial*, 1st ed.(New York: Pantheon Books, 1985); Castleman, *Asbestos: medical and legal aspects*.

47   Malcolm Ross and Robert P. Nolan, "History of asbestos discovery and use and asbestos-related disease in context with the occurrence of asbestos within ophiolite complexes," in *Geological Society of America Special Paper* (Geological Society of America, 2003).

48   Geoffrey Tweedale, "Asbestos and its lethal legacy," *Nature Reviews Cancer* 2, no. 4 (2002): 311.

49   Ibid.

50   William E. Cooke, "Fibrosis of the lungs due to the inhalation of asbestos dust," *British Medical Journal* 2, no. 3317 (1924): 147.

compensation process registered cases of death for lung cancer, as Tweedale reports.[51] In 1931, the Trades Union Congress "was warned of a possible link between asbestos and lung cancer."[52] Further evidence that asbestos could cause lung cancer was gathered in the 1940s in Germany. Alerted by the emergence of such evidence, the Nazis decided in 1943 to list lung cancer as an occupational disease for Aryan asbestos workers.[53] The Nazi imprint on lung cancer as an occupational disease might have worked against public health in the post-World War II era. As an attorney suggested during an interview, the fall and the unraveling of the atrocities committed by the Nazi regime discredited the evidence that a link between asbestos and lung cancer had been proven. The governments of the countries that prevailed at war wanted a fresh start, which unfortunately included refuting whatever the fascists regimes that were defeated during the war, had done. Evidence that asbestos caused lung cancer followed that path. Ten years passed since the end of the war before new evidence was published. This happened in 1995 when Sir Richard Doll published the paper "Mortality from lung cancer in asbestos workers" in the *British Journal of Industrial Medicine*.[54] The study concluded that "lung cancer was a specific industrial hazard of certain asbestos workers and that the average risk among men employed for 20 or more years has been of the order of 10 times that experienced by the general population."[55] In 1964, Selikoff and colleagues furtherer supported Doll's findings: of the 632 insulation workers that comprised Selikoff's cohort, "forty-five died of cancer of the lung or pleura, whereas only 6.6 such deaths were expected."[56]

Scientific knowledge of the link between pleural mesothelioma and asbestos was published only in the 1960s. The credit for exposing the deadly consequences of asbestos goes to J.C. Wagner, a determined scientist appointed by the South Africa Department of Mines to explore occupational diseases in asbestos mines.[57] While initially his research explored the link between the magical mineral and asbestosis, over time Wagner realized that an off-the beaten path idea was very promising: the link between asbestos and cancer. He collected data on mesothelioma cases among men and women who had lived close to the mines. He included in the study thirty two cases with proven exposure to asbestos. Interestingly, only eight victims had experienced occupational exposure. The remaining victims grew

---

51   Geoffrey Tweedale, "Sources in the History of Occupational Health: The Turner & Newall Archive," *Social History of Medicine* 13, no. 3 (2000).

52   Tweedale, "Asbestos and its lethal legacy," 321.

53   McCulloch and Tweedale, *Defending the indefensible: The global asbestos industry and its fight for survival.*

54   Richard Doll, "Mortality from lung cancer in asbestos workers," *British Journal of Industrial Medicine* 12, no. 2 (1955).

55   Ibid.

56   Irving J. Selikoff, Jacob Churg, and E. Cuyler Hammond, "Asbestos Exposure and Neoplasia," *JAMA—Journal of the American Medical Association* 188, no. 1 (1964).

57   Tweedale, *Magic mineral to killer dust: Turner & Newall and the asbestos hazard.*

up and lived in the surroundings of the mines, a highly polluted environment. Dr. Wagner's groundbreaking findings were published in 1960 in the *British Journal of Industrial Medicine*[58] in a paper that "changed the understanding of the dangers of asbestos and suggested a nexus between work, the environment, and cancer."[59] However, Wagner's career in South Africa came to an end: his research made the industry worried that knowledge of asbestos cancerogenicity would put a halt to toxic mining activities in South Africa and he found it more convenient to move back to Great Britain and work as a pathologist.

Evidence of asbestos toxicity would have become public much earlier. The delay was caused by the industry's active efforts to conceal it. Business historians have demonstrated that the surge in asbestos disease in modern times is attributable to asbestos companies' conspiracy. The industry has concealed, misrepresented, underplayed, and manipulated evidence of asbestos toxicity since the early twentieth century.[60] Evidence of asbestos toxicity thus became public *despite* industry efforts to conceal it.

Asbestos toxicity, aggravated by delay in its public awareness, has killed thousands of people around the world. Asbestos causes annually an estimated 20,000 cases of lung cancers and 10,000 cases of mesothelioma across the population of Western Europe, Scandinavia, North America, Japan, and Australia. Indeed, this has been the case for decades. Asbestos use has in fact caused a true epidemic: one person every two hours dies of mesothelioma in the United States, one every four hours in the United Kingdom, three every day in Italy and Germany, two every day, in France, Japan, and Australia, and one a day in the Netherlands. The number of lung cancer deaths caused by asbestos is at least equal to the number of deaths from mesothelioma, as LaDou reported in 2004: "The ratio may be much higher than 1 to 1, with some reports suggesting up to 7 to 1, so there may be more than a half million asbestos cancer deaths in Western Europe over the next 35 years."[61] Epidemiologists predict that many more deaths will take place for a couple of decades from now, at least. The peak of the epidemic is expected to come between 2015 and 2020 in Europe. It may already have been reached in some countries such as the United States. The peak still has to come in those countries in which asbestos has not been banned.

With asbestos disease spreading throughout the world, societies began reacting to the emergence of the asbestos epidemic. Regulation was the first response. England took the lead and in 1931 the British government introduced dust control

---

58   J.C. Wagner, C.A. Sleggs, and P. Marchand, "Diffuse pleural mesothelioma and asbestos exposure in the North Western Cape Province," *British Journal of Industrial Medicine* 17 (1960).

59   McCulloch and Tweedale, *Defending the indefensible: The global asbestos industry and its fight for survival.*

60   Ibid., passim.

61   Joseph LaDou, "The asbestos cancer epidemic," *Environmental Health Perspectives* 112, no. 3 (2004).

regulations, medical examinations, and workmen's compensation for asbestos victims.[62] In the following decades, the majority of industrialized nations followed the example of England by regulating asbestos and eventually banning it. At the time of the publication of this book (this manuscript was finalized in June 2013), over 50 countries banned all forms of asbestos.[63] Unfortunately, by the time the scientific community could articulate the risks associated with extensive use of asbestos in industrial production and policymakers could react to such knowledge by regulating asbestos use, two generations had been exposed to massive quantities of the magical mineral since the modern use of asbestos began in the 1890s. Further, asbestos became ubiquitous because of the mass production of asbestos-containing products that have been installed in houses, schools, boars, plans, pipes, cars, trains, post offices, and many other places.

Even though asbestos regulations restricted the use of asbestos, many individuals had already been exposed, and many continued to be and still are, to deadly quantities of asbestos. Consequently, the institutional responses to the asbestos epidemic quickly entailed initiatives that were broader than mere regulation. With regulation being an insufficient response, countries thus began establishing mechanisms to compensate asbestos victims. Since asbestos production flourished in many capitalist economies, most of which had adopted some variation of the welfare state, compensation took the forms of no fault administrative compensation. Payments were delivered primarily as workers' compensation payments whose beneficiaries were those who had been exposed to asbestos in the course of their employment. In later decades, two additional mechanisms of compensation were activated: personal injury cases, and *ad hoc* compensations schemes.

## Asbestos compensation as a cultural response to the asbestos epidemic

In this book, I trace the emergence and transformation of asbestos compensation in Belgium, England, Italy, and the Unites States. In the tradition of sociolegal scholarship, this book presents a cultural study of asbestos compensation—a comparative study of the production and reproduction of asbestos compensation as a cultural response of capitalist societies to the asbestos epidemic. I look at the mechanisms that delivered compensation as well as the cultural forces and actors that contributed to its emergence and transformations. The ultimate goal is to advance our understanding of how law "is embedded within the larger framework

---

62    Tweedale, "Asbestos and its lethal legacy," 322.
63    Joseph LaDou et al., "The Case for a Global Ban on Asbestos," *Environmental Health Perspectives* 118, no. 7 (2010). An updated list of asbestos bans is maintained by the International Ban Asbestos Secretariat, a UK-based NGO dedicated to the worldwide ban of all forms of asbestos (http://ibasecretariat.org/alpha_ban_list.php).

of cultural norms, routines, and institutional relations,"[64] the role of victims' compensation in society, how its role changes in different societies, and how these differences ultimately highlight cultural differences among societies. The theoretical framework of the study is influenced by sociolegal scholarship, cultural sociology, comparative sociology, and social theory. These theoretical influences can be grouped in three strands of inquiry: law as a cultural phenomenon; national style of legal culture and convergence or divergence of legal cultures; and law as a form of institutionalized power.

First, law is a cultural phenomenon While, as Nelken points out, "there is little agreement on how best to grasp legal culture,"[65] scholars of legal culture view law as a phenomenon that emerges from the cultural fabric of our societies and it contributes to its constitution. It is produced and reproduced in everyday life through the mutual constitution of agency and structure. Anthony Giddens calls this dialectical relationship between social scientific knowledge and human practices the "double hermeneutic."[66] Culture is implicated in structuration when social actors make reference to perceptual frames in organizing and structuring perceptions about legality. Rather than "static, singular, or essentialized," culture is thus viewed "in terms of its multiplicity and variability across time as well as pace."[67] Structuration processes are highly contextual as time and place shape social life and social institutions. Social interactions are produced and reproduced differently depending on their spacial and temporal context. When applied to the study of law, scholars have explored the circumstances under which citizens turn to the law,[68] the framing of disputes and legal claims as cultural events linked to socially constructed definitions of normal behavior, respectability, responsibility, and the good person,[69] the role of cultural schemas and resources that operate

---

64   Engel and McCann, *Fault lines: tort law as cultural practice*, 6-7.

65   David Nelken, "Comparing legal cultures," in *The Blackwell companion to law and society*, ed. Austin Sarat (Malden, MA: Blackwell Publishing, 2004), 116.

66   Anthony Giddens, *The constitution of society: outline of the theory of structuration* (Berkeley: University of California Press, 1984), 284. See also Anthony Giddens, *Central problems in social theory: action, structure, and contradiction in social analysis* (Berkeley: University of California Press, 1979).

67   Engel and McCann, *Fault lines: tort law as cultural practice*, 9.

68   David M. Engel, "The Oven Bird's Song: Insiders, Outsiders, and Personal Injuries in an American Community," *Law & Society Review* 18, no. 4 (1984); William L.F. Felstiner, Richard L. Abel, and Austin Sarat, "The Emergence and Transformation of Disputes: Naming, Blaming, Claiming ..." *Law and Society Review* 15 (1981); Lawrence M. Friedman, *Total Justice* (New York: Russell Sage Foundation, 1985); William Haltom and Michael W. McCann, *Distorting the law: politics, media, and the litigation crisis* (Chicago: University of Chicago Press, 2004).

69   Sally Merry and Susan S. Silbey, "What Do Plaintiffs Want? Reexamining the Concept of Dispute," *Justice System Journal* 9, no. 2 (1984): 157.

in the constitution of legality in everyday life,[70] the relationship between social position and legal consciousness,[71] and legal mobilization.[72] Law as a cultural response to social problems is certainly affected by other responses. With regard to the asbestos epidemic, the welfare state is certainly a key set of cultural and institutional responses that affected the emergence and transformations of asbestos compensation. Since the institutions of the welfare state were already embedded in industrial economies when the asbestos epidemic emerged, the welfare state contributed to the structuration of asbestos compensation. The welfare state can, in fact, be seen to make a set of responses to the tension between capital accumulation and the human costs that has caused the asbestos epidemic. To this end, it contributed to the social organization of capitalism by providing relief to victims of unemployment, disability, occupational injury and disease, and other life events that prevent them from being active members of the productive working force; it moved classic liberalism "away from individualism and the self-guiding market";[73] it constituted a response to capitalists' fear of uncontrolled class conflict; it meant a departure of possessive individualism towards embracing "an ideal of solidarity to supplement the customary liberal commitment to personal freedom";[74] it justified state intervention in the economy and, during its golden years of the Keynesian Welfare National State,[75] produced a culture of *moral economy* that justified capitalist accumulation in the name of wealth redistribution granting a minimum degree of social reproduction.[76]

Second, the study looks at convergence and variation of legal culture in different societies aiming to identify those cultural underpinnings that are specific to certain geographical contexts and those that are consistent across space. While sociolegal scholars have stressed that legal culture as a unit of study does not have

---

70   The classic reference on legal consciousness is Patricia Ewick and Susan S. Silbey, *The common place of law: stories from everyday life* (Chicago: University of Chicago Press, 1998).

71   Michael W. McCann, *Rights at work: pay equity reform and the politics of legal mobilization* (Chicago: University of Chicago Press, 1994).

72   Lauren B. Edelman, Gwendolyn Leachman, and Doug McAdam, "On Law, Organizations, and Social Movements," *Annual Review of Law and Social Science* 6, no. 1 (2010); Michael W. McCann, "Law and Social Movements: Contemporary Perspectives," *Annual Review of Law and Social Science* 2, no. 1 (2006).

73   John F. Manley, "Theorizing the unexceptional US welfare state," in *Class, power and the state in capitalist society: essays on Ralph Miliband*, ed. Paul Wetherly, Clyde W. Barrow, and Peter Burnham (Basingstoke; New York: Palgrave Macmillan, 2008), 175.

74   James T. Kloppenberg, *Uncertain victory: social democracy and progressivism in European and American thought, 1870-1920* (New York: Oxford University Press, 1986), 7.

75   Bob Jessop, *The future of the capitalist state* (Cambridge, UK; Malden, MA: Polity; Blackwell, 2002), 55-94.

76   William I. Robinson, *Latin America and global capitalism: a critical globalization perspective* (Baltimore: Johns Hopkins University Press, 2008), 14.

to be restricted to national legal systems,[77] the literature on capitalism and the welfare state points to nation states as primary units of analysis of comparative divergence and convergence of legal culture. In fact, not only the Keynesian Welfare National State prioritized the "national scale in economic and social policy-making with local as well as central delivery"[78] but, as Robison contends, they "remain major—perhaps the major—battlegrounds for contending social forces."[79] The boundaries of sovereign nations are thus an important conceptual space in the analysis of the structuration of asbestos compensation in the twentieth century. Among legal scholars who measured cross-national variation with nation states, some have stressed the link between specific cultures and specific types of law and highlighted how unique traits of national legal cultures shape law—Kagan's concept of "adversarial legalism" is particularly pertinent to analyzing asbestos compensation and a purported "exceptionality" of American legal culture.[80] Others have focused on the explanatory power derived from accounting for micro- and macro-level factors and have looked at the power of macro-level factors to push legal systems to converge towards similar cultural practices. Lawrence Friedman in particular argued that industrialized nations are converging towards a single, "modern" legal culture that produces dense and ubiquitous law, in which legitimacy is instrumental, that stresses fundamental human rights, that is strongly individualistic,[81] and that gives special attention to the increasing public demand for legal remedies—what Friedman calls "total justice."[82]

A parallel divide characterizes welfare state scholarship. Scholars of the "varieties of welfare capitalism" focus on national styles of welfare capitalism by emphasizing the relative strength of class-related forces in accounting for cross-national variation in welfare state development and concentrating the analysis on the nuanced categorizations of the institutional arrangements of modern

---

77  Nelken, "Comparing legal cultures."

78  Jessop, *The future of the capitalist state*, 59.

79  Robinson, *Latin America and global capitalism: a critical globalization perspective*, 11.

80  Robert A. Kagan, *Adversarial legalism: the American way of law* (Cambridge, MA: Harvard University Press, 2001). 14-15. See also Barnes, *Dust-up: asbestos litigation and the failure of common sense policy reform*; Jeb Barnes, Thomas F. Burke, and Malcolm Feeley, eds, *The Politics of Legalism*, Law, Courts and Politics Series (Routledge, 2013), passim; Erhard R. Blankenburg, "Civil Litigation Rates as Indicators for Legal Cultures," in *Comparing Legal Cultures*, ed. David Nelken (Brookfield, VT: Dartmouth Press, 1997); Thomas Frederick Burke, *Lawyers, lawsuits, and legal rights: the battle over litigation in American society* (Berkeley: University of California Press, 2002); Eric A. Feldman, "Blood Justice: Courts, Conflict, and Compensation in Japan, France, and the United States," *Law and Society Review* 34, no. 3 (2000).

81  Lawrence M. Friedman, "Is There a Modern Legal Culture?" *Ratio Juris* 7, no. 2 (1994).

82  Friedman, *Total Justice*; Lawrence M. Friedman, *The Republic of Choice: Law, Authority, and Culture* (Cambridge, MA: Harvard University Press, 1990).

capitalism—Esping-Andersen's well known typology distinguishes among three types of welfare regimes: liberal (United Kingdom, United States, Australia), social-democratic (Sweden, Norway, the Netherlands), or corporatist (Germany, Austria, Italy).[83] On a similar vein, the "national values" approach is concerned with the relative strength of class-related forces in accounting for cross-national variation in welfare state development.[84]

Once again, this literature for the most part argues that the American welfare state is an exceptional one—it is less extensive, it developed later than in Europe, it grew slowly slower, and it has been supplemented by private enterprise, which "has performed many social functions ... that long were dominated by government or corporatist bodies in Europe."[85] The other side of the debate pays attention to how micro- (subjects and citizens have a voice)[86] and macro-level factors (for instance, the transition from Fordism to Neoliberalism) created opportunities for convergent transformations of national welfare. Robinson in particular identifies five epochs of capitalism, which have important ramifications for the synchronous transformation of welfare states throughout the industrialized world.[87] This literature emphasizes that the transition from corporate capitalism and the subsequent Keynesian Welfare National State to neoliberalism and global capitalism in the 1970s, when the oil crises resulted in a constriction of private capital's capacity for accumulation, caused significant cultural change. In fact, in the 1970s, capitalists launched a global counterrevolution that reversed the culture of moral economy that the golden years of the welfare state had produced,

---

83   "Varieties of capitalism" scholars argue that the organization of capitalist economies deploys a wide range of possible combinations of economic institutions and that cultural and historical influences have determined the emergence of not one but a variety of welfare regimes. Gosta Esping-Andersen, *The three worlds of welfare capitalism* (Princeton: Princeton University Press, 1990); Gosta Esping-Andersen, *Social foundations of postindustrial economies* (Oxford: Oxford University Press, 1999); Peter A. Hall, "The movement from Keynesianism to monetarism: Institutional analysis and British economic policy in the 1970s," in *Structuring Politics. Historical Institutionalism in Comparative Analysis,* ed. Sven Steinmo, Kathleen Thelen, and Frank Longstreth (Cambridge, MA: Cambridge University Press, 1992); Peter A. Hall and David W. Soskice, *Varieties of capitalism: the institutional foundations of comparative advantage* (Oxford; New York: Oxford University Press, 2001).

84   Seymour Martin Lipset, *The first new nation: the United States in historical and comparative perspective* (New York: Basic Books, 1963).

85   Jacob S. Hacker, *The divided welfare state: the battle over public and private social benefits in the United States* (New York: Cambridge University Press, 2002); Kagan, *Adversarial legalism: the American way of law.* 52.

86   Wim van Oorschot, Michael Opielka, and Birgit Pfau-Effinger, *Culture and welfare state: values and social policy in comparative perspective* (Cheltenham, UK; Northampton, MA: Edward Elgar, 2008).

87   William I. Robinson, *A theory of global capitalism: production, class, and state in a transnational world* (Baltimore: Johns Hopkins University Press, 2004), 2-6.

determined Fordism's decline, favored deregulation, labor market flexibility, economic globalization, and ultimately led to the retrenchment of the welfare state.[88] These cultural transformations, if true, are certainly significant to asbestos compensation.

Finally, this book instigates the role of power, dominance, cultural hegemony, consensus, and resistance in legal structuration. Sociolegal scholars focus on "the power at work in and through law" by addressing the mediating thought processes which local practices area aggregated and condensed into systemic institutionalized power.[89] They analyze legal ideology and how the rule of law is interpreted as a device that serves the interests of the powerful[90] and legal consciousness and how cultural schema sustain legal hegemony and create, or fail to create, opportunities for resistance.[91] Further, it is important to consider how groups struggle in everyday life for the appropriation and use of cultural resources to acquire and exercise power over other social groups and how hegemonic processes generate systems of ideas and beliefs through which the ruling class is able to exert power over society.[92] Gramsci's concept of hegemony and Bob Jessup's concept of ecological dominance showed that, rather than the product of "conscious conspiracy by the powerful to dominate the powerless," cultural dominance is the product of coordination of cultural strategies, which results from different types of groups contributing to the creation of a "hegemonic interpretation that is combined into a single narrative, with each element reinforcing rather than contradicting the others."[93] Dominant cultural schemas, once produced, tend to persist due to the action of various mechanisms of cultural reproduction (what Orlando Patterson calls the "mechanisms of persistence")[94] and become embedded in the social texture of a society. Economic power certainly plays an important role in cultural

---

88   Will Hutton and Anthony Giddens, eds, *Global capitalism* (New York: The New Press, 2000); Robinson, *Latin America and global capitalism: a critical globalization perspective*, 19.

89   Susan S. Silbey, "Making a Place for Cultural Analyses of Law," *Law & Social Inquiry* 17, no. 1 (1992); Susan S. Silbey, "Legal culture and cultures of legality," in *Handbook of Cultural Sociology*, ed. John R. Hall, Laura Grindstaff, and Ming-Cheng Lo (London; New York: Routledge, 2010).

90   Christine Sypnowich, "Law and Ideology," in *The Stanford Encyclopedia of Philosophy*, ed. Edward N. Zalta (Stanford: The Metaphysics Research Lab, 2010).

91   Silbey, "Legal culture and cultures of legality."

92   Steven Lukes, *Power: a radical view*, 2nd ed. (New York: Palgrave Macmillan, 2005).

93   Les Back et al., *Cultural sociology: an introduction* (Chichester, West Sussex; Hoboken, NJ: Wiley-Blackwell, 2012), 29, 113; Antonio Gramsci, *Letters from prison*, 1st ed. (New York: Harper & Row, 1973); Bob Jessop, *State theory: putting the capitalist state in its place* (Cambridge, UK: Polity Press, 1990).

94   Orlando Patterson, "The mechanisms of cultural reproduction. Explaining the puzzle of persistence," in *Handbook of cultural sociology*, ed. John R. Hall, Laura Grindstaff, and Ming-Cheng Lo (London; New York: Routledge, 2010): 139-151.

domination in everyday life.[95] In the context of legal structuration, corporate power is certainly an influential force of ecological dominance—an insight that is illustrated by Roth's idea of "corpocracy,"[96] studies by scholars of corporate power and capitalist elites[97] and sociologists of business who have paid attention to corporations as social actors that engage in direct input into social policy whenever their structural power is insufficient to protect corporate interests.[98]

The focus on these three strands of inquiry does not make the study of black letter law useless. To the contrary, black letter law, with its interpretation and official reasoning by judges and other institutional actors, is seen as an important structural component of social life.[99] In this spirit, each chapter provides up-to-date accounts of the formal laws that regulate compensation mechanisms, eligibility requirements as well as landmark opinions and key legal doctrines that are deployed in litigation. Chapters expanding existing literature on the black-letter elements of asbestos compensation can be found herein. Scholars of the asbestos industry discuss compensation and devote some pages of their books to compensation issues. Castleman's encyclopedic *Asbestos: Medical and Legal Aspects* devotes several pages to comparative developments of asbestos compensation.[100] The same is true also for business historians McCulloch and Tweedale's carefully researched and deeply detailed account of how the asbestos industry covered up knowledge of asbestos toxicity.[101] Science and technology scholars Jasanoff and Perese compare asbestos compensation to

---

95   Jessop, *State theory: putting the capitalist state in its place*.

96   William Roth, *The assault on social policy* (New York: Columbia University Press, 2002).

97   William K. Carroll, *The making of a transnational capitalist class: corporate power in the twenty-first century* (London; New York: Zed, 2010).

98   Kevin Farnsworth and Chris Holden, "The Business-Social Policy Nexus: Corporate Power and Corporate Inputs into Social Policy," *Journal of Social Policy* 35, no. 3 (2006); Chris Holden and Kelley Lee, "Corporate Power and Social Policy," *Global Social Policy* 9, no. 3 (2009).

99   I used some of this literature as part of my effort to research the black letter law of the countries analyzed in this study. See Christian von Bar, *The common European law of torts* (Oxford; New York: Clarendon Press; Oxford University Press, 1998); Bernhard A. Koch and Helmut Koziol, *Compensation for personal injury in a comparative perspective* (Vienna; New York: Springer, 2003); Basil Markesinis, Michael Coester, and Guido Alpa, eds, *Compensation for personal injury in English, German and Italian law: a comparative outline*, Cambridge studies in international and comparative law (Cambridge; New York: Cambridge University Press, 2005); Basil S. Markesinis et al., *Compensation for personal injury in English, German and Italian law: a comparative outline* (Cambridge, UK; New York: Cambridge University Press, 2005).

100   Castleman, *Asbestos: medical and legal aspects*.

101   McCulloch and Tweedale, *Defending the indefensible: The global asbestos industry and its fight for survival*.

investigate political culture and risk regulation in Europe and the United States.[102] Government bodies, practitioners, and activists have reported, with a comparative flare, about legal developments happening simultaneously in various jurisdictions.[103] An important contribution comes from sociolegal scholars Dingwall, Felstiner, and Durkin, who have looked in various publications at the cultural understandings, claim mobilization, and social actors associated with asbestos compensation in England and the United States.[104] However, their research is two decades old. Finally, several monographs are dedicated to the empirical study of asbestos litigation in a single country.[105] Overall, legal scholars' approach to asbestos compensation is often fragmented and rarely comparative. This study expands the existing literature for it includes countries for which no literature on asbestos compensation exists and it extends to a long period of time, spanning early modern use of asbestos to present times.

---

102    Sheila Jasanoff and Dogan Perese, "Welfare State or Welfare Court: Asbestos Litigation in Comparative Perspective," *Journal of Law and Policy* XII, no. 2 (2004).

103    Albert Azagra-Malo, "Los fondos de compensación del amianto en Francia y en Bélgica [Asbestos Injuries Compensation Funds in France and Belgium]," *Indret: Revista para el Análisis del Derecho*, no. 3 (2007); Richard Best, "Liability for Asbestos Related Disease in England and Germany," *German Law Journal* 4, no. 7 (2003); Andrea Boggio, "Comparative Notes On The Asbestos Trust Fund," *Mealey's Litigation Report, Asbestos*, 1, no. 6 (2003); Eurogip, "Les maladies professionnelles liées à l'amiante en Europe. Une enquête dans 13 pays," (Paris: Eurogip, 2006); Eurogip, "Compensation of permanent impairment resulting from occupational injuries in Europe," (Paris: Eurogip, 2010); Laurie Kazan-Allen, "Asbestos: the Human Cost of Corporate Greed" (Brussels: European United Left/Nordic Green Left, 2006); Munich Re, ed. *Asbestos. Anatomy of a Mass Tort* (München: Münchener Rückversicherungs-Gesellschaft, 2009); Laura Salvatori, Alessandro Santoni, and Darren Michaels, "Asbestos: The current situation in Europe" (paper presented at the ASTIN Colloquium, Berlin, August 24-27, 2003).

104    Thomas E. Durkin, "Constructing law: comparing legal action in the United States and United Kingdom" (University of Chicago, 1994); William L.F. Felstiner and Robert Dingwall, *Asbestos Litigation in the United Kingdom: An Interim Report* (Chicago: American Bar Foundation, 1988).

105    The asbestos monographs used and cited in this book are: Barnes, *Dust-up: asbestos litigation and the failure of common sense policy reform*; Stephen J. Carroll et al., *Asbestos litigation* (Santa Monica, CA: RAND Corporation, 2005); Emmanuel Henry, *Amiante, un scandale improbable: sociologie d'un problème public* [Asbestos, an improbable scandal: sociology of a public issue](Rennes: Presses Universitaires de Rennes, 2007); Deborah R. Hensler et al., *Asbestos in the Courts. The Challenge of Mass Toxic Torts* (Santa Monica, CA: The Institute for Civil Justice, 1985); Maria Roselli, *Amiante & Eternit: Fortunes et forfaitures* [Asbestos & Eternit. Fortunes and Forfaitures], trans. Marianne Enckell from German (Lausanne: Editions d'en bas, 2008); Nicholas J. Wikeley, *Compensation for industrial disease* (Aldershot, Hants; Brookfield, VT: Dartmouth, 1993).

**From theory to the field**

The translation of theory to field work was methodologically seamless. The inherently multidisciplinary nature of cultural analyses of law translates into field work informed by a method that mixes social science with history. Blending historical inquiry with the methods of social science inquiry, data were gathered from primary and secondary sources as well as semi-structured interviews with experts and practitioners who provide insights on past and current practices of asbestos compensation. Field research was conducted in Belgium, England, Italy, and the United States by consulting a variety of primary and secondary sources as well as by conducting semi-structured interviews with experts and practitioners. I selected these jurisdictions because of my familiarity with their legal systems, culture, and language as well as considerations of availability and accessibility of data, the substantial presence of the asbestos industry (as discussed in the next section), and the distinctive legal traditions that they represent. My familiarity with these countries is rooted in my biography. I live and teach in the United States. I hold degrees in law from both common law (United States) and the civil law (Italy) traditions: American law finds its roots in English common law, and Belgian and Italian law find their roots in Roman law and the codification efforts of the Napoleon era.[106] I am fluent in English, Italian, and French.[107] While French is the first language of roughly 40 percent of the population, the most widely spoken language of Belgium is Dutch. However, in the nineteenth century, the language of law was French. "For lawyers it was easier to keep working with the French codes. That way, they could have a free ride by copying French laws, quoting decisions of French courts and using French literature, sometimes in pirated editions of French works printed in Bruxelles," as Dirk Heirbaut notes.[108] I also lived and engaged in the legal profession or teaching both in Italy and England. Finally, I grew up about one hour away from one of Europe's largest manufacturing asbestos plants (the one in Casale) and the largest asbestos mine in Europe (Balangero). The asbestos operations of Casale are also linked to Belgium through Eternit's corporate network, as the chapter on asbestos firms will demonstrate. Second, my biographical traits contributed largely to my ability to access data, especially with regard to Belgium and Italy, whose asbestos compensation is largely ignored in scholarship in English. I was in fact able to connect with a critical number of lawyers, experts, academics, and activists to conduct meaningful fieldwork in all four countries and to access and read publications in their native language. Third, in all four countries asbestos use was copious and the asbestos industry flourished with the result that significant levels of asbestos disease have been recorded, as discussed in the next section.

---

106   Dirk Heirbaut, "The Belgian Legal Tradition: Does it Exist?" in *Introduction to Belgian law*, ed. Hubert Bocken and Walter de Bondt (Bruxelles; The Hague; Boston: Bruylant; Kluwer Law International, 2001).

107   All translations are mine unless noted.

108   Ibid., x.

I conducted semi-open interviews in all four countries. I did not draft a rigid interview protocol. This would have been inadequate given the wide array of experiences and views that respondents had with asbestos compensation. No single set of questions would have helped me capture such complexity. Rather, the interviews were based on pre-interview research and notes on possible questions, and then conducted in an open-ended fashion so that the "voice" of the respondent would lead the inquiry. The bulk of interview questions can be grouped into the following categories: the role of social security, workers' compensation and other compensation schemes; information on the lawyers' involvement with asbestos litigation and the number and nature of any asbestos cases handled by the firm; the role played by various social actors (victims, advocacy and support groups, experts, insurance companies, judges); issues of substantive (theories of law, causation, damages, and the rules of liability) and procedural (aggregation of claims; settlement negotiations, and litigation strategies) law; issues of funding (fees, expenses, and other costs when claiming asbestos compensation); participants' perceptions of the process. The majority of interviews lasted between 30 and 60 minutes.

The interviews along with the reading of primary and secondary sources have drawn my attention to certain recurring themes, strategies, situations, and processes. As data collection progressed, stories began overlapping and the pieces of the puzzle fell together. Jurisdictions such as England provide an endless supply of stories and judicial cases: while each of them has its specific ingredients (and carries the seeds of the suffering of a particular individual, his or her family and caring network), generalization can be drawn without studying all cases. Similarly, asbestos cases in Italy are numerous and they all follow a limited range of schemas. At some point of data collection, I concluded that the need to read new cases, retrieve new documents, and talk to new people was no longer essential. After saturation, I decided to orient my research towards specific issues that needed further investigation. Overall, I conducted 50 interviews—15 in England, 22 in Italy, eight in Belgium, and five in the United States, and shared information and data by email with a number of other experts. I selected respondents based on consideration of balance and convenience. I purposely sought after experts whose experiences and opinions would reflect a wide range of views. I pursued a strategy of diversification by seeking respondents who had been involved both in cases crucial to the continuing development of asbestos litigation and in marginal or routine cases. I also balanced the pool of respondents in terms of pro-victim versus pro-industry bias. For instance, when researching a case, I only interviewed one side if the other was also available for an interview. This goal was however much harder to attain in Belgium, where the spectrum of respondents was limited because of the very small number of cases. Such reality is reflected in the limited number of interviews conducted in Belgium. I also gave consideration to convenience: given the limited amount of time and financial resources, I excluded individuals who were located too far from the mainstream legal community. Therefore, I excluded Scotland, Northern Ireland, Southern Italy, and the Flemish part of Belgium.

Throughout the book I do not disclose the identity of the respondents. At the time the interview was conducted, I promised to keep their identity confidential. This arrangement allowed me to approach and interview individuals who otherwise would have been reluctant to participate in the interview. With few exceptions, the respondents did not know me personally at the time I approached them requesting an interview. On at least two occasions, the interview focused on the early stages of pending litigation, a very delicate moment in the life of a case. In one case, the respondent looked visibly distressed and worried that, as a fake scholar, I was trying to elicit strategic information on behalf of the defendant. In another case, an attorney confessed to engaging in billing practices that were both against the law and professional rules. Other respondents, especially attorneys representing defendants, were afraid that their words could be indirectly attributed to their clients, a possibility particularly worrying in the event the attorney was rhetorically devaluing or dismissing specific claims brought against the client. Confidentiality certainly has a price. In writing this book, I can use their words but I cannot quote the identity of my sources. Readers may (wrongfully) think less of this study because they cannot assess the source of my data. However I believe my choice to privilege access to sources over identifiability is justified by increased approachability and candor of respondents.

## Organization of the material

The four chapters that follow present case studies of asbestos compensation in Belgium (Chapter 2), England (Chapter 3), Italy (Chapter 4), and the United States (Chapter 5). The book then looks at how three transnational asbestos firms (James Hardie, Cape, and Eternit) contributed to the development of asbestos compensation through the lenses of their corporate structures, role in the emergence of the asbestos epidemic, and legal strategies that were implemented to avoid, minimize, or delay accountability for their tortious conduct (Chapter 6). Finally, I discuss how asbestos compensation emerged as a cultural response to the asbestos epidemic by identifying relevant cultural frames used by social actors, exposing the hegemonic impact of cultural frames on actors' legal consciousness, discussing victims' counter-hegemonic efforts, and concluding that law failed to fully redress the asbestos epidemic (Chapter 7).

Methodologically, I decided to present national data on asbestos compensation in country-specific chapters, even though I have reservations as fully relying on comparativists' conventional wisdom that the proper units of research in comparative legal analysis are nation states or "families of law." Nelken rightfully refers to this as "tired categories."[109] National boundaries, however, can be a misleading line to identifying the unit of comparative research. They can

---

109   David Nelken, "Law, Liability, and Culture," in *Fault Lines*, eds. David M. Engel and Michael W. McCann (Stanford: Stanford Law Books, 2009), 23.

in fact be either too narrow or too broad. At the macro-level, major structural changes are rarely confined to national boundaries but have transnational and sometimes global resonance (the oil crisis of the early 1970s or the progressive off shoring of manufacturing production are prime examples). At the micro-level, local circumstances may shape unique patterns of structuration. At the subnational level, Nelken notes, "the appropriate unit of legal culture may be the local court, the prosecutor's office, or the lawyer's consulting room."[110] In the context of asbestos compensation, a community living in close proximity to an asbestos plant may be particularly active in seeking accountability of an asbestos firm for reasons that are peculiar to the locale. On the other hand, Merryman notes that "differences in the legal systems are reflections of the fact that for several centuries the world has been divided up into individual states, under intellectual conditions that have emphasized the importance of state sovereignty and encouraged a nationalistic emphasis on national characteristics and traditions."[111] Mindful of strengths and limitations of designing the study around national boundaries, I use the nation-state as a convenient starting point to organize the materials but I integrate this perspective by looking at specific communities and sub-national realities in each country as well as bringing in transnational themes—the most important being a discussion of how three major asbestos firms, all of them with transnational operations, dealt with legal accountability for their asbestos liabilities. This perspective adds a layer of analysis that is disjoint from the specific traits of a single legal system and that contributes to understanding how law and capitalism operate in transnational environments.

Before getting to the case studies, I want to make a few remarks on language and comparative analysis. Comparative legal scholars face the enormous challenge to translate legal terms and concepts to a different language—to another legal language.[112] Scholars have developed three strategies to deal with this challenge. Legal comparativists on one hand of the spectrum refrain from translating and use terms in their native languages so that historically rooted differences in functions are "properly and distinctly designated and employed."[113] Comparativists on the other side translate the term using the equivalent term in the target language. Since perfect equivalents are rare, scholars commonly identify a functional equivalent. When no equivalent can be found, comparativists create neologisms that capture

---

110   Ibid.

111   John Henry Merryman, *The civil law tradition: an introduction to the legal systems of Western Europe and Latin America*, 2nd ed. (Stanford: Stanford University Press, 1985).

112   Jeanne Gaakeer, "Iudex translator: the reign of finitude," in *Methods of Comparative Law*, ed. Pier Giuseppe Monateri, *Research Handbooks in Comparative Law* (Cheltenham; Northampton, MA: Edward Elgar, 2012).

113   Sofie M.F. Geeroms, "Comparative Law and Legal Translation: Why the Terms Cassation, Revision and Appeal Should Not Be Translated ..." *The American Journal of Comparative Law* 50, no. 1 (2002): 228.

the essence of the concept, which is often expressed in a footnote.[114] In this book, I try to translate all terms (mostly from French and Italian) into English to the best of my ability. Sometimes this is not possible, and therefore I leave the word in the source language. However, throughout the manuscript I use certain terms in a rather improper fashion. These are the words "victim," "plaintiff," "claimant," and "compensation." Here is why.

The term "victim" is used primarily to identify individuals who suffer an asbestos disease. However, I use it to identify also individuals who had been exposed to asbestos but have not developed a disease and individuals who developed a disease for which they received no compensation (either because they failed to successfully claim compensation or because they never claimed compensation). The reader can then see that "victim" is used as a matter of convenience to identify various categories of individuals who may or may not have a claim, the common denominator being exposure to asbestos. Furthermore, the definition offered by the Oxford English Dictionary ("a person harmed, injured, or killed as a result of a crime, accident, or other event or action")[115] suggest that its use does not necessarily entail blame on part of a tortfeasor or some sort of righteousness in the person who is harmed, injured, or killed. In other words, the use of the term is stripped of any ethical consideration.

With regard to "plaintiff" and "claimant," I use the term "claimant" to identify a victim who demanded compensation whether in workers' compensation, torts, a criminal trial, an administrative process, or a compensation fund. This is also consistent with the Oxford English Dictionary (claimant is "a person making a claim, especially in a lawsuit or for a government-sponsored benefit").[116] The term "plaintiff" identifies only a victim who brought a tort lawsuit against an asbestos company. This distinction is mindful of the English usage of the term "claimant" as plaintiff making a claim in a lawsuit. Finally, the term "compensation" is used in a broad sense of "something, typically money, awarded to someone in recognition of loss, suffering, or injury."[117] My use encompasses any payment paid to an asbestos victim to make the victim "whole" (or at least better) after an injury or loss. It certainly refers to damages awarded liquidated in court but also to payments made by social security administration (often in the form of a pension), workers' compensation systems, insurance companies, and settling defendants. Civil law scholars often distinguish the two concepts—*risarcimento* and *indennizzo* in Italian. One refers to payments made because of negligence and the other to no-fault payments. In this book I purposely avoid this nuanced distinction and use "compensation" in reference to all payments made to asbestos

---

114    Gerard-René De Groot and Conrad J.P. Van Laer, "The Dubious Quality of Legal Dictionaries," *International Journal of Legal Information* 34 (2006).

115    Oxford University Press, *Oxford English Dictionary* (Oxford; New York: Oxford University Press, 2000).

116    Ibid.

117    Ibid.

victims. Two reasons support the indicated use: adapting the language to the (almost endless) variety of payments that are made to asbestos victims in the various jurisdictions is very complicated. What matters is the descriptive power of the word "compensation" as payments to victims. Readers are able to attach the proper meaning to the word "compensation" by looking at the context in which the word is used. Second, the more generic use of the term shifts the reader's attention from the technical nature of the payments to the substantive fact that a payment is made. Readers will easily identify, from the context of the discussion, whether a payment was made by somebody because of a judicial finding of fault or as part of a no-fault system of redress.

# Chapter 2

# Asbestos compensation in Belgium

An "historical champion in asbestos consumption"[1] in which 200 people die every year of mesothelioma,[2] Belgium is barely on the atlas of comparative legal scholarship, much less of comparative studies of asbestos compensation. Legal scholars have paid little attention to this small, bilingual country in the heart of Europe. Belgium, as historian Gerd-Rainer Horn pointed out, "remains one of Western Europe's least well-known territorial states, certainly in academic circles outside of its national boundaries."[3] Nonetheless, Belgium is a very interesting case study of asbestos compensation because of its exceptionalism if compared to the other nations researched in this book: remarkably weak claim consciousness, absence of personal injury cases based on occupational exposure, and workers' compensation as (almost) the only path to compensation (almost because in 2011 an asbestos personal injury case based on environmental exposure was successfully litigated for the first time).

The absence of personal injury litigation is remarkable. This is certainly the reflection of black letter law dictating workers' compensation's exclusivity as a remedy, unless the victim can prove that the employer intentionally caused the disease. This is a *de facto* immunity for employers. Furthermore, Belgian victims' efforts to find ways to circumvent or to curb workers' compensation exclusivity have been ineffective. Claim consciousness and mobilization have been weak. The roots of this state of affairs run deep into Belgian legal, political and socio-cultural tradition. The forces that compressed claim consciousness and mobilization include a powerful asbestos industry, slow emergence of medical studies on asbestos diseases, unfriendliness of rules, judicial and doctrinal attitudes towards occupational disease, a system of labor relations that failed to generate interest in asbestos compensation on the part of unions, and a political and legal culture that discouraged demands for justice in favor of quiet acceptance of asbestos disease as a misfortune.

For five decades asbestos victims were not able to collect anything more than workers' compensation, some additional payments from Eternit, and a few settlements. From 1953, the year in which asbestosis was listed in workers' compensation, and 2011, the year in which the first and only judgment in Belgium's history went in favor of an asbestos victim, workers' compensation has been virtually the exclusive source of compensation for asbestos victims.

---

1  Nawrot et al., "Belgium: historical champion in asbestos consumption," 1692.

2  "Au moins 200 morts chaque année à cause de l'amiante" [At least 200 deaths caused by asbestos every year.] *FMP News*, January 21, 2011.

3  Gerd-Rainer Horn, "The Belgian Contribution to Global 1968," *Belgisch Tijdschrift voor Nieuwste Geschiedenis—Revue belge d'histoire contemporaine* 35, no. 4 (2005): 628.

During these five decades, the only payments that were consistently made to asbestos victims were sums paid by the workers' compensation system to victims of occupational exposure. Currently, victims of occupational exposure receive compensation exclusively from the workers' compensation system. Compensation was expanded in 2007 when the *Fonds d'indemnisation des victimes de l'amiante*, an *ad hoc* asbestos fund, was set up to curb some of the limitations of workers' compensation.[4] Victims of secondhand and environmental exposure are not entitled to receive payments from workers' compensation or the 2007 Asbestos Fund. A few cases have been litigated and only one was successful. The chapter looks at each of these determinants of weak claim consciousness and mobilization, at the current workers' compensation and the recent enactment of the 2007 Asbestos Fund, at growing efforts to mobilize claims, which have led to the only case that an asbestos victim has successfully tried. The discussion begins with an historical roots and developments of workers' compensation.

## Origin of workers' compensation

The statutory exclusivity of workers' compensation as means to compensate occupational disease and its conservative judicial interpretation have also contributed to weak claim consciousness and mobilization. Established in 1903, Belgian workers' compensation is rather biased against claimants. This bias is the product of the historical circumstances that led to its establishment. The 1903 statute is the outcome of a contentious policy debate fueled by years of workers' mobilization and fierce opposition on the part of business owners. Since the 1850s, workers had established mutuality companies that operated as small private funds that provided insurance coverage to workers with no direct involvement of government or industrialists. In the first few decades of operations, these funds helped injured workers cope with the dire consequences of industrial accidents and sowed the seeds of a culture of compensation. However, bringing tort cases was not easy: the rules of tort liability required workers to prove the employer's negligence, and workers did not know how they could find this proof.

Progressive scholars engaged in some efforts to change the doctrine governing these cases from negligence to breach of contract. The proposed shift entailed holding employers civilly liable if, at the time of the resolution of the employment contract, the employee was in bodily conditions different from those at the time the employment contract had started. The adoption of this doctrine would have meant a substantial change in workers' ability to recover damages for occupational disease: being based on a breach of contract, the burden of proof would have shifted to the

---

4   *Loi-programme (I) du 27 décembre 2006 portant création d'un Fonds d'indemnisation des victimes de l'amiante [Law (I) December 27, 2006 creating the Asbestos Compensation Fund]*. December 27, 2006, in Moniteur Belge, December 28, 2006 (Belgium).

employer, who, in the event of a worker having suffered a bodily injury in the course of employment, would have escaped liability only upon proof of *force majeure* (an Act of God) or the fault being with the victim (for example, although well trained, the victim failed to properly operate a certain machine). These progressive ideas were well received at the trial court level, but were rejected by higher courts.[5]

When the progressive movement was defeated, industrialists were already facing a new, more threatening danger of becoming accountable for industrial injuries: joining civil claims for damages to criminal trials. In 1878, Belgium adopted a new code of criminal procedure that allowed, for the time, the practice of joining civil claims to criminal trials. Indeed, victims took advantage of the new rules and began claiming compensation in criminal trials. However, as Pétré and De Simone noted, this practice was short lived:

> Wealthy and well respected citizens, who happened to own a business, were increasingly required to appear in front of the tribunal correctionnel to defend themselves in criminal investigation for work-related injuries. This situation needed to change quickly. Workers needed to be discouraged from joining the claims for damages in criminal investigation for the purpose of obtaining compensation for harm caused by work-related injuries.[6]

Since workers did not seem to become "discouraged," the solution needed to be found elsewhere. Therefore industrialists began lobbying Parliament to establish a no fault system that would be the exclusive remedy for injured workers. By 1903, Parliament had favorably received the idea and created a no fault system for the compensation of occupational injuries. This was the solution that industrialists had hoped for: the removal of claims based on occupational injuries and disease from the tort system. While, on its face, the new law looked an attractive social bargain that allowed workers to recover benefits without the need to prove the employer's fault, in reality the 1903 reform crushed the emerging claims consciousness of the Belgian working class and established narrow boundaries for claiming for decades to come. As De Kezel noted, the exclusivity of the remedy was meant to disfavor conflicts among labor and capital by avoiding employees' lawsuits alleging the employer's fault.[7] The system that was established was a

---

5   Marianne Pétré and Enrico De Simone. "L'indemnisation en droit civil et la question de l'immunité de l'employeur [Tort liability and employer's immunity]." Published electronically September 25, 2011. http://www.progresslaw.net/docs/20110502113417WHFV. pdf (citing a verdict issued by the *Court de Cassation* on January 8, 1886).

6   Ibid., 132.

7   Evelien de Kezel, "La Réparation du dommage corporel à la suite d'une exposition à l'amiante [Compensation for bodily injuries caused by exposure to asbestos]," *Revue Générale des Assurances et des Responsabilités* 8 (2001): 13426[8].

closed one, that is, compensation was awarded only for prescribed injuries appearing on a list compiled by the King at his discretion.

## The evolution of workers' compensation

Workers' compensation originated as a weak compromise for workers. In its original form, the system was rather unfriendly to workers: no diseases were included, it was not mandatory, and employers enjoyed tort immunity. For instance, a disease was compensable only in the event the person's working capacity was lost in its entirety. This requirement pushed victims to file claims at a very difficult time of their lives, when they were near to death, or required the initiative of a surviving relative, who in addition to grieving needed to quickly activate the legal process to secure compensation rights. Furthermore, when claiming, victims needed to attach an affidavit signed by the treating physician, usually a general practitioner and not an expert in occupational medicine, certifying that the disease had been caused "with certainty" by occupational exposure. This requirement was particularly harsh. We have already seen how disengaged with regard to occupational diseases Belgian medical professionals had been and continued to be for decades. Also diagnosing an occupational disease is a task that may exceed the expertise and qualifications of general practitioners. It requires specialized knowledge, access to data on exposure to toxic substances in the workplace, and equipment to conduct proper tests. The fact that the affidavit to be attached to the claim did not need to be signed by an expert, often jeopardized the success of the claim because affidavits often failed to meet the medical expectations of the workers' compensation administration. Workers' compensation unfriendliness towards victims was soon noted by commentators. In 1935, Paul Hennebert, a Belgian physician, published in *Travail et Droit*, a magazine edited by the socialist labor union, a critique of workers' compensation warning that many victims of occupational disease would be left with no compensation in the years to come: "To these sick people, the only option left is money paid by the *mutualitées*, as a form of emergency relief, or becoming beggars."[8]

Throughout the years, workers' compensation was to be refined, modified, and expanded. The first major transformation took place in the 1930s when workers' compensation was expanded to include occupational diseases. This happened in 1927 when a separate body, the *Fonds de prévoyance en faveur des victimes de maladies professionnelles*, was established to compensate victims of occupational diseases.[9] Initially, only three diseases were included, and none of them was an

---

8   Paul Hennebert, "Maladies professionnelles. Le point de vue du médecin [Occupational diseases. The doctor's viewpoint]," *Travail et Droit* 2 (1935): 15.

9   *Loi [Law] relative à la réparation des dommages causés par les maladies professionnelles [concerning compensation for injuries caused by occupational diseases].* July 24, 1927, in Moniteur Belge, August 12, 1927 (Belgium).

asbestos disease (the first known US workers' compensation claim for asbestos disease was filed in 1927). A few more were then added in 1932. By the mid-1930s the list comprised diseases due to exposure to lead, mercury, coal, benzyl, sulfur dioxide, phosphorus, and radium. After the 1930s, new diseases were added at a very slow pace. The case of silicosis provides a good illustration: by the time occupational diseases were included in the workers' compensation system, silicosis had been already known to be a lung disease caused by occupational exposure to dust. In the United States, legislation was introduced to protect workers from silicosis in 1919. In 1930, silicosis was discussed at the International Conference on Silicosis. In England, the Medical Research Council recognized increased claims of coal miners by the late 1930s. The Fascist regime listed silicosis in 1943 in an attempt to survival politically by pleasing industrialists who, by then, had been targeted by a growing number of lawsuits brought by silicosis victims. Notwithstanding scientific consensus and regulatory convergence towards compensating silicosis, Belgium prescribed silicosis only in 1963, after countless Belgian miners had already become victims of the disease. The reform was pushed by political pressure coming from Italian immigrants who were becoming sick after moving to Belgium to work in local coal mines. They knew that silicosis could be caused by occupational exposure because they had worked in Italy, where the disease had been prescribed since 1943.

Asbestos diseases were included only in 1950s. When workers' compensation was established, asbestos was not yet a public health issue, and occupational diseases in general were not matters of particular concerns. Business owners were occupied and preoccupied with chopped hands and missing eyes. The asbestos industry was at that time nascent, and the perils of asbestos dust for the most part still unknown. Consequently no occupational disease was included among the range of compensable events. Asbestosis was the first to become listed in 1953 (23 years after England). Additional diseases were added after further delay: mesothelioma in 1982, pleura plaques and lung cancer in 1999, and cancer of the larynx in 2004.[10] Very few applications for workers' compensation benefits followed the inclusion of asbestos among the list of prescribed diseases mostly because of the rather narrow medical and exposure criteria set by the law. As Nay noted, "[b]ilateral parenchymatous lung fibrosis, presence of asbestos bodies in the sputum, and an alteration of either the heart or lung function were required."[11] Furthermore, "[o]nly those employed in the asbestos cement sector, in the asbestos textile industry, or in the manufacture of asbestos products were entitled to compensation."[12] The definition of asbestosis was expanded in 1964:

---

10 *Fonds des Maladies Professionnelles*, "Liste belge des maladies professionnelles [List of occupational diseases in Belgium]," http://www.fmp-fbz.fgov.be/web/pdfdocs/ Lijsten/FR/Liste%20belge%20des%20maladies%20professionnelles.pdf.

11 Salvator Y. Nay, "Asbestos in Belgium: use and abuse," *International Journal of Occupational and Environmental Health* 9, no. 3 (2003): 287.

12 Ibid.

"fibrosis of the pleura and other pleural lesions became compensable occupational diseases."[13]

Workers' compensation became mandatory only in the 1970s. Before that time, employers could choose to be self-insured or to stipulate policies with private insurance companies. For many years employers could choose whether or not they wanted to insure employees. Many did not. The system was restructured in 1971 and only then it became compulsory for employers. The system was reformed again in the 1990s, when it became a mixed system allowing victims of non-listed disease to attempt to recover benefits provided they could establish that their disease was caused by their occupation.[14]

Although workers' compensation was reformed in the twentieth century, some of the structural features that were since unfriendly to victims from its inception— employer's immunity is the most prominent—will never be touched by reform. The slow, conservative transformation of the welfare state is the product of the dynamics of its evolution. Rather than having a state engaged in labor relations as Mussolini's "corporatist" state, the Belgian welfare state was primarily developed by bipartite intersectoral agreements negotiated by labor and trade unions.[15] This system, which governed labor relations from the 1940s to the 1990s, was institutionalized in the form of a hierarchical pyramid in which the top bounds the bottom through a series of intersectoral agreements that established principles and pillars of negotiation at the company level. Power at the pyramid's top was monopolized by "successive generations of political elites" who had strong ties to industrialists, trade and labor union leaders and took personal credit for the socio-economic achievements of high growth, full employment, and a comprehensive welfare system."[16] Belgian political institutions played a weak role. This is not surprising since political power is highly fragmented and Belgians have "shaky confidence in the functioning of democratic institutions."[17] Vilrokx and Van Leemput talk about "vulnerability of institutions,"[18] a vulnerability that is clear in the context of asbestos. The lack of teeth to bite private companies and enforcing workers' rights is evidenced by labor inspectors' difficulty in accessing workplaces to monitor asbestos levels. In a confidential interview with journalist Vandemeulebroucke, a labor inspector indicated that "employer's duty to monitor

---

13   Ibid., 288.

14   *Loi [Law] portant des dispositions sociales [regulating social security and other matters].* December 29, 1990, in Moniteur Belge, January 9, 1991 (Belgium); *Fonds des Maladies Professionnelles,* "Qu'est-ce qu'une maladie professionnelle? [What is an occupational disease?]," http://www.fmp-fbz.fgov.be/web/content.php?lang= fr&target=citizen#/about-occupational-diseases.

15   Jacques Vilrokx and Jim Van Leemput, "Belgium: the great transformation," in *Changing industrial relations in Europe,* ed. Anthony Ferner and Richard Hyman (Malden, MA: Blackwell Publishers, 1998), 318.

16   Ibid., 316.

17   Ibid.

18   Ibid.

the presence of asbestos in the workplace exists only on paper."[19] Enforcing asbestos regulations is almost impossible as employers "do not have the guts" to monitor asbestos.[20] This framework of bipartite agreements and weak state intervention enabled the asbestos industry to dominate labor relations.

## A powerful asbestos industry

Asbestos firms were part of the group of powerful and politically well-connected interests, and they were able to direct the welfare state towards a friendly path of immunity. The asbestos industry has its roots in Belgium's early industrialization. Partly helped by the wealth generated from its colonies, Belgium played a key role in sectors that fueled the second industrial revolution. Mining, shipbuilding, railroads, and textiles are among the industries that flourished. Belgian industrialization was fueled by its propensity to import and transform raw materials. The colonies were excellent sources of imported raw materials, which were logistically moved around the country easily thanks to a well-developed, efficient system of ports and transportations. Asbestos was one of these imports—primarily from Cyprus and South Africa. A prosper industry grew out of the commercial exploitation of the magical mineral in the early twentieth century.

The context in which the asbestos industry has operated is important in understanding the limited claim consciousness among asbestos victims. Although Belgium underwent early industrialization, over time it lagged behind. Its industrial sector was not as rapid in developing and adjusting to modernization and technological advances in each industrial sector. Ron Boschma demonstrated that, following the first industrial revolution, Belgium failed to develop clusters of innovation or developed them with a considerable delay.[21] Slower innovation is linked to the familial, occasionally feudal, structure of corporate governance. The structure of major corporations is such that it concentrates remarkable power in order to exercise intra- and extra-sector influence. The Belgian asbestos industry illustrates these points well.

The asbestos sector was led by Eternit, now part of Etex, which became affiliated with Saint-Gobain of France and more informally to other asbestos-cement manufacturers throughout Europe, exported its asbestos production as far as Brazil and India, and eventually became the world's second largest seller of asbestos products. Eternit's main manufacturing facility was located in Kapelle-op-den Bos, a small town with a railroad and canals around which a host of smaller

---

19   Martine Vandemeulebroucke, "Prends ton indemnité et tais-toi: l'Inspection ignorait la présence d'amiante sur les lieux" [Take your benefits and shut up: the inspector ignored the presence of asbestos in the workplace] *Le Soir*, October 2, 1997, 17.

20   Ibid.

21   Ron A. Boschma, "The rise of clusters of innovative industries in Belgium during the industrial epoch," *Research Policy* 28 (1999): 853-871.

asbestos manufacturing firms also flourished. In the mid-1960s, Eternit also purchased the Coverit asbestos-cement plant, which was located in Harmignies and had employed roughly 200 men, 40 women, and 40 minors.[22]

Eternit shareholders were powerful and influential members of aristocratic circles and the highest ranks of diplomacy. Krols and Teugels also report that the other Eternit shareholders are key players in the political and economic life of the *Royaume de Belgique*:

> The shareholders of Eternit Belgium belong to the old nobility. By the beginning
> of the twentieth century the Emsens were already a wealthy business family
> with connections to the Belgian court. Members of each of its several branches
> occupy, or have occupied, positions at the top of Eternit companies. These
> include Baron Louis de Cartier de Marchienne; Jean-Marie, Stanislas and
> Claude Emsens; and Paul Janssen de Limpens.[23]

Production sites owned and operated by other asbestos firms popped up all over the small country since asbestos was used in a variety of industries. Shipbuilding in particular sustained the industry as the port of Antwerp acquired commercial prominence to then become the third-largest seaport in continental Europe in the first part of the twentieth century and one of the few ports that had not been completely destroyed during World War II.

Foreign influence was also important in the industry's growth. For example, the English clan the Cockerills brought machinery and technology from Britain and was subsequently rewarded with political protection. By 1812, the Cockerills had established in Liège a machine-building plant that employed over 2000 workers.[24] Furthermore, Mol hosted the first overseas plant—producing asbestos-cement—owned and operated by US asbestos giant Johns-Manville from 1928 to 1983.[25] Johns-Manville also owned a plant in Gent from 1962 until 1983. In 1983, the plants employed collectively 540 workers.[26] Finally, the most influential presences consisted of the Schmidheinys—the owners of Eternit Suisse and the most influential family operating in the asbestos business. Tycoon brothers Stephan and Thomas profoundly influenced the Belgian asbestos industry directly, by holding shares and sitting on the board of Eternit Belgium, and though the lobbying activities of the *Comité d'Information de l'Amiante Benelux* (CIAB), which had been operating since 1970 coordinating the lobbying efforts of firms in

---

22  Nay, "Asbestos in Belgium: use and abuse," 288.

23  Nico Krols and Marleen Teugels, "'A Licence to Kill': the Dirty Legacy of Asbestos," *Le Monde Diplomatique*, January 18, 2007.

24  Peter N. Stearns, *The industrial revolution in world history*, 3rd ed. (Boulder, CO: Westview Press, 2007), 56.

25  "Johns-Manville: from a Basement to a Multi-Billion Dollar Business," *The Telegraph*, February 4, 1978.

26  "Johns-Manville To Sell Facility In Belgium," *Toledo Blade*, February 4, 1983.

Belgium, the Netherlands, and Luxembourg. CIAB is still operating, with an office in Brussels.[27] The powerful role of Belgian asbestos firms is also demonstrated by the fact that asbestos was still heavily used when other industrial nations were moving away from it. In 1980, asbestos per capita use, measured in kilos, in Belgium was 3.23 while in the US it was 0.77 and 0.87 in Great Britain. Similarly in 1990 per capita use was respectively 1.61, 0.08, and 0.18.[28] Also, asbestos was banned only in 1997, and that asbestos production completely ended in 2002.[29]

The Belgian asbestos industry avoided public scrutiny for decades. In 1977, two Belgian investigative journalists, Marie-Anne Mangeot and Salvator Nay, sought permission from the management of Coverit, a large cement-asbestos plant located in Harmignies, in the French-speaking part of Belgium, to enter the factory and interview workers. The firm denied the request indicating that it was undergoing substantial renovations to transform the plant into a state-of–the-art facility and that images of a messy plant filmed during renovations would have misled the public and not depicted the reality of the firm.[30] The effects of professional and environmental exposure in Harmignies were only publicly acknowledged in 2005 in an issue of the Belgian weekly magazine *Le Soir Magazine*. The title of the journalistic investigation was simple: *Coverit counts the dead.*[31]

Public scrutiny was avoided by establishing a culture of secrecy. The Eternit Group, which was the major asbestos firm, led these efforts. The Group exercised tight control on its share circulation and its managers were part of the families that owned shares or individuals trusted by those families. As Krols and Teugels point out, its structure was "feudal:" "Top management had far more direct contact with leading political officials than with ordinary workers."[32] Further, the Belgian companies established strong business, corporate, and political connections with the other asbestos firms in Europe. Among them, the Swiss Schmidheiny brothers, who owned a substantial portion of Eternit shares, held corporate interests in several major Swiss companies, including Swissair, Nestlé, Swatch, UBS, ABB, and the cement group Holcim.[33] These international connections made the Belgian industry stronger and well shielded from domestic public scrutiny.

---

27  http://www-energie.arch.ucl.ac.be/cogeneration/cdrom/repertoire/C/48.htm.

28  Data are compiled from different sources by Marc Molitor, "Négociations et tensions autour de la création du Fonds amiante [Negotiations and conflicts surrounding the establishment of the Asbestos Fund]," *Courrier hebdomadaire du CRISP* 3, no. 2048-2049 (2010): 7.

29  Observatoire des Données de l'Environnement, "Chapter 24. Mesotheliome," in *Interface Santé et Environnement* (Bruxelles: IBGE, 2008).

30  Salvator Y. Nay, *Mortel amiante* [Deadly asbestos] (Bruxelles: EVO-Société, 1997), 67-68.

31  Thierry Vanderhaege, "Coverit compte ses morts" [Coverit counts those that are dead] *Le Soir Magazine*, November 9, 2005.

32  Krols and Teugels, "'A Licence to Kill': the Dirty Legacy of Asbestos."

33  Ibid.

Eternit also proactively offered payments to victims in exchange for a release of any claim. These agreements however are confidential and we know very little about which victims signed them and what happened to them. In the 1980s, Eternit set up a compensation fund for similar reasons. This private plan made payments to victims who became sick either because they had worked at the manufacturing plants located in Kapelle-op-den-Bos and Tisselt or because they lived in the proximity of the plant.[34] In its original form, the fund only offered payments to workers below the age of 65 and affected by asbestosis resulting in a degree of disability exceeding 33 percent. They were offered payments equal to the difference between the workers' compensation benefit and their last salary. In 2000, the fund was expanded to include former employees who had developed mesothelioma. The fund was further expanded to victims of secondhand exposure in 2001 and to victims of environmental exposure in 2006. Overall at least two asbestosis victims and 70 mesothelioma victims were compensated, including 12 victims of household exposure and two of environmental exposure. In 2007, the year in which the plan was closed down after the establishment of the 2007 Asbestos Fund, the payment amounted to EUR 43,171.[35]

## Labor unions and their lack of interest for asbestos compensation

Although union membership and union density in Belgium are high if compared to other corporatist welfare capitalist countries, unions have not significantly contributed to the mobilization of asbestos victims. In 2003 Salvator Nay noted that "local unions remained, for most of the twentieth century, ignorant of the problem."[36] In *Mortel Amiante*, his 1997 monograph entirely devoted to asbestos in Belgium, Nay pays very little attention to unions.[37] Unions are mentioned occasionally in interviews with asbestos workers. However, although several victims were union members, none of them acknowledges any substantial contribution of unions in the emergence of claim consciousness among victims. Overall, labor unions have held ambivalent positions with regard to asbestos and their advocacy at the national level has had very little impact in terms of workers' mobilization at the local level. Their agenda did not include workplace safety and asbestos compensation as a priority. The top concern was salary stability and the preservation of the welfare system.

Unions could, however, have made a difference. Labor unions were in fact deeply involved in the highly institutionalized system that dominated labor relations until the 1970s. Unions dominated workers' participation at the workplace level. An incentive to join a union came from a peculiarity of the

---

34    Molitor, "Négociations et tensions autour de la création du Fonds amiante," 17.
35    Ibid.
36    Nay, "Asbestos in Belgium: use and abuse," 292.
37    Nay, *Mortel amiante*, passim.

system. In Belgium, unemployment benefits are paid by unions and not by the government. Hemerijck and Marx further argue that this mechanism increased and maintained workers' loyalty towards unions for decades, even in times of growing unemployment and overall worsening of the working conditions.[38] National leaders would negotiate bipartite agreements at the national level and local representatives would translate intersectoral agreements into agreements at the company level. The top down approach was rarely challenged by local unions and workers. Even among the ranks of socialist unions, which had the strategic objective of workers' control in the 1950s as a "halving of employers," opposition was mostly neutralized.[39]

The top down approach operated so effectively and led to almost uncontested normalization of labor relations, even though socialist and Christian unions had divergent views on how to protect workers' rights, because of what Vilrokx and Van call "compensation democracy." This feature placated the conflict of interest that invested labor unions leaders in negotiations "by acceding to the demands of one interest group while at the same time providing additional resources to compensate the other groups involved."[40] In the end, since labor negotiations resulted in collective agreements that generated sufficient benefits to all of the social actors involved, labor union leaders were justified in giving up some of the original demands in exchange for any negotiated benefit. Unions' activities have been for the most part fragmented and uncoordinated at the local level. Strikes were occasionally organized by asbestos workers. However no union brought together asbestos workers from different companies and mobilized them in demanding better working conditions and more generous compensation as has happened in England and Italy. Union advocacy was primarily directed towards policy reform at the national level with very minimal spillover effect at the plant level.

In the aftermath of 1968, workplace safety issues did not become part of the political discourse of labor relations, as they did in Italy. During the 1968 protest, workers joined students' protests to organize strikes and other initiatives in major industrial sites throughout the country. Labor unions however rarely backed the protests. Workers' protests were essentially coordinated by grassroots organizations that had no tie to labor unions. As Horn noted, official unions frequently refused to sanction strikes and other forms of protests.[41] Ultimately "militant grassroots-impelled labor actions" of the late 1960s failed to shake

---

38   Anton Hemerijck and Ive Marx, "Continental Welfare at a Crossroads: The Choice between Activation and Minimum Income Protection in Belgium and the Netherlands," in *A long goodbye to Bismarck? The politics of welfare reforms in continental Europe*, ed. Bruno Palier (Amsterdam: Amsterdam University Press, 2010), 139-145.

39   Vilrokx and Van Leemput, "Belgium: the great transformation," 331.

40   Ibid., 333.

41   Gerd-Rainer Horn, "The Belgian Contribution to Global 1968," 614.

Belgian politics and society "to its foundation."[42] Its legacy was for the most part lost in translation during the 1970s especially because Belgium was severely hit by the oil crisis of 1973. Because of its high levels of unemployment, its reliance on international trade, and the low rate of innovation, the oil shock brought tougher times to Belgium than to other European economies. Belgium has traditionally had low levels of employment and low levels of poverty, a combination that is often labeled as "welfare without work."[43] In the 1970s, the split between grassroots groups and labor unions became more marked. The radical fringes of grassroots movements converged politically towards the Far Left and the Revolutionary Workers' League, a political group that, although active throughout the 1970s, was never able to have an impact on Belgian political life. The less radical fringes converged politically towards the New Left, which throughout the 1970s adopted a moderate approach towards social issues. The close ties of political parties with the asbestos industry did not allow much room for negotiation of a "new" welfare and labor unions worked towards preserving the "welfare without work" model rather than venturing into the unchartered territory of workplace safety. During the 1970s, the most popular labor union was the *Confédération des syndicats chrétiens*, a Catholic labor union that "appeared to be … prepared … to accept and support the workplace occupations and especially the self-management initiatives."[44] However, Catholic labor unions have traditionally pursued a less adversarial agenda in industrial relations. This approach was well-suited to the difficult economic times that Belgium faced in the aftermath of the 1973 oil crisis. In 1976, bipartite negotiations failed to reach an agreement for the first time in Belgium's history. The state stepped in and forced an agreement on social parties. The state's primary concern was international competitiveness in the face of a weak decade from an economic perspective. As a consequence, throughout the 1970s and 1980s, unions did not favor workers' mobilization but negotiated a progressive shift of the welfare system from a social insurance system for members of the workforce to a minimum income protection system redressing the risk of becoming poor associated with severe unemployment rates that happened in the 1970s. Welfare policies included early retirement for many asbestos workers, and industrial restructuring was facilitated by low resistance from trade unions and workers.[45]

---

42    Ibid., 615.

43    Hans-Jürgen Andress and Henning Lohmann, *The working poor in Europe: employment, poverty and globalisation* (Cheltenham; Northampton, MA: Edward Elgar, 2008), 77.

44    Patrick Pasture, "Histoire et représentation d'une utopie: l'idée autogestionnaire en Belgique," in *Autogestion, la dernière utopie*, ed. Frank Georgi (Paris: Publications de la Sorbonne, 2003), 149.

45    Hemerijck and Marx, "Continental Welfare at a Crossroads: The Choice between Activation and Minimum Income Protection in Belgium and the Netherlands."

In the 1990s, labor relations focused once again on competitiveness which led to the the tripartite agreement of 1966 on "linking wages in Belgium to those of its three main trading partners [France, Germany and the Netherlands], through what by now is called a 'wage norm'."[46] This was seen "as the only possible (consensual) way to restore the country's competitiveness and to halve unemployment by the end of the century."[47] The need to balance wage increase with wages' purchasing power monopolized labor relations in the 1990s. Even at this juncture though, the retrenchment of the welfare state was more modest than in other industrialized nations. Despite the adoption of neoliberal policies, workers, especially those in sectors that had been affected by the economic downturn or, like asbestos, that were on the verge of disappearing, received favorable packages to be "bought off" in affected sectors.[48] This yielded to low industrial conflict and unions' modest interest in asbestos compensation throughout the 1990s.

Low industrial conflict throughout the 1990s had implication for asbestos compensation. Negotiations expanded the list of prescribed asbestos diseases (lung cancer in 1999 and larynx cancer in 2004). However, unions refrained to support workers' compensation litigation, which was by contrast a prominent feature of asbestos compensation in Italy by then. The reasons are several. First, labor unions had operated with a mindset shaped by a culture of compensation democracy that defined the Belgian experience of labor relations. Gains could be obtained only by negotiating them in exchange for giving up certain demands. Litigating workers' compensation eligibility or challenging the administration's decision clashed with this culture. Furthermore, personal injury litigation was feared to be a bottom-up source of unbalance and destabilization of labor relations at national level. Preserving employers' immunity under workers' compensation was necessary, labor unions thought, to preserve the system of compensation democracy that curbed the retrenchment of the welfare state. Finally, litigation of both workers' compensation eligibility and personal injury claims was a threat to the unions' primacy as the legitimate representatives of the working class and to union membership. If courts expanded the class of asbestos victims eligible for compensation, in particular non-union members who were victims of secondhand exposure and environmental exposure, unions would not have been able to claim the legitimacy to represent these victims, a situation that could have led to further decline of union membership and erosion of their ability to effectively represent workers in the political process.

Labor unions' ambivalent attitude towards workplace safety and lack of interest in supporting expansion of asbestos compensation through litigation have certainly

---

46   Vilrokx and Van Leemput, "Belgium: the great transformation," 339.

47   Ibid.

48   Kurt Vandaele, "From the seventies strike wave to the first cyber-strike in the twenty-first century. Strike activity and labour unrest in Belgium," in *Strikes around the world, 1968-2005: case-studies of 15 countries*, ed. Jacobus Hermanus Antonius van der Velden et al. (Amsterdam; Edison, NJ: Aksant, 2007), 196.

deprived asbestos victims of crucial support to foster claim consciousness and mobilization. Workers' compensation policies were never challenged to the extent to which they have been in Italy and England and no efforts were made to find ways for victims to bring personal injury cases to court by circumventing or reforming the rule of workers' compensation exclusivity and employers' immunity. In particular, no attempts were made to use the strategy that brought significant results in Italy—that is, joining civil claims to a criminal trial.[49] The lack of asbestos trials is not the result of Belgian criminal procedure being based on an inquisitorial model. The distinction between adversarial and inquisitorial systems is "outdated" theoretically.[50] The legal framework set up by the Italian code of criminal procedure and the Belgian code are in the end very similar. The Belgian legal system has in fact developed along the same historical trajectories of Italy and France. Historically Belgium has been profoundly influenced by the continental legal culture, and in particular French legal culture. Belgium's Civil Code was enacted by Napoleon in 1804 when Belgium was a French territory. After independence, the Napoleonic Civil Code was not repealed as Belgium's cultural life was still very much dominated by French influence, which was reinforced by the assistance that the French government offered in Belgium's fight for independence from the Dutch in the 1930s and the economic domination of the French-speaking industrial south. Similarities between Belgium and Italy's criminal procedure systems offer to asbestos victims similar incentives to join their claims to public prosecutions. Labor unions also have incentives as they can recover damages, as they do in Italy, for loss suffered indirectly (in Italy this is also possible and labor unions have been able to recover damages for the loss of image suffered as a result of unions' alleged inability to effectively prevent employers' criminal noncompliance).[51] What have been missing in Belgium are the mobilization preconditions that were present in Italy: prosecutors have never targeted asbestos companies (no asbestos firms and executives have ever been tried in Belgium for asbestos crimes) and neither labor unions nor activists took the initiative to press charges and did not contribute to ensuing investigations.

---

49  *Code d'instruction criminelle [Code of Criminal Procedure]* (November 19, 1808 (as amended on November 30, 2011)), ¶¶ 64, 66-70, 145, 182 and 183 (Belgium). See Michel Franchimont, Ann Jacobs, and Adrien Masset, *Manuel de procédure pénale* [Textbook of Criminal Procedure], 4th ed. (Brussels: Editions Larcier, 2012), 163-181; Jean Laenens and George Van Mellaert, "The Judicial System and Procedure," in *Introduction to Belgian Law* ed. Hubert Bocken and Walter De Bondt (Bruxelles; The Hague; Boston: Bruylant; Kluwer Law International, 2001), 123.

50  Denis Salas and Alejandro Alzarez, "The public prosecutor," in *European Criminal Procedures*, ed. Mireille Delmas-Marty and John R. Spencer (Cambridge; New York: Cambridge University Press, 2002), 489.

51  Antionette Perrodet, "The public prosecutor," in *European criminal procedures*, ed. Mireille Delmas-Marty and John R. Spencer (Cambridge; New York: Cambridge University Press, 2002), 453.

Consequently, the few victims that sought compensation in court brought civil claims for damages in civil courts.

The failure of victims to use criminal investigation as a vehicle to bring claims may have also been the result of the doctrinal fragmentation of the Belgian legal system, which fails to provide strong doctrines. Traditionally, Belgian legal culture has been dominated by France. This is particularly true in the areas of liability and insurance law. More recently, as the importance of Dutch language has grown, the influence of law from the Netherlands has become more prominent, causing a fracture between legal mentalities originating from different legal traditions, the French and the Dutch. Legally, Belgium is experiencing a deep identity crisis. This crisis certainly failed to provide asbestos victims with effective legal tools— doctrines and arguments—to mobilize demands.

### Slow emergence of medical studies on asbestos diseases

Despite Belgium's history of asbestos use, epidemiological studies have not been conducted for many years. In 2007 Bianchi and Bianchi in the review of the global incidence of mesothelioma noted that "[s]carce data are available for Belgium."[52] The lack of public scrutiny of Belgian asbestos firms is certainly correlated to the late emergence of epidemiological data on asbestos disease. In addition, gathering medical data was difficult because the Belgian authorities release no individual information contained on death certificates. An *ad hoc* mesothelioma registry has never been established, contrary to the common practice of other European countries.

Surveys of the health conditions among asbestos workers appeared late, and, to further detriment, these early attempts to monitor asbestos disease were sponsored by asbestos firms. Eternit in particular commissioned two studies. In 1950, Clerens found that Eternit's asbestos-cement workers were "in good health."[53] The study was known by Selikoff, who cited Clerens's work in the literature review of one of his landmark papers of the 1960s that established the link between asbestos and lung cancer.[54] As we will see later, in the aftermath of the study, the Belgian legislature decided to include asbestosis among the list of prescribed diseases under workers' compensation. The second study appeared almost two decades after. In 1967, Eternit commissioned a second study looking at mortality in the population

---

52   Bianchi and Bianchi, "Malignant mesothelioma: global incidence and relationship with asbestos."

53   J. Clerens, "Recherches sur l'asbestose pulmonaire en Belgique [Research on pulmonary asbestosis in Belgium]," *Archives Belges de Médecine Sociale* 9 (1950). The paper is cited in Nay, "Asbestos in Belgium: use and abuse," 287.

54   Irving J. Selikoff, Jacob Churg, and E. Cuyler Hammond, "The occurrence of asbestosis among insulation workers in the United States," *Annals of the New York Academy of Sciences* 132, no. 1 (1965).

living in its plant's neighborhood. Van de Voorde and colleagues[55] found that the mortality from cancer was "twice the national rate in the 13 neighboring villages," but they also found similar mortality rates among the residents of the 13 villages included in the control group.[56]

The two Eternit-sponsored studies found very little evidence of asbestos impact on asbestos-cement workers. The first crack in the wall took place in 1973 when Vande Weyer, a pneumologist who had worked for the workers' compensation administration, published a paper that reported statistics discussing the 20-year history of compensation for asbestosis.[57] This is the first time data at national level were made public. The picture that emerged was dramatic. The study, which comprised 138 patients with asbestosis who had received workers' compensation, included 51 patients who had died. Data showed that four out of five deaths had been caused by asbestosis or its complications. In addition, one patient out of five had also developed a form of cancer—lung cancer and mesothelioma in respectively 20 percent and 7 percent of the cases. Although the data clearly showed that asbestos was killing Belgians, the study did not trigger a public debate on the merits of asbestos production. The only study that was conducted immediately after Weyer's publication was done by an unknown physician in a small town, Dr. Modave, who instigated asbestosis studies in the industrial area of the Basse Sambre on a cohort of workers employed in a company that quietly closed down its asbestos production in 1977, thus disappearing from the list of asbestos companies. The authors found 19 cases of asbestosis among the outpatients of a local hospital and were able to assert the occupational origin of all of them. Dr. Modave's findings were published in a low profile journal.[58] His paper remained unknown to professionals and to the general public for years. A copy was retained in Lyon, France, at the offices of IARC, the UN agency devoted to the study of cancer, and retrieved by a British activist, Nancy Tate, only years after its publication.[59] Studies were subsequently published in later years, but medical evidence in Belgium accumulated over time at a rate comparatively slower than in other Western countries. The only opportunity for public debate of asbestos toxicity presented itself when the Belgian press picked up on the news that a group

55  H. Van de Voorde et al., "Doodsoorzaken bij de bevolking woonachtig rond en bij de arbeiders werkzaam in een asbestverwerkende nijverheid in het noorden van Brabant [Mortality in the population living close to, and in employees working in, an asbestos industry in the North of Brabant]," *Acta tuberculosea et pneumologica Belgica* 58, no. 6 (1967).

56  Nay, "Asbestos in Belgium: use and abuse," 288.

57  R. Van de Weyer, "Bilan de l'indemnisation de l'asbestose [An assessment of asbestosis compensation]," *Acta Tuberculosea et Pneumologica Belgica* 64, no. 3 (1973).

58  J.L. Modave et al., "Réflexions à propos de 19 cas d'asbestose fortuitement découverts dans la population d'une collectivité industrielle de la Basse-Sambre [Reflections on 19 cases of asbestosis discovered by chance in the population of an industrial region in the Basse-Sambre]," *Revue de l'Institut d'hygiène des mines* 30, no. 3 (1975).

59  Nay, *Mortel amiante*, 33.

of French consumers had voiced their concerns with regard to asbestos filters that were used by wine producers in neighboring France. As the public became somewhat concerned with the magical mineral, the industry activated its spin doctors and "bought full-page advertisements in the main newspapers to reassure consumers."[60] Furthermore, in statements to the press, industry representatives indicated that any case of asbestosis was "the result of working for *many* years in a *very* dusty environment that had existed *20 years earlier* but that was now a thing of the past" and that no Eternit worker had been affected by mesothelioma.[61]

While the 1970s ended with very little debate about asbestos toxicity, the wind changed in the 1980s. In 1980, Lacquet and colleagues studied the annual chest radiographs, work history and mortality of 1,973 subjects exposed at the Eternit plant of Kapelle-op-den Bos (although the study refers to the plant as an "unnamed asbestos-cement factory").[62] They reported one death due to pleural mesothelioma and 29 cases of asbestosis.[63] In 1981, Weyer published a follow-up to his earlier study. The second study discussed 267 new cases of asbestosis that had been filed in workers' compensation between 1972 and 1981. With respect to the 1973 study, more subjects had died of cancer (19 percent of mesothelioma and 25 percent of lung cancer), bringing the percentage of asbestos victims with cancer to 75 percent of the claimants who had received workers' compensation benefits.

In the 1980s, another significant step forward happened: the routinization of data collection regarding cancer. In fact, in 1983 the government stepped in and established the National Registry of Cancer. Before 1983, data was hard to access. Data on malignancies was not collected systematically and firms were not required to, and thus did not, disclose them. Unions often provided the only source of reliable data. Since the 1950s, unions began to gather medical information on their members by obtaining data from the treating physician and organizing this data into databases. The 1983 implementation of the National Registry of Cancer represented an important step forward because collected data become public and therefore unions and other interested parties could easily access it. Between 1985 and 1992, the Registry recorded 630 cases of mesothelioma.[64] While an excellent new source of data in the asbestos debate, the system was not perfect: data reporting was not compulsory, and doctors and hospitals were not required to report any data. Data reporting become mandatory only in 2003 when the National Health System required that hospitals submitted to the Registry information regarding cancer cases in order to receive any reimbursement from the care provided to cancer patients. In addition, a

---

60    Nay, "Asbestos in Belgium: use and abuse," 288.

61    Ibid., 288 (italics in the original).

62    Nay, *Mortel amiante*, 39.

63    Lacquet, van der Linden, and Lepoutre, "Roentgenographic lung changes, asbestosis and mortality in a Belgian asbestos-cement factory," 783-793.

64    Nay, "Asbestos in Belgium: use and abuse," 289.

standardized form was distributed to the hospitals so that data could be collected more systematically.

Another important, but incomplete, source of data on asbestos disease was represented by the Belgian Fund for Occupational Diseases. Weyer's 1973 and 1981 papers brought to light data on compensation for claims submitted by asbestos victims. However, in the early days only asbestosis was listed and therefore many other asbestos diseases was missed and could not form the basis of a workers' compensation claims. Furthermore, many asbestos victims were not entitled to compensation because they were either working for employers who were not included in the system or victims of household or environmental exposure. The point is clearly illustrated by looking at data from 1985 to 1992: while the National Registry of Cancer recorded 630 cases of mesothelioma, the workers' compensation system recognized 232 claims based on mesothelioma, less than 40 percent of those recorded nationally. Notwithstanding these limitations, the statistics published by the Belgian Fund for Occupational Diseases are an important source of data on asbestos disease. They reveal that, between 2000 and 2004, 203 deaths were attributed to asbestos. Based on this data, Nawrot and colleagues estimated an asbestos mortality of about eight per million men per year[65]—a figure higher than in any of the 33 countries studied by Lin and colleagues, including England and Italy.[66]

Currently, more epidemiologists are studying asbestos disease more closely. For instance, Hollevoet and colleagues, whose primary interest is in biomarker-based early detection of mesothelioma, conducted a multicenter study of more than 500 asbestos victims, some of whom had worked at Kapelle-op-den-Bos and Gent. They note that more than one hundred of the research subjects had been diagnosed with cancer caused by exposure to asbestos.[67] However the protracted lack of access to and publication of epidemiological and pathological data, for which the medical profession is in part to be blamed, has affected asbestos compensation: medical evidence is a key tool in generating the kind of understanding that leads to developing the awareness and desire to demand compensation. Claim consciousness depends upon the realization that an injury exists and that the injury did not occur randomly but that similar harms have affected individuals who share similar features, exposure to asbestos in our case.

---

65   Nawrot et al., "Belgium: historical champion in asbestos consumption," 1692.

66   Ro-Ting Lin et al., "Ecological association between asbestos-related diseases and historical asbestos consumption: an international analysis," ibid., no. 9564: 844-849.

67   Kevin Hollevoet et al., "Diagnostic performance of soluble mesothelin and megakaryocyte potentiating factor in mesothelioma," *American Journal of Respiratory and Critical Care Medicine* 181, no. 6 (2010); Kevin Hollevoet et al., "Serial measurements of mesothelioma serum biomarkers in asbestos-exposed individuals: a prospective longitudinal cohort study," *Journal of Thoracic Oncology* 6, no. 5 (2011); ibid.

## A culture of pragmatic fatalism

An additional determinant has limited the emergence of asbestos victims' claim consciousness and mobilization: a culture of pragmatic fatalism. By their own very nature, Belgians are reserved and private people. Grief is not shared publicly, and tragedies are often accepted as a fact of life. Moreover, Belgians are often described as being "mostly apathetic toward law."[68] Pragmatic indolence is also a trait of internal legal culture among Belgian lawyers and scholars—as Heirbaut and Storme note.[69] Fatalism has been used by scholars and commentators to describe Belgians' attitude towards conflicts in Belgian society and relations between the French-speaking and the Dutch-speaking communities,[70] towards political elections,[71] and reforms of voting laws.[72]

During fieldwork, respondents pointed to Belgians' fatalism as a cultural frame that has likely colored asbestos victims' perceptions of the asbestos epidemic and attitudes towards compensation. For many years, Belgian asbestos workers thought that risks would naturally be associated with employment, especially in an environment where male, blue collar workers are faced with a significantly higher poverty risk than other groups.[73] In 1998, Luc Vandenbroucke, an asbestos victim and early advocate, framed the attitudes towards risky jobs among Belgians in these terms:

> In the minds of many workers, risking life when working is ordinary: working allows gaining a living. One could become sick because of her job, one could die, but that's the way to provide for the dear ones. Many people still think in these terms when then think about asbestos, it's like a veil made of lead, people don't speak up, people keep their jobs and hope to stay dry when it rains.[74]

---

68    Heirbaut, "The Belgian Legal Tradition: Does it Exist?"

69    Ibid., 645-683.

70    Université catholique de Louvain, "Émotions des Belges face à la crise: respect et fatalisme [Belgians' emotions towards the crisis: respect and fatalism]," http://www. uclouvain.be/cps/ucl/doc/ir-ipsy/documents/Communique_dePresse_FR.pdf.

71    Bénédicte De Beys. "Belgique Le fatalisme tranquille? [Belgium: gentle fatalism?]." Published electronically June 13, 2007 http://www.eurosduvillage.eu/708-BELGIQUE-Le-fatalisme.html?lang=fr.

72    Stephanie Baele, "La Belgique: des crises aux opportunités [Belgium, from crises to opportunities]," *Émulations* 10 (2012): 9.

73    Ive Marx and Gerlinde Verbist, "When Famialism Fails: The Nature and Causes of In-Work Poverty in Belgium," in *The working poor in Europe: employment, poverty and globalisation*, ed. Hans-Jürgen Andress and Henning Lohmann (Cheltenham; Northampton, MA: Edward Elgar, 2008), 82.

74    Marie-Christine Lahaye, "Le combat d'un homme. Luc Vandenbroucke [The fight of a man. Luc Vandenbroucke]," *Inter-Environnement Wallonie* 43 (1998).

This picture was recently reinforced by Eric Jonckheere, who referred to Belgian asbestos victims from the pages of the website of ABEVA, the *Association Belge des Victimes de l'Amiante* (Belgian Asbestos Victim Association), as the *indignés silencieux* or silent *indignados* because of their reluctance to voice their demand for justice. Jonckheere further argues that, in the past, this culture of *omerta* or pledge of silence, which persisted for years in Eternit company towns, had been bought out by the company's offer to pay money (*zwijggeld* or hush money) or to hire a relative in need of a job.[75]

Pragmatic fatalism clearly translates into a legal culture adverse to total justice and demands for redress and claiming. It is a cultural schema that somehow clashes with Belgium's highly structured labor negotiations and the emerging belief in interdependence when it comes to harms caused by employment. Indeed, its influence is certainly remarkable and overpowering as Belgium remains a country with very little asbestos litigation.

## Workers' compensation in its contemporary version

Workers' compensation is a mixed system that lists various asbestos diseases among the disease for which, if exposure is proved, causation is presumed. Claims based on unlisted diseases, on the other hand, require proof of a causal link between occupational exposure and disease—a proof that is very difficult to find. In fact, my research shows that no payment was ever recognized to victims of asbestos exposure who had contracted an unlisted disease. The rate of denials of unlisted diseases is generally much higher than for listed diseases: over 90 percent of unlisted disease claims are denied. Very few claims for unlisted diseases are based on cancer or other fatal diseases. The bulk involves "locomotor apparatus disorders ... and muscle disorders, such as tendinitis."[76]

Listed asbestos diseases are asbestosis, mesothelioma, pleura plaques, lung cancer, and cancer of the larynx (see Table 2.1). For victims who are diagnosed with a disease that was caused by occupational exposure, workers' compensation is the exclusive remedy. Negligence and breach of contract claims against the employer are barred.

---

    75   "Amiante – L'Abeva réclame un élargissement des indemnisations et davantage de prevention [Asbestos – L'Abeva calls for expansion of compensation and more prevention]." *LeVif.be*. Published online May 15, 2013. http://www.levif.be/info/belga-generique/amiante-l-abeva-reclame-un-elargissement-des-indemnisations-et-davantage-de-prevention/article-4000303200565.htm; Laurie Kazan-Allen. "Belgium's Asbestos Killing Fields." Published electronically May 23, 2013. http://www.ibasecretariat.org/lka-belgium-asbestos-killing-fields.php.
    76   Niels J. Philipsen, "Industrial Accidents and Occupational Diseases: Some Empirical Findings for The Netherlands, Belgium, Germany and Great Britain," *Tort and Insurance Law Yearbook* 20 (2007).

**Table 2.1    List of occupational diseases that are recognized under workers' compensation**

| Occupational disease caused by substances that are not included in other categories | | Year of inclusion |
|---|---|---|
| 1.301.21 | Asbestosis | 1969 |
| 9.307 | Asbestos-induced mesothelioma | 1982 |
| 9.308 | Asbestos-induced lung cancer | 1999 |
| 9.301.20 | Pleural plaques | 1999 |
| 9.310 | Asbestos-induced larynx cancer | 2002 |

*Source:* Table prepared by the author by assembling governmental data published at *Fonds des Maladies Professionnelles.* "Liste *Belge Des Maladies Professionnelles* [List of occupational diseases in Belgium]." http://www.fmp-fbz.fgov.be/web/pdfdocs/Lijsten/FR/Liste%20belge%20des%20maladies%20professionnelles.pdf.

Workers' compensation benefits are claimed by filing an application. While money to fund compensation comes from employers through direct contributions, the system is managed by the government through the *Fonds des Maladies Professionnelles.*[77] Claimants, or the treating physician on their behalf, must fill in various forms, made available online by the *Fonds* to simplify and standardize the process, and file them with the administration.[78] The filing triggers a process that mirrors closely the processes other administrations throughout Europe follow.[79] The administration adjudicates the claim based on the evidence submitted at the time of the filing.

Overall approximately 50 percent of all workers' compensation claims, whether or not based on asbestos disease, are granted, as shown by a survey conducted in 1997.[80] Virtually all of them (99 percent) are based on a prescribed disease.[81] The rate of success of claims based on a prescribed disease is within the range of other European countries but above the average of England and Italy. A major downside

––––––––––

77    Conversely, occupational accidents are insured by private carriers that operate under supervision of a government agency, the *Fonds des Accidents du travail.*

78    http://www.afa.fgov.be/Pdfdocs/FormulairesF/501F-20060501.pdf (claim form); http://www.afa.fgov.be/Pdfdocs/FormulairesF/503F-20060501.pdf (medical certificate form).

79    The form is available at http://www.fmp-fbz.fgov.be/Pdfdocs/FormulairesF/dmpf.pdf.

80    Eurogip, "La branche 'accidents du travail—maladies professionnelles' dans les pays de l'UE-15. Gestion, organisation, missions" (Paris: Eurogip, 2005).

81    Danielle De Brucq, "Une Vaste Enquête: 'Les Maladies Professionnelles en Europe.' Déclaration, Reconnaissance et Indemnisation [A broad inquiry: 'Occupational diseases in Europe.' Filing, Adjudication and Compensation]," *Revue Belge de Sécurité Sociale* 2 (2001): 378.

of the Belgian system is its length. In fact, the adjudication process is extremely long and adjudication comes on average at least one year after the claim is filed.[82]

Mesothelioma cases are rather straightforward. The *Fonds* grants the benefit whenever a doctor's certification of diagnosis with proper documentation (results of mesothelioma histology test) is filed with the application and confirmed by the *Fonds*'s medical committee. The policy is that, in adjudicating mesothelioma cases, applications are weighted as much as possible in favor of the applicant. If insufficient medical proof is submitted, the *Fonds* will request information from the National Mesothelioma Registry. If no histological analysis is available, the applicant's medical history is acquired from the treating physician. If no evidence of exposure is submitted or is insufficient, an investigation is conducted to determine the extent to which the claimant was exposed to asbestos while employed. Lung cancer cases are compensated even in the absence of asbestosis.[83] The benefit is awarded to applicants who have been exposed to asbestos for at least ten years and if one of the following conditions is met: presence of asbestosis, employment in certain listed occupations that are known to entail significant exposure to asbestos, employment in a workplace where density of asbestos fibers exceed a decennial average 25 fibers/square centimeter, microscopic evidence of a concentration of at least 5,000 units of asbestos per gram of lunch tissues, or microscopic evidence of a concentration of at least 5 million asbestos fibers in the upper part of the lung. In pleural plaques cases, the benefit is awarded whenever a CT scan shows signs of thickening and the medical board assesses that the functionality of the lungs is compromised to a degree equal to or exceeding 85 percent.[84]

Although the medical criteria to be used by the *Fonds*'s medical expert to review applications are clear, a victims' advocate raised in an interview the issue that the medical controls are often "mortifying experiences" for claimants because the experts' panel comes across as being against applicants and claimants are not assisted by counsel. The lack of legal representation throughout the process raises further issues. Since lawyers are not involved and the results of the medical examination are kept confidential, claims are adjudicated in a highly individualized fashion, if compared to other nations. During the interviews, I was told that applicants are not aware of what standards are applied in other cases and the lack of involvement of lawyers in the process diminishes opportunities for comparison of cases and shared awareness of biases or problems with the adjudication process. The absence of attorney also prevents the legal profession from becoming interested in this area of law because there is very little financial incentive associated with advising clients who seek workers' compensation

---

82    Ibid., 380.

83    *Fonds des Maladies Professionnelles.* "Maladies professionnelles provoquées par l'amiante. Critères de reconnaissance et d'indemnisation [Occupational diseases caused by asbestos. Criteria for assessment and compensation]." Published electronically 2007. http://www.fmp-fbz.fgov.be/afa/pdf/afabrochuref.pdf.

84    Ibid.

payments. As discussed above, because of their role in labor relations, labor unions, which in other countries have acted as aggregating and mobilizing forces, were never interested in supporting victims' efforts in workers' compensation, especially if that required being adversarial with the government. The powerful cultural frames of "compensation democracy" and expectations of *paix sociale* pushed unions towards different goals.

If satisfied with the medical evidence presented, the Board awards the benefit and proceeds to determine the exact amount to be paid to the claimant. The amount is calculated by multiplying the wages earned by the victim during the last year of employment before the disease is diagnosed by the degree of loss of the earning capacity, which the Board assesses based on the advice of medical experts appointed to review the case, adjusted in consideration of certain socioeconomic parameters (age of the claimant, acquired professional skills, and job market conditions). The annual gross wage used in the calculation is currently capped at EUR 36,809.73.[85] The resulting figure is fairly low if compared to other European nations. Awards for all occupational diseases—not only to diseases caused by exposure to asbestos dust—do not exceed on average an annual pension of EUR 5,000.[86] The amount, which is taxed as personal income, is adjusted upwards based on increases in cost of living. Denials can be appealed. If the Board rejects an application, the claimant may file a civil lawsuit in the *Tribunal du Travail*, a court specialized in employment-related disputes, and challenge the decision. Paper must be filed within 90 days of the dismissal.[87] The judge of the *Tribunal* reverses the dismissal whenever the workers' compensation board has abused its discretion. Roughly 10 percent of the dismissals are appealed. In approximately 50 percent of the cases the dismissal is annulled or a higher degree of disability is established, and the benefit payment consequently increased.[88]

Data released by the *Fonds des Maladies Professionnelles* show that from 1992 to 2002 benefits were awarded in 1,849 cases of asbestosis, 491 cases of mesothelioma, and 153 cases of lung cancer.[89] In 2003, however, Salvator Nay indicated that the *Fonds* had "paid compensation to some 850 victims of mesothelioma."[90] In 2010, Molitor estimated, based on data released by the *Fonds*

---

85    Eurogip, "Compensation of permanent impairment resulting from occupational injuries in Europe," 13.

86    Philipsen, "Industrial Accidents and Occupational Diseases: Some Empirical Findings for The Netherlands, Belgium, Germany and Great Britain."

87    Labor tribunals are composed of professional and lay judges. Inquisitorial procedural rules apply. See Laenens and Van Mellaert, "The Judicial System and Procedure," 85-86.

88    De Brucq, "Une Vaste Enquête: 'Les Maladies Professionnelles en Europe.' Déclaration, Reconnaissance et Indemnisation," 373.

89    Sénat de Belgique. *Proposition de loi visant à créer un Fonds pour les victimes de l'amiante [Bill aiming to create a Fund to compensate asbestos victims].* June 28, 2004, n. 3-788/1 (Belgium).

90    Nay, "Asbestos in Belgium: use and abuse," 289.

as well as the Mesothelioma National Registry that by 2008, the year in which the 2007 Asbestos Fund became operative, the *Fonds* had awarded benefits to 3,860 victims of asbestosis and 1,368 victims of mesothelioma.[91] Molitor did not report data on lung cancer because these malignancies are not recorded systematically and therefore data is less accurate.[92] Data released by the *Fonds* show that the number of malignancies caused by asbestos is growing and that roughly 100 claims for asbestos malignancies are filed every year with the workers' compensation system (see Table 2.2).

Various groups of asbestos victims cannot receive workers' compensation benefits. Independent contractors and victims of secondhand exposure are the largest groups. Both are excluded *tout court* from coverage. Furthermore, workers in certain sectors are insured by public insurance schemes other than workers' compensation. Thus railroad workers, public employees, and military personnel are precluded from claiming workers' compensation, as they can seek benefits from their separate public insurance scheme. However, compensation is harder to get from these schemes because they have received a much smaller number of asbestos disease applications and therefore have not developed consistent and predictable rules determining when benefits should be granted.[93]

**Table 2.2**   **Belgian workers' compensation data: death from asbestos disease**

| Year | Asbestosis | Mesothelioma | Lung cancer |
|------|-----------|--------------|-------------|
| 1990 | 29 | 38 | 4 |
| 1997 | 33 | 54 | 14 |
| 2000 | 56 | 56 | 15 |
| 2001 | 55 | 63 | 22 |

*Source:* Sénat de Belgique. Proposition de loi visant à créer un Fonds pour les victimes de l'amiante [Bill aiming to create a Fund to compensate asbestos victims]. June 28, 2004, n. 3-788/1 (Belgium). http://www.senaat.be/www/?MIval=/Registers/ViewReg&COLL=S &POS=1&PUID=50332894&TID=50335890&LANG=nl.

## Occupational diseases and employers' and third parties' immunity

Workers' compensation provides the exclusive path to compensation for occupational disease. This means that employers are immune from civil liability. The only exception to employers' immunity is for victims to prove in a civil court that the employer intentionally caused the personal bodily harm. This exception is

---

91   Molitor, "Négociations et tensions autour de la création du Fonds amiante," 21.
92   Ibid., 23.
93   Ibid., 14.

known as *faute intentionnelle*.[94] Codified as Article 51 of Law June 3, 1970, which comprehensively regulates injuries and disease occurring in the workplace, the principle of *faute intentionnelle* limits a worker's standing to sue to cases in which the employer intentionally caused an occupational disease.[95] Article 51 states that an action in tort can be brought only against "an employer who intentionally caused a work related accident or an accident leading in turn to a work related accident."[96]

In the asbestos context, *faute intentionnelle* can be established by showing the employer failed to comply with a governmental injunction that orders the employer to stop exposing employees or other bystanders to asbestos.[97] This proof is however practically impossible because labor inspectors have never issued such injunctions against asbestos firms and therefore victims have never been able to establish *faute intentionnelle* in a court of law. Evidence of gross negligence is not sufficient. The same rules apply to the survivors of the victims, and in particular a spouse, children, or parents, who enjoy the same, narrow standing to sue.[98] This means that, unless a lawsuit is brought by the sick worker in the remainder of her life after diagnosis of an asbestos disease (mesothelioma victims rarely survive more than a year after diagnosis), the claim vanishes.

The consequence of the employee's procedural burden to show the employer's *faute intentionnelle* has important implications. First, it has limited occupational exposure victims' compensation to workers' compensation. However, workers' compensation only redresses certain medical expenses and the loss of capacity to work and to generate income. The net result is thus victims' inability to claim pain and suffering and other forms of damages that are recoverable under general principles of tort law. Second, the rule has resulted in asbestos firms' substantial immunity. By the government's own admission, tort actions based on *faute intentionnelle* do not and cannot exist in the real world of litigation. In 2005 the *Conseil National du Travail* indicated that an employee's personal injury suit based

---

94 *Lois [Laws] relatives à la prévention des maladies professionnelles et à la réparation des dommages résultant de celles-ci, coordonnées le 3 juin 1970 [concerning the prevention of occupational disease and the compensation of damages caused by the disease, coordinated on June 3, 1970]*. June 3, 1970, in Moniteur Belge, August 27, 1970, ¶ 51 (Belgium); *Loi-programme (I) du 27 décembre 2006 portant création d'un Fonds d'indemnisation des victimes de l'amiante [Law (I) December 27, 2006 creating the Asbestos Compensation Fund]*, ¶ 125, sec. 122.

95 *Lois [Laws] relatives à la prévention des maladies professionnelles et à la réparation des dommages résultant de celles-ci, coordonnées le 3 juin 1970 [concerning the prevention of occupational disease and the compensation of damages caused by the disease, coordinated on June 3, 1970]*, ¶ 51.

96 Ibid.

97 Jean-Luc Fagnart, *La responsabilité civile: chronique de jurisprudence 1985-1995* [Tort liability: Case law chronicle of 1985-1995](Bruxelles: Éditions Larcier, 1997), 21.

98 de Kezel, "La Réparation du dommage corporel à la suite d'une exposition à l'amiante," 13426[8].

on the premise that the employer intended to kill her by causing an occupational disease "is merely theoretical."[99] The only two cases to have been brought under this section were unsuccessful. These cases are impossible to win in areas beyond asbestos. In 2005, a group of practitioners who were gathered in the town of Charleroi to discuss sexual harassment in the workplace shared the same view. Their report noted that the group could not think of a single case in the history of Belgian litigation for workplace injuries and diseases in which a plaintiff prevailed at trial in a claim based on *faute intentionnelle*.[100] Finally, *faute intentionnelle* contributed to the failure of claim mobilization in Belgium because it removed from victims the option of civil litigation, which is the process that mobilized all claims in the United States and a substantial number of claims in England and Italy.

Workers' compensation further prohibits third-party lawsuits against other companies that might have negligently contributed to asbestos exposure in the course of employment. These third parties are commonplace in the United States where suits are regularly brought, under product liability theories, against asbestos defendants who manufactured asbestos products used in the victim's manufacturing facility. These lawsuits are barred in Belgium where compensation for occupational diseases must come from the government.[101] Furthermore, even if the employer negligently ignored the fact that any asbestos product was used in the workplace, these cases are automatically absorbed by workers' compensation because the presumption of occupational origins is associated with contracting any asbestos disease that is listed (mesothelioma, lung cancer, pleural plaques and thickening, and laryngeal cancer). Workers' compensation trumps tort law whether the exposure is due to the employer's or a third party's negligence.[102]

Efforts to challenge *faute intentionnelle* were launched. Two personal injury lawsuits were brought by a victim against his former employers. Constitutional challenges to the principle of immunity were raised. Finally legislative proposals to curb it were launched. In addition, asbestos firms' immunity has also been critiqued in academic circles.[103] All of these efforts however failed to achieve

---

99   *Faute inexcusable en cas d'exposition des travailleurs à l'amiante—Proposition de loi ["Faute inexcusable" and asbestos workers' risk—Bill]*, Avis 1.518 (Conseil National du Travail, June 16, 2005) (Belgium). See de Kezel, "La Réparation du dommage corporel à la suite d'une exposition à l'amiante," 13426[7-9].

100   Conférence du Jeune Barreau de Charleroi, *La loi relative à la protection contre la violence et le harcèlement moral ou sexuel au travail: deux années d'application* [The law on sexual harrassment on the workplace: a two-year assessment], Actes de l'après-midi d'étude organisé le 18 février 2005 (Brussels: Kluwer, 2005), 174.

101   Herman Cousy and Dimitri Doshout, "Compensation for Personal Injury in Belgium," in *Compensation for personal injury in a comparative perspective*, ed. Bernhard A. Koch and Helmut Koziol (Vienna; New York: Spinger, 2003), 42.

102   Ibid., 43.

103   Jacques Cless and Vincent Neuprez, "L'appréciation par la Cour d'arbitrage des exonérations de responsabilité civile dans le droit des accidents du travail [The Court d'arbitrage's treatement of immunity in the law of occupational accidents]," *Revue de*

their intended direct purpose, which was to transform the legal environment for occupational disease claims. In fact, the two personal injury cases ended with a judgment for the defendant, the constitutional challenges were rejected by the highest court, and *faute intentionnelle* was never reformed by Parliament. However, mobilization achieved two secondary purposes, as it is often the case with social movements:[104] the establishment of ABEVA, a grassroots organization organizing claim mobilization efforts and advocating policy reform on behalf of asbestos victims, and the implementation of the 2007 Asbestos Funds. I now briefly discuss each of the three efforts to challenge *faute intentionnelle* as they triggered processes that eventually changed asbestos compensation in Belgium.

### Failed attempts to bring personal injury claims for occupational exposure

Only two legal actions were brought under the theory of the employer's *faute intentionnelle*. The first case was brought by Denis Grégoire against Eternit in the 1990s. This case has not left a mark in the history of asbestos litigation as it was quickly dismissed for the plaintiff's failure to prove Eternit's *faute intentionnelle*. Mr. Grégoire appealed the dismissal. However, the appeal too was defeated: "On appeal, the higher court upheld the decision, finding that while serious wrongful acts had indeed been committed, they were not 'intentional'."[105] Although similarly unsuccessful, the second case is more interesting because it initiated victims' mobilization. The case was brought in 1995 by Luc Vandenbroucke.[106] Mr. Vandenbroucke, who developed mesothelioma by his mid-40s, had contracted the disease while exposed to asbestos during the course of his professional life. The victim had worked for two firms: a company that installed and maintained air conditioning and heating systems at various industrial facilities and a bottle cap manufacturer.[107] Mr. Vandenbroucke had been exposed to asbestos fibers at both workplaces and therefore his mesothelioma was "presumed" as a matter of law to be caused by occupational exposure. In fact, Mr. Vandenbroucke was compensated by the *Fonds des maladies professionnelles*. However, his discontent persisted and he decided to begin a lawsuit in the hope of recovering further damages in

---

*Jurisprudence de Liège, Mons et Bruxelles* (2001): 780-785; de Kezel, "La Réparation du dommage corporel à la suite d'une exposition à l'amiante," 13426[8].

104    Idit Kostiner, "Evaluating Legality: Toward a Cultural Approach to the Study of Law and Social Change," *Law & Society Review* 37, no. 2 (2003); McCann, *Rights at work: pay equity reform and the politics of legal mobilization*.

105    Denis Grégoire, "Former asbestos cement workers search for justice," *HESA Newsletter* 29 (2006).

106    de Kezel, "La Réparation du dommage corporel à la suite d'une exposition à l'amiante," 13426[8] .

107    Martine Vandemeulebroucke, "Amiante: un condamné va en justice" [Asbestos: the victim of a deadly disease seeks justice] *Le Soir*, December 18, 1996.

negligence and of forcing the two companies to stop using asbestos-contaminated products and clean up the workplace. He also wanted to send a signal to the public and to Parliament that asbestos was a public health hazard that needed to be banned.[108] The defendants in this case were Axima and Illochroma, the two companies that had employed him from 1973 to 1993. Since neither employer had monitored asbestos fibers or implemented safety protections to protect him from the deadly mineral, the case was brought under the theory that the two companies had disregarded the law so blatantly that the willful disregard constituted *faute intentionnelle*. The pioneering trait of his case was soon captured by the press and was featured in the politically progressive magazine *Imagine demain le monde*, which presented Mr. Vandenbroucke as "*le premier à se lever*," "the first to rise."[109]

The trial court ruled against Mr. Vandenbroucke finding that the defendants had been "grossly negligent" by failing to detect and act upon the presence of asbestos in the workplace but that their misconduct, although deplorable, did not meet the requirements of *faute intentionnelle*. They had not caused the mesothelioma intentionally because they lacked knowledge of the presence of asbestos fibers in the workplace.[110] Mere lack of compliance with existing workplace regulations, even if grossly negligent, was not sufficient to remove employers' immunity.[111] Vandenbroucke appealed and voiced his disappointment with the decision in an interview: "My employers never made me breath asbestos with the intention of killing me!" Journalist Martine Vandemeulebroucke summed up the case in a succinct, yet telling title of her report for *Le Soir*: "Take your benefits and shut up."[112] The appellate court confirmed the trial court's judgment in 1998.[113]

Luc Vandenbroucke died the year after at the age of 48.[114] However, his legacy was not entirely lost. Luc's death and unsuccessful legal struggle turned his son Paul into an asbestos activist. Along with other activists, Paul established and co-chaired ABEVA, an organization mobilizing efforts and advocating policy reform on behalf of asbestos victims.

---

108   Martine Vandemeulebroucke, "Le tribunal déboute le technicien rendu gravement malade par l'amiante. Exposition à l'amiante sans faute intentionnelle" [The court dismisses the technician who asbestos made severally sick. Exposure to asbestos without "faute intentionnelle"] *Le Soir*, October 2, 1997.

109   "Amiante: le premier à se lever" [Asbestos: the first to rise.] *Imagine demain le monde* March 2007.

110   *Jugement définitif [Final order]*, n. *96/7741/A* (Tribunal de Première Instance [District Court], Brussels, October 1, 1997) (Belgium).

111   Vandemeulebroucke, "Prends ton indemnité et tais-toi: l'Inspection ignorait la présence d'amiante sur les lieux."

112   Ibid.

113   *Arrêt [Order]*, n. *1998/4253* (Cour d'Appel [Court of Appeals], Brussels, 4th Chamber, November 2, 1998) (Belgium).

114   Molitor, "Négociations et tensions autour de la création du Fonds amiante," 29.

## Constitutional challenges to employers' immunity

In 2001, challenges to employers' tort immunity were raised in front of the Constitutional Court.[115] The challenges invested the compatibility of *faute intentionnelle* with respect to the constitutional principles of equal protection and nondiscrimination. These principles are formally recognized as fundamental rights respectively by articles 10 and 11 of the Belgian Constitution. Article 10 proclaims that:

> There shall be no distinction according to class in the State.
>
> Belgians are equal before the law; they are the only ones eligible for civil and military service, but for the exceptions that can be made by law for special cases.
>
> Equality between men and women is guaranteed.[116]

Article 11 adds that "Belgians shall enjoy their rights and freedoms without discrimination."[117] Under Belgian constitutional law, the standard of review of violations of the principle of equal protection and nondiscrimination is on a rational basis. Precedents indicated that equal treatment and nondiscrimination do not preclude differentiated treatment among groups if the differences have an objective basis that can be rationally justified.[118]

There were four issues. The first involved the constitutionality of differences of available remedy between victims who suffered an injury in the workplace and victims who suffered an injury outside the workplace. The second issue examined was whether claims based on the defendant's reckless conduct (which is not a sufficient basis to sue) could be treated differently than claims based on intentional conduct (which is a sufficient basis to sue as it gives plaintiffs standing to sue) is constitutional. The third challenge looked at the prohibition to bring suit in the event of the employer's negligent conduct. Finally, petitioners raised constitutional challenges with regard to different treatment of the surviving relatives of victims of occupational exposure, who are barred from suing the employer, versus surviving relatives of victims of non-occupational tortious conduct, who can recover damages in negligence.

In a succinct opinion, the Court rejected the arguments. The differences between victims of occupational, and the departure from the principles of tort liability, were found to be constitutional because grounded on the same sound reasons that were at the basis of the creation of workers' compensation: the legislative intent to benefit victims of occupational exposure who were exempted from proving

---

115    *Arrêt [Order] n. 2001/31* (Cours d'Arbitrage [Highest Court], March 1, 2001) (Belgium).

116    *Constitution.* 1831, as amended in 1994, art. 10 (Belgium).

117    Ibid., art. 11.

118    *Arrêt [Order] n. 2001/31.*

causation in exchange for employers' tort immunity, preserving social peace, and favoring stable labor relations:[119]

> [The establishment of workers' compensation resulted in] the employer tak[ing] responsibility of any harm suffered by a victim as a consequence of a workplace accident, even in the absence of any fault on its part ... victims [being] not only excused from proving—a proof often difficult to offer—the fault of the employer or of its agents and the existence of a causal link between fault and harm suffered but also able to recover even if they were themselves at fault (negligent) or ... caused harm to a third party ... the victim receiving a lump sum payment that compensates the harm suffered by the victim although only partially.

The goal of the system was both to guarantee that workers received an income in the face of a harm associated with a professional risk even if the accident had been caused by the worker's negligence or by a third party, and preserve social peace and labor relations in the workplace by curbing the proliferation of tort lawsuits.[120]

Employers' tort immunity was found to be constitutional and victims' constitutional right to equal protection and due process not breached by the provision that remove personal injury cases from the tort system. The proliferation of asbestos tort lawsuits was indeed avoided.

### Legislative challenges to employers' immunity

Efforts to repeal the principle of *faute intentionnelle* involved the legislative process as well. Various bills aimed at relaxing workers' compensation law were drafted between 2003 and 2008 but none of them made it through and repealed employers' tort immunity. In the late 1900s, asbestos became a political issue due to increased public awareness that no asbestos compensation was delivered though the court system. Bills were therefore drafted by members of Parliament who have developed political sensitivity towards asbestos victims. Support for the various proposals however was never bipartisan, and as a result none of these bills became law because elections trumped the chances of success of all legislative proposals. This happened because elections changed the distribution of power at the time the bills were discussed in Parliament. Belgium, which is a parliamentary democracy, which means that the political majority is a coalition of the parties that win the election, underwent several elections in the 2000s. All asbestos bills were sponsored by a member of one of the political parties that formed the majority coalition at the time the bill was drafted. However, whenever an asbestos bill was pending, elections were held and in all cases they

---

119   Ibid.
120   Ibid.

altered the distribution of power among political parties so that the proponents of the bills found themselves in the minority after the vote. Consequently, all bills failed to be adopted because of political elections that recreated a majority in Parliament.

The effort that came closest to success was the Lizin Bill, which proposed to replace *faute intentionnelle* with *faute inexcusable*, a principle that had been developed by courts in France.[121] The Bill was comprised of a single article that added the following words to article 51: a tort action can be brought "against an employer who acted with *faute inexcusable* consisting of exposing employees to asbestos without protection."[122] Under French law, an employer acts with *faute inexcusable*, which can be loosely translated as gross negligence, if her conduct meets several requirements: the employer acts without coercion, knowing that employees are exposed to an occupational risk, with exceptional recklessness, and without justification. In contrast to *faute intentionnelle*, intent to cause harm is not an element of *faute inexcusable*.[123] Thus French employees do not need to prove the employer's intent to cause an occupational disease to sue in torts. To the lawmakers supporting the Lizin Bill, borrowing the French rule appealed as an attractive move due to the fact that French asbestos victims had been able to bring personal injury claims in court by showing the *faute inexcusable* of asbestos firms.[124]

The Lizin Bill received serious attention on part of the Senate, certainly because the sponsors were representatives of the three political parties that were part of the majority coalition. Anne-Marie Lizin, Johan Malcorps, and Georges Dallemagne were respectively members of the Socialist, the Social Democrat, and the Green parties. When the Lizin Bill was pending, Muriel Gerkens, a member of the Green party with a long-standing sensitivity towards asbestos victims, proposed a bill inspired by a similar philosophy. However, both bills failed to become law because the *Conseil National du Travail*, an advisory body to the

---

121   Sénat de Belgique. *Proposition de loi modifiant l'article 51 des lois coordonnées du 3 juin 1970 relative à la réparation des dommages résultant des maladies professionnelles pour y intégrer la faute inexcusable en cas d'exposition des travailleurs à l'amiante [Bill to amend article 51 of the coordinated laws of June 3, 1970, allowing the compensation of asbestos workers in the event of faute inexcusable].* July 3, 2003, n. 3-22/1 (Belgium).

122   Ibid.

123   Christian Lahnstein, "Asbestos and Other Emerging Liability Risks—Including Some Critical Remarks on Risk Debates and Perceptions," in *European Tort Law 2002*, ed. Helmut Koziol and Barbara C. Steininger (Vienna: Springer, 2003), 536.

124   Gakuto Takamura, "The French Indemnification Fund for Asbestos Victims: Features and Formative Historical Factors: Preliminary Observations for a Comparative Analysis of Asbestos Relief Frameworks," in *Asbestos Disaster: Lessons from Japan's Experience*, ed. Kenichi Miyamoto, Kenji Morinaga, and Hiroyuki Mori (Tokyo: Springer, 2011), 305.

Parliament, issued negative consultative opinions.[125] The *Conseil* thought that the bills, if turned into law, would be unconstitutional because they were planning to craft compensation for occupational disease that would benefit a single class of victims (asbestos victims) and excluded all other victims of occupational disease.[126] However, victims of occupational disease are all in the same position and no special treatment could be held to be constitutionally justified. Compensation for occupational disease, the *Conseil* reasoned, stemmed from a historical comprise between labor and employers that involved all victims of occupational exposure for which employers' immunity was an important attribute.[127] The *Conseil* sent the bills back to Parliament recommending against their adoption and inviting Parliament to engage in a broader political debate of how the Belgian society was managing asbestos compensation.

Even though the Conseil rejected her bill, Ms. Lizin tried a second time to push an identical bill thought the legislative process. This effort came in the aftermath of the establishment of the Asbestos Fund, which expanded asbestos compensation but did not dispose of employers' immunity.[128] This second bill never became law. Ms. Gerkens, still a Member of Parliament, was working in 2012 on proposals to reform *faute intentionnelle*.[129]

Not surprisingly, labor unions did not offer full support to these bills. The ambivalent attitude that labor unions have held towards asbestos compensation was reflected in the mixed reception of the reform proposals. While showing some sympathy for the bills, labor unions fear that reform would compromise peaceful labor relations. Allegiance to the long-standing principle, labor unions argued, allowed them to better represent workers in negotiating their rights. Allowing workers to sue their employers would have likely compromised the equilibrium of labor relations in ways possibly unfavorable to workers. Unions were further ambivalent towards the proposal to create a compensation fund for all victims of mesothelioma, whether or not exposed in the workplace. The fund was on the one

---

125   *Faute inexcusable en cas d'exposition des travailleurs à l'amiante—Proposition de loi ["Faute inexcusable" and asbestos workers' risk—Bill]*, Avis 1.517 (Conseil National du Travail, June 16, 2005) (Belgium); *Faute inexcusable en cas d'exposition des travailleurs à l'amiante—Proposition de loi ["Faute inexcusable" and asbestos workers' risk —Bill]*.

126   *Faute inexcusable en cas d'exposition des travailleurs à l'amiante—Proposition de loi ["Faute inexcusable" and asbestos workers' risk—Bill]*.

127   Ibid., p. 6.

128   Sénat de Belgique. *Proposition de loi modifiant l'article 51 des lois coordonnées du 3 juin 1970 relative à la réparation des dommages résultant des maladies professionnelles pour y intégrer la faute inexcusable en cas d'exposition des travailleurs à l'amiante[Bill to amend article 51 of the coordinated laws of June 3, 1970, allowing the compensation of asbestos workers in the event of "faute inexcusable"]*. October 1, 2008, n. 4-934/1 (Belgium).

129   A bill sponsored by her and two other colleagues at the Green Party is being examined by the Parliament as I am completing this manuscript (2013).

hand seen as a positive initiative for union members whose claims in workers' compensation were rejected. On the other hand, labor unions saw the proposed fund as a threat to unions' legitimacy in representing workers. As the various bills made their way through Parliament, unions had internal discussions, which resulted in them neither endorsing nor opposing the proposals.[130] In the political arena, labor unions' lack of unconditional support for the proposals weakened the push towards expanding asbestos compensation. The 2007 Asbestos Fund will in fact be successfully proposed not by labor unions but by a nonpartisan asbestos victims' group.

**Victims' mobilization and the establishment of a victims' advocacy group**

By the mid-1990s, asbestos victims' claim consciousness had slowly risen. As a greater number of asbestos workers, both active and retired, were becoming sick on a daily basis, victims began realizing that workers' compensation had substantial limitations and that it was an insufficient means of redress for the asbestos epidemic. Financially, workers' compensation was little more than a form of unemployment benefit. Considerations of horizontal justice were also increasingly perceived as urgent: workers' compensation benefits were only paid to some workers, leaving out uninsured and self-employed victims, victims of household exposure, and residents of neighborhoods adjacent to manufacturing facilities using asbestos. Furthermore, the system never forced employers to take responsibility for the epidemic, asbestos was still used, and Parliament had no plans to take action and ban it.

The most prominent outcome of this historical moment was the establishment of the *Association Belge des Victimes de l'Amiante* (ABEVA), a grassroots organization devoted to mobilizing claims and advocating policy reform on behalf of asbestos victims. ABEVA was established in late 2000 by Paul Vandenbroucke— son of Luc, the mesothelioma victim who had unsuccessfully sued his former employers in torts—and Xavier and Eric Jonckheere—sons of mesothelioma victims Pierre Jonckheere and Françoise Jonckheere van Noorbeeck (Françoise van Noorbeeck is the only plaintiff who has successfully litigated an asbestos personal injury case in Belgium to date).

The legal actions bought by Luc Vandenbroucke and Françoise van Noorbeeck generated a breakthrough moment in legal consciousness among asbestos victims in Belgium. Ms. van Noorbeeck, who had lost her husband and two sons to asbestos, was particularly determined in mobilizing victims. Her son described her thinking with these words:

> It is during her disease and after learning that her five sons had their lungs also filed with this poison, that my dear mom, revolted beyond belief, pushed for the creation of ABEVA … She knew she was the tree hiding the forest, the voice

---

130   Molitor, "Négociations et tensions autour de la création du Fonds amiante," 40.

for good of other victims which disappeared in ignorance after having endured atrocious pains. We were thus at the beginning with seven, all in excellent health and the assessment is dramatic today: three amongst U.S. have died prematurely and four remain, all with dust levels of asbestos in the lungs well above average. Among these four, two present pleural plates.[131]

Since the beginning, the grassroots organization has been active in raising awareness and mobilizing asbestos victims by setting up a website (http://www. abeva.be), publishing a newsletter and various booklets, organizing events to raise awareness among communities in which asbestos exposure is an environmental problem, and organizing marches to raise awareness of the asbestos legacy among the general population. Three marches were organized, and in 2006 over 500 participants took part.[132]

ABEVA lobbied the government to expand access to courts for asbestos victims by getting rid of the need to prove the employer's *faute intentionnelle* in court and to create an *ad hoc* asbestos compensation fund that would compensate other categories of victims in addition to those who were entitled to benefits under workers' compensation. ABEVA worked in conjunction with members of the legislature who were sensitive to these issues. At the beginning pressure on the Belgian legislature was fruitless. As we have seen earlier various proposed bills were never approved by the Parliament. The political environment was still opposed to creating a fund dedicated to asbestos victims.[133] Over the years, ABEVA narrowed its strategy merely towards expanding administrative compensation so that asbestos victims not qualifying for workers' compensation could receive some money. Eventually these efforts were successful and led to the establishment of the *Fonds d'indemnisation des victimes de l'amiante* in 2007.[134]

---

131   Eric Jonckheere, "Actions and achievements of Belgium asbestos victims and their families," in *2007 International Asbestos Conference for fair and equal compensation for all asbestos victims and their families* (Yokohama, Japan 2007).

132   "Pour les victimes de l'amiante" [To asbestos victims] *Le Soir*, May 14, 2007.

133   "La parole à … Xavier Jonckeere, président de l'Abeva (Association belge des victimes de l'amiante) [The microphone to … Xavier Jonckeere, president of Abeva (Belgian Asbestos Victims Association)]." *Le Bulletin de l'Andeva* 22. Published electronically March 31, 2007. http://andeva.fr/?La-parole-a-Xavier-Jonckeere.

134   *Loi-programme (I) du 27 décembre 2006 portant création d'un Fonds d'indemnisation des victimes de l'amiante [Law (I) December 27, 2006 creating the Asbestos Compensation Fund]*; *Arrêté royal [Royal Decree] portant exécution du chapitre VI, du titre IV, de la loi-programme (I) du 27 décembre 2006 portant création d'un Fonds d'indemnisation des victimes de l'amiante [for the implementation of the Asbestos Victims Compensation Fund]*, Moniteur Belge, May 11, 2007 (Belgium).

## The only successful asbestos personal injury case in Belgium's history

The growing ferment among asbestos victims provides the context for the appearance of the only personal injury case that has been successfully litigated against an asbestos defendant in Belgium. Personal injury litigation was increasingly seen as the only path to compensation for victims who could not receive workers' compensation. Furthermore, litigation promised to deliver legal acknowledgment of pain and suffering that victims were experiencing and legal accountability of those responsible for the asbestos epidemic. In this climate, Françoise van Noorbeeck, married Jonckheere, decided to go against the odds and try to recover damages in tort for environmental exposure to asbestos when living in the proximity of Eternit's manufacturing facility in Kapelle-op-den-Bos. Ms. van Noorbeeck certainly knew that the odds of winning were scant since, in the two other personal injury cases that had been filed previously, courts ruled against the plaintiffs.

Not discouraged by the grim record of personal injury litigation, Ms. van Noorbeeck began litigation in 2000 just a few months before dying of mesothelioma. After her death, her son stepped in as plaintiff and after 11 years of litigation, the court ruled for the plaintiff. This historical victory in court, the first for an asbestos victim, originated from non-occupational exposure. Ms. van Noorbeeck never spent a single day of her life in an asbestos manufacturing facility and became sick because her house in Kapelle-op-den-Bos was located very close to Eternit's asbestos plant. Her husband Pierre Jonckheere, who had started working at Eternit in 1952 and had succumbed to mesothelioma in 1987, was a facility supervisor. The company's policy mandated that all supervisors lived close to the workplace so that they could quickly reach the facility in case something was not working properly. To honor this policy, the Jonckheeres made Kapelle-op-den-Bos their home. When five of her children were growing up, Ms. van Noorbeeck often spent time with them along the canal on which asbestos was brought in from the sea to be processed and become asbestos-cement, Eternit's signature product. Environmental exposure to asbestos was certainly significant as demonstrated by the fact that mesothelioma struck not only Ms. van Noorbeeck but also two of her sons, who died respectively in 2003 and 2009.

Eternit could not seek the dismissal of Ms. van Noorbeeck's claim under the doctrine of *faute intentionelle* because her mesothelioma had not been caused by workplace exposure to asbestos. Her tort suit was based on environmental exposure, and therefore the general principles of tort liability applied. The Belgian Civil Code recognizes the right to seek recovery in courts against a tortfeasor for negligently causing bodily harm. Under article 1382 of the Civil Code, "any act by which a person causes damage to another makes the person through whose fault the damage occurred liable to repair such damage."[135] The action can be brought against corporations and any other business entities, which may be held liable for the acts of their agents, and a plaintiff may recover pecuniary damages (past and future lost wages, medical expenses, cost of care, loss resulting in the inability to work) and non-pecuniary damages (pain and suffering, disfigurement, loss of enjoyment of life, impairment of sexual activities, loss of a partner or relative, and bystander's pain and suffering).[136]

The case moved ahead very slowly as it took 11 years for it to be fully litigated. Eleven years after the complaint was filed, the Civil Court of Brussels found Eternit liable in torts and awarded damages to Ms. van Noorbeeck's heirs. This opinion was historical not only for its significance in terms of asbestos claims' mobilization but also from a doctrinal point of view. This is the first case that looked at issues of the statute of limitations in cancer cases. The court rejected Eternit's argument that the statute of limitations had run. Under Belgian law, the Court concluded, the statute of limitations runs from the day the disease is diagnosed rather than the day in which exposure to a toxic substance begins. This principle, which is consistent with the law of many other industrialized nations, had never been clearly formulated before in a judicial opinion in Belgium. Furthermore, the opinion spells out new principles of tort liability in the event of asbestos exposure, which may constitute the foundations for future claims. Eternit was found liable based on a complex doctrinal argument that touches upon tort principles, the constitutional right to health, the constitutional right to privacy, and principles codified in international treaties:

> Section 23 of the Constitution guarantees the right to a dignified existence. This right is understood as encompassing the right to a healthy environment. These constitutional rights were not only violated by the defendant during the period in which the [victim] first became ill, but also throughout the 35 years during which the [victim] first lived in proximity to Eternit's factory. Similarly, the European Court of Human Rights in Strasbourg considers that Article 8 ECHR (European Convention on Human Rights), which states literally that everyone is entitled to respect for private life, family life, his home and his correspondence, also protects the living environment of citizens. It is recognized that this article has indirect horizontal applicability.[137]

---

135   *Code Civile [Civil Code].* March 21, 1804 (as amended on April 6, 2012) (Belgium). See Hubert Bocken, "Tort Law," in *Introduction to Belgian law*, ed. Hubert Bocken and Walter de Bondt (Bruxelles; The Hague; Boston: Bruylant; Kluwer Law International, 2001), 247-249.

136   The liability of multiple negligent defendants is joint and several. Contribution and indemnification actions among joint defendants are possible and based on the causal contribution to the injury rather than on the degree of fault. Pure comparative fault applies as well: no compensation if the victim is at fault. See Bocken, "Tort Law," 267.

137   Jonathan Lefèvre. "Eternit: 'Maintenant c'est aux politiques d'agir' [Eternit: Now is up to the politicians to act]." *Parti du Travail de Belgique.* Published electronically

In its opinion, the Court noted that Eternit's negligence was particularly egregious. Evidence presented at trial showed that Eternit knew about asbestos toxicity since 1967 and, rather than implementing strategies to protect the population, it engaged in an extensive cover up to avoid facing the legal consequences of asbestos dangers:[138]

> … the incredible cynicism with which Eternit, in its quest for profit, has put aside the knowledge that it used a potentially fatal substance and has nonetheless exposed to it not only its employees but also local residents, and worse has made every effort to continue this harmful activity without the need to implement safety precautions to any significant degree.[139]

The Court awarded EUR 250,000 to the surviving sons, who had demanded Euro 399,500. In the aftermath of the case, Eric, one of Françoise's sons, shared his excitement with the press: "This is a historical day. For the first time a humble small family wins a case of this sort against a multinational corporation. We never doubted it but the victory comes as a huge relief."[140] He also expressed his hope that "more victims will have the courage to face Eternit."[141] By contrast, Eternit issued a press release arguing that case constituted an anomaly that could jeopardize asbestos compensation's stability. The company wrote that the award:

> … is much higher than [compensation] granted to victims by the Asbestos Fund and [compensation] normally granted by the courts in Belgium. Therefore, this ruling threatens the principles of compensation that have emerged from negotiations among employers' organizations, trade unions, representatives of asbestos victims and the government negotiated and guiding the operations of the Asbestos Fund.[142]

---

November 29, 2011. http://www.ptb.be/nieuws/artikel/eternit-maintenant-cest-aux-politiq ues-dagir/.

138   "Eternit condamné à dédommager les victimes de l'amiante [Eternit will pay damages to the victims of asbestos]." *Lalibre.be*. Published electronically November 28, 2011. http://www.lalibre.be/actu/belgique/article/703028/eternit-condamne-a-dedommager -les-victimes-de-l-amiante.html.

139   Lefèvre, "Eternit: 'Maintenant c'est aux politiques d'agir'."

140   "Eternit condamnée: 'C'est un jour historique' [Eternit found liable: 'An historical day']." *Lavenir.net*. Published electronically November 28, 2011. http://www. lavenir.net/article/detail.aspx?articleid=DMF20111128_036.

141   Ricardo Gutierrez. "La Justice a osé résister au lobby belge de l'amiante [A court dared to oppose the asbestos lobby]." *Lesoir.be*. Published electronically November 28, 2011. http://www.lesoir.be/actualite/belgique/2011-11-28/la-justice-a-ose-resister-au-lobby-belge-de-l-amiante-879930.php.

142   "Eternit fera probablement appel [Eternit will likely appeal]." *Le Soir*. Published electronically November 28, 2011. http://www.lesoir.be/actualite/belgique/2011-11-28/la-justice-a-ose-resister-au-lobby-belge-de-l-amiante-879930.php.

## The 2007 Asbestos Fund

In addition to standing by the side of the Jonckheeres in the long-lasting litigation against Eternit, ABEVA was active on the policy front, trying to increase the public and political visibility of asbestos compensation. The number of ABEVA's members was growing steadily, and its initiatives were becoming increasingly visible by the public. A series of articles that had appeared in the newspapers and magazines both in French and Dutch contributed to the growing awareness among Belgians of the asbestos epidemic. The most compelling initiative was the publication of a series of articles in the *Het Laatste*, the most widely read Belgian newspaper. In conjunction with the third ABEVA march, *Het Laatste* published articles in which the author Frieda Joris interviews Xavier Jonckheere, Paul Vandenbroucke, and Luc Cortebeek, a journalist who in 2004 had published a story about deaths among for Coverit's employees. There were interviews with politicians and labor union leaders. Another important contribution was the publication in the magazine *Knack*, and then republished in *Le Monde Diplomatique*, of a series of articles written by Marleen Teugels and Nico Krols on the misdeeds of Eternit and other firms.[143] The articles also touched upon the criminal conviction of an Eternit executive in Italy. This was the first time the Belgian public linked the asbestos industry to legal responsibility. The reportages published in *Het Laatste* and *Knack* caused a "choc," as Marc Molitor noted.[144]

In this context of increasing concerns and outrage for the legacy of asbestos, the then Prime Minister Guy Verhofstadt gave a substantial push to the idea of legislative reform of asbestos compensation. A leading figure in the Flemish liberal political party, Mr. Verhofstadt put together a bill that proposed the establishment of an *ad hoc* fund that would compensate mesothelioma and asbestosis victims of occupational and environmental exposure. The bill owed considerable debt to drafts previously proposed by Mr. Gerkens; an early version was reviewed by both ABEVA and Eternit. These drafts never became law though because they also aimed to repeal employers' tort immunity, which is an issue that has always failed to attract sufficient political traction. The Prime Minister's initiative was probably inspired by political and personal motives. Politically, a reform of asbestos compensation would have liberated new funding and thus more spending power for his government. Also, the proposal would have cast a good light on the Green Party, which was a likely political ally in upcoming political elections. On a personal level, Mr. Verhofstadt had lost one of his advisors to mesothelioma. This loss motivated him to do something about asbestos while in office.[145]

---

143   Nico Krols and Marleen Teugels, "The dirty legacy of asbestos," *Le Monde Diplomatique*, January 22, 2007; Krols and Teugels, "'A Licence to Kill': the Dirty Legacy of Asbestos."

144   Molitor, "Négociations et tensions autour de la création du Fonds amiante," 45-47.

145   Ibid., 47.

The first draft of the bill however encountered significant opposition. The *Fonds*'s advisory committee was particularly negative about the proposal. The *Fonds* was skeptical of the financing aspects of the proposed Fund and of its consistency with existing workers' compensation regulations. The sticking point was the provision that allowed mesothelioma victims to sue employers in tort without the need to prove *faute intentionnelle*. This provision, the *Fonds* argued, created a potentially disastrous tension between asbestos victims and victims of other occupational diseases.

The Verhofstadt team however was determined and drafted a second bill that addressed all criticisms raised by the *Fonds*. To do so, they proposed a compromise: the proposed Fund would compensate all mesothelioma and asbestosis victims but all victims would be barred from bringing a civil lawsuit unless they could establish the defendant's *faute intentionnelle*. Tort immunity was extended to mesothelioma and asbestosis victims of secondhand and environmental exposures to asbestos.[146] ABEVA opposed this second Bill. However, the Prime Minister decided to push it through the legislative process. It gained the recommendation of the *Fonds*, the vote of the majority of Members of Parliament and in May 2007 it became law.[147]

The 2007 Asbestos Fund was born. Administered by *Fonds des Maladies Professionnelles*, the Fund is currently in operation and makes payments to mesothelioma and asbestosis victims of occupational and non-occupational exposure. The 2007 Fund is the first mechanism in Belgium's history that allows victims of non-occupational exposure to receive compensation. Victims who receive payments from the Fund are "barred from claiming damages from third parties that may be liable in torts."[148] On the other hand only mesothelioma and asbestosis victims are eligible to receive payments. Victims with pleural plaques, lung cancer, and larynx cancers are not eligible. Parliamentary debates show that asbestos firms successfully lobbied against creating a presumption of a causation link between asbestos exposure and lung and larynx cancers, by pushing the argument, in many cases, that exposure to asbestos is only one of the contributing factors of lung and larynx cancers. With regard to pleural plaques in particular, the lawmakers reasoned that these fibroses do not lead to diminished working capacity or need for medical treatment. Therefore, they fail to qualify as "diseases" that deserve compensation. Companies preferred to lobby for narrowing eligibility to

---

146  Fagnart, *La responsabilité civile: chronique de jurisprudence 1985-1995*, 21.

147  *Loi-programme (I) du 27 décembre 2006 portant création d'un Fonds d'indemnisation des victimes de l'amiante [Law (I) December 27, 2006 creating the Asbestos Compensation Fund]*; *Arrêté royal [Royal Decree] portant exécution du chapitre VI, du titre IV, de la loi-programme (I) du 27 décembre 2006 portant création d'un Fonds d'indemnisation des victimes de l'amiante [for the implementation of the Asbestos Victims Compensation Fund]*.

148  *Loi-programme (I) du 27 décembre 2006 portant création d'un Fonds d'indemnisation des victimes de l'amiante [Law (I) December 27, 2006 creating the Asbestos Compensation Fund]*, ¶ 125.

mesothelioma and asbestosis victims, and so facing a chance of litigation for other asbestos diseases, rather than seeing the share of financial contribution to the Fund increase (see Table 2.3).

**Table 2.3    Comparison of asbestos diseases compensated under workers' compensation versus the Asbestos Fund**

| Disease | Workers' compensation | Asbestos Fund |
| --- | --- | --- |
| Asbestosis | Yes | Yes |
| Pleural plaques | Yes | No |
| Diffuse, bilateral pleural thickening | Yes | Yes |
| Mesothelioma | Yes | Yes |
| Lung cancer | Yes | No |
| Larynx cancer | Yes | No |

*Source:* Table prepared by the author by assembling governmental data published at http://www.fbz.fgov.be/afa/afa_fr.html#med1.

The process to obtain compensation mirrors the process of adjudication of workers' compensation claims. A formal application must be filed by filling out a standardized form.[149] The applicant must demonstrate exposure to asbestos. The victim's doctor must also certify the diagnosis of mesothelioma or asbestosis.[150] Once received by the *Fonds*, the claim is evaluated and adjudicated. In light of the deadly nature of mesothelioma, adjudication of mesothelioma claims is expedited. The rules mandate that the application is reviewed within 15 days from reception of the application and that a decision must be issued within two months.[151] However, victims have no remedy in the event of a delay. If the application is rejected, the asbestos victim can file an appeal with the *Tribunal du Travail*.

The 2007 Asbestos Fund is jointly financed by government and employers— *all* employers, not only companies employing workers that were or are exposed to asbestos. In 2007, the government allocated approximately 1 million dollars to the Fund.[152] Employers' share is collected as a premium that is added to regular social security payments. Employers' contribution is currently set by law at 1 percent of their regular annual contribution to social security. Insurance companies are not required to contribute.

---

149    http://www.fbz.fgov.be/afa/pdf/afaform01f.pdf.

150    http://www.fbz.fgov.be/afa/pdf/afaform02f.pdf.

151    *Arrêté royal [Royal Decree] portant exécution du chapitre VI, du titre IV, de la loi-programme (I) du 27 décembre 2006 portant création d'un Fonds d'indemnisation des victimes de l'amiante [for the implementation of the Asbestos Victims Compensation Fund]*, ¶ 8.

152    Ibid., ¶ 2-3.

In 2012, the Fund was disbursing monthly payments in the amount of EUR 1,689 to mesothelioma victims and EUR 16.89 per point percent of disability to victims of asbestosis.[153] If the disease was caused by occupational exposure, the Asbestos Fund's award is reduced by 50 percent and added to workers' compensation benefit. For deceased victims, their relatives and domestic partners receive a lump sum payment ranging from EUR 16,893 to EUR 33,786 if the claim is based on mesothelioma and ranging from EUR 8,446 to EUR 16,893 in the event of asbestosis. All payments are tax free.

In its first year of operation, the Fund paid compensation to approximately 700 asbestos victims: 521 claims for asbestosis and pleural plaques and 151 mesothelioma cases.[154] By the end of 2009, the number of mesothelioma awards increased to 532. Of these 532 cases, 158 would not have been compensated if the Fund had not been established. Among them, there are 17 independent contractors, 15 spouses who became ill through secondhand exposure, 11 victims of environmental exposure, and 15 victims who were exposed to asbestos-containing products at home. The other cases are not categorized.[155] By 2012, 1505 had received payments from the Fund, 887 for mesothelioma and 618 for asbestosis.[156]

In the best tradition of "compensation democracy," the establishment of the 2007 Fund is a victory for both victims and asbestos companies. From the victims' point of view, the Fund extends compensation to classes of victims who had never been able to recover benefits prior to 2007. Independent contractors and housewives in particular had unsuccessfully tried to recover damages in court in the years that preceded the establishment of the Fund. Furthermore, victims of exposure to asbestos that took place in more than one country can claim compensation provided some exposure took place in Belgium. From the asbestos companies' perspective, the victory is twofold. First, all mesothelioma victims are now barred from bringing tort claims against asbestos defendants. All mesothelioma cases, which are most feared by defendants, are removed from the court system. Legislative proposals to remove the Fund's exclusivity as a remedy for mesothelioma have been pursued in 2012. However, the *Conseil d'État* issued a negative opinion concluding that any amendment that would give victims, compensated by the Fund, a negligence claim against asbestos companies would be unconstitutional because of a breach of the principle of separation of powers.[157] This seems to close the door to legislative

---

153  Ibid., ¶¶ 9.

154  ABEVA, "Un an de fonctionnement de l'AFA (Fonds amiante)" [A year of operations of the AFA (Asbestos Fund).] *ABEVA News* 2008.

155  Molitor, "Négociations et tensions autour de la création du Fonds amiante," 57.

156  "Publication du rapport des 5 ans du Fonds amiante" [Publications of the five report on the Asbestos Fund.] *FMP News*, March 28, 2012.

157  *Proposition de loi complétant l'arrêté royal du 11 mai 2007 portant exécution du chapitre VI, du titre IV, de la loi-programme (I) du 27 décembre 2006 portant création d'un Fonds d'indemnisation des victimes de l'amiante, en vue d'augmenter la cotisation à payer par les employeurs dont la responsabilité a été retenue dans le cadre du Fonds amiante*

reform. Second, tort immunity for mesothelioma deaths indirectly undermines victims' claim mobilization. In all jurisdictions, asbestos litigation has developed around mesothelioma cases, which are the most successful cases and therefore are cases that open the door to legal doctrines and courts' reception of claims based on asbestos exposure. In Belgium, this has not happened yet, and it is likely to never happen, although the 2011 victory of the Jonckheeres against Eternit offers some hope to victims. However, this is the only case that has been successful and it is indeed a mesothelioma case. Furthermore, it was filed before the implementation of the 2007 reform, which means that its relevance as a precedent may be limited. Although highly publicized, one case is hardly sufficient to mobilize victims of diseases that are not compensated by the Fund (pleural plaques, asbestos-induced lung and larynx cancers). Asbestos litigation is therefore likely to remain patchy.

## The future of asbestos compensation in Belgium

Salvator Nay points out that in Belgium every social phenomenon develops with great delay. Asbestos compensation is certainly no exception to this rule. Although various asbestos diseases were included in the list of prescribed diseases covered under workers' compensation in 1953, the regulation of asbestos exposure in working environments only emerged in the late 1970s, and it was enacted only in the 1980s. Asbestos was also banned in 1997 and completely dismissed only in 2002. The delay in banning asbestos and recognizing asbestos disease under workers' compensation has had ramification for asbestos litigation, which has struggled to emerge and that, after the establishment of the 2007 Asbestos Fund, is unlikely to develop much further. Over the years, just a handful of tort cases have been filed, and only one has led to a damage award. A criminal complaint was also filed, but no criminal investigation originated from it. Overall, the political, institutional, and cultural environment that limited victims' claim mobilization has not changed substantially in the past 50 years. The asbestos industry is still influential. Labor unions are divided, and in general preoccupied with maintaining "peaceful labor relations" rather than pushing litigation and other adversarial strategies. Finally, courts are "unsympathetic" to asbestos victims, as suggested by journalist and activist Salvator Nay.[158] Over the years, there has been no erosion of the doctrine of *faute intentionnelle*, which has been found to be constitutional and narrowly construed by courts. To the contrary, the 2007 Asbestos Fund has

---

*[Bill supplementing the Royal Decree of May 11, 2007 on the implementation of Chapter VI of Title IV of Law (I) of December 27, 2006 establishing a compensation fund for asbestos victims, to increase the contribution payable by employers whose responsibility has been found in the context of the Asbestos Fund]*, Avis 51.636/1 (Conseil d'État, July 26, 2012) (Belgium).

158    Laurie Kazan-Allen. "London Asbestos Meetings, April 2002." Published electronically May 3, 2002. http://ibasecretariat.org/lka_london_meetings_rep_0402.php.

reestablished its legitimacy. ABEVA itself has expressed reservations with regard to seeking compensation in court. In 2007, its newsletter stated that "ABEVA will not encourage [or at least] certainly not in a systematic fashion victims to throw themselves in this adventure [a lawsuit], now that the Asbestos Fund has been established."[159]

Although some mobilization has taken place among Belgian asbestos victims and consciousness of the medical and legal implications of exposure to asbestos is more widespread, the basic traits of Belgian legal culture are unchanged: limited expectation of redress, silence, and avoidance are predominant among asbestos victims. As one activist suggested to me in the course of an interview in 2002, "Belgians are reluctant to publicly expose misconducts, and to publicly blame somebody for their misfortunes." Problems are dealt with in the private sphere, and it is unlikely that this distinctive trait of Belgian legal culture will disappear soon. All of these factors are powerful reasons for preserving the *status quo*.

---

159  ABEVA, "Oui a un fonds d'indemnisation, non à l'immunité" [Yes to a compensation fund, no to immunity.] *ABEVA News* 2007, 2.

# Chapter 3
# Asbestos compensation in England

The relationship between England and asbestos compensation is a long and difficult one. One of the countries that made use of asbestos in the late nineteenth century, England is the first country in which asbestos toxicity was recorded. In 1898, the Factory Inspectorate listed asbestos production among occupations that were deemed to be "unhealthy or dangerous."[1] The first cases of asbestosis were recorded by English doctors in 1910, in conjunction with the death of a 33-year-old who had worked in the carding room of an asbestos factory for ten years prior to his admission to hospital, and in 1924, after the death of a woman in her thirties who had worked in asbestos factories since the age of 13.[2] The legacy of asbestos use is tragic indeed. England has one of the highest rates of asbestos diseases among industrialized nations. A person dies every five minutes of mesothelioma. The number of annual cases of mesothelioma is elevated and on the rise. Since 1968, the year in which the British Mesothelioma Register was established, mesothelioma deaths have risen rapidly, with deaths in 2001 12 times higher than in 1968.[3] By 2050, there will have been approximately 90,000 deaths from mesothelioma in Great Britain, 65,000 occurring after 2001.[4] Asbestos disease is distributed in many parts of the country, in urban and coastal communities, in blue collar and white collar workers, in England as well as in all other regions of the United Kingdom.

England was also the first in the world to recognize, in 1931, asbestos as an occupational hazard and grant compensation to victims of asbestosis. Since 1931, asbestosis has been part of asbestos compensation in England. All subsequent major reforms have never touched compensation eligibility for this disease. Administrative compensation for asbestos disease expanded in the aftermath of World War II as medical evidence of asbestos toxicity extended to mesothelioma and lung cancer. These diseases become liable for compensation under the umbrella of the Industrial Injuries Disability Benefit (IIDB), the English system of workers' compensation, which was created as part of the establishment of the

---

1   Factories and Workshops, "Annual Report of the Chief Inspector of Factories and Workshops for the Year 1898," (London 1898), 160.

2   Cooke, "Fibrosis of the lungs due to the inhalation of asbestos dust," 147; William E. Cooke, "Pulmonary asbestosis," *British Medical Journal* 2, no. 3491 (1927).

3   Hodgson et al., "The expected burden of mesothelioma mortality in Great Britain from 2002 to 2050."

4   Ibid.

welfare state.[5] After decades of experience with the legal implication of asbestos toxicity, England now has rather stable although partially contested mechanisms of asbestos compensation which involve a mix of payments from the IIDB, *ad hoc* schemes, and litigation.[6]

The IIDB, which is currently paid to victims with asbestosis, mesothelioma, lung cancer with pleural thickening or with asbestosis, or bilateral diffuse pleural thickening who developed the disease because of occupational exposure to asbestos, has been traditionally the cornerstone of English asbestos compensation in England because its payments have been an important source of compensation for victims of occupational exposure, its expansion a pressing matter for asbestos victims' advocates, and its award a precondition for victims to access to courts. Although in recent years its importance has somewhat decreased (primarily because asbestos victims have access to alternatives to fund litigation and because a growing number of victims are not eligible to receive it because their exposure was not occupational), I will start the discussion of asbestos compensation in England from the IIDB. The IIDB has in fact played a central role in the development of asbestos compensation in England. Since claim consciousness and litigation management strategies rose in its shadow, administrative compensation occupies a key role in asbestos compensation. I will then look at the emergence of personal injury litigation and at other sources of compensation for asbestos victims. The unique blend of administrative compensation and litigation makes England an interesting case study of asbestos compensation compared with Continental Europe and the United States.

## The Industrial Injuries Disability Benefit (IIDB)

English law has recognized asbestos toxicity and compensation for asbestosis since 1931.[7] It is after World War II however that workers' compensation became more widely used by asbestos victims. The causal link between asbestos and cancers was established only in the 1950s and 1960s. By then, the newly established IIDB had become an integral part of the welfare state established in the late 1940s. The footprint of its architecture was based on the 1897 and 1931 regulations. However, after World War II a broad set of welfare interventions were implemented and workers' compensation was absorbed by the nascent welfare state. This new democratic project in which the state guaranteed a social

---

5   I refer to the Industrial Injuries Disability Benefit as "workers' compensation." The reference is technically improper because England chose not to have a workers' compensation system. However, as a matter of substance, the IIDB is a functional equivalent of workers' compensation.

6   Asbestos victims are also entitled to access health care free-of-charge.

7   *Asbestos Industry (Asbestosis) Scheme of 1931* (England).

safety net was inspired by an influential report authored by Sir William Beveridge in 1942.[8]

The decades that followed the Beveridge Report of 1948 saw the emergence of "a bewildering variety of benefits within the British social security scheme for people who are unable to work because of illness."[9] This wide range of social security benefits has undergone significant reforms since the 1940s resulting in asbestos victims' eligibility to receive a variety of benefits connected to the illness and inability to work. Welfare benefits, including IIDB, are reformed, transformed, and reformed again very often. In fact, one of the challenges that I have experienced in writing this book relates to perennial, subtle change in social security laws in England. Proposals for reform are routinely put forward by newly elected politicians, and some make it as far as becoming law thus altering the *status quo* of social benefit entitlements. England in particular seems prone to instability in this area as echoes of the tormented political life of social security with British people conflicted between the civility of an entitlement society and the reality of its cost. Indeed the cost of the system for English taxpayers is substantial. In contrast, several other European countries mandate that employers periodically pay a premium. IIDB and other social benefits are noncontributory, that is, neither workers nor their employers are required to make contributions. Originally benefits under the IIDB scheme were paid out of the Industrial Injuries Fund, a fund financed by contributions from employers and employees. The Industrial Injuries Fund was then abolished, and liabilities were transferred in 1990 to the National Insurance Fund. In 1993, Wikeley noted that social security was the "largest element in the government's public expenditure program, accounting for 29 percent of planned government spending."[10] The general taxation funds the system.[11] The IIDB is a non-means-tested benefit, that is, the earnings or other income of the asbestos victims affects neither the claimant's eligibility nor the amount awarded. The benefit is not taxable unless it is received by the surviving spouse or other third parties.

Political controversy over the welfare system contributes greatly to a constantly changing picture, thus posing a challenge to scholars who try to give a precise account of the British welfare system. Since I started working on asbestos compensation in the early 2000s, names, requirements, processes, and laws have constantly changed. In 2012, the list of benefits comprised Disability

---

8   William H.B.B. Beveridge, *Social insurance and allied services: utilisation of Approved Society Administration under the alternative scheme proposed by the National Conference of Friendly Societies, and other Approved Society organisations: detailed plan: report* (London: Twentieth Century Press, 1943).

9   Wikeley, *Compensation for industrial disease*. 58.

10   Nicholas J. Wikeley, "Social Security Appeals in Great Britain," *Administrative Law Review* 46 (1994): 184.

11   Currently the Secretary of State through the benefits agency administration is responsible for payments.

Living Allowance, Attendance Allowance, Constant Attendance Allowance, Exceptionally Severe Disablement Benefit, Statutory Sick Pay, Employment and Support Allowance, and the Carer's Allowance. While an important component of the safety net of asbestos victims, analyzing these benefits does not add much to understanding how asbestos compensation developed in England, I therefore refrain from discussing them further in detail.

To be eligible, asbestos victims must have suffered a specific type of asbestos disease and the disease must have been caused by occupational exposure to asbestos. English adopted a prescribed-diseases workers' compensation system. Only victims of disease that are listed, or "prescribed" by law are eligible. In 1948, the list only included asbestosis, which had already been thought of as a disease entitling sufferers to administrative compensation by the path breaking Asbestos Industry (Asbestosis) Scheme 1931.[12] The 1931 Scheme played an important role in the development of asbestos compensation: it created a statutory duty of care towards employees and created a presumption that asbestosis was occupational whenever exposure had been protracted for more than five years.[13] The presumption is still one of the pillars of the system.[14]

The current list of prescribed asbestos diseases comprises pneumoconiosis, asbestosis, mesothelioma, primary carcinoma of the lung (when accompanied by asbestosis or, in absence of asbestosis, when there is evidence of exposure to asbestos for a certain time), and bilateral pleural thickening.[15] New asbestos diseases were included progressively as stronger evidence of a causal link between asbestos and these diseases emerged. Mesothelioma was added in 1966, lung cancer with asbestosis in 1985, and lung cancer following asbestos exposure but with no evidence of asbestosis was added in 2006.[16] The 2006 reform added to the list of prescribed diseases cases of carcinoma of the lung in workers with no sign of asbestosis but with a record of occupational exposure lasting more than ten years (five if any of the exposure took place before 1975) in the course of the manufacture of asbestos textiles, spraying asbestos, asbestos insulation work, or applying or removing materials containing asbestos in the course of shipbuilding. The 1975 timeframe originates from a recommendation of the Industrial Injuries Advisory Council, which noted that occupational exposure to asbestos before the 1970s was much higher than in subsequent years:

---

12   *Asbestos Industry (Asbestosis) Scheme of 1931* (England).
13   Ibid., 5.
14   Department of Work and Pensions, "Prescribed diseases," http://www.dwp.gov.uk/publications/specialist-guides/technical-guidance/db1-a-guide-to-industrial-injuries/prescribed-diseases/.
15   *The Social Security (Industrial Injuries) (Prescribed Diseases) Regulations 1985 as amended by the Social Security (Industrial Injuries) (Miscellaneous Amendments) Regulations 1997* (England).
16   *The Social Security (Industrial Injuries) (Prescribed Diseases) Amendment Regulations 2006* (England).

... the risk of lung cancer in asbestos workers fell after the introduction of the 1969 Asbestos regulations, probably as a consequence of a reduction in the use of and associated exposure to asbestos, particularly amphiboles.[17]

In the 2000s, the government considered but rejected the call for adding new diseases to the list of prescribed diseases. These diseases are laryngeal cancer, retroperitoneal fibrosis, and symptomatic pleural plaques. In each case, the Industrial Injuries Advisory Council reviewed the epidemiological evidence and concluded that it would be insufficient to recommend to the legislature to include these diseases among those compensable with an IIDB.

Claimants are eligible to receive the award if they meet three requirements. First, they were diagnosed with prescribed asbestos disease. Second, exposure to asbestos took place "out of and in the course of the employment." Claims are commonly based on evidence of direct exposure to asbestos or any mixture of asbestos or of employment in facilities manufacturing articles containing or composed of asbestos or cleaning any machinery or plant used in manufacturing products containing asbestos. Third, they meet a certain impairment threshold. Since 1986, the threshold of minimum disability associated with asbestosis, pneumoconiosis, and diffuse mesothelioma is set at 1 percent and at 14 percent if diffuse pleural thickening or asbestos-related lung cancer are claimed. If the request is based on more than one disease, each disease is assessed and added to the other. The combined percentage is the basis for determining the benefit. Independent contractors are eligible.

To receive an IIDB benefit, a sick worker must fill out a claim form, which can be downloaded online, and submit it to the local Industrial Injuries Branch or the local Social Security or Jobs and Benefits Office. Eligibility is determined by a benefit officer. Her determination takes into account the results of a medical examination performed by a doctor appointed by the IIDB Board. The examination is intended to confirm the diagnosis of the prescribed disease and assess the percentage of physical impairment that affects the claimant. Upon completion of the medical assessment, the case goes to an adjudication officer who decides whether a benefit must be awarded and its amount.[18] Adjudication officers decide claims based on regulations, case law and "on papers before them."[19] Officers do not hold hearings or interview the claimant. The agency's decision indicates the percentage of disability recognized and how much benefit (if any) the claimant will receive and for how long. As Table 3.1 shows, the amount is determined using a sliding scale based on the age and level of disability of the claimant: higher

---

17 A.J. Newman Taylor, "Asbestos-related Diseases: Report by the Industrial Injuries Advisory Council in Accordance with Section 171 of the Social Security Administration Act 1992 Reviewing the Prescription of the Asbestos-related Diseases" (The Stationery Office, 2005).

18 Wikeley, "Social Security Appeals in Great Britain," 183, 191, 193-195.

19 Ibid.

percentages of disability lead to higher award. The benefit is ordinarily paid in the form of a weekly disability pension. Since 2006, awards that do not exceed GBP 9,980 can be paid as a lump sum payment. This is particularly attractive to asbestos victims with a relatively short life expectancy, mesothelioma and lung cancer sufferers in particular, who may end up receiving less benefit than victims with a nonfatal disease (see Table 3.1).

**Table 3.1    Industrial Injuries Disablement Benefit's weekly payments**

| Disease | Workers' compensation | Asbestos Fund |
|---|---|---|
| Asbestosis | Yes | Yes |
| Pleural plaques | Yes | No |
| Diffuse, bilateral pleural thickening | Yes | Yes |
| Mesothelioma | Yes | Yes |
| Lung cancer | Yes | No |
| Larynx cancer | Yes | No |

*Source:* Table prepared by the author by assembling governmental data published at http://www.fbz.fgov.be/afa/afa_fr.html#med1.

In the past years, benefit agencies have tried to pay benefits as quickly as possible. Mesothelioma cases enjoy a fast track system. These claims, and indeed all claims involving a terminally ill claimant, are given priority at all times. Priority means that cases are referred for medical advice immediately after filing instead of waiting for a favorable decision on the question of whether occupational exposure took place. The fast track system was designed to adjudicate mesothelioma claims before the likely death of the sufferer just months after diagnosis of the cancer. Fast track awards were thus intended to assist claimants with severe health care needs and to provide them with a sense of justice and compensation to be enjoyed in the remaining days of their lives. Notice of the award is given to asbestos victims. In the event of dissatisfaction with the outcome of the claim, a victim can petition for a review of the case with the First-tier Tribunal. The most common sources of disputes in IIDB claims are issues concerning the percentage of assessment, particularly where the benefit is not payable because disability has been assessed at less than 14 percent, and the diagnosis, particularly when the claimant is suffering from a condition that is not severe enough to meet the criteria set by the law.[20] The First-tier Tribunal decision is then reviewed, under narrow grounds, by the Administrative Appeals Chamber:

---

20   Ibid., 188.

**Table 3.2     Cases of asbestos disease with IIDB award**

| Year | Diffuse Mesothelioma | Pneumoconiosis with asbestos agent | Primary carcinoma of the lungs (with asbestosis) | Primary carcinoma of the lungs |
|---|---|---|---|---|
| 1986 | 305 | 312 | | |
| 1987 | 399 | 247 | | |
| 1988 | 479 | 202 | | |
| 1989 | 441 | 368 | | |
| 1990 | 462 | 306 | | |
| 1991 | 519 | 330 | | |
| 1992 | 551 | 354 | | |
| 1993 | 698 | 418 | | |
| 1994 | 583 | 376 | | |
| 1995 | 685 | 427 | | |
| 1996 | 642 | 479 | | |
| 1997 | 553 | 344 | | |
| 1998 | 600 | 310 | 50 | |
| 1999 | 620 | 400 | 40 | |
| 2000 | 650 | 450 | 50 | |
| 2001 | 760 | 470 | 50 | |
| 2002 | 1,000 | 580 | 60 | |
| 2003 | 1,170 | 650 | 70 | |
| 2004 | 1,340 | 760 | 80 | |
| 2005 | 1,540 | 830 | 90 | |
| 2006 | 1,470 | 730 | 130 | 40 |
| 2007 | 1,620 | 690 | 110 | 90 |
| 2008 | 1,740 | 810 | 180 | 130 |
| 2009 | 1,880 | 820 | 190 | 190 |
| 2010 | 1,900 | | 190 | 160 |

*Note:* There is no data between 1986 and 1997 for primary carcinoma of the lungs (with asbestosis) and no data between 1986 and 2006 for primary carcinoma of the lungs.

*Source:* Table prepared by the author by assembling governmental data published in various sources: Asbestos, H.C. Research Paper 99/81, 1, 16 (1999), Table 2, Health and Safety Statistics: 1997/98, HSC. http://www.parliament.uk/documents/commons/lib/research/rp99/rp99-081.pdf; *Department for Work and Pensions, Industrial Injuries Disablement Benefit Quarterly Statistics: March 2008*, Table 1.12. http://webarchive.nationalarchives.gov.uk/+/http://www.dwp.gov.uk/asd/asd1/iidb/iidb_quarterly_mar08.xls; *Department for Work and Pensions, Industrial Injuries Disablement Benefit Quarterly Statistics: September 2010*, Table 1.12. http://statistics.dwp.gov.uk/asd/asd1/iidb/index.php?page=iidb_quarterly_sep10; *Department for Work and Pensions, Industrial Injuries Disablement Benefit Quarterly Statistics: September 2011*, Tables 1.10; 1.12; 1.12A. http://statistics.dwp.gov.uk/asd/asd1/iidb/iidb_quarterly_sep11.xls.

Over the past two decades, IIDB claiming rates have increased for all asbestos diseases. Mesothelioma claims in particular have grown sharply, from a few hundred claims filed annually to almost two thousand claims. The reasons of this growth in numbers can be traced to three factors. The rise of asbestos disease is the first reason. Changes in IIDB's structural features: new kinds of asbestos exposure have been incorporated in the "exposure" requirement, new diseases have been prescribed, the adjudication process has been simplified, victims destined to die soon enjoy a fast track and lump sum payments, and the disability threshold has been lowered. The final and third factor is the growth in mobilization of asbestos victims and routinization of claims. Since the 1990s, social security becomes increasingly embedded in claiming patterns of asbestos victims and part of the "ordinary" package of compensation that victims expect (or hope) to recover. This process has been helped by several leaflets and websites that have been made available over time by unions and supporting groups. Plaintiffs' lawyers too routinely advise their clients of the various paths to compensation, which English law envisions as being not mutually exclusive, and to "invest" a chunk of the social benefits to fund litigation (see Table 3.2).

The IIDB is, in many regards, a generous benefit: no contribution is needed while the claimant is or was employed, the award does not bar a tort action, fast track and lump sum payments help the most severe cases of disablement, and more occupations and disease have been prescribed over time. Yet, many asbestos victims were left out. Self-employed victims, secondhand exposure victims, and victims of environmental exposure are not covered. Moreover, victims whose employers were no longer in business and for which no insurance coverage was left were only able to receive the IIDB but had no viable way to recover damages in court. The law did not provide for more generous payments in favor of victims who were out of luck in court. These victims were asked to swallow the bitter truth. As many asbestos victims were able to obtain routinely more compensation than others, the unfairness of the system became obvious to the various legal and social actors who were involved with asbestos compensation: the law treated men and women whose bodies were attacked by the same diseases and who were affected by the same painful, traumatizing experiences differently. To redress this unfortunate state of affairs, two new forms of compensation were specifically targeted for the benefit of asbestos victims who could not recover benefits under workers' compensation. These are the Pneumoconiosis Etc. (Workers' Compensation) Act 1979, the 2008 diffuse mesothelioma payment, and the 2012 mesothelioma payments to victims who cannot trace a liable employer or an employer's liability insurer.

An IIDB award does not remove the possibility for the victim to seek additional compensation in court. The interrelation between litigation, IIDB and no-fault compensation, which aims at avoiding victims going undercompensated and overcompensated, is complex. The following are the four basic pillars: a social benefit claim does not preclude seeking compensation in court; a social benefit award along with inability to recover damages in court is the prerequisite to apply for compensation under the *ad hoc* no-fault scheme; and defendants and insurers must pay a portion of the damages, estimated to be equal to the amount of social benefits payable to the plaintiff, during the five years immediately following the occurrence of the disease to the government rather than the victim;[21] if the victim has already received workers' compensation or other social security payments, a share of damages that otherwise the defendant would pay to the victim is paid to the Secretary of State (recoupment of benefits).[22]

## Turner & Newall and the birth of asbestos personal injury litigation

Parallel to the establishment and expansion of welfare benefit, asbestos personal injury litigation has also flourished. Its early steps are intertwined with the business success of England's major asbestos firm: Turner & Newall. Founded in 1871, the leading asbestos manufacturer Turner & Newall grew to be one of the largest asbestos companies in the world. The firm became involved with asbestos in 1879 when it became the first business in the United Kingdom to weave asbestos cloth with power-driven machinery. By 1939, the firm controlled 20 percent of the asbestos trade in the United Kingdom, a figure that grew to 50 percent in 1960. By then "the firm's net profits were four times as great as its three principal competitors combined."[23] Post-World War II, during the golden years of asbestos production, the group owned and operated 14 plants in Great Britain and owned 16 businesses overseas, including asbestos mines at Havelock in Bulembu in the Kingdom of Swaziland, Southern Africa. Currently owned by the US conglomerate Federal-Mogul, the firm faced significant hurdles in dealing with its asbestos liabilities. The firm was the largest British employer in the asbestos industry and therefore the number of asbestos victims who could link their diseases to exposure to asbestos dust at Turner & Newall is very high. After being acquired, on October 1, 2001, the new owner Federal Mogul filed for voluntary Chapter 11 reorganization in the US and administration under the UK Insolvency Act of 1986, and Turner & Newall ceased paying asbestos claims. After a long legal battle, an English court approved a plan for Turner & Newall to pay asbestos victims and exit the administration process. Overall, UK victims were offered a fraction of the compensation to which they were entitled. In 2007, Laurie Kazan reported that 483 claims had been made and that a total of GBP 4,386,032 had been paid out in compensation for 147 claims.[24]

---

21　W.V.H. Rogers, John A. Jolowicz, and Percy H. Winfield, *Winfield and Jolowicz on tort*, 15th ed. (London: Sweet & Maxwell, 1998), 779.

22　The Social Security (Recovery of Benefits) Act 1997 mandates that "benefits are deducted in full (for a period) from the plaintiff's damages but the deduction is used to reimburse the Secretary of State." See ibid.

23　Nicholas J. Wikeley, "Turner & Newall: Early Organizational Responses to Litigation Risk," *Journal of Law and Society* 24, no. 2 (1997).

24　Laurie Kazan-Allen. "Update on T&N Ltd." *British Asbestos Newsletter* no. 68. Published electronically Autumn 2007. http://www.britishasbestosnewsletter.org/ban68.htm.

In 2007, Federal-Mogul Corporation emerged from Chapter 11 and its stocks are not listed on NASDAQ.

Turner & Newall is implicated in the emergence of both knowledge of asbestos toxicity and asbestos compensation. With regard to knowledge of asbestos toxicity, the second recorded case of asbestosis involved a Turner & Newall's employee, who was diagnosed with asbestosis in 1924.[25] The victim was a female in her 30s who had worked in asbestos factories since the age of 13.[26] The employee, Nellie Kershaw, tried to recover compensation for her personal injury by contacting the employer. The company denied any liability and refused compensation in a rather cold letter:

> We repudiate the term "asbestos poisoning". Asbestosis is not poisonous and no definition or knowledge of such a disease exists. Such a description is not to be found amongst the list of industrial diseases in the schedule published with the Workmens' Compensation Act. This case was not due to an accident.[27]

The letter set the tone for how the firm would deal with the growing number of instances of asbestos disease: 80 cases of asbestosis were registered in the 1930s, the first lung cancer case was diagnosed in 1932, and the first mesothelioma was diagnosed in 1958, after approximately ten cases of suspected mesothelioma appeared among the firm's employees in the 1930s and 1940s.

By the late 1920s asbestosis became recognized as a disease associated with occupational exposure. At that time England had already established a policy tradition of compensation for occupational injuries and diseases. The idea of a non-contributory, no-fault scheme for occupational diseases came to fruition in the midst of the Second Industrial Revolution with the enactment of The Workmens' Compensation Act 1897. The spirit of the Workmens' Compensation Act 1897 was translated into the Asbestos Industry (Asbestosis) Scheme 1931, a path-breaking piece of legislation that, the first in the world, recognized asbestos as an occupational hazard and granted right to compensation to victims of asbestosis.

More invasive regulation and the growth of asbestos disease cases pushed Turner & Newall to set up a self-funded Asbestosis Fund in the 1940s. The Fund was administered by an external insurance company, Commercial Union, so that the company did not have to confront its employees or former employees directly. Turner & Newall's Fund was designed as an alternative to purchasing insurance to cover surging asbestos liabilities. The company shopped around for quotes but concluded that a self-funded arrangement would have been cheaper and more efficient. Other companies however began insuring their asbestos liabilities, thus dragging insurance companies into the asbestos compensation arena. Early

---

25   Cooke, "Fibrosis of the lungs due to the inhalation of asbestos dust," 147.

26   Ibid; Cooke, "Pulmonary asbestosis."

27   Letter from Turner Brothers Asbestos to Newbold Approved Society, December 15, 1922, cited in Tweedale, *Magic mineral to killer dust: Turner & Newall and the asbestos hazard*, 16.

involvement of insurance companies in asbestos liability influenced the way in which victims' compensation developed throughout the years.

Between 1931 and 1948, the Asbestosis Fund paid GBP 87,938 to 140 asbestosis victims.[28] These payments represent the first steps of asbestos compensation in England more so than workers' compensation since Turner & Newall's employees comprised the majority of early victims of asbestos exposure. The Fund was gradually wound down after 1948 when administrative compensation for occupational disease was reformed with the abolishing of workers' compensation and the creation of the IIDB, which integrated compensation for occupational diseases in the larger institutional network of the welfare state. Turner & Newall's decision was grounded on the predictions that asbestosis cases would decline, the State would provide compensation for all of them, and victims would not turn to courts.[29] Yet, the company did not take into account the possibility that asbestos could cause other diseases. As we know, this is in fact the case. The major setback to the company came in 1954 when Sir Richard Doll found a link between asbestos dust and lung cancer after studying asbestos disease among Turner & Newall's employees. Doll published the findings in 1955 after fighting corporate opposition to the publication.[30] The paper established for the first time the link between asbestos and lung cancer. The second setback came in 1960, when Dr. Wagner published findings that established a link between mesothelioma and asbestos.[31]. Once again the company unsuccessfully tried to block the publication of the findings.[32]

## The emergence of personal injury litigation

Although asbestosis settlements were not publicized, news of them spread among workers by word of mouth and slowly reached labor unions, which mobilized victims against Turner & Newall. This mobilization led in 1950 to *Kelly v. Turner & Newall Ltd*, the first asbestos personal injury lawsuit in England's history.[33]

---

28  Wikeley, "Turner & Newall: Early Organizational Responses to Litigation Risk."

29  Ibid.

30  Doll, "Mortality from lung cancer in asbestos workers."

31  J.C. Wagner, C.A. Sleggs, and P. Marchand, "Diffuse pleural mesothelioma and asbestos exposure in the North Western Cape Province," ibid. 17 (1960).

32  Letter from J.C. Wagner to G. Tweedale, dated October 27, 1998, in Tweedale, *Magic mineral to killer dust: Turner & Newall and the asbestos hazard.*

33  Wikeley provides a thorough account of the case in two papers, which were possible to Chase Manhattan Bank, which had collected documents from the Turner & Newall's archives as part of extensive discovery that took place in connection with a federal lawsuit in which Chase Manhattan Bank sued Turner & Newall for property damage. See Wikeley, "Turner & Newall: Early Organizational Responses to Litigation Risk"; Nicholas J. Wikeley, "The First Common Law Claim for Asbestosis: Kelly v Turner & Newall Ltd (1950)," *Journal of Personal Injury Litigation* (1998).

The case was brought by the father of Nora Dockerty Kelly, a machine assistant in the carding and spinning department of Turner Brothers Asbestos Co. Ltd., a union member, and the victim of deadly asbestosis at the young age of 31. The day after her death, her father accidentally bumped into a coroner who, moved by the story, investigated Nora's case further. After the pathologist had found evidence of asbestosis in her lungs, the coroner "duly recorded the cause of death as 'Generalised Tuberculosis accelerated by the presence of Asbestosis'."[34] Some days later her father spoke to an official of the local union communicating his intention to sue the company. "The official indicated that the family would have to gather the evidence in order to make out a case."[35] The necessary material, once collected, was passed on by the family to the union, which instructed a solicitor to act for the family against Turner & Newall. The attorney contacted the company, which, as Wikeley reports, did not offer to settle the case in the mistaken hope that the family would not decide to sue the firm. Legal papers were in fact filed in the summer of 1951. However, the writ named the wrong company as defendant Turner & Newall instead of Turner Brothers Asbestos. Nonetheless, Turner & Newall's attorney decided against seeking dismissal for lack of standing. The case however did not go to trial: the substantial uncertainty with regard to the outcome for both parties was conducive to a settlement. The case settled for GBP 375 plus costs, putting an end to the first asbestos personal injury case in England.

After *Kelly*, more and more evidence of asbestos hazards cropped up in medical literature. By 1953, the Factory Inspectorate was listing asbestos as a carcinogen.[36] In 1955, Doll published data that confirmed lung cancer risk for asbestos workers. In 1960, Wagner and colleagues established a causal link between asbestos and mesothelioma. The rising mortality from asbestos disease in the 1960s pushed the government to take action and enact new asbestos regulations that applied to a broader set of occupations involving exposure to asbestos fibers.[37] Asbestos firms also agreed to stop importing blue asbestos. The scope of the regulations was further expanded in 1974 to cover asbestos workers in all workplaces.[38]

Claim mobilization grew parallel to the expansion of benefits for occupational disease. In contrast to the pre-1948 regime, the IIDB system does not bar personal injury claims based on an occupational disease. The permissibility of personal injury lawsuits against the employer has certainly shaped asbestos compensation in unique ways if compared to other industrialized countries. First, personal injury cases were selected for litigation based on the success of an IIDB claim.

---

34    Wikeley, "Turner & Newall: Early Organizational Responses to Litigation Risk," 260.

35    Ibid., 261.

36    Tweedale, "Asbestos and its lethal legacy."

37    *Asbestos Regulations (1969)*, Statutory Instrument 1969 No. 690 (England).

38    *Health and Safety at Work etc Act 1974* (England).

Traditionally, administrative compensation acted as a gatekeeper of claims to the court system and victims filed a personal injury suit only after successfully pursuing an IIDB claim: "[u]nions, defendants, and insurers used IIDB decisions to cheaply reduce organizational uncertainty about claim validity."[39] The IIDB award was seen as a precondition of viable claims in courts. It validated the claim and reassured unions that the claim was serious and worth funding. In fact, defendants too took these claims seriously. Second, the conservative attitude of the IIDB administration has slowed down and compressed the scope of litigation. For many years the government acted mostly as a negative gatekeeper as it assessed rather conservatively any application for IIDB filed by asbestos victims. The administration rejected many applications based on the failure to meet the medical criteria that government's experts thought were needed to successfully claim benefits. As Durkin's research in the early 1990s demonstrated, the tendency was conservative:

> If a disease was subject to an alternative diagnosis, not explicitly on the list
> of recognized occupational diseases, or the claimant was not employed in a
> designated occupational, [the administration] would reject the claim.[40]

Negative gatekeeping led to a slow surge in asbestos personal injury cases. The administration's denial in the event of borderline cases set higher standards for access to courts since only the stronger claims would reach courts. Over time, the administration has approached cases less conservatively and asbestos victims have an easier time securing administrative compensation. Almost twenty years after Durkin conducted his research, the disability requirements have been lowered, an *ad hoc* compensatory scheme has been added to the portfolio of government-funded asbestos compensation (the 2008 Diffuse Mesothelioma Scheme) and thus to victims' claim-funding options, attorneys have access to richer databases of asbestos exposure, and overall the outcome of any application is much more predictable to applicants that two decades ago. Finally, construing an IIDB award as a prerequisite for claim viability has framed personal litigation primarily as a matter of occupational exposure. For many years, claim mobilization has not touched cases involving take-home or secondhand exposure and premises exposure, and the overwhelming majority of lawsuits has originated from diseases caused by occupational exposure.

---

39  Durkin, "Constructing law: comparing legal action in the United States and United Kingdom", 113.
40  Ibid., 109.

**A litigation environment favorable to asbestos victims**

Overall, negative gatekeeping however has slowed down but not prevented the emergence of personal injury litigation. Contrary to Wikeley's assertion,[41] the mobilization of asbestos victims nonetheless took place earlier than in other European nations. Some lawsuits were brought in the 1950s,[42] and asbestos litigation emerged more prominently in the late 1960s. This happened because the English legal system has been traditionally friendlier to plaintiffs than those of Continental Europe. The emergence and success of personal injury litigation, which is unmatched in Europe, is partly due to various features of the English legal system, including the early statute of limitations relaxation and rather straightforward proof of liability due to the fact that the employers' duty to control asbestos dates back to 1931. Courts' overall benevolent attitude towards victims and labor unions' activism, which will be discussed in the next section, also contributed to the rise of asbestos personal injury litigation.

First, in 1963 legislative reform relaxed the statute of limitation. Until 1963, victims were required to commence a legal action within three years from the date when the cause of action arose. This rule put asbestos victims in a difficult position because of asbestos diseases' long latency period. The Limitations Act of 1963 reformed the rule and established the principle that the statute of limitations would not start to run until the victim became aware of the disease.[43] When the statute of limitation was relaxed, unions were able to build on the knowledge about asbestos toxicity gathered up until then and contribute to the early mobilization of asbestos victims and several cases were soon filed.[44] The post-1963 wave of lawsuits led to the 1971 landmark opinion in *Smith v. Central Asbestos Company*, in which the Court of Appeal embraced a liberal construction of the statute of limitations thus validating claims filed many years after the exposure to asbestos. In later years, legislation was further adapted to the peculiar nature of toxic torts. The Limitation Act 1980 provides three years' delay for initiating action for damages with respect of personal injuries, defining the limitation period as that running "from the date of the cause of action or, if later, the date when the plaintiff knew that her injuries were significant and resulted from some act of omission on the part of the defendant."[45] Since then, courts have exercised their discretion in allowing claims filed long after the time of the exposure to the benefit of asbestos victims, especially in the

41   Wikeley, *Compensation for industrial disease*, 37-38.
42   *Kelly v Turner & Newall Ltd* was filed in 1950. See Wikeley, "Turner & Newall: Early Organizational Responses to Litigation Risk."
43   *Adams v Bracknell Forest BC* [2005] 1 AC 76 (England).
44   *Sales v Dicks Asbestos and Insulating Co Ltd*, unreported opinion cited in Lord Denning M.R., Edmund Davies L.J., and Stamp L.J., "Sales v. Dicks Asbestos and Insulating Co. Ltd.," *Managerial Law* 11, no. 4 (1972).
45   *Limitation Act 1980*, sec. 33 (England); Wikeley, "The First Common Law Claim for Asbestosis: Kelly v. Turner & Newall Ltd (1950)," 40.

early years. In 1988, Felstiner and Dingwall wrote that "[i]nformants on both sides thought that this provision had been exercised generously and could not conceive of a substantial case being ruled out on a technical breach of the limitation rules."[46] More broadly, Jane Stapleton noted that technicalities have not been invoked against asbestos victims:

> The regime now accommodates the typical reasons for disease victims not claiming promptly: latency of symptoms; the degenerative ill health itself; euphemistic or incorrect medical advice; inadequate or inordinately discouraging legal advice from lawyers inexperienced in such under-litigated area as disease; difficulty in identifying the potential defendants; a belief that compensation being received from one source—typically from the Industrial Injuries Fund— was all the victim was legally and morally entitled to.[47]

Second, asbestos victims' cases have been facilitated by rather straightforward proof of liability due to the fact that the employers' duty to control asbestos dates back to 1931. Occupational exposure cases are legally straightforward and comparatively easier to try than occupational exposure cases in Italy and product liability cases in the United States. English plaintiffs can establish liability based on a breach of a statutory duty: an employer is liable if she disregards regulatory requirements aimed at creating a safe environment for workers. The long-standing regulation of asbestos in the workplace, dating back to 1931, makes it relatively easy for the plaintiff to establish liability in court. Indeed most employers disregarded asbestos regulations, including Turner & Newall, which focused its compliance efforts in Rochdale, the only plant that factory inspectors visited regularly. These laws "were widely ignored and largely unenforced until the 1960s, so that employers are liable in tort for their breach of a statutory duty."[48] Statutory duties also extended to contractors, who were able to bring lawsuits with regularity against hiring contracting firms. Occasionally, asbestos lawyers encounter a defendant who was not subjected to health and safety regulations or in which a victim employed by an asbestos producer was not directly exposed to asbestos as part of her job description but who was nonetheless exposed to dangerous levels of asbestos. In these cases, plaintiffs claim damages under strict liability. Product liability is routinely used in cases in which the victim was exposed to asbestos while wearing an asbestos-insulated robe intended to protect her from the heat. Here, the plaintiff claims that the robe is a defective product and that the manufacturer failed to warn her of the risks associated with wearing it.

---

46  Felstiner and Dingwall, *Asbestos Litigation in the United Kingdom: An Interim Report*, 12.

47  Jane Stapleton, *Disease and the compensation debate* (Oxford; New York: Clarendon Press; Oxford University Press, 1986), 26.

48  Felstiner and Dingwall, *Asbestos Litigation in the United Kingdom: An Interim Report*, 12.

Asbestos victims have however faced litigation hurdles. Proof of exposure and identification of the proper defendant was, and sometimes still is, problematic. Identifying the victims' former employer or employers is difficult if the plaintiff worked under various small contractors or changed job frequently. In these cases, identifying all potential defendants is a complex task, especially if the firms are no longer in business, have merged with another business, or changed their trade names. With regard to proving exposure, if the exposure dates back several decades, very few documents are available and proving the level of exposure to asbestos for certain jobs may be difficult. Some of these hurdles have been resolved through information sharing practices among plaintiff firms and between lawyers and unions.

### The activism of labor unions

Unions were largely instrumental to the emergence to asbestos litigation.[49] They contributed by raising awareness of the harmful consequences of exposure to asbestos among workers and by creating a referral network that sent a large number of cases to a small number of law firms and providing financial support to workers who could not afford the litigation.[50]

In early claiming, unions were the natural mobilization actors as the first wave of asbestos victims comprised primarily workers who handled raw asbestos. Union membership in these occupations was fairly highly and workers routinely turned to unions when they need help to confront issues relating to their jobs. *Kelly*, the first personal injury case in England, involved a union member whose father turned to the union for help, the local official establishing a contact between the family and a solicitor who successfully negotiated the settlement. For years, unions constituted the primary source of funding for personal injury claims and source of information for lawyers representing victims. Unions' support facilitated claiming and removed financial obstacles that victims were facing when determined to claim damages in courts. Unions' money was the surrogate to US-style fee-sharing agreements between clients and lawyers for legal representations, which was essential to the emergence and growth of asbestos litigation in the United States. As P.S. Atiyah noted in the late 1980s, unions "behave[d] more like American attorneys pursuing a tort claim, except that they [did] not demand any proportion of the tort recoveries."[51]

Not all unions and not all local offices of unions were however active in claim mobilization. Unions that were engaged were those that considered health and safety issues a priority and that had sufficient means to engage in public awareness

---

49    Ibid., 5-6. The authors list "most active unions."
50    Ibid., 6.
51    P.S. Atiyah, "Tort Law and the Alternatives: Some Anglo-American Comparisons," *Duke Law Journal* 6 (1987): 1029.

campaigns directed towards their members as well as training local officials to recognize asbestos disease and activate the professional links needed for them to secure compensation. Sometimes unions required that relatives of members handled the result of an autopsy; some others expected members to claim disability before seeking help from a union to secure legal representation. Overall all unions active in mobilization considered the disability award a prerequisite for assistance and funding of members who wanted to pursue compensation in court. Once the precondition was met, unions would favor contacts of members with doctors and lawyers who would assist them.

Unions however never monopolized claim mobilization. Since the beginning, cases were mobilized by supporting groups without significant union involvement. These groups began appearing in the 1970s to help mobilize claims that unions were not interested in pushing forward mostly because the victim was not a union member or because the government was turning down disability application at a higher rate than in other regions.[52] An example of the first group is the *Society for the Prevention of Asbestosis and Industrial Diseases* (SPAID), an asbestos awareness group founded in 1978 by Nancy Tait, the widow of a telephone engineer who had died in 1968 from pleural mesothelioma and the author of the 1976 self-published booklet *Asbestos Kills*.[53]

Mobilization of claims was rarely facilitated by the medical profession. Doctors serve as expert witnesses in litigation and thus develop an expertise in assessing asbestos cases from a legal point of view and become familiar with the litigation process. These critical skills have been exploited by American plaintiff firms. This has rarely happened in England where doctors "generally do not become involved in the transformation of a medical case to a legal action."[54] This is in part due to the features of the English legal system and to cultural traits of the medical profession. First, under English procedural rules, experts are not as partisan as experts in the American legal process: they testify "to help the court on matters within [their] expertise."[55] Furthermore experts are paid by clients rather than by attorneys thus creating weaker ties between experts and attorneys than in the United States. Second, the culture of general practitioners too was not conducive to mobilization. Durkin found that doctors were "highly reactive" rather than proactive, which led victims to see doctors as "distant and

---

52   Durkin, "Constructing law: comparing legal action in the United States and United Kingdom", 120.

53   Nicholas J. Wikeley, "Nancy Tait. Tenacious campaigner for the victims of asbestos diseases," *The Guardian*, February 22, 2009.

54   Durkin, "Constructing law: comparing legal action in the United States and United Kingdom", 107. Felstiner and Dingwall also noticed that it is "uncommon" for doctors to get involved in claim mobilization. See Felstiner and Dingwall, *Asbestos Litigation in the United Kingdom: An Interim Report*, 10.

55   *Civil Procedure Rules* (1998), sec. 35.33 (England).

unapproachable."[56] Doctors' diagnosis was never questioned and always accepted by patients: doctors "did not offer explanations, and victims did not ask for them."[57] Furthermore the profession, at least in the 1970s and 1980s, was inclined towards paternalism: doctors felt that their duty was to "protect the worker" and often kept "victim conditions secret" so that the victims did not have to worry.[58]

Even though some claims were mobilized without union involvement, unions' early contribution to the emergence of asbestos litigation has dramatically shaped asbestos compensation and current trends in asbestos compensation still unfolded along the trajectory carved by early mobilization. In fact, disability benefits are still at the center of asbestos compensation. Asbestos victims are routinely advised to consider claim disability benefits as the gateway to compensation. Asbestos disease is still very much perceived by legal actors in terms of occupational exposure. In early mobilization, unions only funded claims of members who had paid their membership dues and preferably who were still part of the workforce. Unions rarely supported claims coming from other kinds of victims. Consequently, for two decades the only cases that reached courts were claims based on occupational exposure. Indeed for several years plaintiff lawyers were not interested in developing a client base of asbestos victims independent from the referrals coming from unions. Once the relationship was established, "there appeared to be little incentive for a lawyer to actively and independently develop claims."[59] Finally, unions contributed to transforming asbestos into a political issue. The issue of asbestos is recurrently discussed in Parliament, which has often acted upon these debates by reforming workplace safety regulation, compensation for occupational disease, and asbestos compensation itself.

## The routinization of asbestos litigation

Throughout the 1980s and the 1990s, asbestos litigation became part of the routine of asbestos compensation. Much of its evolution was determined by its genesis, which was characterized by lawsuits targeted against employers for causing occupational diseases that the government had formally recognized as valid for the purpose of the industrial disability benefit. Traditionally the number of asbestos defendants named in litigation is relatively small, concentrating on the few major companies that have dominated the asbestos market for years (Cape and Turner & Newall polarized the most litigation), the government, and a handful of smaller companies. In recent years, as the third wave of asbestos disease strikes among those who were exposed to asbestos while working outside the asbestos industry,

---

56    Durkin, "Constructing law: comparing legal action in the United States and United Kingdom", 100.

57    Ibid., 101.

58    Ibid., 104.

59    Ibid., 151.

the range of defendants that have been sued has expanded. Interestingly, litigation can also be filed against a company that no longer exists. This mechanism known as restoring the defendant to the register of companies under the Third Parties (Rights against Insurers) Act of 1930 has been routinely and effectively sought in asbestos litigation.[60] The mechanism does not give new life to a dissolved company, but it allows asbestos victims to collect damages from the insurance company that provided coverage to the defunct company when it was in operation, taking advantage of an exception to contractual privity. As in all other tort claims, the plaintiff must first establish the liability of the defunct company in order to receive any payment from the insurance company. In fact, the insurer's liability in contract is triggered only if the former client is found liable.

As personal injury litigation became a routinized part of asbestos compensation, unions' role in mobilizing claims shrank and was supplemented by victims' support groups and a more active plaintiff bar. In the early days of the litigation, a handful of law firms established links with unions and cooperated in representing asbestos victims. These firms often considered the "real client" to be the union "[l]awyers had to satisfy union leaders," Durkin reports.[61] The working relationship between unions and law firms is still active nowadays although its relevance as to overall claim mobilization is much smaller. The third wave of asbestos disease is finding its victims outside the workplace, and fewer victims are union members.

As unions' contribution to claim mobilization declined, law firms and supporting groups have become more active and effective in campaigns to raise awareness of asbestos disease and in engaging victims interested in personal injury litigation. Asbestos plaintiff lawyers become more independent of unions and more visible to victims. Since the 1990s plaintiff firms have developed stronger personal injuries practices, thus fearing less domestic competition. Some of these are firms that have been involved with asbestos litigation for decades and that, as referrals from unions started declining, launched asbestos practices based on proactive recruiting strategies. Law firms began advertising their asbestos practices and recruiting clients directly and increasing networking among themselves. Other firms are latecomers and became involved only in the late 1980s. Some of the original firms that had strong ties to unions still receive occasional referrals but are on the sidelines of asbestos litigation. Many firms started advertising asbestos litigation as a specialty, consolidated their legal expertise, and developed a reputation for representing asbestos victims. Generally law firms that carry a sizeable asbestos practice have a strong personal injury or asbestos litigation practice, with a team of lawyers who devote their full practice to representing asbestos victims. The number of players is, however, relatively limited on both the defense and plaintiff sides. Only a small number of firms handle asbestos cases occasionally and most

---

60  *Third Parties (Rights against Insurers) Act*, sec. 1-5 (England).

61  Durkin, "Constructing law: comparing legal action in the United States and United Kingdom", 151.

firms are repeat players. Plaintiff firms usually represent asbestos plaintiffs both as social security claimants and plaintiffs in personal injury suits.

The role of supporting groups has also grown. Even in the early days of asbestos litigation, these groups "were the best hopes for the vast majority of U.K. victims who did not have ties to professionals or active unions."[62] Advocacy groups have been active in advising asbestos victims and linking them with lawyers, doctors, and members of Parliament, thus generating "the ability to blame and mobilize claims."[63] The British Asbestos Newsletter compiled by Laurie Kazan-Allen in particular provides a periodic update of the developments of litigation, and lawyers have adopted more "American" marketing strategies and participated in both national (The Association of Personal Injury Lawyers) and international personal injury lawyer associations (The Pan European Organisation of Personal Injury Lawyers). Victims' support groups are generally self-financed and organize a variety of fundraising activities, such as publishing books or booklets or sponsoring shows and performances. Generally, they refer cases to a set of solicitors known to the groups and who, on occasion, offer legal assistance *pro bono*.

Cases are handled individually and rarely aggregated.[64] The lack of aggregation is not the reflection of legal obstacles—English procedural law offers aggregation tools and group litigation has been ongoing since the 1980s.[65] Individualized treatment of claims stems from the practice of considering IIDB awards as a prerequisite for access to court. When an IIDB application is filed, the administration assesses one claim at a time, in isolation from claims filed by victims in a similar position. Each victim ultimately has a unique history of asbestos exposure, with different employers, different years of exposure, different employment tasks to perform. Furthermore, insurers, who ultimately decide the fate of a claim by agreeing whether to settle it, find these differences to be critical in deciding the amount of settlement offers, as discussed in the next section. Insurers have actively engaged in settlement negotiations on behalf of employers since the early days of litigation.

The individual treatment of cases has limited the need for law firms to collaborate with other firms in litigation. In contrast to the United States, English plaintiff firms face less financial risk than Americans and did not need to collaborate

---

62    Ibid., 134-135.

63    Ibid., 135.

64    A noticeable case of aggregation is the litigation brought by South Africa miners against Cape and it is due to the fact that all plaintiffs were foreigner victims and that their attorneys sought funding of all claims collectively from Legal Aid. See Andrea Boggio, "The Global Enforcement of Human Rights: The Unintended Consequences of Transnational Litigation," *The International Journal of Human Rights* 10, no. 4 (2006).

65    In the 80s, group litigation was limited to mass accidents in transports and pharmaceutical or medical devices' product liability litigation. Since the mid-90s, group litigation also interested the areas of insurance or investor protection, environmental and housing litigation. See Christopher J.S. Hodges, "Introduction," in *Multi-Party Actions*, ed. Christopher J.S. Hodges (Oxford; New York: Oxford University Press, 2001).

to share the financial risks of litigation. Also England is certainly a smaller legal market than the United States and the liberal rules of venue permit filing a claim in any court throughout England, even if the court is located in a city other than the place where the exposure relevant to the suit took place or where the plaintiff and defendant reside. As a result, lawyers do not need to litigate cases far away from their home office, thus making referrals, co-representation, and information sharing less important than in the United States. The lack of collaboration has resulted in an asbestos plaintiff bar that is financially and politically more powerful than the American. English plaintiff lawyers seem also to have rejected entrepreneurial habits of American lawyers. In 1994 Durkin noted that there was "a marked professional distaste among U.K. plaintiff lawyers for what were seen as unseemly tactics of the US lawyers ... One lawyer gave the reason that such cooperation [among unions and lawyers] smacked of 'ethical wrongdoing and creeping Americanism.'"[66] However, since the late 1990s, plaintiff firms have increased information sharing, thus overcoming "the general reluctance amongst plaintiff personal injury lawyers to pool information."[67] Networking is a byproduct of unions' loss of their centrality in claim mobilization. As union membership declined and asbestos workers retired, victims would meet lawyers at informational meetings or would be referred to law firms by former co-workers already involved with litigation. Information sharing was also needed in the wake of the destruction of Inland Revenue records of employment (these records constituted the primary source of evidence of occupational exposure), so collaboration became vital. A big help came from documents made public by discovery in asbestos litigation in the United States. Discovery in *Chase Manhattan Bank, N.A. v. Turner & Newall, PLC*,[68] was particularly helpful. Discovery found around two million documents discussing Turner & Newall's practices and involvement with asbestos for almost half a century.[69]

Lawsuits were filed against a plurality of companies whenever the victim was employed in more than one occupation that entailed exposure to asbestos or whenever more than one insurer provided coverage for an occupation over time. Because of defendants' joint and several liability and claim individualization, all former employers and their insurers participated in litigation and contributed to any payment made to plaintiffs. Apportionment of liability among multiple defendants is governed by the principle of joint and several liability. This principle has been

---

66   Durkin, "Constructing law: comparing legal action in the United States and United Kingdom", 105.

67   Wikeley labeled this reluctance as "one of the weaknesses of the British approach." Wikeley, "The First Common Law Claim for Asbestosis: Kelly v. Turner & Newall Ltd (1950)," 47.

68   *Chase Manhattan Bank, NA v Turner & Newall, PLC*, 964 F. 2d 159 (2nd Cir. 1992) (USA).

69   Tweedale, "Sources in the History of Occupational Health: The Turner & Newall Archive," 515-533.

implemented throughout the years by the adoption of the "time employed sharing" club—a well-established, informal arrangement adopted by asbestos firms and the insurance industry based on which liability was allocated "on the basis of the length of a plaintiff's employment with each, without regard to the actual intensity or date of exposure to asbestos in each employment."[70] This mechanism has been highly efficient, as defendants have rarely disputed their share of liability as long as it had been determined by applying it. Consistently with data on personal injury cases,[71] asbestos personal injury cases seldom come to trial. Practitioners indicated that the parties generally settle whenever the limitation period has not expired and sufficient evidence supporting the existence of the injury, the exposure to asbestos, and causation is offered. Occasionally, defendants raise legal arguments, which is up to the judge to resolve.

Settlement amounts are often very close to the amount of damages a plaintiff would reasonably recover at trial. The incentive for defendants to settle comes from the prospect of avoiding paying the plaintiff lawyer's fees and other costs associated with the litigation (experts' fees, barristers' and solicitors' fees). Felstiner and Dingwall provide the following explanation:

> The resistance of British judges to reopening liability issues which have previously been litigated to judgment in asbestos cases, the greater predictability of calculations of awards and the shorter time from filing to trial, all suggest that plaintiffs have less reason to discount the acceptable level of settlement for the delay of risks of trial.[72]

The predictability of the settlement value is also influenced by the consistent involvement of repeat players on both sides—a limited number of plaintiff firms, asbestos firms, and insurance companies. Interviews also suggest that several actors appreciate the social value of compensating asbestos victims, especially in fatal cases. Defendants can also put pressure to settle by making a "payment into court" in satisfaction of the plaintiff's claim.[73] A "payment into court" entails offering to make a payment of an amount that is sufficient to pay for the damages suffered by the plaintiff and her lawyer's fees. If the payment is accepted and

---

70 Felstiner and Dingwall, *Asbestos Litigation in the United Kingdom: An Interim Report*. 8.

71 In 1968, the Passenger Transportation Board to the Winn Committee on Personal Injury Litigation reported that 90 percent of cases were settled out of court. Similarly, in 1994, Hazel Genn reported that "[o]ne in ten claims ... were awarded by a court decision or a judge's ruling, the rest were settled by reaching agreement with the other side." Hazel Genn, "Personal Injury Compensation: How Much is Enough?," in *Report n. 225* (London: Law Commission, 1994), 247.

72 Felstiner and Dingwall, *Asbestos Litigation in the United Kingdom: An Interim Report*, 24.

73 After the Lord Wolf Reform, payments into court or "Pt 36 payments" are regulated by *Civil Procedure Rules*, Part 36 (Offers to Settle and Payments into Court).

the case settled, the plaintiff is entitled to her costs of the proceedings up to the date of serving notice of acceptance.[74] On the other hand, if the plaintiff refuses the defendant's payment and fails to obtain a damage award more advantageous than what the defendant offered, "… the court will order the [plaintiff] to pay any costs incurred by the defendant after the latest date on which the payment or offer could have been accepted."[75] The defendant may always increase the amount of the payment if the plaintiff refuses the offer.[76] Ultimately, if the case goes to trial, the offer is not disclosed to the judge, who takes no role in negotiations.

The "time employed sharing" club is also used to determine which firm will take the lead in defending the claim. Ordinarily, the defendant with higher financial stakes takes the lead in litigating and negotiating the claim. Other defendants will play a limited role, often saving money in defense costs, as they trust that the firm in charge will effectively defend the claim and that the time employed sharing mechanism will lead to a fair allocation of financial responsibility. The time employed sharing club grew out of the insurance industry's early involvement in asbestos compensation and its willingness to indemnify defendants and was formalized in guidelines issued by the Association of British Insurers, which in 2003 issued the *Guidelines For Apportioning and Handling Employers Liability Mesothelioma Claims*,[77] and it is still used as the norm by co-defendants to handle mesothelioma cases. Many asbestos firms maintained insurance since the 1940s. Furthermore, since 1972 almost all private employers in England have been required to maintain employers' liability insurance under the Employer's Liability (Compulsory Insurance) Act of 1969. Except in litigation against self-insured firms like Cape and Turner & Newall, insurers participate in litigation by retaining and paying counsel for asbestos defendants, shaping settlement practices, and paying out claims. Asbestos defense lawyers thus have stronger ties to insurers than to the companies they represent in court. Ten to twelve insurance companies are implicated in about half of the cases.[78]

Tracing an employer's liability insurer can, however, be difficult. Policies date back several decades and discovering them is a difficult task. In 2012, the Government estimated that approximately 300 mesothelioma victims per year had failed to recover damages because of the failure to trace a liable employer or

---

74   Ibid., Part 36.13 (Costs consequences of acceptance of a defendant's Part 36 offer or Part 36 payment).

75   Ibid., Part 36.20 (Costs consequences where claimant fails to do better than a Part 36 offer or a Part 36 payment); ibid., Part 36.37 (Offer to settle a claim for provisional damages).

76   For some of the tactical uses of payments into courts, see Stephen Oliver-Jones, "Payments into Court," in *Personal injury handbook*, ed. Daniel Brennan, Patrick Curran, and Matthias Kelly (London: Sweet & Maxwell, 1997), 340-341.

77   Association of British Insurers, "Guidelines For Apportioning and Handling Employers Liability Mesothelioma Claims" (London 2003).

78   Felstiner and Dingwall, *Asbestos Litigation in the United Kingdom: An Interim Report*. 7.

employer's liability insurer.[79] To redress this problem, the Minister for Welfare negotiated with the Association of British Insurers the establishment of a new scheme that will make payments to mesothelioma victims whose disease was caused by occupational exposure and for which no employer's insurance can be found to seek contribution.[80] Payments are made only to mesothelioma victims which disease was diagnosed on or after July 25, 2012. The plaintiff bar and asbestos advocates have welcomed the announcement of the scheme with mixed feelings, pointing out that, while many mesothelioma victims of occupational exposure will receive money that otherwise would not be recovered, many others are left out: those with other asbestos diseases and those sick because of secondhand or environmental exposure.

**Damages**

Successful asbestos victims may recover pecuniary and non-pecuniary damages. English law traditionally distinguishes general damages from special damages, which are both compensatory in nature, that is, awarded to compensate the plaintiff for the loss caused by the defendant's negligence. General damages are awarded for a loss that is "incapable of precise estimation."[81] The main components of general damages are pain and suffering, future loss of earnings, and loss of amenities of life, which one author defines as "the loss or reduction of a plaintiff's mental or physical capacity to do the things he used to do, suffered as a result of personal injuries."[82] Under exceptional circumstances, victims are awarded "aggravated damages" in the event the defendant's conduct or the circumstances surrounding the accident increases the injury to the plaintiff by subjecting her to "humiliation, distress, or embarrassment, particularly in such torts as assault, false imprisonment, and defamation."[83] Aggravated damages, which are the English version of punitive damages, have never been used in asbestos litigation. In 1989, Felstiner and Dingwall reported their inability "to trace any instance of them arising in asbestos litigation ... at the time of our interviews ... there was too little experience of the new provisions to make a detailed assessment of their effects."[84]

---

79   Department of Work and Pensions. "£300m support for future mesothelioma victims." *Newsroom*. Published electronically July 25, 2012 https://www.gov.uk/govern ment/news/300m-support-for-future-mesothelioma-victims. At the time the manuscript was finalized, the scheme was not yet approved by Parliament.

80   Ibid.

81   Jonathan Law and Elizabeth A. Martin, *A dictionary of law*, 7th ed. (Oxford; New York: Oxford University Press, 2009).

82   Ibid.

83   Ibid.

84   Felstiner and Dingwall, *Asbestos Litigation in the United Kingdom: An Interim Report*.

To date, I have not been able to find an asbestos case in which exemplary damages were awarded. Commentators suggested that they could have been awarded in the Armley case.[85] Exemplary damages are however given some consideration in settling cases. One attorney suggested in the course of an interview that exemplary damages are occasionally used in settlement negotiations whenever the plaintiff could offer evidence at trial that the defendant knew about the toxicity of asbestos and made a conscious business decision not to change the manufacturing policies.

Assessing these damages is a complicated task, but over time, governmental guidelines have simplified calculating general damages.[86] The *Guidelines for the Assessment of General Damages in Personal Injury Cases*, published by the Judicial Studies Board, are in fact widely used in litigation and in settlement negotiations, and even proposed by companies such as Cape as evidence of the "usual range of awards."[87] The rationale behind the Guidelines is "to provide a lump sum sufficient, when invested, to produce an income equal to the lost income, when the interest is supplemented by withdrawals of capital."[88] The Guidelines devote an entire section to several asbestos-related diseases: mesothelioma, lung cancer, asbestosis, and pleural thickening. For each disease, a range of compensation is suggested and indications on how to reach the appropriate assessment within the suggested range are offered. For instance, in mesothelioma cases, the intensity and length of pain and suffering are the principal factors that must be taken into account. In asbestosis cases, the degree of respiratory disability and mobility impairment play a role. Finally, the least serious cases of pleural thickening may be compensated with provisional awards, that is, awards compensating the condition diagnosed at the time of the payment but allowing the asbestos victim to seek further compensation should she develop mesothelioma, lung or other cancer, and asbestosis. The 2010 version of the Judicial Studies Board's *Guidelines* recommend the following

---

85    The president of the Law Society and former President of the Association of Personal Injury Lawyers pointed out that, "in view of the findings in this judgment, it would have been appropriate to seek an award of exemplary damages if only this was permitted by law." Cited in Laurie Kazan-Allen. "Mesothelioma: A European Epidemic." *British Asbestos Newsletter* no. 34. Published electronically Spring 1999. http://www. britishasbestosnewsletter.org/ban34.htm.

86    Judicial Studies Board, *Guidelines for the assessment of general damages in personal injury cases*, 10th ed. (Oxford; New York: Oxford University Press, 2010), 22-23.

87    For a discussion of how the Guidelines are used in litigation and in the settlement process, see Christopher Sprague, "Damages for Personal Injury and Loss of Life: The English Approach," *Tulane Law Review* 72 (1997): 1005-1006. With regard to Cape, see Cape plc, "Proposal for a Scheme of Arrangement under Section 425 between Cape plc and the other Scheme Companies and their respective Scheme Creditors," http://www.capeplc. com/media/81625/proposed%20scheme%20of%20arrangement%20-15%20march%20 2006.pdf.

88    David A. Kemp, "Damages for Future Pecuniary Loss," in *Damages for personal injury and death*, ed. David A. Kemp (London: Sweet & Maxwell, 1998), 163-187; Rogers, Jolowicz, and Winfield, *Winfield and Jolowicz on tort*, 768-773.

damage ranges: GBP 35,000 to 83,750 for mesothelioma; GBP 51,500 to 66,000 for lung cancer; GBP 31,500 to 69,500 for asbestosis; GBP 25,250 to 51,500 for pleural thickening; and provisional awards for the least serious cases of pleural thickening in the range of GBP 4,350 to 7,250.

By contrast, special damages comprise all damages for losses that may be quantified. These include out-of-pocket expenses and earnings lost "during the period between the injury and the hearing of the action."[89] As a general rule, the plaintiff's attorney submits to the court a highly detailed schedule of damages, reporting all monetary losses suffered by the client and a broad outline of any likely future losses. Past lost earnings are damages equal to the net loss from the accident date to the trial date less any sum that that the plaintiff has received from sources such as the Social Security Administration, insurance, and contractual provisions.[90] Additionally, a claimant may recover medical, nursing, and other health care-related expenses "that have reasonably been incurred or will reasonably be incurred as a result of injuries arising from a tort."[91] In England, the National Health System provides health care for free, and empirical research shows that only a small percentage of claimants use private medical treatment exclusively.[92] However, a significant portion of asbestos victims receive some private care. Furthermore, damages are paid for any care gratuitously provided by family members and friends, which occurs frequently with asbestos victims.[93] The plaintiff is also entitled to recover the loss of ability to work in the home,[94] reasonable costs that are incurred by family members in visiting the victim while in hospital, and the costs of purchasing new accommodation or of adapting the existing property to the needs required by the disablement.[95]

---

89   Law and Martin, *A dictionary of law*.

90   Kemp, "Damages for Future Pecuniary Loss," 158-159. Kemp points out that there may be complications if the plaintiff's remuneration is based on commissions on orders or when the plaintiff is self-employed or suffered a drawback in her business caused by the injury.

91   *Law Reform (Personal Injuries) Act 1948*, (England); *Cunningham v Harrison* [1973] 1 QB 942 (England); *Lim Poh Choo v Camden and Islington Area HA* [1980] AC 174 (England); Law Commission, "Damages for Personal Injury: Medical, Nursing and Other Expenses; Collateral Expenses" (London: Law Commission, 1999), sec. 2(4).

92   Law Commission, "Personal Injury Compensation: How Much is Enough" (London: Law Commission, 1994), 145-146; Law Commission, "Damages for Personal Injury: Medical, Nursing and Other Expenses;" in *Consultation Paper* (London: Law Commission, 1996), paragraph 2.9.

93   *Hunt v Severs* [1994] 2AC 350 (England).

94   *Daly v General Steam Navigation Co Ltd (The "Dragon")* [1979] 1 Lloyd's Rep 257 (England).

95   *George v Pinnock* [1973] 1 WLR 118 (England).

In 2009, Thompson Solicitors reported settling a mesothelioma case for GBP 400,000 to a retired 56-year-old asbestos worker,[96] another for GBP 650,000 to the benefit of a wife who had survived her 65-year-old husband,[97] a lung cancer case for GBP 140,000, also to the benefit of the widower of a 72-year-old retired asbestos worker,[98] and a disabling pleural thickening for an undisclosed five figure amount.[99]

Damages are usually awarded in a lump sum at the end of the trial. However, plaintiffs may apply for provisional damages, which are also awarded at the end of the trial but which can be revised in favor of the successful plaintiff in case she develops some serious disease or other serious deterioration of her physical or mental condition after the trial.[100] If the court grants a motion for immediate damage award, the plaintiff may apply for a further award if the asbestos condition worsens within a specified time. The structure of provisional damages is often incorporated in settlement agreements: the parties settle based on the present condition provided the settlement is reformed should the condition worsen or a new asbestos-related disease develops. However, settlement agreements are not enforceable unless the court approves them. Interviews with practitioners suggest that asbestos plaintiffs often settle damages at the time litigation occurs and courts often issue orders that reflect settlement agreements. If the new condition develops, the plaintiff is entitled to claim further damages. Plaintiff lawyers routinely advise elderly clients against provisional damages. Their recommendation is "to take as much as they could at the time of the settlement," as one plaintiff attorney put it. By contrast, younger clients are advised to "take the chance" offered by provisional damages. In provisional damage cases, defendants and insurers also face a financial bet—choosing between a certain but lower payment at the present time and an uncertain but substantially higher payment in the future.

---

96 Thompsons Solicitors. "Successful fight for asbestos compensation." Published electronically May 8, 2009. http://www.thompsons.law.co.uk/ntext/successful-fight-asbestos-compensation.htm.

97 Thompsons Solicitors. "BPD 650,000 damages for mesothelioma widow." Published electronically April 29, 2009. http://www.thompsons.law.co.uk/ntext/damages-for-mesothelioma-widow.htm.

98 Thompsons Solicitors. "MOD settle Devonport asbestos claim." Published electronically May 26, 2009. http://www.thompsons.law.co.uk/ntext/mod-settle-devonport-asbestos-claim.htm.

99 Thompsons Solicitors. "Five figure compensation for lagger's asbestos disease." Published electronically March 16, 2009. http://www.thompsons.law.co.uk/ntext/lagger-pleural-plaques-pleural-thickening.htm.

100 Peter Mantle, "Pre-Trial Considerations," in *Damages for personal injury and death*, ed. David A. Kemp (London: Sweet & Maxwell, 1998), 18.

## Litigation funding and attorney's fees

In England, fees are ultimately borne by the losing party—so-called "English Rule" or "loser pays" rule. Under this regime, the losing party pays litigation costs, her lawyer's fees, the expert's fees, and the opponent counsel's fees.[101] The plaintiff lawyer receives neither a portion of the damages awarded nor any extra compensation because of the positive outcome of the litigation.[102] The application of the "loser pays" rule is not automatic; the court must order so. Judges have the discretionary[103] "full power to determine by whom and to what extent costs are to be paid."[104] Generally, counsel for both sides are paid on an hourly rate.

Up to 1998, plaintiffs had three avenues available in order to fund their claims: cases were either funded by unions,[105] by the Legal Aid, which is a system used to offer legal representation subsidized or free of charge, or self-funded. Over time, unions have lost their interest-funding litigation and, after a long debate and various consultations,[106] personal injury cases are no longer eligible for full funding by Legal Aid since 1999.[107] In addition, Legal Aid presents substantial downsides to lawyers: bureaucratic oversight throughout the litigation and fees below the market rate. Thus, some plaintiff lawyers dislike working with clients funded by the system. Some practitioners even commented that Legal Aid "confer[s] an unfair bargaining advantage on plaintiffs." Thus, specialist firms prefer representing clients who are not funded by Legal Aid.[108] Self-financing is an option that only few victims can afford.

Over time, some law firms worked on an informal success fee arrangement, under which they could "assure clients of modest means that a bill would not be presented if the case were unsuccessful."[109] The process was somehow formalized in 1998 with the recognition of Conditional Fee Agreements or "no

101   Fees are not paid to the winning party in *pro bono* cases or in cases in which the lawyer agreed not to be paid unless the claim is successful.

102   Clients bear a greater financial risk than their lawyers do. See John Peysner. "A Revolution By Degrees: From Costs to Financing and the End of the Indemnity Principle." *Web Journal of Current Legal Issues* 1. Published electronically. http://webjcli.ncl.ac.uk/2001/issue1/peysner1.html.

103   *Supreme Court Act 1981*, sec. 51(51) (England).

104   Ibid., sec. 51(53).

105   Felstiner and Dingwall, *Asbestos Litigation in the United Kingdom: An Interim Report*.

106   "The Government's plans for reforming legal services and the courts," (Lord Chancellor's Department, 1998).

107   Funding is limited to obtaining basic legal information and advice. *Access to Justice Act 1999*, c.22, schedule 22 (Community Legal Service: Excluded Services) (England).

108   Felstiner and Dingwall, *Asbestos Litigation in the United Kingdom: An Interim Report*.

109   Ibid.

win, no fee" arrangements. These agreements between client and attorney provide that "fees and expenses, or any part of them, [are] payable only in specified circumstances."[110] The circumstances in which the fees are to be paid are indicated in the agreement. The general practice is that fees are not paid unless the plaintiff recovers money. In exchange for not getting paid if the claim is unsuccessful, the client may agree to pay an extra percentage ("success fee" or "uplift") on top of the fees in the event the claim is successful. The success fee is calculated by applying a multiplier of normal costs and not as a split of damages and cannot be higher than 100% of the fees. Since 1998, the Law Society has recommended "an additional voluntary cap of 25% of damages," now a widely accepted practice.[111] In 2012, a bill with changes to the "no win, no fee" in England and Wales will prevent lawyers claiming "success fees" from the losing side.[112] The money will come from the damages awarded to the client, much more like contingency fees in the United States. The reform is said to act as a disincentive to bring "spurious cases" and force defendants to settle under the pressure of a large bill in the event of unfavorable outcome at trial.[113] However, the Government is studying the possibility of carving out an exception for mesothelioma victims, whose "illness's severity is indisputable."[114]

The English version of contingency fee agreements, "no win, no fee" arrangements have become increasingly important in personal injury litigation. "No win, no fee" arrangements have gained popularity because, as a practical matter, plaintiff lawyers recover money also if unsuccessful. Solicitors are personally liable for barristers' fees, which they usually recover from the client.[115] However, solicitors only agree to represent asbestos victims who are insured for legal costs in the event of an unsuccessful outcome. Known as "after the event" insurance, this form of insurance is widely available. Unfortunately, insurance premiums are often not affordable by all plaintiffs. Practitioners expressed concerns regarding the ability of asbestos victims to secure access to justice in the long run. Sometimes, plaintiffs solve the problem by reaching an agreement with the insurer to defer payment of the premium until the end of the litigation in exchange for a higher premium.

---

110   *The Courts and Legal Services Act 1990*, sec. 58 (England).

111   Gary Slapper and David Kelly, *The English legal system*, 11th ed. (Abingdon, UK; New York: Routledge, 2010). 480.

112   *Legal Aid, Sentencing and Punishment of Offenders Act 2012* (England).

113   BBC News. "'No-win, no-fee' changes announced by Ken Clarke." Published electronically March 29, 2011 http://www.bbc.co.uk/news/uk-12890256.

114   BBC News. "Asbestos exemption to 'no-win, no-fee' changes." Published electronically April 24, 2012. http://www.bbc.co.uk/news/uk-politics-17833607.

115   Peysner, "A Revolution By Degrees: From Costs to Financing and the End of the Indemnity Principle."

## Contested issues

The great majority of asbestos personal injury cases settle, and very few issues are contested and litigated in court. These include certain issues of causation in mesothelioma and lung cancer cases. The causal contribution of multiple defendants has been contested for a long time. Courts have established rules that differ from disease to disease. In asbestosis cases, courts concluded that it is the burden of the plaintiff to show that a specific defendant materially contributed to the injury.[116] Asbestosis is in fact seen as a dose-response disability, that is, a disability that worsens any time the body is exposed to asbestos, and a divisible injury, that is, the product of consecutive exposures, each of which has acted separately and independently to produce part of that disability. Based on these assumptions, a defendant is liable only for the portion of harm to which she has materially contributed.

Mesothelioma cases are however treated differently as courts construe it as an indivisible injury, that is, a disease that must be taken as a whole even in the event the victim's exposure took place in different jobs. If the periods of exposure are several, the disease is considered to be caused by exposure to asbestos as a whole, without the need for assessing the contributory of various periods of exposure. The House of Lords held that any employer is liable for the harm resulting from the illness because each had "materially" increased the risk of mesothelioma.[117] An asbestos victim claim is thus successful as long as it is shown that there was exposure at different times from different employers, that all of the employers were negligent, and that "any cause of [the claimant's] mesothelioma other than inhalation of asbestos dust at work can be effectively discounted."[118] The Compensation Act 2006, section 3 established the rule that "each person who has, in breach of duty, been responsible for exposing the victim to a significant quantity of asbestos dust and thus creating a 'material increase in risk' of the victim contracting the disease [is] held to be jointly and severally liable in respect of the disease."[119] Another contested issue is the causal contribution of smoking in lung cancer cases. Courts have consistently concluded that lung cancer cases are caused by asbestos if there is evidence of asbestosis or of exposure to asbestos dust sufficient to cause asbestosis.

Another highly contested issue was the viability of pleural plaques claims. Until 2007, damages for asymptomatic pleural plaques were routinely awarded according to the aggregation theory. Under this theory, claimants who had been exposed to asbestos and fear developing an asbestos disease had a viable claim.[120]

---

116    *Holtby v Brigham & Cowan (Hull) Ltd* [2000] 3 All ER 421 (England).

117    *Margereson and Hancock v J.W. Roberts* [1986] PIQR 358 (England).

118    Ibid.

119    *Compensation Act of 2006*, section 3 (England). The quotation is from *Durham v BAI (Run Off) Ltd (in Scheme of Arrangement)* [2012] UKSC 14 (England).

120    *Church v Ministry of Defence* [1984] 134 NLJ 623 (England); *Patterson v Ministry of Defence* [1987] CLY 1194 (England). See also General Insurance Practice

Practitioners reported settling pleural plaque cases with a provisional damage award that allow for further claims in the event the victim developed an asbestos disease.[121] Successful pleural plaques cases used to lead to provisional damage awards between GBP 5,000 and GBP 7,000, with final damage awards between GBP 12,500 and GBP 20,000.[122] In 2007, the House of Lords however set the aggregation theory aside.[123] The risk of future illness and the anxiety associated with having pleural plaques were found to be an insufficient basis for claiming damages as a matter of law. Since 2007, courts have, however, been somewhat receptive of cases in which pleural plaques result in some degree of disability associated with asbestosis.[124] The leading case, *Johnston v NEI International Combustion Ltd*, was certainly informed by policy arguments for fair allocation among asbestos victims of the limited funds available to compensation these victims. At the time *Johnston* was decided, insurers had estimated that future pleural plaques claims were worth collectively a sum ranging from GBP 4 billion to GBP 28 billion.[125] Since the case was decided, legislative initiatives aimed at providing individuals with pleural plaques some financial assistance have been launched. None of these proposals has become law though, contrary to the experience of Scotland and Northern Ireland where *Johnston* has been overruled by law.[126]

## Asbestos-specific benefits: The Pneumoconiosis Etc. (Workers' Compensation) Act 1979

Enacted in 1979, the Pneumoconiosis Etc. (Workers' Compensation) Act 1979 sets up a no fault compensatory scheme which aims to "provide compensation for sufferers (or their dependents) of certain dust-related diseases, who are unable to claim damages from the employers where the dust exposure which caused the

---

Executive Committee and UK Asbestos Working Party, "Pleural Plaques," in *Consultation Paper* (London: Ministry of Justice, 2008), 4.

121   Felstiner and Dingwall, *Asbestos Litigation in the United Kingdom: An Interim Report*.

122   General Insurance Practice Executive Committee and UK Asbestos Working Party, "Pleural Plaques," 4.

123   *Johnston v NEI International Combustion Ltd* [2007] UKHL 39 (England).

124   In 2009, a court in Newcastle allowed claims of pleural plaques that compromised 5 percent of the bodily function with asbestosis making a small contribution to the cause of breathlessness of the asbestos victim to be tried. *Beddoes v Vinters Defence Systems & Others* and *Cooksey v Vinters Armstrong & Others*, both discussed in Thompsons Solicitors. "Insurers challenge asbestosis compensation." Published electronically March 20, 2009. http://www.thompsons.law.co.uk/ntext/insurers-challenge-asbestosis-compensation.htm.

125   General Insurance Practice Executive Committee and UK Asbestos Working Party, "Pleural Plaques," 33.

126   *The Damages (Asbestos-related Conditions) Act of 2009* (Scotland); *The Damages (Asbestos-related Conditions) Act of 2009* (Northern Ireland).

disease occurred, as they have gone out of business."[127] The 1979 Act provides for a one-time lump sum payment only. The 1979 Act is not based on contributions from employers, but instead is funded by the Treasury.

The 1979 Act followed a long campaign led by Welsh miners. One of points of political leverage used by the proponents of the scheme was that in 1974 the National Coal Board's compensation scheme for pneumoconiosis sufferers had been established. This scheme departed from the established principle that no category of workers would benefit from social security benefits that were intended to be received by a single group of workers. Coal compensation was the first exception to the traditional idea. It compensated former miners who had had ten years in the coal industry and who had been diagnosed with pneumoconiosis certified by a Benefits Agency Medical Board. The coal miners' scheme was an important cultural shift as it broke IIDB's monopoly of compensation for occupational injuries and diseases. It opened up different thinking about these issues, especially in a time of economic recession, unemployment, and closure of coal mines and asbestos plants. Parliament set up the 1979 scheme to provide "a faster and cheaper means of obtaining compensation, with lump sums being awarded according to the severity and starting date of the condition, and weekly payments made in appropriate cases to compensate for loss of earnings."[128] Still nowadays, the 1979 scheme "is designed for [those] who do not have a realistic prospect of bringing a successful claim against a previous employer, either because the employer is no longer in business or it seems likely that it would be difficult to prove that the period of employment made material contribution to the development of the disease."[129]

To be eligible to receive a payment, an asbestos victim must be diagnosed with an asbestos disease caused by occupational exposure, the recipient of IIDB payments, and not have been the plaintiff in a personal injury case.[130] In addition, the relevant employer must no longer be in business. The administrative agency verifies this requirement by conducting a search via the company register.[131] The 1979 Act provides compensation only if there is no prospect of recovering damages in tort. Compensation is not available if the claimant has already sued for damages in relation to the same disease. The rule applies when the court heard the case in

---

127   *The Pneumoconiosis etc. (Workers' Compensation) (Payment of Claims) (Amendment) Regulations 2007* (England).

128   Written answer submitted by Mr. Battle, *Parliamentary Debates*, Commons, 6th series, Vol. 123 (1997) (England).

129   Tim Williams, Pippa Slade, and Jack Raeburn, "Lump sum compensation for asbestos related lung disease," *Thorax* 53, no. 7 (1998): 535; ibid.

130   Former coal industry workers that suffer from pneumoconiosis are covered by a separate scheme. The Pneumoconiosis Act also covers byssinosis if associated with cotton dust exposure.

131   In rare cases, an asbestos victim may recover more than just the lump sum because, although the company no longer exists, there is insurance coverage for the alleged disease.

full (even if the court ruled against the plaintiff and awarded no damages) or if the claimant reached an out of court settlement. However, if the plaintiff withdrew the lawsuit before the facts of the case were heard in court, or if the claim was dismissed for procedural reasons, the agency may still award compensation. If the claimant receives payment and later discovers the possibility of filing a civil claim against a defendant who was unknown at the time of the application, the government cannot recover an already paid payment from the claimant. However, courts have established that the damage award will be reduced to the extent compensation under the 1979 Act has been paid.[132]

The procedural steps that an asbestos victim must complete mirror the administrative path of all disability claims. The asbestos victim must file a claim with the benefit agency. In the majority of cases the claimant files the application without seeking the assistance of an attorney. However, representatives of the agency routinely visit asbestos supporting groups and others with the purpose of expanding the knowledge of the scheme among the population. Moreover, asbestos lawyers often remind claimants that they are entitled to claim the Pneumoconiosis Act benefit. Even though lawyers consider the level of compensation inadequate, they advise filing the application because the compensation payment does not preclude a subsequent civil lawsuit and the payment might help the claimant in funding the litigation. If the claim is denied, the decision can be challenged, and the administrative agency reviews the case. The agency routinely reconsiders denied applications where IIDB was first rejected but subsequently awarded on appeal. However, if the agency denies reconsideration, no other remedy is available. Neither courts nor tribunals have jurisdiction to hear cases challenging the denial of this benefit.

Claims have increased in the last few years. The scheme did not hit off right away. Wikeley notes that the government began promoting the scheme in leaflets and other publications only in 1993.[133] Increasing popularity and use of the scheme is in part due to the sympathetic attitude of governmental bureaucrats towards claimants, which was confirmed to me in interviews in London. In fact, the liberal philosophy that inspired the 1979 scheme—bridging torts and welfare aspirations—results in very few rejections. Interviews with some of the administrators of the Scheme reveal that government officials make a concerted effort to accept as many claims as they can. The determination of who the "relevant employer" is has been more relaxed than with IIDB claims (with reference to the 1979 scheme, "relevant employer" is a crucial concept because claims are granted only if there is no recovery in tort against the "relevant employer").[134] Moreover,

---

132    *Ballantine v Newalls Insulation Co Ltd* [2001] ICR 25 (England).

133    Nicholas J. Wikeley, "The New Mesothelioma Compensation Scheme," *Journal of Social Security Law* 16, no. 1 (2009): 30-42, citing research conducted by Fitzgerald in the 1990s.

134    Ibid., 30-42.

occasionally the benefit is granted also in the even the application filed the claim after the expiration of the limitation period.

Roughly 87 percent of claims led to a payment.[135] The few unsuccessful cases involve cases in which evidence is presented that the former employer is still in operation or in which the IIDB claim is also rejected. The high success rate and the sympathetic attitude maintained by bureaucrats are certainly associated with the fact that the majority of claims are filed by victims who have been diagnosed with mesothelioma. In fact, approximately 80 percent of claims paid under this scheme involve the deadly cancer.

By 2000, 12,247 victims had sought payments and 8,468 payments made since 1980, the year in which the 1979 Scheme became operative. The number of claims has increased on average by 20 percent each year in recent years. In 2001 alone, the number of applications increased by 50 percent. The increase was likely due to victims' increased awareness of the existence of the scheme. Between 2008 and 2012, 3,887 victims received the benefit. From 1980 to February 2001, the 1979 Act made payments for a total among of GBP 83 million. Expenditure between 2008 and 2012 amounted to roughly GBP 54 million.

**Table 3.3    Lump sum payments under the 1979 Scheme**

| Year | Amount (GBP) | Cases |
|------|--------------|-------|
| 2008-2009 | 5,164,697 | 370 |
| 2009-2010 | 14,760,789 | 1078 |
| 2010-2011 | 15,569,636 | 1097 |
| 2011-2012 | 17,702,849 | 1342 |
| Total | 53,197,971 | 3887 |

*Source:* Table prepared by the author by assembling governmental data published at http://www.dwp.gov.uk/other-specialists/compensation-recovery-unit/performance-and-statistics/mesothelioma/.

The average payment to dependents is currently around GBP 6,000.[136] There is no possibility of a second payment if the health conditions worsen. The amount paid fixed as income is not factored in. The lump sum payment can also be made to the asbestos victim's dependents after his or her death, but in this case a lesser amount is paid. The payment is calculated using charts that apply two criteria: the claimant's age at the time the IIDB Medical Board first confirmed, and the level of disability as assessed by the IIDB Agency. In 2001, the average payment

---

135  *Parliamentary Debates*, Commons, 6th series, General Committee Debates, Third Delegated Legislation Committee, col. 5 (1997) (England).

136  *Parliamentary Debates*, Lords, 5th series, Column GC115, February 26, 2008, http://www.publications.parliament.uk/pa/ld200708/ldhansrd/text/80226-gc0001.htm

to sufferers was around GBP 14,500, and it rose from an average of GBP 12,669 in the early 2000s.[137] In 2012, draft legislation aiming to increase payments by 5.2 percent was pending (see Table 3.3).[138]

## Premises owner liability and secondhand exposure

Not all asbestos victims can claim payments as IIDB or under the 1979 Scheme. Victims of secondhand exposure and environmental exposure have traditionally been never given an opportunity to participate in the safety net of the welfare state because their exposure to asbestos had not been occupational. For many years, welfare state programs had not been extended to them because union mobilization had favored routinization of occupational exposure cases to the detriment of other cases. Traditionally, the only path to compensation for victims of environmental exposure and secondhand exposure was to bring a tort case against the owner of the premises contaminated with asbestos. Not surprisingly, these cases are infrequent and hard to prove. For many years, courts were reluctant to allow these kinds of claims as they maintained that this exposure was just "occasional" exposure and thus not sufficient to sustain a viable claim.[139] To redress the unfair treatment of victims of environmental exposure, Parliament established in 2008 a compensation fund (known as Diffuse Mesothelioma Scheme) for the benefit of all mesothelioma victims who cannot claim compensation based on an occupational exposure case.[140] Before looking into this fund, I discuss case law owner premise liability cases and secondhand exposure cases.

Courts' unfriendliness towards premise owners' liability however did not deter activists from trying to push the issue of the public health risk associated with asbestos pollution in the public arena. A breakthrough moment came when the dangers of dispersion of asbestos fibers in the environment were featured in two studies: Nancy Tait, *Asbestos Kills* (1977) and Alan Dalton's *Asbestos Killer Dust* (1979). A few years after the appearance of these books, national TV broadcast a documentary featuring Alice Jefferson, a 47-year-old woman who had contracted mesothelioma when working for a few months at Cape's Acre Mill asbestos plant. This documentary, which aired in 1982, had a significant impact on the

---

137   Ibid.

138   *The Pneumoconiosis etc. (Workers' Compensation) (Payment of Claims) (Amendment) Regulations 2012* (England).

139   *Cherry Tree Machine Co Ltd and Shell Tankers UK Ltd v Dawson, Shell Tankers UK Ltd v Jeromson* [2001] EWCA Civ 101 (England); Laurie Kazan-Allen. "Asbestos Compensation in Europe." Published electronically July 7, 2000. http://ibasecretariat.org/lka_eu_comp.php.

140   *The Mesothelioma Lump Sum Payments (Conditions and Amounts) Regulations 2008* (England).

English public.[141] As the sensitivity towards asbestos disease in the population grew and asbestos litigation became routinized, lawyers became more inclined to try premises owner cases. The cases however proved hard to win. Up until the mid-1990s, victims were able to obtain only a handful of out of court settlements. We know for instance that Cape paid GBP 45,000 to Gordon Prior, a man who had alleged that he had contracted mesothelioma living next door to Cape's East London asbestos factory.[142] The breakthrough in litigation came in 1995 with the Armley case. Two residents of Armley, a small town in the suburbs of Leeds, began litigation against J.W. Roberts, a Turner & Newall's subsidiary, alleging that the defendant negligently caused their mesotheliomas by exposing them to asbestos coming from the plant. Both victims had been exposed to asbestos in the 1930s during their childhood while playing on sacks of asbestos which had been "disposed of" by the company simply by leaving them behind in a residential neighborhood near the plant.[143] The victims could not recover from workers' compensation because exposure to asbestos had not taken place "in the course of the employment." Litigation, which was the only chance of recovery, became possible because the two plaintiffs were able to secure funding through Legal Aid.[144] The case did not settle and the court returned a judgment in favor of the two mesothelioma victims. The trial court found that Turner & Newall had breached its duty of care and that the breach had been the proximate cause of the plaintiff's mesothelioma. The Court of Appeal confirmed the findings of the trial court and established, for the first time in history of English law, the principle that asbestos firms' duty of care extends beyond the factory walls.[145] The damage awards were on par with awards for occupational exposure. June Hancock was awarded GBP 65,000 and the widow of Mr. Margereson was awarded GBP 50,000.[146]

In the aftermath of the Court of Appeal's decision, other residents of Armley brought suits and settled. John Battle, a Member of Parliament, stated in the course of a parliamentary debate that "some 15 or 16 people were paid compensation, but others are in train and waiting to go through the process."[147] In December 1996,

141	James Cutler, "Asbestos and the media," *British Medical Journal* 285, no. 6344 (1982): 814.

142	Kazan-Allen, "Asbestos Compensation in Europe."

143	Jenny Steele and Nick Wikeley, "Dust on the Streets and Liability for Environmental Cancers," *The Modern Law Review* 60, no. 2 (1997): 266-267.

144	Geoffrey Tweedale, "Management strategies for health: J.W. Roberts and the Armley Asbestos Tragedy, 1920-1958," *Journal of Industrial History* 2 (1999): 72-95.

145	Gerrit Betlem and Michael Faure, "Environmental Toxic Torts in Europe: Some Trends in Recovery of Soil Clean-up Costs and Damages for Personal Injury in the Netherlands, Belgium, England and Germany," *Georgetown International Environmental Law Review* 10 (1998): 875.

146	Kazan-Allen, "Asbestos Compensation in Europe."

147	Statement by John Battle MP in *Parliamentary Debates*, Commons, 6th series, col. 71WH (January 16, 2002) (England).

Irwin and Mitchell, the law firm that had represented June Hancock confirmed the settlements:

> T&N agreed to settle eight of our 16 remaining Armley Environmental claims. Seven out of the eight were ... cases [of] people who as children played in the yards and loading bays around the factory. In addition, T&N also agreed to settle one of our "Clock School" cases, where there was no evidence that the deceased had played any closer to the factory than the school playground, which was on the other side of the road from the factory.[148]

Even if courts have been more open to victims of environmental exposure after the Armley opinion, premises owner cases are nonetheless hard to prove. Not many law firms are willing to put in the work given the uncertainty of the outcome. Since the *Margereson* and *Hancock* cases, very few cases were brought and victims compensated. For instance, in 2013, the High Court dismissed the claim for damages of a female mesothelioma victim who had sued a local council and a contractor for exposure to asbestos that came from a demolition site next to a playground where she had played as a child.[149]

To address concerns arising out of under compensation of victims of environmental exposure, the government established in 2008 the Diffuse Mesothelioma Scheme. The payments under the scheme are modest but compensation is certain. Victims of environmental exposure can still pursue any claim in litigation, but these cases are far from being routinized.[150]

Secondhand exposure cases, which are brought by victims who were exposed to asbestos dust at home because of close contact with an asbestos worker, are also infrequent and difficult to prove, as illustrated by *Maguire v Harland & Wolff plc and Another*.[151] The lawsuit was brought by an asbestos worker's wife who had contracted mesothelioma after years of secondary exposure to asbestos in connection to cleaning her husband's working clothes. By a majority of two to one, the Court of Appeal rejected the claim holding that the state of knowledge at the time when the claimant was exposed to asbestos did not allow for a reasonable person to have foreseen the injury. Ms. Maguire died while the case was pending.

While ultimately unsuccessful, the case pushed the Court to establish the principle that after 1965 employers should have had knowledge of the risks posed by take-home exposure and other kinds of secondary exposure. Indeed a few

---

148 Laurie Kazan-Allen. "T&N plc: News." *British Asbestos Newsletter* no. 27. Published electronically Spring 1997. http://www.britishasbestosnewsletter.org/ban27.htm.

149 *Garner v. Salford City & Anor* [2013] EWHC 1573 (QB) (England).

150 Wikeley, "The New Mesothelioma Compensation Scheme," 16. For instance, in 2009, a victim was able to recover damages based on her exposure low level of exposure to asbestos while attending a school at the age of 11. See *Willmore v Knowsley Metropolitan BC* [2009] EWCA Civ 1211 (England).

151 *Maguire v Harland & Wolff plc and Another* [2005] EWCA Civ 01 (England).

victims of secondhand exposure succeeded. One of these victims is Barry Welch, a father of three, who died aged 32 of mesothelioma. His exposure occurred during childhood because of daily contacts with his stepfather who worked as scaffolder at a power station in the south east of England. In litigation, the company's insurance conceded negligence and paid the victim's surviving relatives.[152] In another case, the widow of a roofer who had worked for a number of small firms, making use of products manufactured by Turners Asbestos Cement filed and settled a case with Turned & Newall for an amount of GBP 335,000.[153] Finally, in 2006, Michelle Campbell, the granddaughter of a shipyard worker, settled a lawsuit for mesothelioma due to exposure during the frequent visit of her grandfather Charles Frost. The case, which had been brought against the Ministry of Defense, settled for GBP 145,000.[154]

Other victims of secondhand exposure have claimed damages under product liability law. Although infrequent, these cases are commonly brought by self-employed plaintiffs and have a good chance of settlement if supported by good evidence of exposure. In 1999, Laurie Kazan-Allen reported that "Turner & Newall had been "paying out 100% of well-founded product liability claims for several years now."[155]

## The 2008 Diffuse Mesothelioma Scheme

The problem of secondhand exposure and environmental exposure has been addressed at the legislative with the establishment on the diffuse mesothelioma payments. This mechanism compensates victims who are not eligible under IIDB laws. As we have seen, they could only hope to recover damages in a court of law. However, this is an uncertain and expensive path, especially if there is no IIDB that provides start-up funds for the litigation. The different treatment of victims of mesothelioma depending on the source of exposure became a matter of public debate in the 2000s. By 2008, Parliament decided to step in to fill the gap in compensation.[156] The diffuse mesothelioma payments were thus created with the support of trade unions and the plaintiff bar.[157] The 2008 Regulations set up a one time, lump sum payment for the benefit of mesothelioma victims who are unable to

---

152   BBC News. "Damages won after asbestos death." Published electronically December 13, 2006. http://news.bbc.co.uk/2/hi/uk_news/england/6176641.stm.

153   Kazan-Allen, "Mesothelioma: A European Epidemic."

154   Laurie Kazan-Allen. "One Step Forward, Two Steps Back." *British Asbestos Newsletter* no. 65. Published electronically Winter 2006-2007. http://www.britishasbestosnewsletter.org/ban65.htm.

155   Kazan-Allen, "Mesothelioma: A European Epidemic."

156   *The Mesothelioma Lump Sum Payments (Conditions and Amounts) Regulations 2008.*

157   Wikeley, "The New Mesothelioma Compensation Scheme," 30-42.

make a claim under IIDB or the 1979 Scheme and who have not received payment in respect of the disease from an employer, a civil claim, or another source.

The eligibility requirements are two: evidence of some asbestos exposure that had taken place in the United Kingdom and a diagnosis of diffuse mesothelioma (a primary neoplasm of the mesothelium of the pleura or of the pericardium or of the peritoneum). The scheme does not require an independent assessment of the medical condition: the government makes a decision exclusively based on the medical records submitted by the claimant. The law also went further: during the first year, all victims were entitled to compensation regardless of the year of diagnosis of mesothelioma. After the first year of operation, claims have been accepted only if filed within 12 months from the date of diagnosis. Relatives of a deceased victim are also entitled to compensation. They must file the claim within a year of the death of their relative.

The amount of the award is set by law and depends in on the age of the claimant at the time of the diagnosis. Thus, a victim who is diagnosed at the age of 40 receives GBP 72,991. If the diagnosis comes later in life, the amount is reduced as follows: GBP 59,896 at the age of 50, GBP 36,422 at the age of 60, GBP 15,088 at the age of 70, and GBP 12,040 for victims aged 77 or more. Data on the number of claims and lump sums awarded are summarized in Table 3.4.

**Table 3.4     Lump sum payments under the 2008 Diffuse Mesothelioma Scheme**

| Year | Amount (GBP) | Cases |
|---|---|---|
| 2008-2009 | 165,071 | 11 |
| 2009-2010 | 1,326,788 | 94 |
| 2010-2011 | 2,814,296 | 216 |
| Total | 4,306,155 | 321 |

*Source:* Table prepared by the author by assembling governmental data published at http://www.dwp.gov.uk/other-specialists/compensation-recovery-unit/performance-and-statistics/mesothelioma.

The inclusive philosophy that inspires the scheme and the fact that the government does not need to conduct a medical assessment of the case makes the process rather quick. In fact, the government sets a rather ambitious target—that payments are made within six weeks after receiving the form. Also the government ambitiously envisioned the scheme to be financially self-sufficient. The hope is that the money paid as compensation is recovered, through the recoupment of benefit system, from the tortfeasor in the event a lawsuit is successful or settled since these payments are intended to be used by beneficiaries to fund personal injury litigation.

# Chapter 4

# Asbestos compensation in Italy

A major producer and user of asbestos, Italy's asbestos compensation emerged in the 1980s and bloomed in the 1990s combining workers' compensation payments, social security benefits, and criminal trials to which a growing number of personal injury claims were joined.[1] Asbestos compensation matured along the lines of the rigid distinction between cases of occupational exposure and cases in which the exposure was no occupational-secondhand exposure, environmental exposure, but also exposure in the workplace in occupations that, although risky, the law has not recognized as occupations entailing proper exposure to asbestos. This trajectory, which has resulted in exclusion of many asbestos victims from compensation, is rooted in the important role that unions have played in mobilizing claims and in the strict requirements that victims of asbestos personal injuries must meet to seek recovery in torts.

The exclusion of victims of non-occupational exposure from workers' compensation and social security is certainly problematic and it has been both litigated and debated at great length since 1994, the year in which all major asbestos diseases were listed as compensable under workers' compensation. A high volume of cases were brought to challenge the definition of "occupational" exposure as well as other eligibility requirements under workers' compensation. While eligibility criteria have been relaxed as a consequence of judicial intervention, victims on non-occupational exposure have substantially lower expectations of recovery than victims of occupational exposure. Even the 2011 Asbestos Fund, which advocacy groups had supported in the hope that the compensation gap would be filled, was set up only to the benefit of victims of occupational exposure. As a way to overcome some of these restrictions, many victims resorted to the criminal system for answers. This resulted in a lively and rather unique series of criminal investigations and trials against officers of asbestos firms that have

---

1  In the European tradition, Italy guarantees universal access to health care. Therefore, all asbestos victims are entitled to medical care and medical monitoring free of charge. See *Decreto Legislativo [Legislative Decree], Attuazione delle direttive n. 80/1107/ CEE, n. 82/605/CEE, n. 83/477/CEE, n. 86/188/CEE e n. 88/642/CEE [Enacting Directives n. 80/1107/CEE, n. 82/605/CEE, n. 83/477/CEE, n. 86/188/CEE e n. 88/642/CEE].* August 15, 1991, n. 277 (Italy); Elisabetta Chellini, Alessandro Marinaccio, and Massimo Nesti, "La sorveglianza dei casi di mesotelioma maligno e la definizione delle esposizioni ad amianto: i dati ReNaM 1997 [Malignant mesothelioma monitoring and asbestos exposure requirements: ReNaM 1997 data]," *Epidemiologia e Prevenzione* 27, no. 3 (2003).

opened the door to compensation also to victims whose claims were not based on occupational exposure.

The legal framework that has emerged from the resilient stream of cases and the legislative reaction to incessant litigation is, in the words of Franco Lotito, the chairman of the advisory board of the workers' compensation administrative body, highly "redundant, fragmented, and largely pushed by considerations of emergency" to the strenuous litigation rather than a clear policy vision.[2] Lotito adds that "this state of affairs creates a dense institutional curtain of fog filled with confusion and uncertainty that workers and firms are forced to navigate with difficulty."[3]

Lotito's words are also very useful to frame my account of asbestos compensation in Italy. Although I am a scholar trained in the Italian legal academia, conducting research and drafting this chapter was not easy: the legal environment is unclear, redundant, ever changing, and difficult to grasp; reform and litigation and further reform densely populated the story of asbestos compensation. This chapter represents my best effort to account for a complex and purposely unclear legal framework.

## Asbestos regulation and the lack of asbestos compensation

Asbestos compensation emerged in the 1980s. However, the regulation of asbestos dates back to the early twentieth century. In 1909, a royal decree mentioned asbestosis as one of the occupational hazards that women and minors working in dusty environments face.[4] In 1917, Adolfo Mazza patented a form of asbestos-cement pipe that developed the ideas of Hatschek, Eternit's inventor, and launched an asbestos-cement manufacturing facility in Casale that would soon attract foreign investment from entrepreneurs linked to the Eternit group and expand the production to one of the largest in Europe. In 1918, the largest chrysotile mine in Europe opened in Balangero. Extraction at this site positioned Italy as second after Russia on the list of European asbestos producers.

By 1943, in the midst of World War II, asbestosis made its appearance as one of the "prescribed" diseases that workers could develop if exposed to asbestos dust. In 1929, Mussolini had extended the mandate for employers to purchase insurance for occupational injuries, which had been established in 1898,[5] to six occupational

---

2  Franco Lotito, "Considerazioni introductive [Introductoty remarks]" (paper presented at the conference "A che punto è la notte", Turin, April 28, 2011).

3  Ibid.

4  *Regio Decreto [Royal Decree], Regolamento per l'applicazione del testo unico sulla legge per il lavoro delle donne e dei fanciulli [Regulations implementing the framework law on working conditions of women and minors]*. June 14, 1909, n. 442 (Italy).

5  *Legge [Law]* March 17, 1898, n. 80 (Italy).

diseases, none of which was linked to asbestos exposure.[6] The new legislation framed compensation for occupational injuries by deploying two principles which are still at the basis of contemporary policies compensation only for "prescribed" diseases and presumption that, in the presence of exposure to a known toxic industrial risk, the prescribed disease was caused by said industrial risk. Between 1933 and 1935, Mussolini took the further step of establishing a workers' compensation administration with automatic coverage of workers involved in dangerous occupations.[7] Workers' compensation provided the exclusive remedy for victims of prescribed disease and victims lost the right to sue the employer.

These laws were part of Mussolini's master plan to resolve labor disputes, and the entangled class conflicts, with "corporatism."[8] Proposed as a third way between capitalism and socialism, this approach entailed state control of labor relations by harmoniously coordinating and resolving, sector by sector, disputes between capital and labor in the economic interest of the nation. Mandatory insurance for occupational diseases, which awareness was growing among public health scholars and the medical profession, was a step towards state interventionism in labor disputes. History tells us that corporatism was more ideology than praxis: its implementation betrayed its spirit since Mussolini used the interventionist approach undemocratically to suppress free labor unionism and to "reestablish discipline ... within the factory," a promise that he had made to rubber and tire tycoon Alberto Pirelli in 1922 before rising to political power.[9] Yet, the seeds were sewn for interventionist policies in labor relations and compensation for occupational injuries.

In 1943, before losing political power and projecting Italy into a two-year civil war, the Fascist majority in Parliament voted to extend workers' compensation to asbestosis.[10] Its recognition as a prescribed disease was rooted in the political alliance with Nazi Germany. A few months earlier, Nazi Germany had listed lung cancer with asbestosis as an occupational disease covered by its workers' compensation. German public health officials had in fact concluded that there

---

6  *Regio Decreto [Royal Decree], Assicurazione obbligatoria contro malattie professionali [Mandatory insurance for occupational diseases].* May 13, 1929, n. 928 (Italy). The six diseases were conditions caused by exposure to lead, mercury, phosphor, benzene, and ammonia as well as hookworm, a disease caused by a parasite.

7  *Legge [Law], Unificazione degli istituti per l'assicurazione obbligatoria contro gli infortuni degli operai sul lavoro [Merger of workers' compensation administrations].* June 22, 1933, n. 860 (Italy); *Regio Decreto [Royal Decree], Disposizioni per l'assicurazione obbligatoria degli infortuni sul lavoro e delle malattie professionali [Regulations pertaining to mandatory insurance of occupations injuries and diseases].* August 17, 1935, n. 1765 (Italy).

8  Cyprian Blamires and Paul Jackson, *World fascism: a historical encyclopedia*, vol. 1 (Santa Barbara, CA: ABC-CLIO, 2006), 150-151.

9  Robert O. Paxton and Julie Hessler, *Europe in the twentieth century*, 5th ed. (Boston, MA: Wadsworth/Cengage Learning, 2012), 276.

10  The law also added silicosis to the list of prescribed diseases.

was sufficient evidence to link asbestos exposure to lung cancer. This path-
breaking initiative had very limited impact in those countries that were fighting
Germany, mostly because of the lack of scholarly exchange between scientists on
opposed war fronts.[11] Italians, who were war allies and engaged in free flowing of
information with Nazi allies, followed the path of Germany and listed asbestosis
as an occupational disease.[12]

After the end of the war, the word Fascist was dropped from the name of
the workers' compensation administration and it was renamed[13] but the regime
envisioned by Mussolini and implemented during his ruling remained untouched for
over twenty years. The first major post-war reform took place in 1965. Parliament
rewrote the Fascist law, and, in consolidating laws on occupational injuries and
disease, confirmed the inclusion of asbestosis as a prescribed disease.[14] By then, a
wave of epidemiological studies was showing that asbestos was killing workers in
factories. Researchers had reported cases of asbestos disease since 1955.[15] In the
1960s, various epidemiological studies showed that Italian asbestos workers were
becoming sick. In 1967, Donna linked a death due to lung cancer with the patient's
exposure to asbestos.[16] In 1972, Rubino and colleagues published an early case
control study that confirmed several cases of mesothelioma in patients who had
been exposed to asbestos.[17] This demonstrates that Italian epidemiologists were
well aware of the findings of Doll and Wagner and that they worked towards

---

    11    Based on personal correspondence Wilhelm C. Hueper, the director of the
Environmental Cancer Section of the National Cancer Institute, Castleman notes that the
war with Germany "precluded his knowing that the German government had formally
recognized lung cancer associated with asbestosis as a compensable disease." Castleman,
*Asbestos: medical and legal aspects*, 45.

    12    *Legge [Law], Estensione dell'assicurazione obbligatoria contro le malattie
professionali alla silicosi ed all'asbestosi [Workers' compensation extension to silicosis
and asbestosis]*. Aprile 12, 1943, n. 455 (Italy).

    13    From *Istituto Nazionale Fascista contro gli Infortuni sul Lavoro* (INFAIL) to
*Istituto Nazionale contro gli Infortuni sul Lavoro* (INAIL).

    14    *Decreto Presidenziale [Presidential Decree], Testo unico delle disposizioni per
l'assicurazione obbligatoria contro gli infortuni sul lavoro e le malattie professionali
[Unifying law pertaining to mandatory insurance of occupational injuries and diseases]*.
June 30, 1965, n. 1124 (Italy).

    15    G. Rombola, "Asbestosi e carcinoma polmonare in una filatrice di amianto (spunti
sul problema oncogeno dell'asbesto) [Asbestos and pulmonary carcinoma in an asbestos
worker (problems of carcinogenic action of asbestos)]," *Medicina del Lavoro* 46, no. 4
(1955): 242-250.

    16    A. Donna, "Considerazioni su un nuovo caso di associazione fra asbestosi e
neoplasia polmonare [Considerations on a new case of asbestosis associated with lung
cancer]," ibid. 58, no. 10 (1967): 561-572.

    17    G.F. Rubino et al., "Epidemiology of pleural mesothelioma in North-western Italy
(Piedmont)," *British Journal of Industrial Medicine* 29, no. 4 (1972).

confirming them on Italian cohorts. Nonetheless, the growing body of evidence did not equate lung cancer with mesothelioma.

Legislative action lingered to the point that these diseases would become prescribed only in the 1990s, mesothelioma and carcinoma of the lungs became prescribed in 1994;[18] pleural thickening in 2008.[19] Why such a long delay? During the 30 years, the growing consciousness of asbestos disease translated into political and legal action at a very slow rate because unions thought they could promote workers' health and safety by working from within the factory and cooperating with the state institutions. The 1970 *Statuto dei Lavoratori*, or Workers' Charters, shaped the legal framework of such strategy. It prohibited employers from hiring a doctor to assess occupational diseases and demanded the assessment is completed by a doctor employed by the state agency responsible for industrial disease. It also established workers' unalienable right to unionize and to have a representative at the plant. This statute is seen as a policy victory for labor, which had become strong after the mobilization of 1968, and a partial institutionalization of *operaismo* or workerism, that is, movement fostering the affirmation of workers' rights in autonomy from "the dictates of the labour movement and capital."[20] Labor's idea was to protect workers' health through unionization and dialogue with the institutions without jeopardizing full employment. Occupational health became integrated in labor relationship. Some issues were discussed at the national level as part of collective bargain negotiation. Other issues were negotiated by unions at the manufacturing facility level in direct dialogue with management. This strategy however resulted in a partial sacrifice of health and safety issues, which become conflated in broad collective bargaining negotiations and was often the object of unions' concessions to management to secure workers' full employment or better economic conditions. At national level, demands for employment stability and salary increase trumped health and safety considerations. Asbestos disease was one of the issues that were lost in translation. However, at European level and at the local level things operated differently.

---

18   *Decreto Ministeriale [Ministerial Decree], Normative e metodologie tecniche di applicazione dell'art. 6,comma 3, e dell'art. 12, comma 2, della legge 27 marzo 1992, n. 257, relativa alla cessazione dell'impiego dell'amianto [Rules and regulations pertaining to art. 6, sec. 3, and art. 12 , sec. 2, of Law March 27, 1992, n. 257, banning asbestos uses].* September 6, 1994 (Italy); *Legge [Law], Regolamento recante le nuove tabelle delle malattie professionali nell'industria e nell'agricoltura [New charts regulating occupational diseases in the manufacturing and agricultural sectors].* April 13, 1994, n. 336 (Italy).

19   *Decreto Ministeriale [Ministerial Decree],* (April 9, 2008) (Italy).

20   Steve Wright, *Storming heaven: class composition and struggle in Italian autonomist marxism* (London; Sterling, VA: Pluto Press, 2002), 3.

## The birth of asbestos compensation

The negotiated equilibrium that kept asbestos cancers off the list of prescribed diseases was cracked only when the European Union took legislative action to tightly control asbestos exposure and eventually ban the magical mineral. Since 1983, the EU passed several pieces of legislation focusing on the issue of exposure to asbestos. Directive 83/477/EEC set limits for asbestos exposure at work, limits that were further lowered in 1991.[21] The two directives clearly indicated that the days of asbestos manufacturing in Europe were numbered. The prospect of the entire industrial sector being shut down changed the approach to negotiations of national unions that could no longer hope for collective bargaining negotiations to deliver full employment and salary increases. This led to the awakening of interest of labor unions' national managers for the asbestos issue in the early 1990s. Yet, the most significant contribution to the emergence of asbestos disease consciousness and compensation advocacy came from grassroots initiatives that took place at the plant and community level in Casale Monferrato. A small blue collar town in Piedmont, the city of Casale hosted a large asbestos-cement plant owned and managed by the Eternit group. Since the early 1980s a group of local union organizers and of Eternit employees began keeping track of all cases of mesothelioma and started realizing that a significant epidemic was afflicting the community. The public health risks were particularly severe because substantial amounts of asbestos dust flew daily over the city as asbestos was transported from the railroad station to the plant and back to the station—a poor logistical choice that contributed to the high rates of mesothelioma in the city's population.

Grassroots activities in Casale were led primarily by members of local branches of major labor union organizations and began by helping mobilization victims in their quest for compensation in workers' compensation and in torts. The activists also realized early on that the proper way to address the asbestos epidemic, in addition to compensation, entailed banning the use of asbestos and cleaning up any contaminated area. Therefore these activists soon embraced a broader political agenda that aimed at creating a safety net for the soon-to-be unemployed or retired asbestos workers and their family. The prospect of financial hardship was certainly tangible as retired and retiring sick workers were experiencing major difficulties in securing workers' compensation. Yet, activists thought that the answer was not in keeping asbestos in the community but by building a safety net for victims and

---

21   *Council Directive 91/382/EEC of 25 June 1991 amending Directive 83/477/EEC on the protection of workers from the risks related to exposure to asbestos at work (second individual Directive within the meaning of Article 8 of Directive 80/1107/EEC),* 91/382/ EEC. March 27, 1992 (EU). In 2003, Directive 2003/18/EC prohibited the extraction of asbestos as well as its manufacture and processing. A general ban on the production and marketing of asbestos materials is in place since 2005 and, since 2006, it is illegal to handle asbestos.

relatives who were about to face unemployment and, in some cases, illness and death.

Activists therefore pushed a multifaceted agenda that combined supporting litigation, advocating an asbestos ban, expanding workers' compensation, and creating *ad hoc* compensation that could reach victims of all forms of exposure to asbestos.[22] This agenda was however challenged both at the local level, by those members of the Casale community who argued that an asbestos ban would have had devastating effects for the local economy that heavily relied on the asbestos-cement factory, and at the national level by labor unions' headquarters that resisted the idea of a local group trying to dictate the political agenda at national level. Activists however did not desist in their lobbying efforts, which became increasingly strenuous with regular trips to Rome to demonstrate in front of the Parliament.

Eventually the national leadership of labor unions became involved, but only after asbestos had been banned. Unions' labor relations agenda narrowly focused on full employment and wage increases were no longer viable: the wave of rising unemployment rates among union members as well as the generalized trend towards greater flexibility of the labor market, led unions to shift their strategy finally embracing the quest for compensation of asbestos victims. While unions understood the immediate need to effectively represent union members who were employed in the asbestos industry, their change of posture is also a consequence of broader changes in labor relations. By the 1990s, world capitalism had entered into a new epoch, one of transnational capital and neoliberal policies that greatly relied on job flexibility. Labor unions became caught in this new wave of capitalism and in 1992 they agreed to "an emergency industrial relations reform that abolished wage indexation and temporarily banned enterprise-level bargaining."[23] Once job security and salary increases were no longer the pillars of negotiations between labor and capital, health and safety issues, along with issues of preservation of the safety net that had been built since the end of World War II, attracted much more political attention among labor unions leaders.

The asbestos campaign that connected local activists with labor unions leaders brought home significant results. Chrysotile was banned in 1992.[24] The law banning asbestos established social security payments to the benefit of already retired or newly unemployed asbestos workers in the form of a pension multiplier (the pension of each retiree was automatically increased by a certain percentage).

---

22   Mirco Volpedo and Davide Leporati, *Morire d'amianto: l'Eternit di Casale Monferrato: dall'emergenza alla bonifica* [Dying of asbestos: The Eternit at Casale Monferrato: from emergency to clean-up] (Genova: La clessidra, 1997), *passim*.

23   Lucio Baccaro and Sang-Hoon Lim, "Social Pacts as Coalitions of the Weak and Moderate: Ireland, Italy and South Korea in Comparative Perspective," *European Journal of Industrial Relations* 13, no. 1 (2007): 29.

24   *Legge [Law], Norme relative alla cessazione dell'impiego dell'amianto [Regulations pertaining to the ban of asbestos use]*. March 27, 1992, n. 257 (Italy).

Mesothelioma and carcinoma of the lungs became prescribed in 1994.[25] Moreover, labor unions began supporting asbestos victims' efforts to secure workers' compensation awards. They did so by providing the financial support and expertise to challenge benefit denials and in lobbying for further expansion of the various compensatory schemes.

The early 1990s mark the birth of asbestos compensation. The emergence of asbestos compensation is certainly due to a reactive necessity rather than proactive vision. Political inertia reigned for many years and contributed to late governmental recognition of asbestos disease. Policymakers were not interested in asbestos and labor unions at the national level did not push the agenda for years. Since then, labor unions have played a central role in the political mobilization of asbestos victims. As the labor market readjusted to the disappearance of the asbestos industry, labor unions embraced asbestos compensation as a vehicle to maintain control of labor relationship in times of declining union membership and increasing job mobility: expanding compensation for asbestos victims, whether in the form of a higher pension or of greater compensation for disease, allowed labor unions to retain the (almost monopolist) role of the representatives of the working class. As noted earlier in the chapter, unions' support has profoundly shaped the current legal framework of compensation, which is highly biased in favor of victims of occupational exposure and almost silent about victims of other kinds of exposure. A review of the litigation that emerged after the establishment of asbestos compensation mechanisms, as well as the informational material posted on websites of labor unions and administrative agencies discussing the mechanisms, reveals that labor unions greatly influenced and shaped victims' expected path to compensation. Equality of treatment among workers and prioritization of occupational exposure over other kinds of asbestos exposure were championed by labor unions and became embedded in the legal struggle for greater compensation. Labor unions pushed the compensation agenda of asbestos victims towards social benefit and away from personal injury compensation in ways more pronounced than in other countries. This process of structuration led to interesting effects, such as the further expansion of the pension multiplier model: it has not been extended to non-occupational exposure victims but it has been used to accommodate demands for compensation of workers in other industries. In fact, 1,250 workers who had been exposed to chloride-nitro-ammonia, which similarly to asbestos is associated with reduced life expectancy, are now entitled to the same pension multiplier that was made available to victims of occupational exposure to

---

25   *Decreto Ministeriale [Ministerial Decree], Normative e metodologie tecniche di applicazione dell'art. 6,comma 3, e dell'art. 12, comma 2, della legge 27 marzo 1992, n. 257, relativa alla cessazione dell'impiego dell'amianto [Rules and regulations pertaining to art. 6, sec. 3, and art. 12, sec. 2, of Law March 27, 1992, n. 257, banning asbestos uses]; Legge [Law], Regolamento recante le nuove tabelle delle malattie professionali nell'industria e nell'agricoltura [New charts regulating occupational diseases in the manufacturing and agricultural sectors].*

asbestos in the early 1990s.[26] Victims of occupational exposure currently receive compensation in the form of the pension multiplier, workers' compensation, and, under narrow circumstances, damages in court. The next segment of the chapter discusses the details of each of these paths to compensation.

## The pension multiplier

Negotiated as part of the political process that led to banning asbestos and the disappearance of the asbestos industry, the benefit was viewed as a social welfare measure for retired, unemployed, or soon-to-be unemployed asbestos workers. As for other Italian regulations in the area of asbestos compensation, deciphering eligibility under the scheme is complex and complicated. The legal framework and subsequent amendment is an intricate quagmire.[27] Rules have been significantly amended over time, and eligibility requirements are difficult to map. In essence, victims of occupational exposure to asbestos dust, whether or not they developed an asbestos disease, may apply for a social benefit in the form of a pension multiplier, which operated as an additional payment on top of the recipient's pension liquidated at retirement. It is applied only to the years of exposure to asbestos dust not to the entire professional life of the retiree.

The multiplier is either 1.50 percent or 1.25 percent. The higher figure applies to victims whose exposure ended on or before October 2, 2003, to those who filed an application to receive the benefit on or before June 15, 2005, and to those who are affected by an asbestos disease. The 1.50 percent rate applies to both the retirement age and to the pension amount. The result is that these workers could reach retirement age early. Eligibility is further restricted to cases in which exposure lasted for more than ten years and the asbestos firm was required to pay an asbestos supplemental premium for workers' compensation coverage.[28] These include a limited number of firms that the workers' compensation administration had singled out because their manufacturing process involved significant and direct exposure to asbestos. The 1.25 percent multiplier is applied to all other victims, that is, those who were exposed after 2003, who failed to file a claim by 2005, or who worked for firms that were not required to pay the supplemental asbestos premium. To these victims, the

---

26   Paola Scola, "All'Acna stessi benefici di chi lavorò l'amianto" [ACNA workers will receive the same benefits of those who worked with asbestos] *La Stampa (Nord-ovest)*, December 6, 2003, 45.

27   For a recent, well written account of the legislation, see Luigi Pelliccia, *Le nuove pensioni* [The New Pensions], 2 ed. (Santarcangelo di Romagna: Maggioli Editore, 2011).

28   This hypothetical illustrates how the multiplier works: victims hired in 1978, exposed to asbestos for 12 years during 1978 and 1990. This victim receives a pension that is increased by adding to the ordinary pension an amount of money equal to six extra years of employment ($12 \times 1.5 = 18$). An asbestos worker who was exposed to six of those 12 years, receives a lower pension than in the previous case ($6 + 6 \times 1.5 = 15$).

1.25 percent multiplier is applied only towards the pension amount not to retirement age.[29] Self-employed victims are not eligible to receive the pension multiplier. The benefit is not paid to independent contractors and small business owners (such as artisans). The rationale, embraced by courts in the numerous attempts to be defeat the exclusion, has its foundations in the notion that self-employed victims were not legally required, by contract, to work in dusty environments, on a schedule set by the firm, and without proper protection against dust, in contrast to the many victims who were forced by their employers to be exposed.[30]

The 1.50 multiplier is notably applied to the pensions of "walking worry" victims, that is, individuals who are healthy but in fear of developing an asbestos disease because of substantial exposure to the magical mineral. The exposure is substantial because the benefit can only be paid to victims whose exposure is certified by the workers' compensation administration as having lasted for at least ten years. Considerations of social welfare formed the basis for their inclusion as a means to rebalance the safety net of gainfully employed members of society who became unemployed in the aftermath of the disappearance of the asbestos industry. Over time, as the labor market readjusted to the rise of unemployment caused by the asbestos ban, policymakers and courts revisited the rationale behind the benefit, shifting its justification from a social welfare measure redressing unemployment to compensation for reduced life expectancy.[31] The Constitutional Court has in fact held that "walking worries" are eligible to receive compensation on the assumption that prolonged occupational exposure to asbestos might have reduced their life expectancy.[32]

This benefit has been heavily contested since its appearance. With the support of unions, victims have extensively challenged eligibility requirements at the administrative level as well as in court, and have lobbied Parliament for their extension to new classes of victims. The current discipline is the outcome of legislative reforms, guidelines issued by the workers' compensation authority, court cases that have clarified, refined and expanded the scope of entitlement in the course of the past twenty years. Extensive litigation, supported by labor unions, targeted the validity of four requirements: the 10-year exposure; the employer's failure to pay the addition premium; eligibility under workers' compensation (state

---

29   *Legge [Law], Norme relative alla cessazione dell'impiego dell'amianto [Regulations pertaining to the ban of asbestos use]*, sec. 13; *Decreto Legge [Law Decree], Disposizioni urgenti per favorire lo sviluppo e per la correzione dell'andamento dei conti pubblici [Urgent rules to promote development and to address public finances' issues]*. September 30, 2003, n. 269, sec. 47 (Italy).

30   *Sentenza [Opinion] n. 10722/98*, INPDAI v. Vianco (Corte di Cassazione [Highest Court], October 27, 1998) (Italy); INPS, "Comunicazione [Communication]" (Rome: INPS, 2004).

31   *Sentenza [Opinion] n. 127/02* (Corte Costituzionale [Constitutional Court], April 11, 2002) (Italy). In Italy, universal health coverage covers, with no charge or a nominal charge, health care and medical monitoring services dispensed to asbestos victims.

32   Ibid.

employees and other categories were excluded from eligibility because the benefits were administered by a different system); and certification of exposure issued by workers' compensation officials, which the workers' compensation administration has often denied.

The first strand of cases challenged the constitutionality of the 10-year exposure requirement based on equal protection and due process considerations. Victims who did not qualify argued that the law failed to treat all victims equally because no consideration to the severity of the exposure to asbestos was given. The aim was to extend entitlement to asbestos victims who had been exposed to shorter periods of time. The Constitutional Court disagreed and ruled that the law was constitutional.[33] The Court reasoned that setting a minimum length of time for exposure was constitutional since the benefit was meant to compensate the risk of developing a disease and that the its length (10 years) was a reasonable approach to identify any exposures that were "substantial" and therefore sufficient to create the risk that the law compensates.[34]

The second strand of cases challenged eligibility exclusion for victims who had worked for firms that had not paid to the workers' compensation administration the supplemental premium for asbestos risks. These firms did not pay the supplemental premium either because the workers' compensation authority had assessed the premium ignoring that asbestos was used in the manufacturing process or because the firm had simply failed to make payments. Pushed by an abundant stream of lawsuits that lasted a decade and that ultimately gained the court's sympathy, Parliament ultimately embraced this challenge in 2003 and reformed the law so that asbestos victims could be compensated even if no payments had been made.

The third strand of cases was brought by asbestos victims who had been employed in sectors that had a pension system administered by a specialized agency. State employees (postal service, military police, and railroads) and maritime workers were among them. Once again in the wake of a robust stream of cases, some categories were able to push the argument further and gain enough political support that, at some point, they were granted eligibility. For instance, workers of the state-owned railroad firm raised due process and equal protection issues, which were eventually embraced by the Constitutional Court in 2002.[35] The opinion extended to all state employees, who can now claim the pension multiplier. To this extent, in 2004, the Department of Labor issued guidelines that expressly explained the eligibility requirements for railroad workers.[36] In similar ways, maritime workers

---

33   *Sentenza [Opinion] n. 5/00* (Corte Costituzionale [Constitutional Court], January 12, 2000) (Italy).

34   Ibid.

35   *Sentenza [Opinion] n. 127/02* (Corte Costituzionale).

36   Ministero del Lavoro e delle Politiche Sociali [Department of Labor and Social Policy]. *Decreto Ministeriale [Ministerial Decree], Benefici previdenziali per i lavoratori esposti all'amianto [Asbestos workers' benefits]*. October 27, 2004, in Gazzetta Ufficiale December 17, 2004, n. 295 (Italy).

(not shipyard workers but employees of companies offering public transportation services by boat) fought to remove certain barriers to compensation. In their case, a special statute of limitations applied: to claim a benefit or compensation for an occupational disease they were required to file a claim within five years from the day of retirement. If applied to the context of asbestos diseases, which have long latency and, in many cases, victims become aware of being sick only years after leaving employment, the statute of limitations resulted in ineligibility for compensation in mesothelioma or lung cancer cases. The inequity was litigated extensively until it reached the Constitutional Court. Once again, the Court found that the statute of limitations constituted an unreasonable restriction and indicated that the five-year limitation runs from the moment of diagnosis.

The last strand of litigation targeted the procedural requirement that workers' compensation "certifies" asbestos exposure. Originally, victims were required to attach to their application an affidavit, signed by the employer, certifying both asbestos and payment of the additional premium. However, many employers refused to sign this document in fear that it could later be used in courts as evidence of exposure. Consequently, their applications were often rejected. Dismissals have been routinely challenged arguing that, even in the absence of the employer's affidavit, exposure to asbestos could be demonstrated. Victims thus began submitting an employee's generated record of exposure based on documentation, testimony, and other evidence. Local labor unions and victim support groups often helped victims by creating databases with data on exposure levels for each occupation and by contributing to the legal costs of challenging the workers' compensation's denial.[37]

These employee-generated records are currently considered to be sufficient to meet the procedural requirement. However, applications are often denied because of the workers' compensation administration's failure to certify exposure for certain industries and certain occupations. Once again maritime workers are a case in point. The workers' compensation authority often dismissed requests for certification because the agency could not assess the amount of exposure of maritime workers on commercial boats. Lack of expertise on the part of the agency was often indicated as the reason for rejecting these claims. The problem with maritime workers was resolved by Parliament. In 2005, a law transferred the authority to certify asbestos exposure to the agency responsible for managing the pension system of maritime workers.[38] This specialized agency is in a better position to assess which occupation involved exposure to asbestos. Unfortunately this reform has not made the process completely smooth. The agency processes requests at a very slow pace (a speedy turnover is often critical in asbestos cases due to the deadly nature of asbestos-induced cancer) and, in a discreet number of cases, rejects the request, in part

---

37   This statement is based on field interviews.

38   *Legge [Law], Legge finanziaria del 2006 [2006 Annual Budget Act]*. December 23, 2005, n. 266, article 1, section 567 (Italy). The specialized agency to which the authority to certify asbestos is called IPSEMA (*Istituto di previdenza per il settore marittimo* or *Social Security Institute for the Maritime Sector*).

because it experiences difficulties tracing down asbestos exposure that took place in boats that are no longer in use. Denials are often challenged in court. Some of these claims were even filed in the United States, with the assistance of US plaintiff lawyers who recruited clients in Italy, in the event victims had worked on an American vessel throughout their professional lives. The case for navy personnel is even harder because the authority to certify exposure has not been transferred to the specialized agency but it still with the workers' compensation authority.

Other asbestos victims who had to resort to litigation to pursue their claims are former employees of oil refineries, aluminum, chemical, and steel plants, who came into contact with asbestos-containing products although asbestos was never manufactured there. The former employer does not release documentation proving asbestos exposure and the workers' compensation authority claims that it has no basis for assessing the level of exposure in industries that are not typically categorized as "asbestos firms." Consequently, many of these requests are dismissed and the dismissals challenged in courts. Railroad workers are also a case in point to illustrate the second issue of the workers' compensation certification: often, the agency certifies exposure only if the worker had been employed in certain specific occupations. So, requests submitted by victims who worked in repairs are granted only if the applicant's duties focused on insulating issues. Requests from co-workers, who shared the same working environment but with different responsibilities, are denied. These dismissals have been routinely challenged in courts with mixed results.

The social security administration does not make the statistics regarding this benefit available to the public. Thus it is only possible to retrieve partial data. The data that I gathered show that claiming rates have substantially grown since 1992. This was certainly to be expected given the rise of asbestos disease and the progressive relaxation of the eligibility requirements in the past 20 years. In 2003, Cazzola reported that, since 1999, the filing rate doubles every year (see Table 4.1).[39]

**Table 4.1    Pension multiplier claims: trends (all claims) (1998-2003)**

| Year | Number of new claims filed | Total number of applications |
|------|----------------------------|------------------------------|
| 1998 | – | 91,000 |
| 1999 | 5,000 | 96,000 |
| 2000 | 12,000 | 108,000 |
| 2001 | 21,000 | 129,000 |
| 2002 | 50,000 | 179,000 |
| June 2003 | 31,000 | 210,000 |

*Note:* 2003 data are incomplete.

*Source:* Table prepared by the author by assembling data published in Cazzola, Giuliano. "La Miniera d'amianto." *Il Sole-24 Ore*, November 17, 2003.

---

39   Giuliano Cazzola, "La miniera d'amianto [The asbestos mine]". *Il Sole-24 Ore*, November 17, 2003, 23.

Furthermore, the percentage of applications filed by unimpaired claimants is growing. In 2003, in 40 percent of the cases, benefits were claimed by unimpaired applicants. In 1999, only 17 percent of claimants were unimpaired (see Table 4.2).[40]

**Table 4.2    Pension multiplier claims: trends (unimpaired claims) (1999-2003)**

| Year | Number of applications filed by unimpaired claimants | Percentage of applications filed by unimpaired claimants |
|------|------------------------------------------------------|----------------------------------------------------------|
| 1999 | 16,000 | 17 |
| 2000 | 27,200 | 25 |
| 2001 | 42,300 | 33 |
| 2002 | 70,000 | 39 |
| June 2003 | 83,818 | 40 |

*Note:* 2003 data are incomplete.
*Source:* Table prepared by the author by assembling data published in Cazzola, Giuliano. "La Miniera d'amianto." *Il Sole-24 Ore*, November 17, 2003.

Claims are not very successful if compared to the workers' compensation system. So far, roughly 50 percent of the applications were processed and approved. Claims are routinely rejected. In 2003, the board had rejected roughly one third of the claims (69,159 out of 200,750).[41] From these approximately 70,000 cases of denial, two thirds were determined by the lack of evidence that exposure to asbestos took place. Data from 2004 are consistent: increase in filings and only half of the claims led to a benefit award.[42]

Furthermore, cases are processed slowly. Roughly one quarter of the applications are still pending. As of 2009, 565,000 claims had been filed, 167,000 accepted, 300,000 rejected, and 185,000 were pending.[43] In 2004, 254,703 had been filed, 87,302 rejected and 45,727 were pending (see Table 4.3).[44] Once the request for benefits is rejected, the unsuccessful claimant may sue the governmental agency.

---

40    Ibid.

41    Diego Rughi, "Benefici amianto: una tutela in evoluzione [Asbestos benefits: evolving regulations]," *Dati INAIL* 7 (2003): 27.

42    INAIL. "Dati previdenziali per lavoratori esposti all'amianto ex ¶ 132, comma 8, legge n. 257/93 e successive modifiche [Coverage data for workers exposed to asbestos under ¶ 132, section 8, law n. 257/93 and following amendements]." Published electronically 2009. http://www.amiantomaipiu.it/files/amiantomaipiu_page_6_resource_file3_orig.pdf.

43    Data are based on author's note taken at a conference on asbestos disease held in Rome on April 28, 2010.

44    INAIL, "Dati previdenziali per lavoratori esposti all'amianto ex ¶ 132, comma 8, legge n. 257/93 e successive modifiche."

**Table 4.3**     **Pension multiplier claims: status of applications as of June 2003**

| Applications | Number of applications | Percentage (out of total applications) |
|---|---|---|
| Total applications | 221,684 | |
| Applications granted | 111,143 | 50% |
| —Impaired applicants | 27,146 | 12% |
| —Unimpaired applicants | 83,997 | 38% |
| Applications denied | 81,249 | 37% |
| Applications pending | 29,292 | 13% |

*Note:* 2003 data are incomplete.

*Source:* Table prepared by the author by assembling data published in Cazzola, Giuliano. "La Miniera d'amianto." *Il Sole-24 Ore*, November 17, 2003.

The system is funded by taxpayers. In the early years, the government allocated several million dollars each year. After the initial funding of roughly USD 3 million in 1992, funding has become more generous. In 1993, funding grew to USD 50 million and in 2004 additional USD 40 million were allocated.[45] Over time, funding exceeded greatly the original estimates in great part because of the growing number of claims and increase in the value of pensions due to periodical adjustment of the cost of living.

In 1992, policymakers were advised that the projected number of applications would have been limited to 1,200! Consequently, the estimates indicated that USD 250 million were required to compensate all future claimants. Political opportunity may have led to such a grossly inaccurate prediction. Policymakers were trying to minimize the impact of banning asbestos on the employment rates. Asbestos victim advocates played with low numbers to contain fears that the scheme would be financially disastrous—yet knowing that the benefit would over time become the primary source of compensation for thousands of asbestos workers. By the year 2000, the financial coverage required was substantially higher than the amount originally allocated. In 2003, the government paid benefits to 51,400 former asbestos workers for an amount equal to 800 million dollars (roughly 15,500 dollars per beneficiary). In 2004, over USD 10 million were allocated annually for these payments,[46] USD 15 million in 2008 and 2009, and USD 35 million in 2010.

In 2008, the government proposed converting the pension multiplier into the broader Asbestos Victims' Fund (*Fondo per le vittime dell'amianto*), so that payments could be distributed to all asbestos victims including those who cannot

---

45    *Sentenza [Opinion] n. 5/00* (Corte Costituzionale).

46    Lino D'Orta, "La matassa di leggi sul 'killer' amianto [The puzzle of regulation of 'killer' asbestos]," *IL - Bimestrale di informazione dell'INAIL* 6 (2003): 3-4.

recover from workers' compensation.[47] The Fund was established in 2011 but eligibility was limited to victims of occupational exposure who can recover from workers' compensation. The pension multiplier survived.

### Workers' compensation

Workers' compensation is the cornerstone of the compensation system for occupational disease. The system is compulsory, public, no-fault insurance, reinforced with fines levied against employers who fail to make periodical contributions to the system. The system is triadic: the government insures any worker exposed to an occupational risk for the physical and economic damages caused by workplace accidents or occupational diseases; the employer pays a premium; and the worker receives compensation. Workers' compensation is also a no-fault system: the employer's negligence—as well as the contributory negligence of the employee—is irrelevant. However, the employer's fault is relevant with regard to the agency's indemnification rights.[48] In fact, if the employer is found criminally liable of manslaughter or negligent infliction of a bodily injury, the government can recoup the awards paid to a victim of an occupational disease. Workers' compensation payments compensate lost wages, loss of working capacity, medical expenses, and loss of bodily integrity (bodily integrity is discussed later in the chapter). Since 2011, these victims also receive additional payments out of the Asbestos Victims' Fund.

While the system originally recognized only prescribed diseases, in 1988 the system has become a mixed one. In this mixed system, victims of occupational exposure to asbestos dust who develop one of the asbestos diseases prescribed by the law must only prove exposure. Causation is presumed. Victims of nonprescribed diseases must prove both exposure to an industrial risk and causation between the risk and the disease. The transformation of workers' compensation from a list system to a mixed one is the product of judicial intervention. In 1988, the Constitutional Court held that the ineligibility of nonprescribed disease offended

---

47    Senato della Repubblica Italiana. *Proposta di legge [Bill], Estensione delle prestazioni previste per gli infortuni sul lavoro e le malattie professionali ai soggetti danneggiati dall'esposizione all'amianto [Extension of benefit entitlements for occupational injuries and diseases to individuals exposed to asbestos].* October 17, 2006, n. 23.

48    *Decreto Presidenziale [Presidential Decree], Testo unico delle disposizioni per l'assicurazione obbligatoria contro gli infortuni sul lavoro e le malattie professionali [Unifying law pertaining to mandatory insurance of occupational injuries and diseases]*, 10-11; *Legge [Law], Misure in tema di tutela della salute e della sicurezza sul lavoro e delega al Governo per il riassetto e la riforma della normativa in materia [Regulations pertaining to workplace health and safety and assignment of power to the Executive to reorganize regulation in this matter]. August 3, 2007*, n. 123 (Italy).

due process.[49] The opinion intended to push a system inherited from the Mussolini era towards modernization. The emergence of new forms of occupational risks, the increasing scientific knowledge of occupational diseases, and technological advances in medical diagnosis tools made prescription-based eligibility obsolete and unconstitutional. The Court reasoned that, if workers' protection and compensation ought to be taken seriously, the system must be more flexible and contemplate the possibility of recovery for new occupational risks and diseases. However, the Court did not reject the achievements of the old system. Diseases that were prescribed in 1988 remained prescribed even after the reform, the reason being that their pre-1988 inclusion as occupational disease was assumed to be the result of legislative scrutiny of well-established scientific evidence.

Under the current regime, several asbestos diseases are prescribed. Asbestosis has been prescribed since 1943, mesothelioma and carcinoma of the lungs since 1994[50] and pleural thickening since 2008.[51] To receive compensation for any of the prescribed diseases, asbestos victims must show that they meet two requirements: they must prove that they have been exposed to asbestos in the course of their employment and that they have been diagnosed with a prescribed asbestos disease. Because of the mixed nature of the system, asbestos victims can also seek compensation for an asbestos disease that is not prescribed. In this case, they victim must offer evidence of a causal link between occupational exposure and the disease. These claims are seldom successful.

To claim the benefit, victims must follow certain procedural steps, some of which are unique to Italy. First, the victim must give notice to the employer, who then files a claim with workers' compensation and notifies local public safety authorities, which in turn give notice to the prosecutor of the jurisdiction where the disease occurred or the exposure took place. The law mandates that notice must be given to the agency within 15 days from the day when the first symptoms appear. However, the workers' compensation administration routinely

---

49 *Sentenza [Opinion].* February 18, 1988, n. 179 (Corte Costituzionale [Constitutional Court]) (Italy).

50 *Decreto Ministeriale [Ministerial Decree], Normative e metodologie tecniche di applicazione dell'art. 6,comma 3, e dell'art. 12, comma 2, della legge 27 marzo 1992, n. 257, relativa alla cessazione dell'impiego dell'amianto [Rules and regulations pertaining to art. 6, sec. 3, and art. 12 , sec. 2, of Law March 27, 1992, n. 257, banning asbestos uses]*; *Legge [Law], Regolamento recante le nuove tabelle delle malattie professionali nell'industria e nell'agricoltura [New charts regulating occupational diseases in the manufacturing and agricultural sectors].*

51 Ministero del Lavoro e delle Politiche Sociali [Department of Labor and Social Policy]. *Decreto Ministeriale [Ministerial Decree], Nuove tabelle delle malattie professionali nell'industria e nell'agricoltura [New occupational disease charts for the manufacturing and agricultural sectors].* April 9, 2008, in Gazzetta Ufficiale July 21, 2008, n. 169 (Italy).

accepts late notices.[52] However, late filing is taken into account in determining the amount of the compensation: each day of delay reduces the award. Notice was set as a requirement when workers' compensation was first created during the Fascist era. It served a precise purpose: to ensure government involvement in the management of occupational diseases. This was part of Mussolini's plan to establish "corporatism" as a common practice in labor relations so that workers' opportunities for mobilization could be minimized.

Claims are adjudicated by an agency's official, and denials can be challenged in administrative courts for abuse of discretion. If the claim is successful, the victim receives periodical payments in compensation for lost wages, loss of working capacity, medical expenses and any loss of bodily integrity that is unrelated to diminished working capacity.[53] The number of claims submitted throughout the years is substantial: an estimated 20,000 claims were filed between 2001 and 2010.[54] The asbestos claims filed were 2,294 in 2010 and 2,250 in 2011.[55] Workers' compensation claims for asbestos disease have risen over time. Published data suggest that claims for mesothelioma have increased between 5 and 10 percent since 2001. 2011 data show that the rate of workers' compensation claims for an asbestos disease rose 7 percent between 2010 and 2011, 21 percent since 2005, and 53 percent since 2001.[56] The coverage of mesothelioma under workers' compensation did not immediately turn into victims claiming benefits. The effect on victims' consciousness was not immediate, and was mediated by doctors and labor unions that made victims progressively aware of the existence of the remedy. Slowly, asbestos victims began claiming workers' compensation benefits as they were becoming sick. The number of mesothelioma claims recognized in Italy is a case in point. After mesothelioma became listed, the number of claims increased at a regular but slow pace. There was no explosion of filings. Indeed, claims started growing only after the ban on asbestos and the forced retirement of the asbestos industry workforce after 1992.

---

52    *Decreto Presidenziale [Presidential Decree], Testo unico delle disposizioni per l'assicurazione obbligatoria contro gli infortuni sul lavoro e le malattie professionali [Unifying law pertaining to mandatory insurance of occupational injuries and diseases]*, sec. 52.

53    Ibid., sec. 66.

54    Franco D'Amico. "Malattie da amianto: il bilancio di un dramma senza fine [Asbestos disease: numbers of a never ending tragedy]." Published electronically August 10, 2012. http://www.anmil.it/Chisiamo/ReteeServiziANMIL/IlPatronatoANMILpresentein79Sedi/Malattiedaamianto/tabid/2191/language/it-IT/Default.aspx.

55    Ibid; INAIL, "Rapporto Annuale 2011: Parte quarta/statistiche Infortuni e malattie professionali" (Rome: INAIL, 2012).

56    D'Amico, "Malattie da amianto: il bilancio di un dramma senza fine"; Eurogip, "Asbestos-related occupational diseases in Europe. Recognition, Figures, Specific systems" (Paris: Eurogip, 2006); INAIL, "Rapporto Annuale 2010 con analisi dell'andamento infortunistico" (Rome: INAIL, 2011).

Workers' compensation claims based on a prescribed disease are often successful. Approximately 75 percent of claims based on a prescribed disease are accepted. Among all asbestos diseases, mesothelioma has the highest success rate. However, comparatively, asbestos diseases have a tougher time than non-asbestos diseases. In fact, on average, 90 percent of the claims for prescribed diseases are granted versus 75 percent of mesothelioma claims.[57] Furthermore, mesothelioma claims filed by victims in traditional "asbestos" jobs have higher rates of success than claims filed by mesothelioma victims who were exposed in industries or jobs that have weaker connection with asbestos. For instance, Merler and colleagues report that the rate of success of claims filed by mesothelioma victims exposed in the construction industry is roughly 50 percent.[58]

**Table 4.4**     **Workers' compensation claims and awards (2001-2011)**

| Condition | Filed/ Awarded | 2001 | 2002 | 2003 | 2004 | 2005 | 2006 | 2007 | 2008 | 2010 | 2011 |
|---|---|---|---|---|---|---|---|---|---|---|---|
| Asbestosis | F | N/A | N/A | 511 | 553 | 621 | 567 | 626 | 609 | 570 | 533 |
| Meso-thelioma | F | 644 | 680 | 696 | 754 | 840 | 904 | 583 | 505 | 658 | 650 |
| | A | 486 | 538 | 536 | 560 | 591 | 582 | 446 | N/A | N/A | N/A |
| Pleural thickening (added in 2003) | F | N/A | N/A | 643 | 488 | 605 | 439 | 468 | 545 | 710 | 803 |
| | A | N/A | N/A | 576 | 428 | 475 | 321 | 193 | N/A | N/A | N/A |

*Source:* Table prepared by the author by assembling data made publicly available by INAIL and published in Fabiola Ficola, "La tutela INAIL per i lavoratori esposti all'amianto". Paper presented at the Annual Assoamianto Workshop (September 2008). Available at http://www.assoamianto.it/RELAZIONI%20SEMINARIO%20NAZIONALE%20AMIA NTO%20FERRARA%2026%20SETTEMBRE%202008/FICOLA.pdf.

Providing evidence of an economic or bodily loss is relatively easy. Victims of mesothelioma and lung cancer qualify for compensation of economic loss with any degree of disability. In fact, a diagnosis of cancer suffices to meet the

---

57  De Brucq, "Une Vaste Enquête: 'Les Maladies Professionnelles en Europe' Déclaration, Reconnaissance et Indemnisation," 372.

58  Enzo Merler, Vittoria Bressan, and Anna Somigliana, "Mesoteliomi negli edili: frequenza, stima del rischio, carico polmonare di fibre di amianto, domande e riconoscimenti per malattia professionale nel Registro regionale veneto dei casi di mesotelioma [Mesothelioma in construction workers: risk estimate, lung content of asbestos fibres, claims for compensation for occupational disease in the Veneto Region mesothelioma register]," *Medicina del Lavoro* 100, no. 2 (2009): 120-132.

threshold. In pleural plaques and pleural thickening cases, only claimants whose physical impairment exceeds 6 percent receive compensation. Bodily integrity is compensated when the loss exceeds 5 percent. On the other hand, providing evidence of occupational exposure to asbestos dust is much harder. In fact, this has become a major hurdle for asbestos victims, and many victims have failed to recover in workers' compensation because they were unable to present an accurate record of exposure. These challenges mirror those already examined with reference to the pension multiplier. Employers have access to exposure data but are afraid of making them accessible as they could be used in criminal and personal injury litigation against them. Workers struggle with collecting these data and meeting the burden of proof—a burden that is partially alleviated by the efforts of unions and doctors who often keep a record of exposure in various occupations at various firms. The administration is a reactive institution and lacks investigative power so it cannot conduct independent inquiries to assess exposure. Victims often challenged denials of coverage in court. Over the years courts have somehow eased up the requirement by construing the statute more liberally. Case law has forced the administration to accept claims based on any form of exposure to asbestos that took place in the working environment—whether the victim was directly exposed as part of her duty to manufacture or handle asbestos-containing products or was exposed as a bystander working on premises where occasional exposure to asbestos was possible.

One of key elements of compensation is the loss of working capacity. The workers' compensation board uses charts to award benefits.[59] These charts are divided into three columns: diseases; job functions involving occupational hazards; and limitation period between the appearance of the disease and the last exposure. This column does not apply to asbestos diseases because the statute of limitations starts running at the time of the manifestation of the disease. The amount calculated using the charts reflects the severity and length of the disablement as well as the victim's average salary in the year preceding the disease.[60] Loss of income consists of a percentage of daily wages lost because of the impairment. Impairment is assessed based on the degree of inability to perform job-related duties. This is measured on a 0-100 percent scale where 100 percent is total inability. The periodic payment may be updated if the degree of inability changes over time.[61] Life-long payments are made periodically to victims who become permanently unable to work as a consequence of the disease.[62] The law does not contemplate lump sum payments.

---

59    *Decreto Presidenziale [Presidential Decree], Testo unico delle disposizioni per l'assicurazione obbligatoria contro gli infortuni sul lavoro e le malattie professionali [Unifying law pertaining to mandatory insurance of occupational injuries and diseases].*

60    Ibid., sec. 2-3.

61    Ibid., sec. 83.

62    The 60 percent of the average daily wage from day 1 to day 90 of illness and the 75 percent of the daily wage from day 91 on. The compensation is reduced by one third in case of inpatient hospital care.

The loss of bodily integrity is determined by charts developed by the Department of Labor.[63] For each bodily or mental loss—the list of losses comprises approximately 400 items from loss of a limb to paralysis, from contracting HIV to diabetes—the government sets a degree of loss. Once the degree of loss is determined, victims who lost between 6 and 16 percent of their bodily integrity receive a lump sum payment (Table 4.5). If the loss is equal or greater than 16 percent, the victim receives a fixed amount, monthly payment (Table 4.6). These amounts are increased in the event bodily integrity deteriorates further after the award is assessed. An increase can be granted once, and victims must apply to receive it.

**Table 4.5**  **Lump sum payments (in EUR) for loss of bodily integrity suffered by male beneficiaries (6% to 15%)**

| Loss (%) | Age group | |
|---|---|---|
| | **61-65** | **66 and above** |
| 6 | 5,280 | 4,800 |
| 7 | 6,545 | 5,950 |
| 8 | 7,920 | 7,200 |
| 9 | 9,405 | 8,550 |
| 10 | 11,000 | 10,000 |
| 11 | 13,310 | 12,100 |
| 12 | 15,840 | 714,400 |
| 13 | 18,590 | 16,900 |
| 14 | 21,560 | 19,600 |
| 15 | 24,750 | 22,500 |

*Source:* Ministero del Lavoro e delle Politiche Sociali [Department of Labor and Social Policy]. *Decreto Ministeriale [Ministerial Decree], Approvazione di "Tabella delle menomazioni," "Tabella indennizzo danno biologico," "Tabella dei coefficienti," relative al danno biologico ai fini della tutela dell'assicurazione contro gli infortuni e le malattie professionali [Adoption of "Injury Chart," "'Danno Biologico' Awards Chart," "Coefficient," pertaining to "danno biologico" in relation to occupational injuries and diseases].* July 12, 2000, in Gazzetta Ufficiale, July 25, 2000, n. 172 (Italy).

---

63   Ministero del Lavoro e delle Politiche Sociali [Department of Labor and Social Policy]. *Decreto Ministeriale [Ministerial Decree], Approvazione di "Tabella delle menomazioni," "Tabella indennizzo danno biologico," "Tabella dei coefficienti," relative al danno biologico ai fini della tutela dell'assicurazione contro gli infortuni e le malattie professionali [Adoption of "Injury Chart," "'Danno Biologico' Awards Chart," "Coefficient," pertaining to "danno biologico" in relation to occupational injuries and diseases].* July 12, 2000, in Gazzetta Ufficiale, July 25, 2000, n. 172 (Italy).

**Table 4.6    Annual payments (in EUR) for loss of bodily integrity (16% to 100%)**

| Loss (%) | Payment (per year) |
|----------|--------------------|
| 16       | 2,000              |
| 20       | 2,800              |
| 30       | 4,900              |
| 40       | 8,000              |
| 50       | 12,000             |
| 60       | 16,000             |
| 70       | 16,400             |
| 80       | 19,500             |
| 90       | 22,500             |
| 100      | 25,500             |

*Source:* Ibid.

The workers' compensation agency exercises its indemnity rights either by joining an ongoing criminal trial or by filing a civil lawsuit in the aftermath of the criminal trial. Overall, the system is financed by the periodic contributory payments made by the employers in order to insure employees for the specific risks related to the employment. As we have seen earlier, workers' compensation awards are not based on the premium paid by the employer but on the severity of the disease, as assessed by the charts issued by the government. Also, the worker is entitled to receive compensation regardless of whether the employer has paid the periodic premium to the government. In 2011, the workers' compensation administration claimed, in an indemnification claim joined to the criminal trial against Eternit, EUR 272,518,026 plus interests in relation to workers' compensation made to 1,651 victims formerly employed by Eternit.

**The Asbestos Victims' Fund**

Since 2011, asbestos victims receive an additional payment from an Asbestos Victims' Fund, which was set up to increase the benefits available to victims of an asbestos disease (asbestos exposure alone is not sufficient so "walking worries" are not compensated).[64] Some proponents of the Fund, and in particular asbestos victims' organizations, intended to set up a compensation mechanism for all victims

---

64   *Legge [Law], Legge finanziaria del 2008 [2008 Annual Budget Act]*. December 24, 2007, n. 244, sec. 241-246 (Italy); Ministero del Lavoro e delle Politiche Sociali [Department of Labor and Social Policy]. *Regolamento concernente il Fondo per le vittime dell'amianto [Guidelines for the Asbestos Victims' Fund]*. January 1, 2011, n. 30, in Gazzetta Ufficiale, March 29, 2011, n. 72 (Italy).

of mesothelioma, irrespective of the nature of the exposure. Mesothelioma is a signature disease that is caused only by asbestos. Therefore, exposure to asbestos is certain whenever a victim develops mesothelioma. However, as we have seen, victims of mesothelioma have substantially different chances of recovery depending on whether the exposure to asbestos was occupational or not, with occupational cases having much higher chances of recovery than all other victims. Proponents of the Fund intended to redress this unbalance. However, the eligibility requirement laid out in the rules as approved by the Government exclude from compensation victims of non-occupational exposure. This outcome reflects the fact that labor unions' lobbying prevailed. Labor unions were in fact interested in a Fund to the exclusive benefit of victims of occupational exposure so that workers could see that unions were still important political agents of workers' rights.

The payment is added automatically to benefits awarded to eligible victims without the need to submit additional paperwork. The benefit, which is paid retroactively to victims who qualified for workers' compensation since 2009, is calculated as a percentage of the benefit already awarded to the victim. The percentage was set at a 20 percent rate for years 2008 and 2009 and at 15 percent for year 2010. From 2011, the percentage fluctuates depending on the actual money that the Fund collected from the Treasury and selected firms. Payments by the Fund are in fact conditional upon the Fund having sufficient funds.

Three quarters of the funds come from the Treasury and the remainder from certain firms whose workers have been exposed (and still are) to asbestos after the asbestos ban was enforced in 1992. The law mandates that, after an initial contribution of EUR 30 million for 2008 and 2009 each, the Treasury transfer EUR 22 million each years. In addition, firms are required to contribute with EUR 10 million for the first two years and then with 7.333 million for each of the subsequent years. To guarantee a regular stream of money, firms' contributions are collected in the form of a supplemental workers' compensation premium (roughly 1 percent) rather than with *ad hoc* payments. The firms that are required to contribute to the Fund are identified by Government. These firms are businesses that employ more than 2,000 workers in jobs that entailed or entail exposure to asbestos dust.

Because of the fluctuation of the rate and the uncertainties regarding the cash flow, the law sets up an *ad hoc* governance body to monitor the cash flow and sets, every year, the appropriate rate for calculation of the supplemental benefit. The 16 members of the Board of Trustees are appointed by the Department of Labor and must include four representatives of major labor unions, four representatives of industry trade groups, and two representatives of the victim's advocacy groups with the largest number of members at national level.[65]

---

65  Ministero del Lavoro e delle Politiche Sociali. *Regolamento concernente il Fondo per le vittime dell'amianto*, art. 5.

## The emergence of asbestos personal injury litigation

In the current legal environment, personal injury litigation is the primary path to compensation available to victims of exposure to asbestos who are not eligible for compensation under workers' compensation. This group comprises victims of environmental exposure and secondhand exposure as well as all victims of occupational injury whose claims were rejected by workers' compensation administration. Lawsuits can also be brought by victims of occupational injury. However, if they are the beneficiaries of workers' compensation payments, their claims are very thin as they can only seek in court damages that have not been redressed by workers' compensation. Considering that their economic and bodily harm losses are almost entirely absorbed by workers' compensation, the only damages left to be claimed are "moral" damages that the victims of a crime can collect from the perpetrator when found guilty.

This has not always been the case though. Until 2000, occupational exposure victims could seek more substantial damages in court because the loss of bodily integrity had not been absorbed by workers' compensation. Occupational exposure's ability to claim in court damages for the loss of bodily integrity had played a key role in the birth of asbestos personal injury litigation in the 1990s. The loss of bodily integrity, or *danno biologico*, is a complex concept that is hardly translatable into the Anglo-Saxon legal vocabulary. Loosely translating as "injury to health," this compensable concept redresses any negligently inflicted loss of bodily and mental integrity. Originating from case law that embraced the idea, developed during the 1970s by a conspicuous body of scholarship, this new tort claim was the result of the Italian law's need to adapt to Italian society's new understanding of person that emerged from the dramatic cultural change of the 1960s and 1970s. Under the Italian Constitution, the right to health is a fundamental right, and since its enactment, Parliament and courts have progressively realized it by expanding the range of remedies available to tort victims. As part of this movement towards fundamental rights, the Constitutional Court created the harm to bodily integrity in 1986, which is seen as harm to the personal and social development of a person.[66] Up until the 1980s, the law would only compensate personal injuries if the injuries resulted in loss of bodily functionality (for instance the loss of limbs or organs) and loss of earning capacity. The law was silent on other aspects of human life such as the ability to enjoy a good life, to exist as a distinct individual, to pursue a life plan. The loss of bodily integrity was developed to correct the traditional view and adapt tort law to a renewed vision of the person. Scholars identify the harm as an injury to the "self-fulfillment of the individual in private and social life."[67] Federici summarizes the current understanding of this loss as follows:

---

66 *Sentenza [Opinion]*. July 14, 1986, n. 184 (Corte Costituzionale [Constitutional Court]) (Italy).

67 Markesinis et al., *Compensation for personal injury in English, German and Italian law: a comparative outline*. 85-91.

> Loss of bodily integrity refers to ... a person's inability or difficulty of a relation
> with herself or other persons, with the internal and the external worlds, caused by
> an inherited or acquired change of her whole bodily and psychological integrity.[68]

The "integrity" and right to self-fulfillment of the person became compensable
in itself independently from earning capacity and loss of bodily functionality.
Until 2000, victims of occupational exposure to asbestos could use loss of bodily
integrity as a basis for pursuing personal injury litigation in courts. This right was
instrumental to the emergence of asbestos personal injury litigation in the 1990s.

The first published asbestos case was however brought in 1992 by a victim
who could not claim compensation under workers' compensation.[69] Litigated
in Pordenone, a town in the northeast of Italy well known for shipbuilding and
currently the stage of a large asbestos criminal trial, the case was brought by a
mesothelioma victim who had not worked in a traditional asbestos occupation. He
had been employed by a company that sold, installed, and serviced elevators. The
elevators had breaks containing asbestos that the victim periodically inspected and
replaced. At that time, victims of a nonprescribed asbestos disease (mesothelioma
became prescribed in 1994) in non-traditional occupations were practically unable
to recover from workers' compensation. The novelty of the case certainly worked
against the victim and the judge found the company's executive not guilty because
the evidence of a causal link between the employer's conduct and the victim's
mesothelioma was insufficient. Needless to say, the civil claim for damages, which
had been joined to the criminal trial, was unsuccessful.

The significance of the case did not go unnoticed to *Il Foro Italiano*, one of the
leading legal publications. The case thus became the first published opinion of a
claims for damages connected to an asbestos disease. However, this was not the
first asbestos case. In 1906, when asbestos was taking its first steps in Italy, a court
was asked to deal with the asbestos problem for the first time. The opinion raised
the issue of asbestos toxicity in unequivocal terms:

> An international conference that took place in Milano [in 1906] on occupational
> disease ... highlighted the fact that "dusty" occupations [involving exposure to
> dust] are among the most dangerous for workers, and among these those involving
> mineral dust, and silica and asbestos in particular, are among the deadliest because
> they affect the respiratory tract and sometimes even reach the lungs.[70]

---

68   Antonio Federici, *Il danno biologico nel sistema previdenziale* [Social security
and "danno biologico"] (Milan: Giuffrè, 2009).

69   *Sentenza [Opinion]*, Virga (Pretura [District Court], Pordenone, July 7, 1992)
(Italy).

70   Roberto Riverso, "La difficile giustizia per i lavoratori esposti all'amianto [Tough
justice for asbestos workers]," *Questione Giustizia* 1 (2009): 20 (citing *Sentenza [Opinion]
n. 1197/06*, Società Anonima The British Asbestos Company Limited v. Avvocato Carlo
Pich (Tribunale [District Court], Torino, 1906)).

The 1906 case is important as an historical marker as it led to the adoption of the 1909 royal decree that singles out asbestosis as an occupational disease that could arise when working in dusty environments.[71] However, for decades no asbestos case was filed. They made their appearance after the recognition of the compensability of loss of bodily integrity. This "new" right opened the door to courts to asbestos victims because it granted access to litigation for victims with the strongest asbestos claim—those based on occupational exposure in traditional asbestos occupations. Often with local support from unions and lawyers paid by unions—initially the national headquarters of labor unions were not supportive of asbestos compensation—victims started exploring the potential and sued former employers seeking damages for loss of bodily integrity. In 2000, however, legislative reform barred victims of occupational disease from claiming damages for the loss of bodily integrity in court, and expanded the scope of workers' compensation to include such loss.[72] The reform, which in the United States would be labeled "tort reform," aimed to reduce personal injury litigation. To this end, Parliament balanced inability to seek damages in court and relatively lower awards to be expected in workers' compensation with increased likelihood of receiving some compensation. In fact, the threshold for receiving some compensation is set at 6 percent.[73]

Victims of occupational exposure are now barred from bringing a personal injury lawsuit under the loss of bodily integrity theory, and they have standing to sue the employer for damages only in the event the employer is found liable of a crime.[74] In this case, victims can recover the so-called "moral" damages—damages awarded to victims of a crime in reparation for the psychological harm caused by the offender. No proof of physical injuries or emotional distress is needed. Claimants may recover these damages without the need of offering specific proof of any loss whenever a criminal defendant is convicted of a crime that affects the interests of the asbestos victim. The loss of bodily integrity is still very much relevant in the context of personal injury cases brought by victims of non-occupational exposure. These victims are not eligible for damages under workers' compensation and can file a civil lawsuit or join a criminal trial to claim all types of losses directly caused by the asbestos disease.

The emergence of asbestos litigation in civil courts had however been curbed by courts' unfriendly treatment of asbestos plaintiffs. Roberto Riverso, a trial

---

71    *Regio Decreto [Royal Decree], Regolamento per l'applicazione del testo unico sulla legge per il lavoro delle donne e dei fanciulli [Regulations implementing the framework law on working conditions of women and minors].*

72    *Decreto Legislativo [Legislative Decree], Disposizioni in materia di assicurazione contro gli infortuni sul lavoro e le malattie professionali, a norma dell'articolo 55, comma 1, della legge 17 maggio 1999, n. 144 [Regulations pertaining to mandatory insurance for occupational injuries and diseases].* February 23, 2000, n. 38 (Italy).

73    Ibid.

74    Federici, *Il danno biologico nel sistema previdenziale.* 232.

judge in Ravenna, talks about "tough justice" for asbestos victims in civil courts.[75] The bases of this tough justice are primarily doctrinal. First, civil and criminal courts have developed different standards in mesothelioma cases. Civil courts consider mesothelioma disease that is independent of the dose of exposure, that is, that can be caused by any exposure, even a trivial exposure, to asbestos dust. When this standard, which is referred to as "trigger dose" doctrine, is combined with evidentiary standards, the consequences are not beneficial to victims. Civil courts maintain that, unless the plaintiff shows that with "qualified probability" the defendant is responsible for the trigger dose, the tort action is dismissed.[76] Qualified probability—a doctrine developed to deal with cases in which there is no certainty that a conduct caused the harm—is defined as "serious and reasonable probabilistic basis grounded on scientific evidence" that allows the court to conclude that a negligent act or omission caused the mesothelioma.[77]

Developed to favor plaintiffs who cannot establish causation with absolute certainty, the standard has not proved to be unfriendly to victims: exposure to massive quantities of asbestos dust is immaterial unless the plaintiff can also prove that the triggering dose was part of that massive exposure. Defendants ordinarily argue that, if the victim was exposed to asbestos from other sources (other employers or environmental exposure, other companies may be responsible for the "trigger dose." Based on this doctrine, many civil courts have dismissed tort actions. Asbestos claimants have had more luck in establishing damage claims in criminal trials because criminal courts have increasingly adopted a different legal standard to decide causation issues. In mesothelioma trials, criminal courts have in fact concluded that evidence of exposure to asbestos dust for a long time is sufficient to establish criminal negligence in manslaughter cases.[78] Criminal courts see mesothelioma as dose-dependent: the more intense and longest the exposure was, the more likely it caused mesothelioma.[79] Consequently, long exposure affects latency by anticipating the appearance of the disease. This is one of the reasons why asbestos victims have preferred to engage in criminal trials rather than bringing civil lawsuits.

Second, civil courts in particular have been particularly unfriendly to victims also with regard to statutory interpretation of asbestos regulations. Civil courts read

---

75  Riverso, "La difficile giustizia per i lavoratori esposti all'amianto."

76  Alessia Muratorio, "La declinazione della probabilità causale qualificata nell'esposizione all'amianto [Qualified probability as standard of proof for harm caused by asbestos exposure]," *Argomenti di diritto del lavoro* 1, no. 2 (2010): 239-246.

77  *Sentenza [Opinion] n. 2729/08*, M.V. v. Croce Rossa Italiana (Corte di Cassazione [Highest Court], Lavoro, February 5, 2008) (Italy).

78  Luca Masera. "Danni da amianto e diritto penale [Asbestos damages and criminal law]." *Diritto Penale Contemporaneo*. Published electronically October 29, 2010. http://www.penalecontemporaneo.it/materia/2-/23-/-/134-danni_da_amianto_e_diritto_penale/.

79  *Sentenza [Opinion] n. 317/08*, Cozzini et al. (Corte d'Appello [Court of Appeals], Trento, June 10, 2008) (Italy); *Sentenza [Opinion]*, Stringa (Tribunale [District Court], Bari, June 16, 2009) (Italy).

the language of the 1956 statute that gave a mandate to firms whose employees worked in a "dusty" working environment certain safeguards. If the word "dusty" is interpreted as including asbestos dust, plaintiffs could prove negligence by showing lack of compliance with the 1956 statute. However, courts' dominant statutory interpretation goes in a different direction: for reasons that obviate an easy translation into English, courts conclude that asbestos dust cannot be considered "dust" under the 1956 statute because asbestos must be considered "fiber" rather than "dust." This line of reasoning has led courts to dismiss many cases in which victims tried to establish the failure to comply with the 1956 regulations.[80]

## The practice of joining tort claims to criminal trials

As a consequence of civil courts' tough treatment of asbestos personal injury claims, asbestos victims often turn to criminal courts, where they have better chances of recovering damages in tort. Asbestos victims can seek damages by filing a civil lawsuit or by joining an ongoing criminal trial. By activating both, with a preference for joining a criminal trial, victims have slowed down maturity because the two procedural avenues have created two sets of legal expertise, resources, law firm specialization, and court opinions that do not always match and pull in the same direction. While not unique to Italy, the coexistence of these two procedural paths surface only in Italian asbestos litigation. Although complex, it is interesting to explore it further.

Claiming damages in criminal trials has a long tradition in Italy and the 1988 reform of the Code of Criminal Procedure, shifting the process from the inquisitorial model to the adversarial model, certainly enhanced the role of civil claimants in the criminal trial. In criminal trials, the civil claimant is represented at trial by a counsel and are entitled to offer evidence—witnesses, expert witnesses, documents—in support of and relevant to the claims for damages. Civil liability arises only if a guilty verdict is returned. Success is subordinate to criminal conviction. Because of that, prosecutors play a leading role at trial. Civil claimants' counsel often limit their advocacy role to the civil aspects of the case.

Civil claims can be grounded on various theories (negligence, intentional tort, or on the breach of the employment contract).[81] Breach of contract cases can only be heard by civil courts. Negligent and intentional torts can be heard by both civil and criminal courts. Furthermore, there is a special kind of damages that can be claimed exclusively if a defendant is tried in criminal trial and found guilty. These are moral damages, which can be claimed by joining the criminal trial or filing

---

80   *Sentenza [Opinion] n. 7362/05* (Corte di Cassazione [Highest Court], Civile, April 11, 2005) (Italy).

81   To date, no asbestos case has been brought under product liability theory.

a civil claim in the aftermath of the conviction.[82] Awards for moral damages are usually not large but they are important because victims of occupational exposure can claim them as they are not absorbed by workers' compensation payments.

Asbestos victims cannot litigate damages simultaneously in a civil trial and in a criminal one. They must choose one of the two paths. A victim who has not yet filed a civil claim can join the criminal proceedings by "joining" the case before or at trial. If a civil proceeding for damages is already pending at the time a criminal trial starts, the claimant can "transfer" her claim for damages by "joining" the criminal case.[83] In this scenario, the pending civil case "stays" until the criminal trial ends[84] and the criminal court acquires jurisdiction over the defendant's civil liability in addition to the criminal liability and may award damages to the benefit of the civil claimant.[85] Alternatively, the victim may also decide not to join the criminal trial and to file a civil lawsuit independently while a criminal trial is ongoing.[86] An asbestos victim may also file a civil lawsuit in the aftermath of a criminal conviction. While the standard of proof in civil and criminal trials had been identical for decades—courts had discretion to decide the case for either litigant as long as they could demonstrate that evidence presented by the prevailing party was "sufficiently persuasive"[87]—in 2006, the Code of Criminal Procedure was reformed and the standard of "beyond reasonable doubt" was introduced in criminal trials.[88] Therefore, under current procedural laws, the civil case and the criminal trial that see the same defendant tried for the same conduct may end with inconsistent verdicts *à la* O.J. Simpson.

---

82    Ennio Amodio and Eugenio Selvaggi, "An Accusatorial System in a Civil Law Country: The 1988 Italian Code of Criminal Procedure," *Temple Law Review* 62 (1989); Louis F. Del Duca, "An Historic Convergence of Civil and Common Law Systems—Italy's New Adversarial Criminal Procedure System," *Dickinson Journal of International Law* 10 (1991); Stephen P. Freccero, "An Introduction to the New Italian Criminal Procedure," *American Journal of Criminal Law* 21 (1993); William T. Pizzi and Luca Marafioti, "The New Italian Code of Criminal Procedure: The Difficulties of Building an Adversarial Trial System on a Civil Law Foundation," *Yale Journal of International Law* 17 (1992).

83    *Codice di Procedura Penale [Code of Criminal Procedure]*. 1929, sec. 75 (Italy).

84    Ibid.

85    Ibid.

86    Ibid.

87    The reform was strongly advocated by legal scholars. Federico Stella in particular argued that differentiating the standard of proof in civil and criminal trials would channel occupational disease litigation towards civil litigation, thus improving the protection afforded by the victims. See Federico Stella, *Giustizia e modernità: la protezione dell'innocente e la tutela delle vittime* [Justice and modernity: protecting the innocent and compensating the victim], 2 ed. (Milano: Giuffrè, 2002).

88    *Legge [Law], Modifiche al codice di procedura penale, in materia di inappellabilità delle sentenze di proscioglimento [Amendments to the code of criminal procedure, with regard to appellability of acquittals]*. February 20, 2006, n. 46 (Italy).

In addition to less unfriendly doctrinal views, choosing the criminal path presents other advantages for victims, which help to explain the prevalence of asbestos criminal trials over civil trials. The first and most important factor is that prosecutors investigate the misconduct. Criminal investigations are done at the prosecutors' expense, with no financial burden for the asbestos claimant, even in cases where the assistance of medical and technical experts is needed.[89] Second, in the absence of an American-style pre-trial discovery, prosecutors have investigating powers that are greater than private parties. Prosecutors have the power to conduct searches and seizures by accessing private residences, offices, factories and then seizing documents. They can take depositions, which, under exceptional circumstances, can be offered at trial as evidence without further scrutiny. For instance, if a person is at risk of not being able to offer testimony at trial, or locations and physical evidence are at risk of being irreversibly modified before trial, prosecutors may depose the witnesses, document the state of locations and physical evidence, and request expert testimony on the same issues. The resulting information becomes evidence by operation of law and can be used at trial in the event the person, location or physical evidence becomes unavailable. The procedural tool, unavailable in civil trials, is useful in asbestos litigation to secure the possibility to use at trial, evidence that time may tamper with or erase. For instance, asbestos plants are for the most dismissed and therefore physical evidence of asbestos contamination needs to be secured as soon as possible. Third, criminal trials put great psychological pressure on the defendant, and civil claimants may use it as leverage for settlement purposes. Fourth, the average time of adjudication of civil claims brought into criminal trials is shorter than in civil proceedings. Fifth, the adversarial environment reinvigorates the presentation of evidence and testimony at trial. Parties have more control on the case and the evidence presented. Finally, since criminal trials may lead to the issuance of criminal sanctions in addition to a monetary award, this path fulfills better than civil trials the quest for justice as demanded by asbestos victims: monetary awards coupled with the shame of a criminal conviction is a powerful, retributive cocktail.

## The criminal path to compensation: uncertainties and successes

Since criminal trials certainly offer a procedural advantage over civil trials, asbestos victims often preferred the criminal trial path. However, the extent to which asbestos victims can truly secure compensation in connection to criminal trials greatly depends upon prosecutors' ability and willingness to prosecute cases. The Italian Code of Criminal Procedure establishes that prosecutors may begin investigations of crime at any time, perhaps because the crime is a matter of public knowledge or its knowledge was acquired in the course of other investigations, but are mandated to investigate criminal charges whenever they receive "notice"

---

89   *Codice di Procedura Penale [Code of Criminal Procedure]*, sec. 327.

that a crime was allegedly perpetrated. The mandate to prosecute is however just "on the books." While prosecutors are sanctioned if they do not investigate upon notice, they have the discretion not to seek an indictment in the event they believe there are no grounds to pursue the matter further. In these cases, prosecutors move to set the investigation aside and to dismiss any charge already issued. Prosecutors may also fail to prosecute cases by merely "sitting" on the file for months, even years, up until the statute of limitations has passed thus removing the possibility of a trial.

During the interviews, victims and activists told me that cases were often assigned to prosecutors who were not eager to investigate the crimes, formalize an indictment, and try the defendants. A case in point concerns victims of exposure at shipbuilding facilities in Monfalcone. When victim mobilization took place in the early 2000s, asbestos disease in the area had been documented for years. The prevalence of asbestos disease was and still is high, and the region is rightfully considered one of the major clusters of asbestos disease in Italy. In the face of a significant number of asbestos victims and their willingness to come forward and participate in legal proceedings, local prosecutors—the court sits in Gorizia— were very reluctant to prosecute asbestos cases. It is estimated that in 2008 the pending criminal complaints or investigations for asbestos deaths in Gorizia were approximately 600.[90] Local prosecutors invoked, as justification for slowing investigations, understaffing and insufficient resources to prosecute these cases. Mr. Carmine Laudisio, a prosecutor in Gorizia, used the following words:

> [I] repeatedly denounced the objective organization challenges, to be attributed to the decade-long understaffing of judges, which has substantially compromised the operations of the office or resulted in a substantial obstacle to a rapid resolution of the asbestos issue. Furthermore, I raised the issue of the need of more efficient means to deal with asbestos but with no discernible results.[91]

Investigations and trials stalled for a few years until Chief Prosecutor Beniamino Deidda—the head of the regional office of the prosecutors—mandated that the files and criminal "information" concerning 42 asbestos deaths and pending in Gorizia without the prospect of going to trial, should be transferred to his office for further investigation. Simultaneously, Mr. Deidda created a working group on asbestos comprising members of his office and outside experts. The working group reactivated the investigation of some of the pending matters and indicted several executives who, at some point of their career, were employed as managers

---

90  Guido Barella, "Morti d'amianto, un pool d'indagine [Asbestos deaths, a team of prosecutors]," *Il Piccolo*, June 26, 2008.

91  "Precisazione di Laudisio: 'Amianto, il grosso dei processi è rimasto a Gorizia' [Laudisio's remarks: 'Asbestos, the bulk of the trials remained in Gorizia']." *Il Messaggero Veneto*. Published electronically August 7, 2008. http://moriredicantiere.wordpress.com/2008/08/07/precisazione-di-laudisio/.

at the shipbuilding firm Italcantieri, later renamed Fincantieri. Mr. Deidda's and collaborators' efforts started to materialized, although have not really paid off yet: the office of the chief prosecutor is now investigating the death of approximately 300 victims; a trial verdict for manslaughter against an executive ended with a not guilty verdict, later upheld by the Court of Appeal;[92] a major trial against 41 executives charged of causing asbestos disease in 87 victims started in 2010 and is scheduled to end in 2013.[93] This trial is a remarkable achievement, which is however tainted by the spectrum of bankruptcy. In fact, in early 2011, Fincantieri froze all payments to victims, mostly made as part of out of court settlements.[94]

In other instances, prosecutors dutifully investigated any asbestos crimes, indicted asbestos executives, and tried the cases. While asbestos cases are certainly sophisticated and demanding in terms of professional dedication and office resources, some prosecutor's offices have been more receptive of asbestos criminal complaints arising out of asbestos diseases and deaths. One prosecutor's office in particular has been at the forefront of asbestos criminal litigation and has eagerly taken up the challenge of prosecuting asbestos cases. It is the office located in Torino and led by Raffaele Guariniello, a seasoned prosecutor who has developed an expertise in trying occupational injury and disease cases. Torino is a large industrial town in the northwest located not far from Balangero mine and the cement-asbestos plant of Casale Monferrato, which is the area with the highest prevalence of asbestos disease in Italy. While Casale is in a different judicial district and therefore prosecutors in Torino have limited jurisdiction over the asbestos deaths in Casale, Mr. Guariniello has found creative ways of becoming involved with Casale. Mr. Guariniello has been professionally sensitive to injuries and death among workers for years and is a prolific scholar on the same topic. In 1985, he published a monograph on occupational diseases, which anticipated many of the issues that had kept courts busy in the 1990s and 2000s.[95] A few years after, in 1992, Mr. Guariniello established a Cancer Unit (*Osservatorio sui Tumori*) to prosecute criminal conduct causing occupational disease. Still operational, the Unit has worked exclusively towards uncovering cases of occupational diseases occurring within the office's jurisdiction. It combines diverse expertise: criminal

---

92    "Amianto, confermata in Appello l'assoluzione di Fanfani [Asbestos, Fanfani's acquittal upheld on appeal]." *Il Piccolo*. Published electronically July 23, 2011. http://ilpiccolo.gelocal.it/cronaca/2011/07/23/news/amianto-confermata-in-appello-l-assoluzione-di-fanfani-1.742699.

93    "Amianto, riparte il maxi-processo [Asbestos, the super-trial resumes]." *Il Messaggero Veneto*. Published electronically October 30, 2012. http://messaggeroveneto.gelocal.it/cronaca/2012/10/30/news/amianto-riparte-il-maxi-processo-1.5947880.

94    "Morti d'amianto, la Fincantieri congela i risarcimenti [Asbestos deaths, Fincantieri freezes payments]." *Il Piccolo*. Published electronically January 25, 2011. http://ilpiccolo.gelocal.it/cronaca/2011/01/25/news/morti-d-amianto-la-fincantieri-congela-i-risarcimenti-1.20597.

95    Raffaele Guariniello, *Se il lavoro uccide: riflessioni di un magistrato* [If working kills: reflections of a prosecutor]. Nuovo politecnico (Torino: G. Einaudi, 1985), *passim*.

investigators, doctors, occupational health and safety experts, and engineers. The thinking that brought the Unit into being is that sick workers were treated in public hospital where occupational diseases were diagnosed, but that the diagnosis never reached courts because of the missing link between hospitals and courts. Over the years, the Unit has established the missing link by keeping track of five types of cancer (mesothelioma, bladder cancer, angiosarcoma, adenocarcinoma of the septum of the nose, and laryngeal cancer), linking medical records shared by hospitals with employment and safety data, and referring possible cases of occupational diseases to Mr. Guariniello along with an expert report outlining the findings and documents of biographical, medical and employment information for each deceased worker. Upon receipt of the file, Mr. Guariniello has often requested further investigations to the police, which routinely interviews co-workers of the victim and other informants to fill any gap in the employment history. Between 1992 and 2000, data collected during the interviews reveal, the Unit referred more than 10,000 cases of cancer, 700 of which were cases of mesothelioma, to the prosecutors.

The referrals led to the indictment and subsequent trial against executives of the firm that owned the asbestos mine of Balangero[96] and other asbestos firms. Some of them are cement-asbestos firm Eternit, industrial oven manufacturer Humbert, two large retail firms Rinascente and Lagrange, a railroad contractor providing maintenance and insulation services, break manufacturers Riff and Galfer, asbestos-containing pipe manufacturer Saca, chemical company Montefibre, and asbestos-textile manufacturer Bender & Martiny.[97] The major prosecutorial accomplishment of Guariniello's office is certainly the Eternit trial, which has led to the conviction, currently being appealed, of two executives of foreign parent companies of the Eternit group. The case was brought in Torino even though the Eternit plant was located in Casale. Mr. Guariniello was able to assert jurisdiction and prosecute two businessmen who had participated in the management of four cement-asbestos plants in Italy. Since one of these plants operated within the jurisdiction of Mr. Guariniello's office and some of the victims became sick when living in Switzerland—the rules of prosecutors' power to investigate are relaxed if crime or part of it took place abroad,[98]—the prosecutor was able to bring the defendants to trial.[99] The trial lasted for over a year and ended in 2012 with a guilty

---

96  *Sentenza [Opinion] n. 3101/98*, Giannitrapani (Corte d'Appello [Court of Appeals], Torino, September 17, 1998) (Italy).

97  *Sentenza [Opinion]*, Barbotto Beraud et al. (Pretura [District Court], Torino, February 2, 1995) (Italy); *Sentenza [Opinion] n. 660/00*, Santullo et al. (Corte d'Appello [Court of Appeals], Torino, February 10, 2000) (Italy); *Sentenza [Opinion] n. 1522/00*, Humbert (Corte d'Appello [Court of Appeals], Torino, March 14, 2000) (Italy).

98  *Codice di Procedura Penale [Code of Criminal Procedure]*, sec. 8-10.

99  *Richiesta di Rinvio a Giudizio [Indictment]*, *Case 24265/04*, Schmidheiny and De Cartier De Marchienne, (Procura della Repubblica [Office of the Prosecutor], Torino, October 10, 2008) (Italy).

verdict. Both defendants were found guilty of criminal negligence and sentenced to 16 years in jail.[100] The conviction was upheld by the Court of Appeals, which, on June 3, 2013, increased the sentence for Stephan Schmidheiny to 18 years.[101] It is however uncertain whether and when victims will actually receive payments. So far no payment has been made, and victims' efforts to enforce the provisional award have been fruitless. Schmidheiny is a wealthy individual whose assets are scattered around the world and buried in banks, trusts, and businesses.[102] Enforcing the judgments will be expensive, complex, timely, and ultimately the outcome is uncertain. On his part, Mr. Guariniello did not rest on his laurels: his office is currently investigating the deaths of roughly 2,000 additional asbestos victims who were not included in the first criminal trial. More charges are likely to be brought in the future since approximately 50 cases of asbestos disease are recorded every year in the areas in which Eternit's operations were located.

The successes of Mr. Guariniello, which are the results of dedicated professionalism and unique circumstances, have not been replicated in other districts, even in parts of the country in which epidemiological studies show high rates of asbestos deaths. While no other prosecutor's office has been able to investigate and try this number of asbestos cases, asbestos trials have nonetheless popped up throughout Italy. A review of published opinions indicates that verdicts in at least 40 asbestos trials have issued in trails courts other than Torino, the court in which Mr. Guariniello has jurisdiction.[103] In Bologna, the office of the prosecutor organized an asbestos task force akin to the one set up in Torino and investigated 42 asbestos-related deaths among railroad workers employed by Casaralta, a contractor providing asbestos insulation for train carriages.[104] The investigation led to a trial. Before the trial began, the victims had settled their claims with Firema,

---

100   *Sentenza [Judgment] n. 5219/09*, Schmidheiny and De Cartier De Marchienne, (Tribunale [Trial Court], Torino, February 13, 2012) (Italy).

101   *Sentenza [Judgment] n. 5621/12*, Schmidheiny and De Cartier De Marchienne, (Corte d'Appello [Court of Appeals], Torino, June 3, 2013) (Italy). Louis de Cartier de Marchienne died on May 21, 2013 at the age of 92, few days shy from the appeal sentence of the Turin trial.

102   "Signori Ministri vi chiediamo formalmente aiuto [Gentlemen, we formally ask you for help]." *Alessandrianews.it*. Published electronically November 4, 2012. http://www.alessandrianews.it/politica/signori-ministri-vi-chiediamo-formalmente-aiuto-15457.html. With regard to de Cartier de Marchienne's liability, victims' only remedy is to file a lawsuit for damages against Etex in Belgium, a jurisdiction notoriously unfriendly to asbestos victims.

103   A list of published opinions deciding asbestos cases is available at http://www.studiolegalestella.it/eng/news_scheda.php/titolo=asbestos-decision-s-listing/idsottocat=9/idnews=17 (November 16, 2010).

104   Fernando Pellerano. "Avviato il censimento dei morti per l'amianto killer [Asbestos victims' census is under way]." *La Repubblica (Bologna)*, March 13, 2001.

the company that had purchased Casaralta. Each family received approximately EUR 200,000, for a total amount close to EUR 7 million. At trial, a Casaralta executive was sentenced to a year in jail after being found guilty of manslaughter in relation to 16 of the mesothelioma deaths. "This is a verdict for the future ... the verdict ... is a warning so that things that happened in the past do not happen in the future," a union representative stated at the end of the trial.[105] In Pavia, again in the north, charges of manslaughter associated with the deaths of 12 workers were brought against the former CEO of Fibronit, a producer of pipes and tiles containing asbestos. The trial ended with a sentence of thirty months' jail time for the 81-year-old former executive. In Bologna, a court convicted the manager of the Officine Grandi Riparazioni, a facility owned by the national railroad where carriages are checked and fixed accordingly, for the deaths of 12 workers. After being awarded damages in compensation for the loss of reputation suffered by the local union throughout the years (EUR 50,000), the union stated that the money would go to the advocacy group that had supported asbestos victims in Bologna.[106] In Vicenza, the owners of Metalcarpen, a small roofing company that used cement asbestos as part of its operations, were sentenced for the death caused by mesothelioma of one of their carpenters, 54-year-old Claudio Cerantola.[107] In Taranto, a total of thirty individuals—including owners and managers—of ILVA, the largest European steel plant, are under investigation for the death of 15 employees.[108] Thirty individuals are under investigation.

Asbestos prosecutions, while preferred to and overall more successful than civil litigation, also come with failures. Asbestos defendants who are indicted and then tried have often been acquitted. It is often a matter of proof of *mens rea*. Ordinarily, criminal courts are more liberal than civil courts in weighing evidence of causation-in-fact. However, courts are often dissatisfied with regard to proof of criminal intent or negligence. This is in part due to the fact that criminal liability is individual and therefore prosecutors must establish specific instances of misconduct that can be criminally linked to each defendant. Moreover, the statute of limitation runs independently for each defendant. Consequently, prosecuting managers who led the company in the 1960s and 1970s is arduous because

---

105   Statement by Bruno Papignani in Luciano Nigro. "Un processo che non s'è arenato la sentenza è un monito per tutti [A trial that did not stop is a warning for everybody]." Ibid. Published electronically November 23, 2004.

106   "Amianto, condannati cinque dirigenti FS [Asbestos, five railroad executives found guilty]." *Corriere della Sera (Bologna)*. Published electronically March 13, 2009. http://corrieredibologna.corriere.it/bologna/notizie/cronaca/2009/13-marzo-2009/amianto-condannati-cinque-dirigenti-fs-1501085490317.shtml.

107   "Morte da amianto, solo due colpevoli [An asbestos death, only two defendants guilty]." Published electronically June 10, 2009. http://www.cartiglianonews.it/rassegna-stampa/morte-da-amianto-solo-due-colpevoli.

108   Mimmo Mazza. "Taranto, 30 indagati per i morti all'ILVA [Taranto, 30 people under investigations for deaths at ILVA]." *La Gazzetta del Mezzogiorno*. Published electronically May 25, 2011. http://www.lagazzettadelmezzogiorno.it/notizia.php?IDNotizia=429364.

gathering and presenting incriminating evidence for past decades is difficult (making criminal prosecution challenging), because managers have often died (making criminal prosecution impossible), and because the statute of limitations might have expired for some deaths and some managers (making criminal prosecution vacuous). As a general trend, proof of culpability is more accessible with regard to plant managers and it is much harder with regard to directors of the company that owns the plant—and even more with regard to executives and directors of the parent company. Some of these asbestos firms brought to the bar are large companies or conglomerates. Breda is a case in point. Founded in 1886, this company has manufactured locomotives, railway machinery, armaments, and aircraft for decades in the Milano metropolitan area and in Pistoia near Florence, Tuscany, and has been involved with the shipbuilding industry in Monfalcone. Various managers have been tried in courts in all three cities. The verdicts are inconsistent: managers were sometimes convicted and other times acquitted. Throughout the years, acquittals protected managers of several large companies.

## Asbestos personal injury litigation fragmentation

The picture that emerges after twenty years of asbestos litigation is a fragmented one. Asbestos personal injury litigation has never routinized, it has not reached maturity. Maturity of mass torts is a concept developed by Professor Francis McGovern in the 1980s to frame the stage in which litigation involving consistent personal injury claims becomes routinized.[109] Maturity entails some predictability and consistency in claiming patterns and ways in which victims, defendants, and courts approach litigation. This has not happened in Italy where the asbestos litigation has been fragmented since its emergence.

As discussed in the previous pages of this chapter, fragmentation is the product of multiple factors, including the rigid divide in treatment of victims of occupational exposure and non-occupational exposure, the coexistence of different paths to compensation, the civil and the criminal, the removal from the tort system of occupational exposure victims' actions based on the loss of bodily integrity, which had been instrumental in the rise of asbestos litigation, civil courts' deployment of doctrines and statutory interpretations unfriendly to plaintiffs, the varying degrees of expertise and willingness on part of prosecutors' offices to investigate and try defendants for asbestos crimes, and the ever-changing nature of the welfare system, which ultimately provides the bulk of compensation to Italian asbestos victims.

The fragmentation is such that a full picture of how many cases have been tried is difficult to patch together. There are no statistics or official data on the number of asbestos cases filed each year and of their distribution among civil and criminal

---

109   Francis E. McGovern, "Resolving Mature Mass Tort Litigation," *Boston University Law Review* 69 (1989).

proceedings. In 2009, Beniamino Deidda, a well-known prosecutor, tried to gather this data and provided this account of his efforts:

> With regard to criminal trials, any in depth analysis is undermined by the fact that knowing how many proceedings are pending is almost impossible. Nobody can tell with sufficient reliability how many asbestos criminal cases are tried every year in Italy. I personally tried to gather some data by inquiry with various District Attorneys and Chief Judges at several district courts about pending criminal proceedings involving deaths or diseases caused by exposure to asbestos and their reaction, as I experienced it, was of surprise at the idea that somebody would ask for these data.[110]

Deidda also adds that "one can only say, as a general statement, that criminal proceedings are very infrequent and certainly must less frequent that the instances of mesothelioma or lung cancer that kill workers." Empirical data shows that not all instances of asbestos disease are mobilized and result in a claim for damages; that, when claims are mobilized, criminal trials are both favored over civil lawsuits; and that civil claim joined to criminal trials are more likely to lead victims' compensation than civil lawsuits. A review of opinions in asbestos criminal trials in which civil claims were joined, published between 1992 and 2010, indicates that verdicts have been issued in at least 30 trials, that the courts of appeal issued at least 20 opinions and that the highest court issued 21 opinions.

Occasionally, victims bring civil lawsuits for damages against the employer. The interviews reveal than in the majority of these cases the decision to sue in a civil court is heavily influenced by the expertise of the attorney representing the victims. These attorneys are usually experts in labor law and cases are referred to them by unions. The cases are usually victims who had sought the help of unions to recover the pension multiplier and workers' compensation benefits and were denied coverage. They are then referred by unions to attorneys who have stable professional links and have developed an expertise in dealing with labor disputes. The fact that the Civil Code shifts the burden of proof to the defendant seems to be immaterial with reference to the choice to file in a civil court rather than a criminal court. In fact, the Civil Code provides that, in breach of contract cases— damages claims for a disease caused by occupational exposure to asbestos dust are usually tried simultaneously as breach of contract and tort cases[111]—the breaching party must be found liable unless he or she proves that the breach or delay was

---

110 Beniamino Deidda. "Il fondo per il risarcimento delle vittime dell'amianto: opportunità, necessità, prospettive [The Asbestos Victims Compensation Fund: opportunities, needs, perspectives]." Published electronically April 10, 2009. http://olympus.uniurb.it/index.php?option=com_content&view=article&id=2807:2009-deidda-beniamino-fondo-per-le-vittime-da-amianto-in-italia&catid=29:approfondimenti-tematici&Itemid=40.
111 *Codice Civile [Civil Code]*. 1942, sec. 2087 (Italy).

caused by impossibility to perform with no fault on his or her part.[112] Overall, the professional background and the strong tie to unions are the primary determinants affecting victims' decision to work with a prosecutor to bring criminal charges and eventually join in the claim for civil damages rather than investigating and trying a tort case in civil court.

The major losers of asbestos litigation are victims of non-occupational exposure cases. The great majority of cases discussed so far involve claims brought by victims of occupational exposure, whether or not the recipient of workers' compensation payments. Victims of non-occupational exposure have had much tougher times than other victims. These cases have been rarely successful. Weak mobilization is in part to be blamed. Non-occupational exposure cases have been considered for a long time as second-class citizens, and understandably so. Prosecutors pushed further occupational exposure cases because these cases are relatively easier to investigate and try, and have higher chances of success. The criminal negligence link between an employer's conduct and the employee's disease is easier to prove that the link between the owner of an asbestos site and a bystander's disease. Labor unions have also pushed occupational exposure cases in the political process as well as the legal process: unions have no direct vested interest in representing these claimants and coordination among the claimants is not easy to achieve. Furthermore, many of the asbestos lawyers have strong professional ties with labor unions and therefore have often followed the client's "wisdom," which entailed advancing occupational cases rather than the other cases.

The legal consciousness of non-occupational exposure victims has been less oriented towards seeking compensation. Occupational exposure captured for years collective consciousness of asbestos disease. Asbestos workers became ill before other victims, and found support in activists and unions since the early days of asbestos compensation. Non-occupational exposure cases often strike among relatives of these workers, who were the breadwinners, which meant that the need to secure compensation for their diseases was more immediate than in the case of other victims. The realization that asbestos could strike also those who had nothing to do with it and had lived all of their lives outside the perimeters of asbestos factories and mines also came late. Epidemiologists focused for many years on cohorts of workers, unions promoted workers' compensation, and lawyers, often paid by unions, were more willing to represent asbestos workers than other victims.

Slowly, throughout the years, victims of environmental exposure and secondhand exposure found their sponsors in activists' groups. For instance, the victims' support group in Casale advocated compensation for all victims since its early days. *Medicina Democratica*, an activists' group from the radical left, which had advocated stronger workers' health and safety protection since the early 1970s, often in attrition with national labor unions, pushed compensation for all victims

---

112   Ibid., sec. 1218.

of asbestos exposure. However, their efforts have had a more limited impact than support of occupational disease cases. The (few) cases that have been litigated, are in the end somehow connected to occupational cases. Many litigated cases were brought by relatives of asbestos workers, who had been themselves claimants or beneficiaries of asbestos compensation. Successful non-occupational cases are often linked with occupational exposure cases. The case of the wife of a railroad worker illustrates the point. The woman was diagnosed with a mesothelioma and the only meaningful exposure that she could identify was the exposure to asbestos fibers on her husband's clothes at the time he would come home at the end of a shift at the factory or at the time she handled them to wash them. Her mesothelioma claim was filed and aggregated with claims brought by various railroad workers against their employer. The procedural strategy was effective and she recovered damages from the husband's employer based on the argument that the employer had negligently failed to take all necessary precautions to prevent innocent victims from being exposed to asbestos. The fact that the woman had never set foot at the husband's workplace was immaterial to the court.[113]

This case shows that liability for secondhand exposure has been occasionally recognized by courts. However cases have not been routinized, and their legal fate is becoming more problematic as disease keeps rising among these victims and courts' attention is primarily allocated to occupational exposure victims. Over the years, several bills have been introduced aiming to make compensation available to all victims, including victims of non-occupational exposure, on a no fault basis.[114] However, in establishing the Asbestos Victims' Fund, Parliament decided to limit no fault compensation to victims of occupational exposure, even if the language of the proposed bill asked compensation for the benefit of "citizens affected by disease associated with asbestos exposure." The proponents of the bill aimed to make compensation available to victims who were ineligible under workers' compensation and were facing a hard time in courts. Parliament approved the bill in a modified version, leaving victims of non-occupational exposure out.

While a legislative solution is unlikely, non-occupational exposure victims have nonetheless reason for hope. A clear success, which may ease access barriers to tort compensation, comes from the Eternit trial. Defendants were convicted for disease suffered, in addition to thousands of asbestos workers, by 261 victims of environmental exposure and six victims of secondhand exposure. The case was tried as a "criminal disaster" case. The precise boundaries of the elements of the crime of "disaster" are controversial. The Criminal Code fails to expressly define what "disaster" means.[115] Courts have construed "disaster" as an event or series

---

113 *Sentenza [Opinion] n. 5037/00*, Camposano (Corte di Cassazione [Highest Court], March 30, 2000) (Italy). See also Raffaele Guariniello, "Dai tumori professionali ai tumori extraprofessionali da amianto [From occupational to non-occupational asbestos cancers]," *Foro Italiano* 126, no. 5 (2001).

114 Senato della Repubblica Italiana. *Proposta di legge [Bill]*, n. 23/2006.

115 *Codice Penale [Criminal Code]*. 1930, sec. 434 (Italy).

of events creating a risk of harm for an undetermined number of members of a protected class of individuals.[116] Taking the more liberal interpretation of the letter of the law, Mr. Guariniello successfully argued that any innocent bystander is included in the protected class and that defendants' duty not to harm was breached by letting asbestos dust spread beyond the perimeters of the manufacturing facility. Eternit executives were then found liable of criminal disaster by the extent to which they put at risk of developing as asbestos disease an undetermined number of individuals, which was comprised of those who had worked in the plants, had lived in proximity of the plants, or had lived under the same roof as plant workers.[117] If upheld by Italy's highest court, the *Corte di Cassazione*, the legal conclusion of the trial court will offer the doctrinal support needed by victims of non-occupational exposure to win more cases on a regular basis.

116   *Sentenza [Opinion] n. 19342/07*, Rubiero et al. (Corte di Cassazione [Highest Court], February 20, 2007) (Italy).
117   *Schmidheiny and De Cartier De Marchienne, Case 24265/04.*

# Chapter 5
# Asbestos compensation in the United States

Asbestos compensation in the United States is highly controversial. Compensation is delivered to asbestos victims primarily by deployment of litigation. Thousands of claims have been filed year after year since courts established that asbestos victims had viable personal injury claims under product liability theories in the early 1970s.[1] By 1999, the US Supreme Court called asbestos litigation "an elephantine mass [that] defies customary judicial administration and calls for national legislation."

Initially, victims only obtained compensation in the form from workers' compensation benefits or money paid out of confidential settlements with large asbestos manufacturers. In 1973 asbestos litigation took a turn when courts recognized the viability under product liability law of asbestos personal injury claims against asbestos manufacturers. This second wave of asbestos litigation targeted leading manufacturers of asbestos insulation materials, including industry titan Johns-Manville and ended when all major defendants had disappeared after filing for bankruptcy. The litigation however did not stop. New targets were found in firms that had manufactured, distributed, sold, or applied any products containing asbestos. As defendants crumbled under the pressure of the heave number of cases filed against them, asbestos victims found news litigation targets in firms that manufactured boilers, pumps, valves, automobiles that incorporated components that contained asbestos. Litigation also targeted owners of industrial facilities that had products containing asbestos in their manufacturing plants and employers whose workers brought asbestos into the home thus causing household exposure.

As the various waves of litigation were coming and going, legislative and other attempts to establish alternative compensation paths that would stop filings of traditional personal injury cases have been unsuccessfully tried for decades. Congress examined a number of bills barring asbestos claims and offering administrative compensation to asbestos victims. None of these bills became law. Although state workers' compensation systems pay out asbestos victims (and many victims do claim these benefits), the bulk of compensation comes from personal injury cases that are either settled out of court or reach a verdict as well as payments made by the various bankruptcy trusts that have been set up by bankrupt asbestos defendants and are endowed with substantial reserves to allegedly compensate victims/creditors for the foreseeable future. In this chapter I discuss

---

1 *Borel v. Fibreboard Paper Prods Corp.*, 493 F.2d 1076 (5th Cir. 1973), cert. denied, 419 U.S. 869 (1974) (USA).

the use of asbestos in the United States, the emergence of asbestos compensation and its developments, with particular attention to the various waves of litigation and the controversy that they generated.

## Asbestos use and disease epidemic in the United States

Asbestos was extensively mined in the United States. One of the chrysotile asbestos mines was located near Coalinga, California (now a US EPA Superfund reclamation area). The world's largest vermiculite mine was located near the town of Libby, Montana. The mine opened in 1923, and was owned and operated by the W.R. Grace & Company from 1963 until it closed in 1990. Finally, the Great Valley of California hosted at least 26 asbestos mines or asbestos prospects.[2] Asbestos was also easily imported from neighboring Canada.

The consumption of asbestos in the United States has been massive. With over 20 million tons, its cumulative use between 1920 and 1970 is the highest of the world: four times more than the United Kingdom, 10 times more than Italy, and 20 times more than Belgium.[3] Interestingly for the purpose of comparative analysis, the historical use pattern of the United States differed from that of other countries.

> The United States recorded the earliest and maximal peak use at 4.2 kg per capita/ year in 1950, followed by progressive reduction over four decades and approaching 0.02 kg per capita/year in 2003, equating to a reduction rate of −1.9%/year.[4]

Asbestos use grew significantly in the 1940s due to the need to build ships and submarines to be deployed in World War II. This wave of asbestos consumption caused disease among Navy soldiers and shipbuilding workers. Cities with large ports were major asbestos consumption sites. The incidence of pleural mesothelioma among white males residing in Seattle, San Francisco-Oakland, and Hawaii was higher than other parts of the country. Asbestos use continued to grow in the aftermath of the war. Nishikawa and colleagues add that the "'bubble' in asbestos use occurred in the mid-twentieth century because of early manufacturing research, industrial demand, and ready supply from Canada."[5] During these years asbestos was installed in America's homes, offices, post offices, and schools.

These are golden years for manufacturers of insulating products containing asbestos. The major player in this industry was Johns-Manville. The largest asbestos

---

2　Ross and Nolan, "History of asbestos discovery and use and asbestos-related disease in context with the occurrence of asbestos within ophiolite complexes."

3　Eun-Kee Park et al., "Global Magnitude of Reported and Unreported Mesothelioma," *Environmental Health Perspectives* 119, no. 4 (2011).

4　Kunihito Nishikawa et al., "Recent mortality from pleural mesothelioma, historical patterns of asbestos use, and adoption of bans: a global assessment," ibid.116, no. 12 (2008).

5　Ibid.

firm in the United States and one of the major asbestos companies at the global level, Johns-Manville was established in 1858 by entrepreneur Henry Ward Johns, who at that time was 21 years old. Henry Ward Johns, who was starting up a roofing business, began creating roofing products with asbestos that he had found in deposits in Staten Island, New York, The products become a success. In 1881 Scientific American profiled the products and by 1990s Henry Ward Johns had entered into an agreement with the Manville Covering Company, which distributed the products in the Midwest. In 1901, three years after Henry Ward Johns's death in 1898, the two businesses were merged and Johns-Manville was born.[6] Its major manufacturing plant was located in New Jersey in the town of Manville, which was formed by an act of the New Jersey Legislature in 1929 and named after the company that brought jobs to the community. Throughout the years, the firm expanded the range of its products by manufacturing asbestos textiles, roofing, and insulation materials.

After World War II, its profits grew significantly. The company stopped producing products containing asbestos only after the growing number of lawsuits forced the company to file for bankruptcy on August 26, 1982. It did so reluctantly since only two years before its CEO had told Forbes Magazine that "[t]he day asbestos isn't good business for us, we'll get out of it."[7] With all asbestos liabilities transferred to the Manville Personal Injury Settlement Trust, the firm emerged from bankruptcy in 1988. Its business, which was reoriented towards commercial and industrial fiberglass insulation and roofing systems during the bankruptcy, was acquired by Warren Buffet's Berkshire Hathaway in 2001.

In the twentieth century, other firms manufactured asbestos in the United States: Raybestos-Manhattan (a leader in asbestos friction products and textiles), Owens-Illinois and its successor Owens-Corning Fiberglass (manufacturers of Kaylo, a pink insulation material made of asbestos and quartz mixed together), Unarco and its successor Pittsburg Corning (manufacturers of Unibestos, an insulating material that contained amosite fibers extracted in South Africa and supplied by Cape Asbestos), United States Gypsum (manufacturer of insulating materials), Southern Textile and its corporate successors Thermoid and H.K. Porter (manufacturers of asbestos-cement), Eagle Picher (manufacturer of asbestos-cement), and W.R. Grace & Company. This last company, also (in)famous for its role in the Woburn contamination case on which the 1996 non-fiction novel by Jonathan Harr *A Civil Action* is based,[8] acquired an asbestos brake lining business in 1954 and the Libby vermiculite mines, the largest in the world, in 1964.[9]

---

6  "Johns-Manville: from a Basement To a Multi-Billion Dollar Business," *The Telegraph*, February 4, 1978.

7  Kalanik, Lynn M., Mary McNulty, and Christina M. Stansell, "Johns Manville Corporation," in *International Directory of Company Histories*, ed. Tina Grant and Miranda H. Ferrara, Vol. 64, 209-214 (Detroit: St. James Press, 2005).

8  Jonathan Harr, *A civil action*, 1st ed. (New York: Vintage Books, 1996).

9  For a full account of the asbestos industry in the United States, see Castleman, *Asbestos: medical and legal aspects*.

## The first wave of litigation

The first wave of asbestos litigation involved asbestos workers filing workers' compensation claims and receiving money by the way of occasional settlements with asbestos manufacturers. Asbestos workers started getting sick in the late 1920s. This wave of asbestos disease, the first one, occurred in other industrialized nations (particularly in England) in which asbestos had been extensively used since the late nineteenth century. In 1929, the widow of a Johns-Manville's employee and mother of six began legal proceedings in federal courts in New Jersey seeking damages for the asbestosis that killed her husband.[10] This case, *Pauline Lasin v. Johns-Manville Corporation*, is the first personal injury case for an asbestos disease recorded in the United States. The case never went to trial though as Ms. Lasin abandoned the case.

The industry's reaction to the emergence of asbestos victims' claiming was twofold. First, companies put pressure on plaintiffs to abandon the litigation or, if pressure was ineffective, to settle the cases with confidential awards. In 1933, Johns-Manville settled cases involving 11 employees with asbestosis. Fearing the settlement could fuel more litigation, the company settled on the condition that their attorney would never "directly or indirectly participate in the bringing of new actions against the Corporation."[11] Johns-Manville was not the only target of litigation. In the 1940s, Unarco paid off the widow of a former employee who had died of mesothelioma. Raybestos-Manhattan, on the other hand, paid compensation to employees for disability from asbestosis since the 1930s, from carcinoma since the 1950s, and from mesothelioma since the 1960s. Overall, this strategy successfully contributed to asbestos companies' efforts in limiting their liability exposure. John Fabian Witt noted that very few cases reached large monetary awards or settlements: "With rare exceptions, settlement and judgement values appear to have remained low or medium-sized."[12] Witt's research reveals that the largest asbestos verdict of this wave of litigation was rendered in *Jacque vs. Lock Insulator Corporation*. The award amounted to USD 15,000. However the Second Circuit reversed it on appeal.[13]

Second, the engagement in a campaign of suppression of evidence of asbestos toxicity and of dissemination of questionable studies that disproved asbestos dangers. Along with Raybestos-Manhattan, a leader in asbestos friction products and textiles, Johns-Manville executives edited an article about the diseases of asbestos workers written by Anthony Lanza, a doctor at Metropolitan Life

---

10 McCulloch and Tweedale, *Defending the indefensible: The global asbestos industry and its fight for survival*.

11 Brodeur, *Outrageous misconduct: the asbestos industry on trial*.

12 John Fabian Witt, "US asbestos and silica litigation in the 1930s," in *Asbestos. Anatomy of a Mass Tort*, ed. Munich Re (München: Münchener Rückversicherungs-Gesellschaft, 2009).

13 *Jacque v. Locke Insulator Corp.*, 70 F.2d 680 (2nd Cir. 1934).

Insurance Company, and instructed the editor of the magazine *Asbestos* to publish nothing about asbestosis.[14] Indeed, the most effective way to contrast the growing body of medical evidence was to gain control of the production of scientific knowledge itself. To this end, Johns-Manville along with other asbestos firms established the Trudeau Foundation's Saranac Laboratory in Saranac, NY, for the purpose of studying the health effects of asbestos dust. Research at Saranac led to important discoveries. In 1942, its director Leroy Gardner discovered that white mice exposed to asbestos experienced excessive incidence (81.8 percent) of malignant tumors of the lungs.[15] However, Gardner was not able to publish his findings right away. For years, the firms behind the Saranac Laboratory, which stopped funding research on the link between asbestos and lung cancer, withheld their consent to publication.[16] The findings were published only in 1951 in redacted form that contained no reference to cancer. In the 1950s and 1960s other companies contributed to the cover up. These firms, which included Armstrong Cock, Fibreboard, Ruberoid and its successor GAF, and Philip Carey Manufacturing and its successor Celotex, become concerned with their asbestos liabilities as an increasing number of workers were becoming sick and filed workers' compensation claims.

The most significant help to minimize exposure to asbestos liabilities came from state legislatures. Encouraged by asbestos companies' lobbying efforts, most states expanded the exclusive remedy provisions of workers' compensation statutes to include industrial diseases such as asbestosis and silicosis. Workers' compensation put an end to the first wave of asbestos litigation. In fact victims were no longer able to bring a claim for damages under common law. For three decades the exclusive source of compensation would be workers' compensation.

### The second wave of litigation

Since the late 1930s, victims could only claim exclusively workers' compensation benefit since state laws barred common law claims against the employer. However, towards the late 1960s, a second wave of asbestos cases hit the courts as a consequence of how the asbestos epidemic had developed and of changes in the legal environment of asbestos compensation. A new wave of asbestos disease and the publication of evidence that strengthened our understanding of asbestos toxicity changed the counters of the asbestos epidemic. In the 1960s asbestos, the consumption of which had reached its peak in the 1950s, was causing more deaths that ever before. Victims were increasingly counted among veterans who had been

---

14   Brodeur, *Outrageous misconduct: the asbestos industry on trial.*

15   Tweedale, "Asbestos and its lethal legacy."

16   Gerrit W. H. Schepers, "Chronology of asbestos cancer discoveries: Experimental studies of the Saranac laboratory," *American Journal of Industrial Medicine* 27, no. 4 (1995).

exposed to asbestos while serving the military in World War II. Furthermore, new medical studies reinforced the notion that asbestos was linked to various diseases. The publication of epidemiological studies in particular contributed to asbestos disease awareness among medical professionals and beyond. In New York, Selikoff and colleagues conducted research that changed our perception of asbestos.

Beginning in the early 1960s, with financial support from sources as diverse as the insulation workers' union and (from 1968) the Johns-Manville Corporation, Selikoff and his colleagues produced a stream of publications indicating, among other things, that insulators who worked with asbestos material in the USA faced an "important risk" of contracting asbestosis, lung cancer or mesothelioma, and possibly also gastrointestinal cancer.[17]

Parallel to these changes in the asbestos epidemic, significant changes had also taken place in legal culture. The most important innovation was the gradual emergence of product liability in courts. Since Cardozo's path-breaking opinion in *MacPherson v. Buick Motor Co.* in 1916,[18] courts throughout the country had recognized innovative new paths to tort compensation that eroded contractual privity, the lack of express warranties, and the requirement to establish negligence and other obstacles that had traditionally barred recovery at common law. These changes were eventually captured in Section 402A of the second edition of the American law Institute's *Second Restatement of the Law of Torts*:

> One who sells any product in a defective condition unreasonably dangerous to the user or consumer or to his property is subject to liability for physical harm thereby caused to the ultimate user or consumer, or to his property, if (a) the seller is engaged in the business of selling such a product, and (b) it is expected to and does reach the user or consumer without substantial change in the condition in which it is sold.[19]

The revolutionary idea that liability followed a defective product rather than privity of duty of care offered creative opportunities to pursue compensation beyond the narrow confines of workers' compensation. This opportunity was soon grabbed by attorneys engaged in representing the new wave of asbestos victims who pioneered a new litigation strategy—suing asbestos manufacturers as third party producers of a defective product. The first case that successfully established the viability of such claims is *Borel v. Fibreboard Paper Products Corporation*. Clarence Borel, who had worked for over thirty years as an insulator of steam pipes, boilers, and other devices in shipyards and oil refineries, was diagnosed with mesothelioma, asbestosis, and pneumonia at the age of 57. A father of six, Borel, when alive, received approximately USD 13,000 after settling his workers'

---

17 Peter W.J. Bartrip, "History of asbestos related disease," *Postgraduate Medical Journal* 80, no. 940 (2004).

18 *MacPherson v. Buick Motor Co.*, 271 N.Y. 382 (N.Y. 1916) (USA).

19 *Restatement (Second) of Torts (1965)* (USA).

compensation claim. After receiving the settlement money and realizing that it was not sufficient to pay for his medical bills and provide for his family, Borel approached Ward Stephenson, a Texas trial lawyer who had recently settled a case on behalf of another pipe insulator and who agreed to represent Borel on a contingency fee basis. Stephenson filed a complaint in federal court for the Eastern District of Texas capitalizing on the recent adoption on part of Texas of section 402A. The case was brought in strict liability under the theory that Fibreboard had failed to warn Borel of asbestos toxicity. The jury returned a verdict in the amount of USD 79,436.24 in favor of Borel thus holding an asbestos manufacturer liable under product liability for the first time in American history. The defendant appealed the verdict and hired tort expert W. Page Keeton, who was the dean of the University of Texas School of Law and became one of the architects of Section 402A, to brief and argue the case. Keeton's advocacy however did not change anything: on September 10, 1973, the Fifth Circuit upheld the verdict and kicked off the second wave of asbestos personal injury litigation.[20]

The Fifth Circuit's opinion did not go unnoticed. The large number of victims becoming ill and approaching lawyers for legal advice as well as a litigation environment that was ripe of opportunities for plaintiff lawyers to start lucrative practices on behalf of injured consumers created a fertile context for law firms to develop asbestos practices. Law firms in Texas and elsewhere in the country followed the litigation template inaugurated by Stephenson and successfully extended *Borel* principles to many other jurisdictions. Many of these lawyers had already been involved with representing asbestos victims in front of workers' compensation boards and administrative judges and expanded their practices to personal injury litigation. Other firms, already specializing in personal injury cases, received referrals from workers' compensation attorneys.

During the first years of post-*Borel* litigation defendants were however able to raise defenses to liability. The strongest was the "state of the art" defense. Under this doctrine, defendants are not required to possess information that goes beyond state of the art knowledge. Asbestos firms raised the defense by claiming that they were unaware of studies demonstrating asbestos toxicity before Selikoff's publication. The defense did not stand the test of time. In the course of discovery in a case against Raybestos-Manhattan, correspondence between the president of Raybestos and asbestos executives at other firms showed that companies had engaged in a cover up of asbestos toxicity since the 1930s. These papers, collectively known as the "Sumner Simpson Papers," put an end to the state of the art defense and allowed asbestos litigation to reach its maturity.

The *Borel* opinion established the principle that asbestos was a defective product and that firms in the business of marketing it were strictly liable for harm caused by exposure to it. Its holding, formally sanctioning the viability of personal injury claims against asbestos manufacturer, constituted the foundation of asbestos

---

20   *Borel v. Fibreboard Paper Prods Corp.*

personal injury litigation for the years to come, which reached its maturity in the 1980s.

Judicial opinions alone do not mobilize claims. Unions and medical professionals were instrumental in the growth and routinization of asbestos litigation. As Durkin demonstrates in his thorough research on asbestos litigation in the early 1990s, in the path to naming, medical research—epidemiologists in particular—used their resources in a particularly powerful and effective manner. Researchers activated their "weak ties lining them to the victims by way of asbestos worker unions. They contacted affected unions directly, persuading union officials to participate in the research."[21] Unions effectively contributed by the growth of litigation by using their networks to distribute and favor sharing of information between doctors, lawyers, and victims. Unions' endorsement made naming information "more trustworthy."[22] In contrast to asbestos litigation in Europe, unions rarely became involved with claiming. They did fund litigation—US lawyers pushed cases ahead by relying on contingency fee agreements and self-funding—and thus they played no role in claiming gatekeeping, litigation strategies, or settlement offers.

Victim support groups played a less prominent role in the United States. In the first years of asbestos litigation, the bulk of the victims secured legal representation by way of networking among lawyers, unions, and medical professionals. As the litigation progressed, plaintiff law firms established asbestos law practices, which directly attracted clients. Victims who were "desperate," as Durkin refers to them, for the most part widows of victims who fell outside the unions/lawyers/doctors complex, created support groups to help other victims in their attempts to receive compensation.[23]

The result was a wave of personal injury cases—the second wave of litigation—targeting leading manufacturers of asbestos insulation materials, including industry titan Johns-Manville. In the 1970s, about 950 cases were filed in federal courts alone.[24] In the mid-1980s, the authors of the first RAND study on asbestos litigation indicated that approximately 30,000 asbestos personal injury suits had been commenced and that these cases made up between 10 to 20 percent of the docket of civil cases in the United States. USD 1 billion had been spent for compensation and litigation expenses.[25] By 1991, the cases numbered 115,000.[26] During the 1980s asbestos litigation underwent a drastic transformation from pioneering litigation to a mature yet contested mass tort.

---

21   Durkin, "Constructing law: comparing legal action in the United States and United Kingdom," 74.

22   Ibid., 85.

23   Ibid., 89.

24   Paul D. Carrington, "Asbestos Lessons: The Unattended Consequences of Asbestos Litigation," *The Review of Litigation* 26, no. 3 (2007): 589.

25   Hensler et al., *Asbestos in the Courts. The Challenge of Mass Toxic Torts.*

26   Suzanne L. Oliver and Leslie Spencer, "Who Will the Monster Devour Next?," *Forbes Magazine*, February 18, 1991, 75.

## The maturity of asbestos litigation

Maturity of mass torts is a concept developed by Professor Francis McGovern in the 1980s to frame the stage in which a litigation involving consistent personal injury claims becomes routinized.[27] McGovern is a proponent of maturity as a prerequisite of courts' use of collective procedures to resolve the mass tort. Whether or not maturity should be used as proposed by McGovern, the concept is helpful in analyzing asbestos litigation. In fact McGovern uses asbestos litigation as an example of a mass tort litigation that reached maturity. Peter Schuck summarizes the point as follows:

> In its early years, asbestos litigation was so fragmented, chaotic, costly, and unpredictable that it resembled an unruly, erratic adolescent. During that period, relatively few asbestos cases went to trial, but those that did, coupled with the numerous settlements, created patterns that the lawyers discerned and used. Asbestos litigation crossed a kind of developmental threshold in the early 1990s; thereafter cases could be resolved more readily in a more systematic, inexpensive, predictable—and therefore equitable-fashion.[28]

What factors contributed to the maturity of asbestos litigation and what were its traits as a mature mass tort? Law firms' specialization and coordination as well as judicial management of the caseload contributed to the high volume of lawsuits.

Lawyers found effective ways to specialize, expand their client base, litigate cases in victim-friendly jurisdictions,[29] and maximize revenues by settling cases without overburdening firms' infrastructure. Forum shopping practices allowed a limited number of law firms to dominate asbestos litigation and concentrate claims to victim-friendly jurisdictions. Three or four firms handled most cases in each litigation-friendly jurisdiction. Over the years, plaintiff firms with most clients have been particularly creative in finding new, more aggressive strategies in stretching the boundaries of asbestos litigation to include within the scope of compensation individuals who had been exposed to asbestos but were not sick and to force companies with minimal involvement with asbestos to share liability. With regard to the first aspect of asbestos compensation expansion, some of the plaintiff firms used litigation screening to recruit as many clients as possible.[30] This practice

---

27　McGovern, "Resolving Mature Mass Tort Litigation."

28　Peter H. Schuck, "Mass Torts: An Institutional Evolutionist Perspective," *Cornell Law Review* 80 (1995): 949-950.

29　Mesothelioma cases are referred to as "portable." See Asbestos Liability Risk Analysis Group. "Asbestos Claims and Litigation: Update and Review: 2011 New Case Filing: Summary and Analysis," 1-11. Published electronically October 15, 2012. http://www.alragroup.com/documents/Asbestos_paper_2012.pdf.

30　Lester Brickman, *Lawyer barons: what their contingency fees really cost America* (New York: Cambridge University Press, 2011), 117-119.

is highly contentious, and has eventually been curbed by courts through structural stratagems such as inactive or non-impaired dockets.[31] Professor Brickman, a very vocal critic of this practice, summarizes it with these words:

> Entrepreneurial screening companies have been hired by lawyers to seek out persons with occupational exposure to dusts such as those containing crystalline silica or asbestos. Mobile X-ray vans are brought to local union halls, motels, or strip mall parking lots where X-rays are taken on an assembly line rate of one every five to ten minutes. In addition to the X-rays, most screening companies also administer pulmonary function tests (PFTs) to determine lung impairment for the sole purpose of generating evidence for litigation purposes.[32]

This practice contributed to the creation of long inventories of asbestos victims. These inventories would be mobilized by mass filing of claims involving a mix of a few impaired and a large number of "exposure-only" cases, that is, claims based on the possibility of developing a disease as a result of exposure to asbestos rather than an actual bodily injury caused by asbestos exposure. Facing the risk of losing the few impaired claims, defendants often opted for settling all claims, thus reinforcing the practice of litigation screening and victim inventories. Among the critiques launched against this practice, two strands are particularly compelling. The first strand of critiques revolves around the fact that these screenings might have generated a multitude of falsely positive results and that defendants have been unable to expose and challenge false positives because plaintiff lawyers refuse to disclose these data, in some cases by refusing to comply with discovery orders compelling their disclosure.[33] The second strand of critiques focuses on questions of equity: assuming that asbestos funds available for compensation are limited, is it fair for victims of asbestos exposure with no medical conditions to subtract these limited resources from victims who are sick, often with deadly forms of cancer? The issue of equity in distribution are particularly compelling to the point that it has divided the plaintiff bar by splitting firms among those who represent both kinds of clients and those who focus on sick asbestos victims.[34]

Whether ethically defensible or not, litigation screening changed the face of asbestos litigation. The issue is not unique to the United States but the relatively low barrier to access the court system and approaching defendants for settlement

---

31   Asbestos Liability Risk Analysis Group, "Asbestos Claims and Litigation: Update and Review: 2011 New Case Filing: Summary and Analysis."

32   Lester Brickman, "Written Statement Filed at the Hearing on How Fraud and Abuse in the Asbestos Compensation System Affect Victims, Jobs, the Economy and the Legal System Held Before The Subcommittee On The Constitution Of The U.S. House Of Representatives Committee On The Judiciary" (2011), 8.

33   Ibid., 14.

34   Francis E. McGovern, "The Tragedy of the Asbestos Commons," *Virginia Law Review* 88, no. 8 (2002): 1749.

negotiations have heightened the problematic nature of these cases. The Manville Trust, as we will see shortly, has been one of the victims of litigation screenings: in 2002, Steven Kazan, a renowned plaintiff lawyer who belongs to the group of firms that has not represented exposure-only victims, reported in a 2002 letter to judges Weinstein and Lifland that "90% of the Trust's last 200,000 claims have come from attorney-sponsored X-ray screening programs ... 91% of all claims [against the Trust] allege only non-malignant asbestos 'disease,' and ... these cases currently receive 76% of all Trust's funds."[35] Over time, the critiques of this practice have found their way in the litigation process, and courts have reacted by establishing institutional barriers directed towards reducing the flow of less meritorious claims. One such barrier is to list exposure-only claims in a deferral docket. Their inclusion in the list preserves the claim against the running of the statute of limitations but postpones the trial at an uncertain future date upon the victim developing some impairment due to asbestos exposure. Another example is represented by the implementation of an inactive asbestos docket: exposure-only cases are added to the inactive docket upon dismissal without prejudice by agreement of the parties, meaning that the case can be re-filed and the defendant cannot raise the statute of limitations defense.

Courts' efficient management of this wave of cases had the unintended effect of contributing the claiming rates' growth. Procedures for handling heavy dockets were streamlined, cases consolidated, and asbestos dockets assigned to single judges who would adjudicate asbestos cases on a full time basis thus developing expertise in how to push the process ahead and speed up litigation. A well-known example of court management of asbestos litigation is the transfer in 1991 of all asbestos personal injury cases to the Eastern District of Pennsylvania ordered by the Judicial Panel on Multidistrict Litigation.[36] By 2008, MDL875 had collected claims of about 110,000 plaintiffs, each of whom had sued, on average, over 50 defendants.[37] In the same year, more than 10,000 of those 110,000 cases were still pending.[38] These judicial management strategies, which were primarily designed for courts to survive with limited resources in the face of high volume litigation, ultimately had the unintended consequence of favoring asbestos plaintiffs in courts.

The defense side also contributed to the growth of asbestos litigation in a mature mass tort primarily by failing to coordinate any litigation strategy. McGovern argues that the lack of cooperation has been a "major factor" in the success of

---

35    Senate Committee on the Judiciary, "Report on S.1125, The Fairness In Asbestos Injury Resolution Act of 2003 (108th Congress)" (Washington, DC, 2003), 68.

36    *In re Asbestos Products Liability Litigation (No. VI)*, 771 F. Supp. 415 (J.P.M.L. 1991) (USA).

37    Eduardo C. Robreno, "Asbestos Personal Injury Litigation in the Federal Courts: MDL-875," http://www.paed.uscourts.gov/documents/MDL/MDL875/MDL%20875%20 Overview.pdf.

38    Ibid.

asbestos plaintiffs: "Some defendants have tried bad cases with disastrously high verdicts being returned, while others have settled cases regardless of merit or risk, thereby funding the litigation against other defendants."[39] Indeed, the great majority of asbestos cases have traditionally being settled rather than litigated at trial, whether or not they would have had a chance should they have been tried in front of a jury. Carrington notes that, between 1982 and 1991, "not more than 5 out of 1000 asbestos cases could be expected to conclude with a trial on the merits."[40]

Large inventories of clients and efficient judicial management of the litigation put workers' compensation in the corner as a path to compensation that lacked appeal. Seeking damages in court became the prevalent path to compensation for asbestos victims. Fewer and fewer workers' compensation claims were filed in the 1980s and 1990s. Field and Victor's research about filing patterns in Massachusetts between 1984 and 1985 revealed that lawyers filed workers' compensation claims in approximately 50 percent of the cases. Their research also showed that, although workers' compensation was "not entirely neglected for asbestos claims," many of the workers' compensation cases were filed (to prevent the statute of limitations from barring the claim) but not actively pursued by lawyers until a settlement in the tort case was reached.[41] Litigation was given priority because workers' compensation state statutes often imposed substantial restrictions, in the form of a lien on any recovery, or on lawyers' freedom to negotiate an out of court settlement with asbestos firms. Field and Victor refer to them as "placeholder cases."[42] The few cases that were actively pursued usually involved serious diseases affecting clients who needed early benefits often because they did not have medical insurance or were not eligible to receive medical care under Medicare.

The result of asbestos litigation becoming a mature mass tort is what McGovern labels as "the worst of all possible worlds: high verdict values, an unlimited supply of plaintiffs, rapid resolution of cases, and well-funded lawyers."[43] The incessant volume of cases, some of which with minimal or no merit, pushed all major defendants of the second wave to seek protection under bankruptcy law. In 1985, Hensler and colleagues indicated that six asbestos producers had already filed for bankruptcy. This early casualties among asbestos firms also triggered more litigation and eventually more bankruptcies. Bankruptcy protection afforded to major asbestos defendants subtracted substantial funds to court-based compensation with the effect of reducing the value of settled claims up to 30 percent less than in the event Manville had not filed for bankruptcy. The

---

39    McGovern, "The Tragedy of the Asbestos Commons," 1743.

40    Carrington, "Asbestos Lessons: The Unattended Consequences of Asbestos Litigation," 589.

41    Robert I. Field and Richard B. Victor, *Asbestos claims: the decision to use workers' compensation and tort* (Cambridge, MA: Workers Compensation Research Institute, 1988), 12.

42    Ibid., 15.

43    McGovern, "The Tragedy of the Asbestos Commons," 1744.

disappearance of major defendants from the court system pushed plaintiff lawyers to creatively pursue new classes of defendants, which over time became the target of high volume of cases and increasingly sought protection under Chapter 11. In 2010, researchers at RAND reported that "claim payments by the 26 largest trusts totaled at least $10.9 billion through 2008."[44]

Because of its undesirable features, asbestos litigation in its maturity became increasingly perceived as a problem that needed to be resolved. Two strategies were attempted, albeit unsuccessfully, to resolve it: global settlements and legislation.

## Global settlements

Between the early 1980s and the 1990s, the amount of filings of asbestos claims grew significantly. By the year 2002, as Senator Hatch reported to Congress, 730,000 personal injury claims alleging personal injuries caused by the use of asbestos had been filed in state and federal courts.[45] Carrington adds more data:

> Approximately 8,400 businesses had been named as defendants in asbestos cases. A total of $54 billion had been paid to claimants. In each of the last three years, over 100,000 additional claims were filed. To date, fewer than two thousand out of almost a million asbestos cases have been tried on the merits.[46]

By the mid-1990s, asbestos litigation was in crisis mode. Courts in victim-friendly jurisdictions were swamped with cases. Judicial management of cases had proven to be ineffective: it did not speed up litigation to guarantee that victims with cancer could see the resolution of the case and it did not slow down the growth of filings. With dubious claiming practices, some firms routinely bundled up claims of sick victims with claims of unimpaired plaintiffs to push defendants to settle all bundled claims in fear of a trial that could result in a significant unfavorable verdict of the single case with a mesothelioma victim.

By the 1990s, debates on the merits of asbestos litigation involved old issues of efficiency and fairness, which RAND researchers had raised issues in the 1980s, and new issues of impact for the economy, abuses on part of the plaintiff bar, and prospects of compensation for future victims. Scholars, practitioners, judges, business associations, and politicians started looking at ways to "resolve" asbestos litigation other than mere reliance on judicial adjudication.

---

44   Lloyd S. Dixon, Geoffrey McGovern, and Amy Coombe, *Asbestos bankruptcy trusts: an overview of trust structure and activity with detailed reports on the largest trusts* (Santa Monica, CA: RAND Corporation, 2010).

45   United States Congress, "Congressional Record, Fairness in Asbestos Injury Resolution Act of 2003" (Statement by Senator Orin Hatch, 2004).

46   Carrington, "Asbestos Lessons: The Unattended Consequences of Asbestos Litigation.", 592-593.

Some of these attempts to resolve asbestos litigation came from practitioners, litigants, and the insurance industry. The first attempt took place in 1985 when 34 asbestos defendants and 16 insurers signed the Wellington Agreement. The Agreement created the Asbestos Claims Facility, an entity that would make offers to claimants who would furnish evidence of exposure to asbestos and of physical harm caused by asbestos. Claimants could accept the offer or reject it and go to court. The signatories of the Agreement agreed to contribute to compensation even if their product had not been named in the complaint or if the claimant could not prove that a product manufactured by the producer caused the injury. Instead they agreed to use a formula based on each producer's previous litigation experience to allocate the liability for each new claim. After accepting and assessing claims for three years, the Facility dissolved after seven producers withdrew their membership as a result of dispute among the signatories of how to allocate shares of costs.

Twenty asbestos defendants, the majority of which had supported the Wellington Agreement, pursued a second attempt to settle all of their asbestos liabilities. In 1988, they established the Center for Claims Resolution, which were to settle pending claims against the signatories. In 1991, the Center's scope was expanded to include all possible future injured parties who had not yet developed any perceptible disease. The plan was backed up by two prominent plaintiff lawyers, Ron Motley and Gene Locks, who represented 14,000 claimants who were offered a USD 215 million settlement, with USD 70 million going to the two attorneys and their co-counsel as legal fees. However, after the proposed class action settlement was filed, more than 236,000 people rejected the proposal. The case was heard as *Amchem Products Inc., v. Windsor* by the Supreme Court in 1997.[47] The Court rejected the settlement holding that due proceed considerations precluded litigants from settling claims of personal injury victims parties who were not yet sick and therefore not in condition to exercise their right to recovery. The settlement agreement did not meet the requirements of "common issue predominance and adequacy of representation."[48]

In 1993, a single defendant, Fibreboard, negotiated the so-called Global Settlement of a class action comprised of approximately 186,000 pending claims and any future claim. The maximum amount of the fund was determined by the defendant's insurance policy limits. To this end, Fibreboard's insurers agreed to allocate USD 2 billion to the settlement. However, class members had very limited opportunities for opting out. Several class members objected to the settlement, which reached the Supreme Court. The Court concluded that the settlement violated the law to the extent to which the allocation of funds negotiated as part of the settlement was in breach of the law because it excluded some potential plaintiffs, it failed to address the conflict of interest between present victims and future victims, and funds' distribution raised questions of fairness.[49]

---

47   *Amchem Products, Inc. v. Windsor*, 521 U.S. 591 (1997) (USA).
48   Ibid.
49   *Ortiz v. Fibreboard Corp*, 527 U.S. 815 (1999) (USA).

In 1998, Owens Corning Fiberglas established a National Settlement Program to resolve claims against Owens Corning and the recently acquired Fibreboard. The Program was successful in the sense that many claimants applied for compensation. However, Owens Corning Fiberglas had underestimated its liabilities and ended up filing for bankruptcy in 2000.

## Legislative efforts to resolve asbestos litigation

Legislative efforts to resolve asbestos litigation date back to the emergence of the second wave of litigation. These reform efforts fall within three of the four labels proposed by Thomas Burke to categorize antilitigation efforts: replacement, discouragement, and management reforms.[50] Efforts at federal level have aimed primarily at either replacing litigation with alternative paths to compensation—workers' compensation, schemes funded and managed by governmental agencies, and private trusts—or discouragement—legislation imposing threshold levels of disablement, medically proven, for personal injury claims to be litigated. Parallel to attempts to legislate asbestos compensation at federal level—all of which fell short of becoming federal law—reforms were pursued and implemented at state level. Before turning to reforms at state level, we shall however look at attempts to pass federal legislation first.

The first effort to implement replacement reform at the federal level took place quite early. Aware that after *Borel* asbestos litigation was there to stay, Millicent Hammond Fenwick, a four-term Republican member of the United States House of Representatives from New Jersey, the state that hosted Johns-Manville's largest manufacturing facility, introduced the first bill that offered a comprehensive, national solution to asbestos compensation in 1977. The Asbestos Health Hazards Compensation Act of 1977, which was supported by Johns-Manville, its workers' union, the International Association of Heat and Frost Insulators and Asbestos Workers, and Dr. Selikoff, proposed the creation of a board that, under this supervision of the Secretary of Labor, provided compensation to impaired victims on a no fault basis. After initial public funding the scheme was supposed to be funded by various "responsible parties," which included "producers and distributors of asbestos products and, since smoking and asbestos diseases are so clearly related, the producers and distributors of cigarettes and cigarette tobacco."[51]

---

50 Barnes, *Dust-up: asbestos litigation and the failure of common sense policy reform, passim*; Burke, *Lawyers, lawsuits, and legal rights: the battle over litigation in American society, passim*.

51 *The Asbestos Health Hazards Compensation Act of 1977*. House of Representatives. H.R. 8689 (USA) (1977); Eugene R. Anderson, Irene C. Warshauer, and Adrienne M. Coffin, "The Asbestos Health Hazards Compensation Act: A Legislative Solution to a Litigation Crisis," *Journal of Legislation* 10 (1983).

The bill did not become law. It was reintroduced in 1981, and once again it failed to become law.

This bill has inaugurated a series of attempts to resolve asbestos litigation with legislative action. The next attempt was the Asbestos Related Disease Screening Act of 1979, introduced by wealthy Democratic Representative Fred Richmond form New York. This bill proposed to establish a federal program to reimburse eligible individuals exposed to asbestos for screening expenses. Richmond's clever plan was to remove from the litigation arena exposure-only claims. In 1980, it was the turn of Senator Gary Hart, who became known for unsuccessfully running in the US presidential elections in 1984 and in 1988. Hart, a senator from Colorado, Johns-Manville's home state, proposed the Asbestos Health Hazards Compensation Act of 1980, which purported to expand workers' compensation by permitting an employer who pays an award to bring other responsible parties into the proceeding to determine the amount they should contribute to the compensation. This Bill also intended to reestablish the principle that workers' compensation is the exclusive remedy for asbestos compensation. The bill did not pass in part because of disagreement over governmental funding. Representative George Miller, a Democrat from California, sponsored a bill that envisioned that all funds would come from the industry and their insurers. Mr. Miller argued that a privately funded system would be "more feasible politically and better financially for taxpayers ... than to 'socialize American industry's losses.'"[52] In 1985 it was the turn of the Asbestos Workers' Recovery Act, which purported to set up a scheme that would have been funded by both government and private entities and have served as an exclusive path to compensation for asbestos victims.

After a few years of bumpy roads, attempts to resolve asbestos compensation were abandoned for several years starting from the mid-1980s. The consensus was that legislation was not needed because litigation itself was expected to deliver a solution to its own problems. The immune system of the litigation process was expected to deliver global settlements as antibodies would not only reduce pending litigation but also address the problem of future victims' compensation. As we have seen earlier, the Supreme Court crushed these hopes and sent the proposed solution back to the litigation arena. Not entirely discouraged by the turn of events, defendants started developing legislative proposals at the federal level to resolve pending asbestos litigation once and for all. The judiciary joined the number of voices calling for legislative action. In 1991, a US Supreme Court Panel chaired by Chief Justice Rehnquist concluded the courts were "ill-equipped to address the mass of claims in an effective manner."[53]

---

52  Barnaby J. Feder, "Paying asbestos damages," *The New York Times*, September 18, 1982.
53  Judicial Conference of the United States. Ad Hoc Committee on Asbestos Litigation, "Report of the Judicial Conference Ad Hoc Committee on Asbestos Litigation," (1991), 3.

Bills were introduced in the House and in the Senate in 1998, 1999, and 2000. The last bill (H.R. 1283) introduced medical criteria as threshold of claims' viability and various alternative dispute resolution options. In the wake of these bills' failure to become law, key actors switched their strategy away from bill drafting towards coalition-building to achieve consensus on reform proposals before submitting them to the Congress. The first of such efforts revolved around the "Asbestos Working Group," a group formed in 2001 by members of the plaintiff bar and some key defendants with the intent to translating the philosophy of global settlements into legislation. By the end of the year, as failure to reach consensus became clear, Steve Kazan and other members of the plaintiff bar along with the American Insurance Association, which represented the insurance industry, began working on building consensus around medical criteria legislation. Although none of the bills containing medical criteria requirement for claim viability became law, the Kazan/AIA initiative was instrumental in changing the public's opinion of asbestos litigation. The unfolding of the initiative offered the opportunity for the popular press to publish several stories focusing on broken aspects of the asbestos litigation, for the Senate Judiciary Committee to hold a hearing in 2002, and for the ABA to adopt a resolution calling for medical criteria legislation. By the end of 2002 and early 2003, "the public had come to view asbestos litigation as a serious problem in itself."[54]

The changed attitude towards asbestos compensation paved the road to the attempt to resolve asbestos compensation with federal legislation that got closer to success than any other proposals in three decades of effort to turn asbestos bills into law. This attempt is the Federal Asbestos Injury Resolution (FAIR) Act (S. 1125), a bill introduced and pushed through the legislative process by Republican Senator Orrin Hatch and aimed at replacing litigation with a USD 140 billion, privately financed, federal national fund. The bill went as far as receiving a favorable 10-8 vote by the Senate Judiciary Committee on July 10, 2003. Although reported, the S. 1125 was in "comatose" state,[55] primarily because several key stakeholders opposed it. This included the AFL-CIO, the largest federation of labor unions in the United States, industry organizations such the NAM Asbestos Alliance and the Asbestos Study Group, and the insurance industry. Senator Hatch rewrote the bill in 2004 after extensive negotiations led by Judge Edward R. Becker of the Third Circuit and introduced it in 2004 as S. 2290. Majority and minority leaders supported it after securing financial commitment up to USD 140 billion. However, the bill was not brought to the floor before the new Congress was installed in January 2005. Two versions of the bill were reintroduced by Senator Arlen Specter, the elected chairman of the Senate Judiciary Committee. The first (S. 852) was introduced in 2005 and failed to obtain sufficient votes (by a single vote) in support of a motion to waive the requirement to assess the bill's compliance

---

54  Patrick M. Hanlon and Anne Smetak, "Asbestos Changes," *N.Y.U. Annual Survey of American Law* 62 (2007): 562.

55  Ibid., 580.

with the budget resolution adopted in 2005. The second (S. 3274) was introduced in 2006 but was never brought to the floor and hopes to have it passed vanished when the Democrats, traditionally protective of the interests of the plaintiff's bar, regained majority. No other notable attempt to introduce comprehensive federal legislation on asbestos compensation has taken place since then. Legislative efforts have in fact focused on aspects—the latest bill targets asbestos trusts[56]— rather than the whole asbestos compensation complex.

While all attempts to legislate asbestos compensation at the federal level fell short of becoming federal law, proponents of asbestos legislation were more successful at state level. Antilitigation legislative initiatives at state level are primarily what Burke classifies as discouragement efforts. The first strand of efforts concentrated on medical criteria legislation. Between 2004 and 2006, Ohio, Texas, Georgia, Florida, Kansas, and South Carolina passed medical criteria legislation at curbing the practice of individuals who had been exposed to asbestos filing a claim when there is no disablement that can be medically ascertained. Some of these bills also had provision requiring that victims of cancer other than mesothelioma submit from the outset of the case evidence of a link between asbestos and the disease. The second strand of initiatives focused on venue reform, that is, laws excluding state courts' jurisdiction in cases in which the plaintiff was not a resident of the state and a substantial part of the tortious conduct had not taken place in the state. Variations of this legislation, or court management disfavoring a finding of jurisdiction, were adopted in Texas, West Virginia, Georgia, Florida, Mississippi, and Illinois. The final strand for reform resulted in tightening up the rules of joint and several liability, which, especially in its pure form, had permitted victims to pursue litigation against peripheral but solvent defendants knowing that these defendants could be eventually liable for the entire harm suffered by the plaintiff and shifted the burden of seeking contribution. New York, Florida, Texas, Ohio, and Mississippi enacted legislation curbing joint and several liability, thus removing plaintiffs' incentive to pursue litigation against defendants with small shares of liability.

Reform efforts at the state level have been more successful because they surfed the political wave of tort reform proposals, which gained much popularity in the 1990s especially at the state level, where policymakers' consensus is less difficult to achieve than at the federal level. At the federal level, the reform attempts that advanced the most further in the legislative process were those that fit by what Jeb Barnes refer to as "politics of efficiency." Politics of efficiency are deployed to build consensus around reforms that aim to fix inefficiency of what is perceived to be a "broken" mechanism. In the case of asbestos reform, proposals to replace litigation with an alternative compensation mechanism were tried "on the grounds that the new administrative remedy would streamline the adjudication process, replace open-ended legal rules and widely variable jury verdicts with more

---

56  *Furthering Asbestos Claim Transparency (FACT) Act of 2013.* House of Representatives. H.R. 982 (2013) (USA).

predictable regulations and administrative procedures, and remove lawyers as intermediaries."[57] However, notwithstanding the fact that several factors that are predictors of success in building winning coalitions were in place, all attempts, even those launched during the 109th Congress (a term in which both chambers had a Republican majority, the same party as President Bush), failed.[58] Barnes's nuanced explanation of this failure against all odds engages on a number of factors: "partisan dynamics in an age of narrow majorities and ideological polarized parties; well-organized trial lawyers' opposition; the quality of leadership inside the Senate; and the interplay between judicial innovation and congressional inertia."[59] In sum, divisive interest group politics are at the roots of failure of any bill to become federal law and change the face of asbestos litigation, by shifting compensation away from litigation and towards a federal trust fund.

## Asbestos bankruptcy trusts

When global settlements and then legislative attempts to replace litigation with an alternative mechanism were attempted, the claim filing surged. Deborah Hensler reports that in the early 2000s, "annual filings were skyrocketing towards 100,000."[60] The increase in asbestos cases was probably pushed by the fear that claims would be removed from the litigation process. "Anticipating the success of an administrative compensation scheme, lawyers filed 'ahead of the bell,' hoping not to be bound by the limits that would likely be incorporated in a new statute."[61] Therefore, lawyers advised their clients to file early to secure a spot in the court system. As the number of claims surged, new law firms got involved on the plaintiff side bringing claims against new, progressively more peripheral defendants. This surge in cases pushed some of these non-traditional defendants, who had never manufactured asbestos products but only used them in their production or assembled them in products for the market after purchasing them from asbestos suppliers, to seek protection under federal bankruptcy law.

Bankruptcy had been used by asbestos defendants since the 1980s to stop the flow of claims. In fact, the filing of a bankruptcy petition results in the automatic stay of all proceedings commenced by creditors to collect their debts. These

---

57   Barnes, *Dust-up: asbestos litigation and the failure of common sense policy reform*, 49-50.

58   During the 109th Congress, President Bush vetoed only one bill, the Stem Cell Research Enhancement Act of 2005.

59   Barnes, *Dust-up: asbestos litigation and the failure of common sense policy reform*, 73.

60   Deborah R. Hensler, "A brief history of asbestos litigation in the United States," in *Asbestos. Anatomy of a mass tort*, ed. Munich Re (München: Münchener Rückversicherungs-Gesellschaft, 2009), 29.

61   Ibid., 31.

include asbestos personal injury claims. The first asbestos bankruptcy is Johns-Manville's in 1982. The decision to file for bankruptcy protection was the direct result of the wave of asbestos claims that inundated the firm, in part as a result of the harsh doctrine deployed by New Jersey state courts. In *Beshada v. Johns-Manville Products Corp.*, the New Jersey Supreme Court threw out the "state of the art" defense for asbestos manufacturers, that is, the defense based on the notion that the danger of which they failed to warn was undiscovered at the time the products were marketed and that it was undiscoverable given the state of the scientific knowledge at that time. The Court held that if the product is in fact dangerous, the knowledge of such danger is implied to the defendants. The court reasoned that "The burden of illness from dangerous products such as asbestos should be placed upon those who profit from its production and, more generally, upon society at large which reaps the benefits of the various products our economy manufactures."[62] The year after, the New Jersey Supreme Court backed away from this position for product liability cases but carved out an exception and preserved it for asbestos cases.[63]

Bankruptcy protection allowed Johns-Manville to emerge from bankruptcy in 1988 as Manville Corporation, a viable business stripped of all asbestos liabilities, which had shifted to a new entity known as the Manville Personal Injury Settlement Trust.[64] Assets for approximately USD 2.5 billion were allocated to the Trust for the purpose of paying off all future claims by virtue of a channeling injunction that barred all future asbestos claimants against the Manville Corporation. The life of the Manville Trust however became turbulent. Claiming rates had been underestimated: the Trust expected to settle a number of claims ranging from USD 83,000 to 100,000. However, by 1992, and in part because of mass screenings that plaintiffs' law firms conducted among workers who had been exposed to asbestos, more than 190,000 claimants were seeking compensation from the trust. As a consequence the Trust soon became insolvent and new litigation arose. In 1995, the new claims were settled with an agreement that will have a "lasting significance for all future asbestos [personal injury] trusts and broad ramifications for public policy regarding the compensation of asbestos claimants."[65] The 1995 settlement:

> … established a new compensation plan that gave priority to the most-seriously ill[,] established processes for resolving disputes between claimants and the trust[, and] created an administrative role for a future claimants' representative

---

62  *Beshada v. Johns-Manville Prods Corp.*, 442 A.2d 539 (D.N.J. 1982) (USA).

63  *O'Brien v. Muskin Corp.*, 463 A.2d 298 (N.J. 1983) (USA); *Feldman v. Lederle Laboratories*, 479 A.2d 374 N.J. 1984) (USA).

64  *Matter of Johns-Manville Corp.*, 68 BR 618 (Bankr. S.D.N.Y. 1986) (USA).

65  *In re Joint E. & S. Dist. Asbestos Litig.*, 878 F. Supp. 473 (S.D.N.Y. 1995) (USA). Dixon, McGovern, and Coombe, *Asbestos bankruptcy trusts: an overview of trust structure and activity with detailed reports on the largest trusts*. 6.

(FCR), whose duty it was to protect the interests of claimants who had not yet filed with the trust.[66]

The framework inaugurated by the Manville Trust was formalized by Congress with the Bankruptcy Act Reform Act of 1994. The 1994 reform, also known as "asbestos amendments," modified bankruptcy law to allow establishing trusts, as part of a debtor's reorganization plan under Chapter 11 of the bankruptcy code, towards which a company targeted with asbestos claims may channel present and future asbestos liabilities. The 1994 reform carved a special discipline for asbestos trusts within the general federal rules of bankruptcy.

These trusts, also known as Section 524(g) trusts, are intended to resolve present and future asbestos liabilities of the company filing for bankruptcy. Asbestos trusts are established in two ways. The first is the traditional practice of having the debtor filing a petition and then negotiating a reorganization plan with the creditors. This traditional model, known among practitioners as "free fall," sees a company facing asbestos liabilities seeking bankruptcy protection by filing a petition with the bankruptcy court. After the petition is filed, the company negotiates a reorganization plan with its creditors. The majority of asbestos victims are usually represented by plaintiff lawyers with large inventories of clients. They propose matrix agreements to be used in reviewing and liquidating claims. The reorganization plan is then submitted to present claimants. If at least 75 percent of present asbestos claimants vote in favor, the plan is then brought to court and, after a public hearing is held, is typically approved. The alternative to traditional free fall bankruptcies is a "prearranged" or "prepackaged" bankruptcy, in which the debtor enters Chapter 11 after negotiating the terms of a restructuring with its major stakeholders. Prepackaged plans, which are a very popular path to establishing asbestos trusts, are typically confirmed by judges.

Judicial ratification of reorganization plans typically binds future claimants. Because of the uncertainty of future claims and the fact that the funds allocated to the trusts are limited yet sufficient to address present and future liabilities, the law requires that courts view proposed plans on their entirety and approve them only if they are fair and equitable to future claims. To further protect the interests of future claims, courts appoint a futures representative, which role, as we will see later, is controversial.

With a "channeling injunction," the court transfers all asbestos liabilities to the newly created trust of the company and the reorganized company is shielded against all current and future asbestos liabilities.[67] In return, the reorganized company usually partially funds the trust with its securities, which also acquired ownership of the majority of voting shares of the reorganized company. The trusts' assets, which are managed by the trustees, must be used for the sole benefit of

---

66  Dixon, McGovern, and Coombe, *Asbestos bankruptcy trusts: an overview of trust structure and activity with detailed reports on the largest trusts*, 6.

67  Ibid., 3.

claimant beneficiaries, that is, to collect, process, and pay all of the valid asbestos claims. Victims-creditors file their claims with the trust. If the claimant meets a trust's exposure requirements relating to a debtors' product, as well as medical criteria, the trust will pay compensation to the claimant.[68] A single victim can file various claims against multiple trusts if asbestos exposure originated from more than one product. The coordination among trusts is minimal, and payments made by one trust are rarely taken into consideration by a second trust. However, since payments amount only to a fraction of the value of the claim, the lack of coordination among trusts is hardly an issue.

Insurance companies usually do not participate in negotiations of reorganization prepackaged plans, whether they are negotiated by following the traditional route of free fall bankruptcies or are prepackaged. Indeed, insurers typically have no standing to challenge the plan or to appeal a court's approvals of reorganization plans. Insurers' interests however are not forgotten. Federal law requires that the negotiated trust respects the principle of "insurance neutrality." This principle imposes a duty to the debtor to leave the interests of its insurers unaltered during the course of its bankruptcy case, particularly in connection with a plan of reorganization, and to preserve insurance coverage disputes for resolution outside of bankruptcy. Trusts ordinarily adhere to the principle of insurance neutrality by refraining from relying on insurance assets in connection with plan funding and by making no assignment of insurance assets. As we will see later, the lack of involvement of insurance companies in negotiations of reorganization plans is controversial since money spent by trusts to compensate claimants is often recouped from insurers in subsequent litigation. While insurers can be forced to indemnify trusts without standing to challenge the overall plan, courts have recently engaged in a more liberal analysis of the boundaries of insurers have standing to sue.[69] In fact they can only challenge the plan's neutrality.[70] In addition, insurers' interests are taken into consideration when courts often issue an injunction prohibiting claimants from suing asbestos insurers without permission by the trust; the trust may not allow such actions unless asbestos claimants agree to the same judgment reduction that is binding on the trust before proceeding against non-settling insurers.

To overcome exclusion from key negotiations, insurance companies often settle all prospective claims that the trust has towards the insurance company during the "packaging" negotiations that precede the filing. When claims against insurers

---

68    Ibid., 4.

69    But see *In re Global Indus. Technologies, Inc.*, 645 F.3d 201 (3rd Cir. 2011) (USA); *Motor Vehicle Cas. Co. v. Thorpe Insulation Co. (In re Thorpe Insulation Co.)*, 671 F.3d 980 (9th Cir. 2012) (USA).

70    *In re Combustion Eng'g, Inc.*, 391 F.3d 190 (3rd Cir. 2004) (USA); *Baron & Budd, P.C. v. Unsecured Asbestos Claimant Comm.*, 321 B.R. 147 (D.N.J. 2005) (USA); *In re Global Indus. Technologies, Inc*; *In re Pittsburgh Corning Corp.*, 453 BR 570 (Bankr. W.D. Pa. June 16, 2011) (USA).

are settled, a lump sum contribution towards the trust's fund is made in return for discharge of any coverage claims. These settlements create a duality between settled insurers and unsettled insurers because courts ordinarily issue an injunction preventing the assertion of contribution claims held by unsettled insurers against settled insurers. This practice is controversial as it raises issues of fair evaluation of insurance coverage for the purpose of settlement. Unsettled insurers often attempt to challenge the injunction barring claims in contribution alleging that the share of liability assumed by settled insurers is unfairly small. To redress the gap between claims' settlement value and their judgment value, courts have developed a multifaceted strategy. First, the trust absorbs the cost of those barred contributions and reduces dollar-for-dollar any judgment obtained against unsettled insurers holding contribution claims. Second, claimants are barred from bringing an action against unsettled insurers unless they agree to the same judgment reduction that is binding on the trust before proceeding against unsettled insurers.

Throughout the years, many asbestos defendants sought bankruptcy protection and asbestos trusts have been extensively used. Researchers at RAND indicated that as of March 2011 "96 companies with asbestos liabilities had filed for reorganization, 56 trusts had been established, and additional trusts are in the pipeline."[71] Collectively these trusts had initial assets exceeding USD 44 billion and paid more than USD 10 billion to claimants. Of these, 14 were allocated initial assets in excess of USD 1 billion.[72] With regard to the compensation, "[t]he largest 26 trusts had paid $10.9 billion on 2.4 million claims through 2008. Trust outlays have grown rapidly since 2005, reaching $3.3 billion in 2008."[73]

While asbestos trusts adopted arrangements to deal with claims that vary greatly, Francis McGovern identified ten elements that trusts typically have: trustees, administration, governance provisions, diseases, exposure criteria, medical criteria, valuation criteria, defenses, payment limitations, and court access.[74] The rules for each of these elements tend to vary greatly from trust to trust, especially with regard to the monetary value assigned to valid claims and the amount eventually liquidated to victims. However consistent patterns can also be traced among trusts. These rules are primarily the expression of the will of the committee of asbestos personal injury plaintiffs appointed by the US Trustee in the bankruptcy and are patterned to reflect how the interests of the personal injury plaintiffs have evolved throughout the years, as McGovern demonstrated in his survey of asbestos personal injury trusts.[75]

---

71   Lloyd S. Dixon and Geoffrey McGovern, *Asbestos bankruptcy trusts and tort compensation* (Santa Monica, CA: RAND Corporation, 2011), 2.

72   Dixon, McGovern, and Coombe, *Asbestos bankruptcy trusts: an overview of trust structure and activity with detailed reports on the largest trusts*, 27-29.

73   Dixon and McGovern, *Asbestos bankruptcy trusts and tort compensation*, 3.

74   Francis E. McGovern, "The Evolution of Asbestos Bankruptcy Trust Distribution Plans," *N.Y.U. Annual Survey of American Law* 62 (2006): 166.

75   Ibid., 165-166.

An important feature of asbestos trusts is their widespread refusal to compensate victims who do not show signs of impairment, which has been a highly contested issue in asbestos litigation since the late 1970s. Whether malignant or non-malignant, a disease is needed for the claim to be approved.[76] Trusts consistently decline to compensate victims who do not meet certain criteria, which are met only in the presence of evidence that a medically recognizable disease is in progress, and those who cannot demonstrate significant occupational exposure. While trusts do not ordinarily object to claims based on mesothelioma, medical criteria for lung cancer are more complex mostly because of the possible contribution of causes other than asbestos. Some trusts have required "chest x-rays read by a B-reader, pathology, underlying bilateral asbestos-related non-malignant disease, and a physical exam."[77] Some others would not need evidence of underlying bilateral non-malignant disease if the record shows that the claimant had been exposed to a significant amount of asbestos.

With regard to the requirement for occupational exposure, Dixon and colleagues[78] point out that the Kaiser Aluminum and Chemical Corporation bankruptcy offers the standard definition of what "significant" occupational exposure is:

> ... employment for a cumulative period of at least five (5) years with a minimum of two (2) years prior to December 31, 1982, in an industry and an occupation in which the claimant (a) handled raw asbestos fibers on a regular basis; (b) fabricated asbestos-containing products so that the claimant in the fabrication process was exposed on a regular basis to raw asbestos fibers; (c) altered, repaired or otherwise worked with an asbestos-containing product such that the claimant was exposed on a regular basis to asbestos fibers; or (d) was employed in an industry and occupation such that the claimant worked on a regular basis in close proximity to workers engaged in the activities described in (a), (b), and/or (c).[79]

With regard to the list of qualifying diseases, trusts ordinarily accept claims if they are grounded on one of the following medical conditions: mesothelioma, lung cancer (in some cases also in the absence of evidence of bilateral non-malignant disease caused by asbestos), other cancers with evidence of bilateral non-malignant

---

76   Dixon, McGovern, and Coombe, *Asbestos bankruptcy trusts: an overview of trust structure and activity with detailed reports on the largest trusts*, 33.

77   McGovern, "The Evolution of Asbestos Bankruptcy Trust Distribution Plans," 172.

78   Dixon, McGovern, and Coombe, *Asbestos bankruptcy trusts: an overview of trust structure and activity with detailed reports on the largest trusts*, xxiii.

79   Kaiser Aluminum and Chemical Corporation, "Third Amended Asbestos Trust Distribution Procedures, November 20, 2007," http://www.kaiserasbestostrust.com/Files/Third%20Amended%20Trust%20Distribution%20Procedures%2000013238.pdf.

disease caused by asbestos, or asbestosis (ranging from severe to asbestosis without significantly restricted pulmonary function).[80] In 2007 and 2008, 86 percent of the total number of claims that these trusts paid were for non-malignant injuries for an expenditure that amounted to 37 percent of the overall expenditure.[81] This amount was "roughly one-tenth that for malignant claims."[82] Over time, the balance of payments has gone against non-malignant claims. McGovern demonstrates this trend by reporting data of the ration of payments of malignant versus non-malignant claims. In the early 1980s, the Manville Trust paid 17 mesothelioma claims and three lung cancer claims for every non-malignant claim. In 2003, the Babcock & Wilcox plan has corresponding ratios of 360:1; 140:1; and 140:1.64. "The shift to the malignants has been dramatic," McGovern concludes.[83]

Dixon and colleagues advance various reasons that explain the diminished appeal of non-malignant cases. A number of legislative reforms and judicial decisions that were adopted in the first half of the 2000s have reduced tort payments on non-malignant claims. Some states barred exposure-only claims or assigned them to deferred dockets; other states barred out-of-state claims with out-of state exposures.

The United States Supreme Court has been unwilling to recognize a cause of action for infliction of emotional distress based on mere exposure to asbestos.[84] It has only allowed plaintiffs with asbestosis to recover damages for a genuine and serious fear of future cancer.[85] Finally US District Court Judge Janice Jack systematically challenged diagnoses from doctors frequently used to support claims for non-malignant injuries.[86] In addition to these reasons, plaintiff lawyers themselves have been instrumental in the loss of appeal of unimpaired and non-malignant claims. In fact, key members of the plaintiff bar have increasingly believed in asbestos trusts as viable mechanisms for the compensation of asbestos victims and have thus participated in their management and influenced their frameworks. These lawyers realized that the funds available to trusts for distribution were limited and that victims with more severe conditions deserved priority. Thus they stopped advising victims to bring claims even if unimpaired and worked as trustees from within the trust organizations to tilt the balance in favor of victims affected by the most severe conditions. McGovern summarizes the shift with these words: "Plaintiffs' counsel have voluntarily strengthened qualification criteria and

---

80    Dixon, McGovern, and Coombe, *Asbestos bankruptcy trusts: an overview of trust structure and activity with detailed reports on the largest trusts*, 17-18.

81    Ibid., 3.

82    Ibid.

83    McGovern, "The Evolution of Asbestos Bankruptcy Trust Distribution Plans," 173.

84    *Metro-North Commuter R. Co. v. Buckley*, 521 U.S. 424 (1997) (USA).

85    *Norfolk & Western R. Co. v. Ayers*, 538 U.S. 135 (2003) (USA).

86    Dixon, McGovern, and Coombe, *Asbestos bankruptcy trusts: an overview of trust structure and activity with detailed reports on the largest trusts*, 34.

altered the balance of payments for discrete diseases to deal with the scarcity of resources in the bankruptcy trust context." [87]

Once filed, the trust's processing facility reviews the claim. Claims are typically accepted when evidence shows that they meet the requirements set by the trust. Accepted claims are then liquidated. Payments are usually made "based upon a schedule with maximum benefits."[88] The scheduled benefits of asbestos trusts set the liquidation value for mesothelioma at USD 500,000. Over time the lowest liquidation value for other asbestos diseases has been reduced from USD 12,000 to zero.[89]

Unfortunately for victims, the trust's acceptance of a claim does not mean full payment of the value based on the benefit schedule set up by each trust. The liquidation value set in the charts does not mean amount paid in compensation. Since most trusts have generous but limited funds available for compensation victims-creditors, they cannot afford to compensate victims in full as the Manville Trust did in the early years—a practice that prematurely emptied its pockets. Trusts have therefore established two sets of limitations on payments. First, trusts ordinarily limit the amount of money allocated in a given year to non-malignant claimants. They do so by setting a maximum percentage of funds that are allocated to non-malignant claims (this strategy is referred to as "collar") or more simply by setting a cap on payments to non-malignant victims. Second, all trusts determine a fixed percentage payout; that is, the percentage amount of a liquidated value. These "payment percentages" vary greatly from trust to trust. Dixon and colleagues report that "[t]he UNR Asbestos-Disease Claims Trust ... applies a 1.1 percent payment percentage [and that] Manville initially paid 100 percent of a claim, [then] renegotiated the payment percentage to 10 percent, reduced ... to 5 percent [and more] recently ... increased to 7.5 percent.[90] After payment percentages are applied, mesothelioma victims receive an average of USD 41,000.

On top of the reduced payment, victims are also responsible for attorneys' fees. These are ordinarily deducted from the payments liquidated by the trust as compensation. Many asbestos trusts cap attorneys' fees at 25 percent of the award, which is lower than what plaintiff attorneys usually demand when claims are litigated. While there is no way for the trust to enforce this limit, Dix and colleagues reported that "[k]nowledgeable parties ... believed that attorneys' fees of 25 percent are typical."[91]

Whenever the trust rejects the claim or the victim-creditor has rejected the results of the trust's claim review and liquidation, the victim-creditor has typically access to an alternative dispute resolution procedure. Some trusts have adopted

---

87    McGovern, "The Evolution of Asbestos Bankruptcy Trust Distribution Plans," 164.

88    Ibid., 173.

89    Ibid.

90    Dixon, McGovern, and Coombe, *Asbestos bankruptcy trusts: an overview of trust structure and activity with detailed reports on the largest trusts*, 21-22.

91    Ibid., 22.

the binding arbitration model, and therefore the decision of the arbitrator is final. For other trusts, the alternative dispute resolution process is nonbinding: victims-creditors who are dissatisfied with the arbitrator's decision can sue the trust. However, typically claims are not pushed thus far in the process. Dixon and colleagues report that "very few claims go to arbitration or to the courts."[92]

## The third wave of asbestos litigation

Four decades after *Borel* recognized the viability of asbestos victims' product liability claims, asbestos litigation is still ongoing and some of its features are controversial and contested. Most recent trends in asbestos litigation include the rapid decline in claim filing, increased individualization in judicial treatment of cases, and cautious expansion of litigation towards new causes of actions.

This rapid decline in claim filing is evidenced by two prominent factors. One if the almost tenfold smaller number of claims filed with the Manville Trust between 2003 and 2005 and bigger than 50 percent of those filed with the Celotex Trust.[93] The second is the fading away of consolidation of cases at the federal level. In December 2011 the Judicial Panel on Multidistrict Litigation ordered the stop to the transfer of new "tag-along" actions (with the exception of cases in the Maritime Docket) to MDL No. 875—a "tag-along" action involves factual questions similar to the questions involved in cases that were already transferred to the MDL.[94] The decision was made primarily because the backlog of cases had been eliminated and the number of newly filed cases was small enough that each federal court could adjudicate them without the need for consolidation:

> ... the backlog of cases in the MDL has been largely eliminated ... and the current rate at which new asbestos-related cases are being brought in the federal district courts stands at approximately 400 per year ... the interests of justice and the "efficient and economical adjudication" of such cases ... would be promoted by discontinuing their transfer to the MDL.[95]

The success of bankruptcy trusts, which freeze adjudication in courts of personal injury claims against the bankrupt company, partially contributed to the declining number of new cases. Along with the success of asbestos trust funds, the claim filing trend was inverted as a result of the disappearance of unimpaired victims' lawsuits. Unimpaired victims' claims disappeared for a number of reasons. First,

---

92   Ibid., 21.

93   Hanlon and Smetak, "Asbestos Changes," 594.

94   *In re Asbestos Prodcs Liab. Litig. (No. VI)*, MDL No. 875, Order Adopting Suggestion To The Panel Concerning Future Tag-Along Transfers (E.D. Pa. December 13, 2011) (USA).

95   Ibid.

it became that much of the medical evidence used to support these claims was the product of widespread fraud, as discussed earlier. Second, asbestos trusts began recognizing only claims that met certain requirements of medically proven impairment and asbestos exposure. This meant that unimpaired victims' claims were no longer economic and therefore were left behind by most firms. Third, inactive dockets and medical criteria legislation adopted at the state level also undermined the procedural viability and economic value of "exposure only" cases.

The second trend—increased individualization of judicial treatment of case— was inaugurated by MDL 875 in the aftermath of the Supreme Court's rejection of a global settlement for all asbestos claims. After *Amchem*, the Eastern District of Pennsylvania approached cases transferred to MDL 875 under a "one plaintiff, one claim" policy. The philosophy was articulated in Administrative Order No. 12, which has set the context for a more aggressive, pro-active approach to case management.[96] The Order has set strict requirements for submissions to the court and deadlines for settlement conferences, motion hearings, and trials. In particular, the Order has required that plaintiffs submit at the outset of the case a "medical diagnosing report or opinion upon which the plaintiff now relies for the prosecution of the claim."[97] Since the Order has also made clear that the evidence contained in the report must be sufficient to "withstand a dispositive motion" such as a motion to dismiss for failure to state a claim or a summary judgment motion.[98] For those familiar with the civil litigation process, this means a rather high standard of proof, certainly more stringent that the practice of using evidence gathered by law firms in litigation screening campaigns. Aggressive case management has resulted in decreased rate of claim filing, which has eventually led to stopping the transfer of new cases to MDL. State courts too seem to move towards increased individualization. An example of this trend is the decision taken by Associate Judge Clarence Harrison, who is responsible for the asbestos docket in Madison County—a jurisdiction that has been traditionally friendly to asbestos victims—to end the practice of reserving trial slots for cases not yet filed and claims filed by exposure only victims and to order that 2013 asbestos cases be set on a "case-by-case basis": Judge Harrison indicated that "the standard jury trial week calendar will be used going forward, and that cases will be set by motion on a case-by-case basis."[99]

With the disappearance of "exposure only" cases and the decline in pulmonary disease, asbestos in particular, due to the fact that high, prolonged exposures to asbestos are no longer common, mesothelioma cases, although slowly declining,

---

96    *In re Asbestos Prodcs Liab. Litig. (No. VI)*, MDL No. 875, Amended Administrative Order No. 12 (As Amended Effectively August 27, 2009) (E.D. Pa. September 3, 2009) (USA).

97    Ibid.

98    Ibid.

99    Ann Maher. "Judge eliminates advance asbestos trial setting in Madison County." Published electronically March 30, 2012. http://www.legalnewsline.com/news/235666-judge-eliminates-advance-asbestos-trial-setting-in-madison-county.

are rising to prominence in terms of litigation priority. Mesothelioma cases are often referred by a counsel to a colleague in a plaintiff-friendlier jurisdiction, filed against a long list of defendants, and occasionally adjudicated at trial. Forum shopping is still an important feature of asbestos litigation with jurisdictions such as Delaware and California experiencing an increase in claim filing. In December 2011, Tom Mikula, a partner in the Washington office of Goodwin Procter and national coordinating counsel for several asbestos defendants, told the National Law Journal that "during the past five years, the number of cases has increased and, this time, they involve a higher percentage of people diagnosed with serious illnesses."[100] Given the seriousness of the injury and the individualized treatment of each claim, cases end up at trial more than in the past. This has resulted in record damage awards. In 2011, "two record-setting jury awards" took place, "one in Mississippi for $322 million and another in Illinois for $90 million."[101] Although claiming rates have fallen, the increased number of jury awards in mesothelioma cases has pushed indemnity costs per case up.[102] In part, this seems also to be "a function if an increase in punitive damages award amounts, as the punitive to compensatory damage ration has continually increased."[103]

Since defendants are further and further removed from asbestos mining and manufacturing of insulation products, establishing liability has however become a harder burden for plaintiffs. In their perpetual quest for new defendants, new friendly jurisdictions, and new causes of action, plaintiff firms have not passively reacted to the success of bankruptcy trusts. To the contrary, they have once again acted creatively. To offset the lost relevance of unimpaired claims, the disappearance of tort defendants who sought protection under bankruptcy law, and increased and individualized judicial scrutiny of claims, plaintiff firms have targeted new defendants and deployed new causes of action. With regard to new defendants, lawsuits have been launched against companies that sold a product to which a component containing asbestos was added with installation that took place after the sale of the product. In these cases, the defendant is not the manufacturer or supplier of the asbestos-containing component: it is the manufacturer of a product not containing asbestos to which an asbestos component is added later. Facing these lawsuits, most courts have been reluctant to expand the liability "beyond that reasonably connected to the sale of the product."[104]

---

100   Amanda Bronstad, "Asbestos is rearing its head; Plaintiffs' firms are injecting life into a once-'sleepy' California docket," *The National Law Journal*, December 19, 2011.

101   Lisa A. Rickard, "Never-ending asbestos quagmire," ibid., November 7.

102   Asbestos Liability Risk Analysis Group. "Asbestos Claims and Litigation: Update and Review: 2010 New Case Filing: Summary and Analysis," 1-15. Published electronically November 1, 2011. http://www.alragroup.com/documents/asbestos%20paper%202011.pdf.

103   Ibid.

104   James K. Toohey and Rebecca L. Matthews, "Liability For The Post-Sale Installation Of Asbestos-Containing Replacement Parts Or Insulation," *Mealey's Litigation*

More success followed the deployment of two new causes of action, both of which had been already successfully used in litigation in Europe: secondhand exposure and premises owners' liability. Secondhand exposure and premises owners' liability match litigation for household exposure that has been somehow successful in Europe. Cases have been tried in multiple jurisdictions. Victims of secondhand exposure have been particularly successful in California. The wife of a pipefitter won a jury award in the amount of USD 11.5 million in 2002.[105] Another mesothelioma victim won an award in the amount of USD 200 million in punitive damages and USD 8.8 million in compensatory damages in 2010 after showing that her husband's clothes brought deadly amounts of asbestos into the home.[106] However, in 2012, the Court of Appeal of the Second Appellate District of California in *Campbell v. Ford Motor Company* held that an employer has no duty to protect family members of employees from secondhand exposure to asbestos used during the course of the employer's business.

> The general rule in California is that "[e]veryone is responsible ... for an injury occasioned to another by his or her want of ordinary care or skill in the management of his or her property or person ... ." In other words, "each person has a duty to use ordinary care and is liable for injuries caused by his failure to exercise reasonable care in the circumstances ... ." In the absence of a statutory provision establishing an exception to the general rule of Civil Code section 1714, courts should create one only where clearly supported by public policy.[107]

Initially cases were also successfully tried in Texas, New York, Maryland, and Missouri.[108] Over time, successes at the trial level have been upheld by appellate courts only in a handful of jurisdictions.

Cases based on the liability of premises owners to the employees of their independent contracts have also been tried. Although these cases have been received

---

Report 25, no. 21 (2010): 44. The authors cite *Simonetta v. Viad Corp.*, 197 P.3d 127 (Wash. 2008) (USA); *Taylor v. Elliott Turbomachinery Co. Inc*, 90 Cal. Rptr. 3d 414 (Ct. App. 2009) (USA).

105   *Gunderson v. A.W. Chesterton Co.*, Case n. 406207, Verdict (Cal. Super., San Francisco Co. December 12, 2002) (USA).

106   *Evans v. A.W. Chesterton Co., et al.*, Case n. 418867, Verdict (Cal. Super., Los Angeles Co. April 29, 2010) (USA); Bryan Redding. "Los Angeles Jury Awards $200 Million in Punitive Damages for Secondhand Asbestos Exposure." *Litigation Blog*. Published electronically April 30, 2010. http://www.lexisnexis.com/community/litigationresourcecenter/blogs/litigationblog/archive/2010/04/30/los-angeles-jury-awards-200-million-in-punitive-damages-for-secondhand-asbestos-exposure.aspx.

107   *Campbell v. Ford Motor Co.*, 206 Cal. App. 4th 15 (Ct. App. May 21, 2012) (USA).

108   Theodore Jr. Voorhees and Eric Hellerman, "Peripheral Defendants As Litigation Targets: Defense Strategies For The Next Wave " (paper presented at the Fourth National Forum: Asbestos Litigation, San Francisco, February 28, 2003), 16-20.

well in some jurisdictions, overall they have faced "significant legal obstacles in many states."[109] In 2009, Strang and Ross's review of secondhand exposure liability and premise owner liability points out that the "emerging majority rule" is that "no duty [is] owed by a premises owner to a 'take-home' claimant."[110] Only a handful of jurisdictions have consistently recognized these claims at appellate level. These are California, Louisiana, New Jersey, and Tennessee. On the other hand, the majority rule is the law of Delaware, Georgia, Iowa, Kentucky, Maryland, Michigan, New York, Ohio, Texas, and Washington. Although disfavored in many jurisdictions, secondhand exposure liability is contested and occasionally courts shift their position as in the case of Illinois. In 2012, the Illinois Supreme Court held that an employer has an obligation to warn workers and their families about the dangers linked to take-home asbestos exposure.[111] Contrary to the European experience, very few cases have been successfully tried based on the theory of community or neighborhood exposure. In 2007, Hanlon and Smetak indicated that "new attention is being paid to community or neighborhood exposures and even exposures resulting from the negligent removal of naturally occurring asbestos," but provided no citation to pending or resolved cases.[112]

## Current controversies

Four decades after *Borel* was decided, it is safe to say that asbestos litigation changed the landscape of tort and product liability litigation in the United States. It solidified the plaintiff bar and transferred to it enormous amounts of money. The accumulated wealth was used by the plaintiff bar to pursue other mass torts and to influence policy at national and local level. Furthermore, this wave of cases showed US courts' failure to deliver efficient and individualized justice for mass torts. The bulk treatment of victims on part of law firms and the standardized life of cases after entering the court system "sacrificed attention to individualized injuries and needs."[113]

Furthermore, a significant portion of the money transacted went to pay for attorneys' fees and litigation expenses. In 1983, Hensler and colleagues estimated that plaintiffs received only 37 cents of every dollar spent to resolve asbestos claims.[114] In 2005, Carroll and colleagues estimated that, from its inception

---

109   Hanlon and Smetak, "Asbestos Changes," 601.

110   Carter E. Strang and Karen E. Ross, "'Take-Home' Premises Liability Asbestos Exposure Claims—2009 Update," *Mealey's Litigation Report* 24, no. 22 (2009): 1.

111   Sanford J. Schmidt, "Supreme Court ruling crucial in 'take-home' asbestos cases," *The Telegraph*, March 25, 2012.

112   Hanlon and Smetak, "Asbestos Changes," 602.

113   Hensler et al., *Asbestos in the Courts. The Challenge of Mass Toxic Torts*, xxvii.

114   James S. Kakalik et al., *Costs of Asbestos Litigation* (Santa Monica, CA: RAND Institute for Civil Justice, 1983).

through the end of 2002, the total spending of asbestos litigation, which was the sum is the amount defendants spent after being reimbursed from insurers plus the amount insurers spent after being reimbursed by reinsurers, amounted to approximately USD 70 billion, with defense transaction costs amounting to more than USD 21 billion (31 percent of total spending) and claimants' transaction costs amounting to USD 19 billion (27 percent of total spending). As a result, claimants' net compensation equaled about USD 30 billion (42 percent of total spending).[115]

After *Borel*, asbestos litigation has however substantially evolved from an initial stage of growing lawsuits targeting major asbestos manufacturers to the surge in claims, in great part fueled to questionable litigation screening practices to recruit masses of clients, leading up to the failed attempt to resolve asbestos litigation with global settlements and, later, legislation, to a third phase characterized by greater individualization and primacy of mesothelioma cases. The third phase is still characterized by a practice, implemented by plaintiff law firms, that is contested: product identification testimony. Testimonial and written evidence exposed plaintiff lawyers' practice to facilitate recollection or implant false memory of exposure to specific asbestos products in clients.[116] The practice entails approaching the client with a list of products that were used at the workplace of the victims and that was generated by the law firms by accessing databases of asbestos product use. A paralegal at Baron and Budd, a first-hour leading plaintiff firm known for its aggressive practices, admitted that client who had no recollection of the product prior to the interview, "identified at least one product they couldn't recall originally" in 75 percent of the cases.[117] There are some allegations that this is still an ongoing practice.

Bankruptcy trusts are another contested area of asbestos compensation. Critics point to victim overcompensation, unequal treatment among claimants, and fair involvement of insurers. With regard to overcompensation, the allegation is that the lack of communication between courts and trust permits victims to recover once in the tort system and again from the trusts. The result is victim overcompensation to the disadvantage of future claimants, and needless to say a double fee for plaintiff attorneys, defendants' true enemies. Also, overcompensation may come from suits against unsettled insurers who worry that that they may be forced to pay more than their proportionate share of liability, and thus want to ensure that they obtain appropriate credits in litigation.[118] To this end, many courts have agreed

---

115   Carroll et al., *Asbestos litigation*, 87-106.

116   Christine Biederman et al., "Toxic Justice," *Dallas Observer*, August 13, 1998, 12; Lester Brickman, "On the Theory Class's Theories of Asbestos Litigation: The Disconnect Between Scholarship and Reality," *Pepperdine Law Review* 31 (2004): 137-153.

117   Biederman et al., "Toxic Justice," 12.

118   Mark D. Plevin, Leslie A. Davis, and Tacie Yoon, H., "Where Are They Now, Part Six: An Update On Developments In Asbestos-Related Bankruptcy Cases," *Mealey's Asbestos Bankruptcy Report* 11, no. 7 (2012): 14.

that information relating to claims against trusts is discoverable.[119] Other courts, including the Judicial Panel on Multidistrict Litigation, have mandated that plaintiffs disclose information submitted to bankruptcy trusts and the amount of payments received from asbestos trusts for the purpose of reducing a judgment entered against the defendant.[120] Finally, other courts "have required claimants' counsel to file or produce any bankruptcy claims that were being contemplated, so that non-debtor defendants could set off from any damages award the amounts received or to be received by the plaintiffs from any bankruptcy trusts."[121] Legislative solutions were also tried. If enacted, the Furthering Asbestos Claim Transparency (FACT) Act of 2013 (H.R. 982) would require trusts set up through a Chapter 11 bankruptcy reorganization caused by asbestos liabilities to submit quarterly reports to the bankruptcy court with the Executive Office for United States Trustees on damage claims and payments and to file all such reports.[122]

Whether these strategies have avoided overcompensation is a vexed question, one that Dixon and his colleagues at the RAND Corporation tried to tackle in their 2011 study of asbestos bankruptcy trusts. Although Dixon and colleagues were unable to provide an answer based on actual court awards and trust payments for lack of data on point, they analyze the communication channels that exist between courts and trusts in six jurisdictions. Their study shows that the legal environment is highly fragmented because of differences on liability regimes, court procedures, and the behaviors of plaintiffs, defendants, and their attorneys, and that different scenarios are possible, some of which contemplate the possibility of over-compensation.

Overcompensation seems less likely in jurisdictions in which a tort claimant must file, before trial, a form disclosing all claim trusts that have been filed and in those in which courts reduce damages to the extent to which the victim received trust payments before the verdict. In some jurisdiction, in which joint and several liability governs the allocation of liability among multiple companies, defendants ordered to pay damages as a result of an adverse judgment can seek indemnity from asbestos trusts for their share of liability. Finally, some trusts developed rules and strategies, or at least "are on the lookout," that prevent trust claimants from obtaining payments for injury that were covered by another source.[123] In the end, Dixon and colleagues conclude that:

---

119   *Shepherd v. Pneumo-Abex, LLC,* 2010 WL 3431663, Memorandum and Order (E.D. Pa. August 30, 2010) (USA); *Ferguson v. Lorillard Tobacco Co.,* 2011 WL 5903453, Memorandum and Order (E.D. Pa. November 22, 2011) (USA).

120   *In re Asbestos Prodcs Liab. Litig. (No. VI),* MDL No. 875, Order Regarding Bankruptcy Claims (MARDOC cases) (E.D. Pa. January 27, 2012) (USA).

121   Plevin, Davis, and Yoon, "Where Are They Now, Part Six: An Update On Developments In Asbestos-Related Bankruptcy Cases," 14.

122   *Furthering Asbestos Claim Transparency (FACT) Act of 2013.* House of Representatives. H.R. 982 (2013) (USA).

123   Dixon and McGovern, *Asbestos bankruptcy trusts and tort compensation,* 29-31.

In some cases, the replacement of once-solvent defendants by trusts increases total plaintiff compensation. This increase in total compensation can come at the expense of future plaintiffs. In addition, we have shown that payments by solvent defendants can increase, sometimes by more than the amount of the bankrupt firms' pre-reorganization liability that is not covered by the trusts. We have also identified circumstances under which total plaintiff compensation decreases, as well as circumstances under which total plaintiff compensation and payments by solvent defendants remain unchanged.[124]

It is fair to say that, in 2013, the jury is still out on the issue of overcompensation.

Problems of unequal treatment among claimants are rooted in the rules that govern asbestos trusts and in the fact that only a handful of law firms represent the great majority of trust claimants and that the appointment of the future claimants' representative is made by these firms.[125] In 2004, Francis McGovern noted that the plaintiffs' bar "is represented by approximately twenty-five lawyers who serve on the various asbestos bankruptcy committees. Roughly seven to fifteen of those lawyers can effectively speak for all of their peers. If those seven to fifteen lawyers can agree among themselves on the details of a prepackaged bankruptcy, there is a substantial likelihood that there will be no critical opposition from the plaintiffs to an eventual plan of reorganization."[126]

Firms have used their power to influence the destiny of prepackaged asbestos trusts in a way that has resulted in unequal treatment of claimants despite the fact one of the requirements of "same treatment for all claimants" is a hallmarks principle of the Bankruptcy Code. First, some prepackaged approvals involved "a large discrepancy between what is paid to claimants who qualify for payment under the pre-petition trust and those who must look solely to the post-petition trust."[127] In some cases, influential firms have conditional support to approval if "claims of the plaintiff lawyers' current inventory of clients [are paid] at values that are considerable inflated when compared to the amounts to be paid out of the §524g trust for similar claims after the approval of the plan and trust."[128] The issue is hard to properly investigate because negotiations of prepackaged plans take

---

124   Ibid., xiv.

125   Five law firms are particularly influential: Kazan, McClain, Satterley, Lyons, Greenwood & Oberman; Baron & Budd, P.C.; Weitz & Luxenberg, PC; Cooney and Conway; and Motley Rice LLC.

126   Francis E. McGovern, "Asbestos Legislation II: Section 524(g) Without Bankruptcy," *Pepperdine Law Review* 31 (2004): 247-248.

127   Mark D. Plevin, Robert T. Ebert, and Leslie A. Epley, "Pre-Packaged Asbestos Bankruptcies: A Flawed Solution," *South Texas Law Review* 44 (2003): 911.

128   Lester Brickman, "Ethical Issues in Asbestos Litigation," *Hofstra Law Review* 33 (2005): 874.

place in secret.[129] Furthermore, pre-petition payments are made based on a "far less stringent evaluation to determine entitlement to compensation."[130]

Second, future claimants may end up receiving less than current claimants. In these cases, the focus of the criticism is on the role of the futures' representative, on the conditions of her appointment, and on her real capacity of truly representing future claimants. Futures' representatives play a critical role in protecting the interests of future victims especially because the funds allocated to the trust are not unlimited and claiming rates difficult to predict. Their presence is certainly more effective in conventional bankruptcies rather than prepackaged. In conventional bankruptcy, the representative participates in all negotiations that allocate all funds. In prepackaged ones, they do not participate in the negotiations that lead to the establishment of the trust: they can only participate in the allocation of what is left, "since half the debtor's value [is] already off the table,"[131] and they can only access the information that "the debtor elects to provide."[132] Furthermore, the effectiveness of the futures representative is questioned because of conflict of interest with regard to her appointment. In prepackaged trust, a futures representative is hired and paid by the debtor during pre-filing negotiations. Once papers are filed, courts often appoint the same person as post-filing futures representative. Since the plans are already set, the "old" representative in new clothes will likely not challenge the proposed allocation of funds.

The last strand of criticism focuses on insurance companies' fair involvement in bankruptcy trusts. The argument is that insurers are not offered a fair opportunity to present their case, participate in the establishment of the trust, and contribute to identifying which creditors are entitled to payments and the amounts of those payments. Rather, insurance companies are asked to pay the bill that assumes insurance coverage. This, critics argue, is a shortcoming of the process, one that could be easily solved by more extensive involvement of insurance companies throughout the process.[133] On the other hand, bankruptcy courts routinely "form a committee to represent ... insurers in the negotiations in a manner similar to the manner in which insurers' interests are represented in all major insurance coverage litigation."[134]

Notwithstanding these issues, twenty years into their implementations, it is not hard to find a positive side to asbestos trust. First, the "asbestos amendments," which were enacted as part of the Bankruptcy Act Reform Act of 1994, are the only successful attempt to reform some aspects of asbestos compensation at the federal level. Asbestos trusts have gone farther than any other effort to find a solution to

---

129 Plevin, Ebert, and Epley, "Pre-Packaged Asbestos Bankruptcies: A Flawed Solution," 909-911.
130 Ibid., 909-912.
131 Ibid., 915.
132 Ibid., 916.
133 Ibid., 919-921.
134 McGovern, "Asbestos Legislation II: Section 524(g) Without Bankruptcy," 255.

asbestos compensation that goes beyond judicial adjudication. They are "the only generally recognized legal vehicle that is currently available for imposing finality on a defendant's asbestos liability"[135] and that guarantees compensation to future claimants. They are usually inspired by principles of fairness and equity among present and future claimants. Compensation comes in its entirety from private pockets, and taxpayer money is not touched. They are rather efficient processes. Finally, they exclude from compensation claims of dubious value that often use money that should go to sicker victims. This has had a positive impact on the tort system because several asbestos firms, who believe in asbestos trusts as vehicle to fair and reasonable compensation, have stopped representing unimpaired victims in courts.

In 2013, hopes for a legislative solution to asbestos compensation are nowhere to be found. Courts have abandoned hyper-management strategies and have rediscovered individual treatment of cases, which is not easy however since for several decades asbestos cases have been rarely tried and often settled in bulk. Most of the compensation comes from the wealthy pockets of asbestos trusts, which are up and running but often paying just cents to the dollar given the unclear projections of future cases and suspicions of conflict of interest, which might have resulted in selling out future claimants. Asbestos disease rates are declining but still steady. This means that asbestos compensation will be an issue for the foreseeable future and that personal injury litigation will likely be an integral part of it for years to come.

---

135   McGovern, "The Tragedy of the Asbestos Commons," 1756.

# Chapter 6
# Asbestos firms and their liabilities

Since the 1800s, asbestos firms have been key actors throughout the history of asbestos and have exercised a substantial influence in asbestos compensation. Firms have hired workers, withdrawn key medical information, lobbied governments, appeared in courts to defend themselves, relocated their business to escape liabilities, filed for bankruptcy, settled cases, set up voluntary compensation schemes, paid damages to asbestos victims—in most cases only after victims had been able to secure verdicts after extensive litigation. Many are the companies that played important roles at different times and in different countries. Most firms have abandoned the asbestos business or more simply disappeared because of bankruptcy or other forms of dissolution. Few of the companies that were in business a century ago have survived or are still connected to asbestos.

This chapter looks at three of these firms that were major players of the asbestos industry since the beginning of the twentieth century and are still in operation: James Hardie, Cape, and Eternit. For each firm, I outline their business model of each company and highlight some of the strategies that they implemented to avoid accountability for their asbestos liabilities. The chapter, which is a break from the country-by-country exposition of the material so far, enriches the data and the analysis with a transnational outlook—these three firms operated in different countries and litigation against them was brought in various jurisdictions—on asbestos compensation as a set of cultural responses to the dark side of industrialization. The stories of the three firms raise important issues of the role of corporate law. In particular, the chapter highlights how adherence to two bedrock principles of corporate law (the limited liability of shareholders and the doctrine of separate and distinct corporate entity) enabled firms to postpone, limit, and even avoid, facing their asbestos liabilities and how victims engaged in legal struggles in which they found themselves catching up with powerful adversaries' use of corporate law to escape the rule of law.

## James Hardie's Machiavellian corporate restructuring

In Australia, James Hardie is synonymous with asbestos. A leader in fiber cement building products with operations in Australia, the United States, New Zealand, Indonesia, Chile, and the Philippines, James Hardie mined, manufactured and distributed the majority of Australian asbestos thus dominating the domestic asbestos industry for decades. The firm assumed the parent/subsidiary structure in the 1930s. James Hardie Industries Limited (JHIL) held all of the shares of two subsidiaries, James Hardie and Company Pty Limited (Coy) and Jsekarb Pty Limited (Jsekarb), which run the operations of the business. Coy manufactured fiber cement building products and asbestos-cement pipes and Jsekarb manufactured brake linings for motor vehicles, railway wagons and locomotives.[1] The company reached the peak of its growth by the mid-1950s when "more than half of the new homes built in New South Wales were made from Hardie's asbestos-cement sheets."[2]

Since its business generated significant asbestos liabilities, Hardie began being targeted by lawsuits in the 1970s. In a matter of a few years, Hardie realized the magnitude of its asbestos liabilities and began enacting stratagems to avoid accountability. The first stratagem involved settling cases of union members for small amounts. This, in 1979, Hardie and the Federated Miscellaneous Workers Union agreed that any Hardie employee who was diagnosed with an asbestos disease recognized by the Dust Disease Board of New South Wales would receive an out-of-court lump sum award of AUD 14,000.[3] The stratagem however was ineffective. Rather than turning off victims, the agreement invited victims to come forward. Asbestos lawsuits increased dramatically and, from 1981 to 2000, James Hardie paid out over AUD 130m to more than 2,000 asbestos victims. This wave of cases led Hardie to enact a second stratagem involving a substantial amount of conglomerate restructuring. This stratagem effectively shielded Hardie from asbestos liabilities for a decade.

The stratagem was put to work in 1996 and consisted of four stages. The first stage (1996-2001) strategy entailed modifying the existing conglomerate structure by transferring the lucrative operating business (that is, all non-asbestos assets of Coy and Jsekarb) to James Hardie NV (JHNV), a subsidiary of RCI Pty Limited, a Dutch company that was fully owned by JHIL (see Figures 6.1 and 6.2).

At the end of this stage, JHIL, which retained all shares in the two subsidiaries, owned two empty boxes soaked in asbestos liability.

The second stage (February 2001) entailed Jsekarb becoming a subsidiary of Coy and Coy's, shares being transferred to the Medical Research and Compensation Foundation (MRCF), a charitable trust set up for the purpose of conducting research on asbestos toxicity and compensating asbestos victims (see Figure 6.3). Later, Coy and Jsekarb were respectively renamed Amaca Pty Ltd and Amaba Pty Ltd. The second stage only entailed the signing of the 2001 Deed of Covenant and Indemnity, an agreement between Coy, Jsekarb, and JHIL under which "JHIL undertook to make payments totaling AUD 112.5m over 42 years in return for an

---

1   David F. Jackson, "Report of the Special Commission of Inquiry into the Medical Research and Compensation Foundation" (Sydney: The Cabinet Office: New South Wales Government, 2004), 123.

2   Jock McCulloch, "The Mine at Baryulgil: Work, Knowledge, and Asbestos Disease," *Labour History* 92 (2007): 113.

3   Ibid., 119.

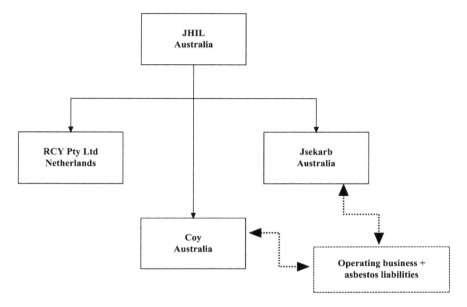

**Figure 6.1    James Hardie (pre-1996)**

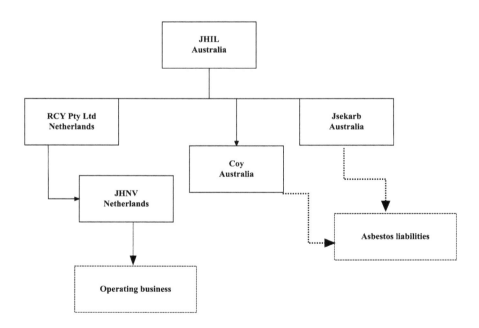

**Figure 6.2    James Hardie (1996-2000)**

indemnity and covenant not to sue in relation to certain asbestos claims and inter-company transactions."[4] As a result, the operating business and asbestos liability were separated into different corporate entities: the asbestos liabilities went to MRCF and the operating businesses stayed with the James Hardie group.

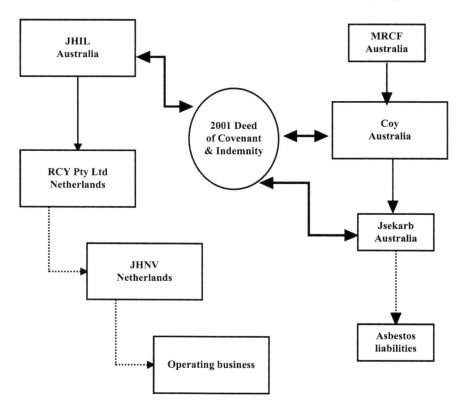

**Figure 6.3    James Hardie (February 2001)**

The third stage (October 2001) entailed rearranging the parent/subsidiary structures within the James Hardie group (see Figure 6.4). To do so, the Dutch company RCI Pty Limited was renamed James Hardie Industries NV (JHINV) and became a subsidiary of JHIL. Its shares in JHNV—the company that held all operating businesses—however were transferred to JHIL. At this point, JHINV became the parent company of the conglomerate, holding, amongst others, all shares in two subsidiaries: JHIL and JHNV.

---

4   *James Hardie (Investigations and Proceedings) Bill 2004.*

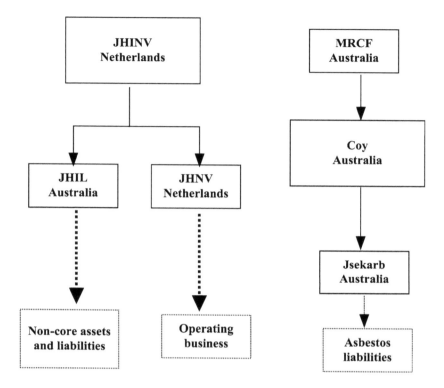

**Figure 6.4      James Hardie (October 2001)**

This meant that AUD 1.9b left Australia for Europe. The small European state had not been chosen randomly: at the time, the Netherlands was one of the few countries around the world that had not signed a treaty for the enforcement of judicial orders with Australia. The fourth and final stage (2003-2004) entailed changing JHIL's name into ABN 60 Pty Ltd (ABN60) and separating it from the (now Dutch-based) James Hardie group (see Figure 6.5).

ABN60 cancelled all shares held in it by JHINV. As a result, ABN 60 became a wholly owned subsidiary of ABN 60 Foundation Pty Limited and ceased to be a member of the James Hardie Group. Immediately prior to the cancellation of shares, ABN 60 entered into a Deed of Covenant, Indemnity and Access with JHINV. The combined reading of the 2003 Deed of Covenant, Indemnity and Access and its 2004 Rectification stipulate that ABN60, which has negligible assets, renounces its right to be indemnified for asbestos claims by JHINV. The legal picture that emerges from the conglomerate restructuring is both frightening and depressing: what was once the parent company of subsidiaries that had dealt in asbestos for more than half a century became a company estranged from the conglomerate, with no operating business, and negligible assets. The four-stage Machiavellian exit strategy left victims with no remedy against a profitable conglomerate that had generated a substantial amount of unmet asbestos liabilities.

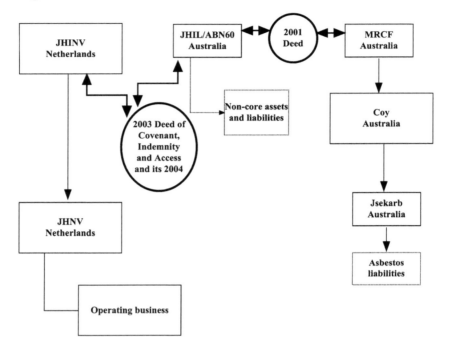

**Figure 6.5     James Hardie (2003-2004)**

The Machiavellian plan, however, did not go unchallenged. In reaction to such grim prospects of recovery, unions and asbestos victim advocacy groups organized public protests and a successful boycott of James Hardie products in 2004.[5] By May of 2005, James Hardie had lost 2 percent in annual net profit as a consequence of the boycott.[6] The loss exceeded AUD 1b.[7] The protests and boycotts also found allies in the political world. The State of New South Wales established a Commission of Inquiry with the mandate to look into MRCF and the circumstances "in which MRCF was separated from the James Hardie Group and whether this may have

---

5    Stephen Gibbs, "Mines and Communities: Boycott call on Hardie gathers pace." *MAC: Mines and Communities*. Published electronically August 4, 2004. http://www.minesandcommunities.org/article.php?a=5544&l=1.

6    AAP. "Boycotts hit James Hardie sales." Published electronically May 16, 2005. http://www.theage.com.au/news/Business/Boycotts-hit-James-Hardie-sales/2005/05/16/1116095891708.html.

7    Ben Hills, "The James Hardie story: asbestos victims' claims evaded by manufacturer," *International Journal of Occupational and Environmental Health* 11, no. 2 (2005).

resulted in or contributed to a possible insufficiency of assets to meet its future asbestos-related liabilities ... and the adequacy of current arrangements available to MRCF under the Corporations Act."[8] The inquiry concluded that James Hardie had engaged in deceptive conduct that misled the stock exchange to understate the extent of future asbestos liabilities. This finding was reinforced in 2012 when the High Court of Australia upheld the conviction of seven Hardie directors, including the former chairman Meredith Hellicar, for making misleading statements, and thus breaching their duties as directors, when in 2001 they shifted the company to the Netherlands with the promise that they had formed a "fully funded" body to meet all future compensation claims.[9] As the inquiry had already established, the Fund was far from being fully funded: "Within three years, the compensation fund cupboard was empty, short by an estimated $1.5 billion."[10]

The inquiry however left James Hardie with few options. In 2006, the conglomerate negotiated the establishment of a new, more generously funded charitable trust with the government of New South Wales. This trust, called the Asbestos Injuries Compensation Fund (AICF), is a public-private partnership between James Hardie and the NSW government and its terms mandated that, after an initial deposit of AUD 184,000, James Hardie would fund it for 40 years with a yearly sum drawn from up to 35 percent of the company's annual cash flow.[11] In 2009, AICF reported that all personal injury claims caused by exposure to asbestos in Australia "in respect of which final judgment has been give against, or a binding settlement has been entered into by [any company of the James Hardie group]" were being paid.[12] Compensation was further guaranteed against corporate stratagems to avoid liability by the provision that events such as bankruptcy and restructuring of the holding company, which is the signatory of the trust deed, would have no effect as to James Hardie's obligation to the Fund.

In 2009, however, James Hardie's willingness to stick to its obligation was tested as the global economic crisis weakened its commitment financially to support the Fund. The collapse of the housing market in the United States, with the resulting collapse of orders in the homebuilding industry, dried up cash flow, and in April 2009 the company made public statements warning that it was unlikely to contribute to the Fund: "With assets of just AUD 140m at the end of March, the fund says it may be unable to meet all of its commitments within two years."[13]

---

8    Jackson, "Report of the Special Commission of Inquiry into the Medical Research and Compensation Foundation," 3.

9    Ian Verrender, "The shameful legacy of James Hardie," *The Sydney Morning Herald*, May 5, 2012.

10    Ibid.

11    James Hardie Industries, "Amended and Restated Final Funding Agreement (Amended FFA), Copy conformed to include all amendments to March 31, 2009," http://www.ir.jameshardie.com.au/public/download.jsp?id=3776.

12    Ibid.

13    Editorial, "Hardie's fund hits trouble," *Newcastle Herald*, April 24, 2009.

Fortunately for asbestos victims, in 2012 Hardie received a generous tax refund in the amount of AUD 369.8 million, 35 percent of which was directed to the AICF.[14] This influx of money replenished the pockets of the Fund, which in the nine months to December 31, 2011 paid out AUD 73.9 million in compensation.[15] In 2011, Hardie relocated one more time, moving its domicile to Ireland allegedly for reasons having to do with taxes and management.[16] Overall the establishment of the Fund is certainly good news for Australian asbestos victims: it is an achievement that was obtained *in spite of* corporate law.

## Cape's successful exit strategy from the American asbestos litigation

Registered in England and Wales, Cape plc is the holding company of a network of subsidiaries that do business in the UK, North Africa, the Middle East and the Far East. Currently this conglomerate specializes in insulation, fire protection, abrasive blasting, refractory, coatings, cleaning, training and other essential non-mechanical services. While its current business is not connected to its asbestos heritage, Cape used to be a leading asbestos firm. The firm was founded in 1893 to control a syndicate that operated South African crocidolite asbestos mines and then expanded to manufacture insulation products containing asbestos. It mined most of the world's amosite asbestos and was a leading producer of crocidolite. Its manufacturing and sales expansion reached its peak after World War II with operations in the UK, the United States, South Africa, France, Germany, and Italy. While the business reach and asbestos liabilities of Cape are global, in this chapter I only focus on corporate restructuring that was implemented by Cape headquarters as exit strategy with regard to asbestos liabilities in the United States.

Cape has done business in the United States since the 1930s. It sold its asbestos to various clients through the Union Asbestos and Rubber Company (UNARCO), which was the exclusive distributor of Cape's asbestos in North America. As a consequence of the success of this business venture, the London headquarters decided, in 1953, to establish a fully-owned subsidiary in Chicago: the North American Asbestos Corporation (NAAC). For several decades, NAAC successfully acted as an "agent" of CASAP, which was based in South Africa and fully owned by Cape, and which in turn fully owned Egnep, another South African part of Cape's conglomerate that ran the mining business. NAAC acted with no authority to bind CASAP contractually and received commission for its service (see Figure 6.6).

---

14   AAP. "Hardie fund to get top-up." Published electronically March 27, 2012. http://www.smh.com.au/national/hardie-fund-to-get-topup-20120327-1vwle.html.

15   Ibid.

16   Elizabeth Knight, "Looking for the joke in logic of James Hardie moving to Ireland." http://www.smh.com.au/business/looking-for-the-joke-in-logic-of-james-hardie-moving-to-ireland-20090616-cgjb.html.

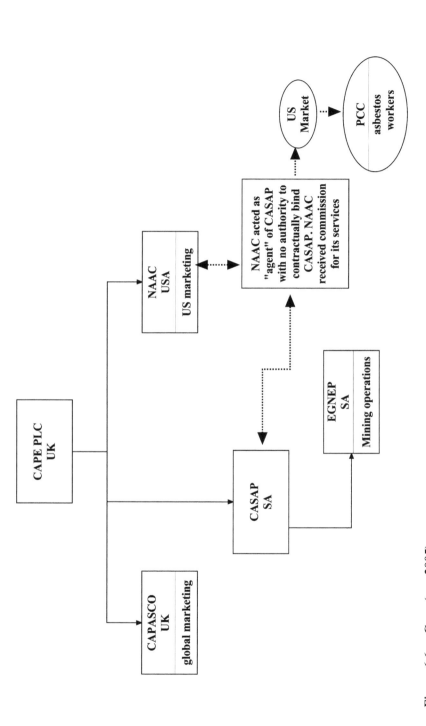

Figure 6.6    Cape (pre–2005)

Between 1953 and the late 1970s, Cape sold "nearly half-a-million tons of asbestos in the United States."[17] One of the buyers of Cape's asbestos was Pittsburg Corning Corporation. Some of the asbestos originating from Cape's mines was used in a Texas-based plant manufacturing asbestos pipe insulation materials.[18] Over the years, many of the employees of this plant developed an asbestos-related disease and, in the early 1970s, approximately 2,000 to 3,000 victims filed tort lawsuits. Cape was named defendant in most of them. One in particular became particularly insidious. In 1977, a group of 462 forced Cape and its business partners to settle the claims for more than USD 20m. Along with NAAC and Egnep, Cape contributed to the settlement with USD 5.2m. Most of the money came from NAAC's insurance. The remaining USD 1.2m was paid by Cape. This settlement, pricey by 1970s standards, exhausted available asbestos insurance for business operations in the United States. Acquiring new insurance looked too expensive to Cape. Very conscious of the implications of settling a case—after the settlement asbestos lawyers would have predictably tried to reach Cape's deep pocket for more—Cape turned to a different strategy just before agreeing to settle: corporate restructuring.

By the time the 1977 settlement was reached, Cape had implemented an exit strategy that involved abandoning the corporation with all the asbestos liabilities, moving the ownership of any business assets left to Liechtenstein, and running the business through new companies owned by trustworthy individuals who had no formal links with the conglomerate. The restructuring, which aimed to separate the conglomerate from its US liabilities by removing the group from the jurisdiction of US courts, was rather simple. The parent company changed its name from Cape Asbestos Company to Cape Industries, sold all of NAAC's assets, and transferred the NAAC share it owned to Cape International and Overseas Ltd. (CIOL), a newly established and vastly undercapitalized English company. All of the parent company's shares in CASAP also went to CIOL with its mining business. On the American front, Cape incorporated Continental Products Corporation (CPC), a corporation set up to market Cape's asbestos in the United States, and established Associated Minerals Corporation (AMC), a Liechtenstein-based company that would appear as the "seller" in all sales of asbestos in the US market. All of CPC's shares were given to Mr. Morgan, the former Vice President of NAAC, and all of AMC's shares were owned by a Liechtenstein lawyer named Ritter, "who agreed to vote as instructed by Cape."[19] The plan was to have CPC acting as "agent" of AMC with no authority contractually to bind AMC in exchange for commission for any service rendered. Through the medium of AMC and with the assistance of CPC, Cape's amosite

---

17    Geoffrey Tweedale and Laurie Flynn, "Piercing the Corporate Veil: Cape Industries and Multinational Corporate Liability for a Toxic Hazard, 1950-2004," *Enterprise and Society* 8, no. 2 (2007): 276.

18    JeVrey L. Levin et al., "Tyler asbestos workers: mortality experience in a cohort exposed to amosite," *Occupational and Environmental Medicine* 55, no. 3 (1998): 156.

19    Tweedale and Flynn, "Piercing the Corporate Veil: Cape Industries and Multi-national Corporate Liability for a Toxic Hazard, 1950-2004," 284.

asbestos continued to be sold into the US until Transvaal Consolidated Exploration Co. Ltd. become the owner of the South African mines in 1979. Yet Cape carefully avoided establishing any link between the conglomerate and the corporate entities created *ad hoc* to operate in the US market so that no contractual or tort liability could flow from its North American operations to the conglomerate.

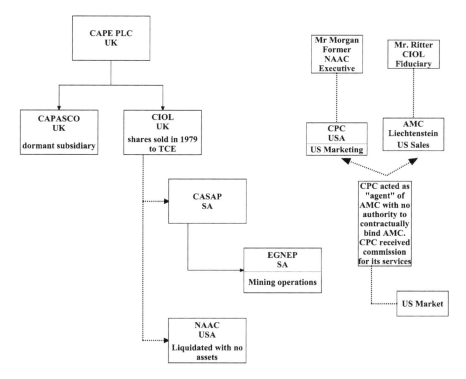

**Figure 6.7     Cape (post-2005)**

While Cape was busy getting its business in order, a new wave of asbestos victims was filing lawsuits. Between April 1978 and November 1979, 206 plaintiffs filed lawsuits naming Cape or one its subsidiaries as defendants. Cape did not appear in court, however, maintaining that the Eastern District of Texas lacked jurisdiction over the company. After securing default judgments against Cape, the asbestos victims (now judgment creditors) tried to enforce them in England. The English judges were confronted with the issue of whether, after the restructuring, Cape conducted business in the United States by using *alter ego* corporations in a way that allowed a US court to pierce the corporate veil and assert jurisdiction over the conglomerate. If indeed Cape had used *alter ego* corporations, the default judgment issued in Texas against Cape would have been proper. The English judges however disagreed with this assertion, and concluded that the facts were insufficient for English courts to disregard the corporate entity, to pierce the corporate veil, and allow the asbestos victims from Texas to attach Cape's assets in England based on the default judgments. Justice Scott contemplated but rejected the argument that Cape had set *alter ego* companies:

> CPC's conduct was much the same as NAAC's had been. It paid the rent for its offices and paid its employees. It received commission from [Associated Minerals Corporation] as well as incurring expenditure and receiving payments in connection with its independent trading activities ... I do not think, on analysis, that the plaintiffs' case is any stronger than their case regarding NAAC. If anything, I think the case is weaker. NAAC was at least a wholly owned subsidiary. CPC, even if incorporated and launched with Cape money, was ... an independently owned company. Like NAAC, CPC acted as agent for the purpose of facilitating the sale in the United States of Cape's asbestos. The seller of the asbestos in NAAC's time was Egnep or Casap. The seller in CPC's time was, nominally, [Associated Minerals Corporation] but, in reality, still, I think, Egnep or Casap. C.P.C., like NAAC, had no authority to bind Egnep, Casap or any other of the Cape subsidiaries to any contract. CPC like NAAC carried on its own business from its own offices at 150, North Wacker Drive. The provision by Cape of the US$160,000 as a starting-up fund does not make the offices Cape's offices or the business Cape's business.[20]

That was the end of the story. The opinion killed US asbestos victims' ambition of satisfying their demand for compensation by attaching Cape's assets in England. Furthermore, the restructuring made any effort to collect money in the United States futile. All assets disappeared, and the few lawsuits in which CPC or Cape were named as defendants, along with dozens of other asbestos defendants, aimed not to obtain enforcement against Cape but to establish its liability in order to trigger coverage of the limited insurance policies from the NAAC period which had not been exhausted (see Figure 6.7).

### Eternit's preemptive corporate structuring

Eternit, the last asbestos firm to be considered in this chapter, provides a rather different yet fascinating case study. In fact, its corporate structure was rather different from the previous two cases. Rather than a conglomerate with subsidiaries propagating from a single parent company, Eternit was structured for its inception as a cartel of companies that coordinated their business activities through the sharing of licenses, shareholders, and directors.

The business history of Eternit began when Ludwig Hatschek, an Austrian businessman, obtained patent protection for a cement-asbestos that he had invented.

---

20    *Adams v Cape Industries plc* [1991] 1 All ER 929 (England).

To exploit the product's profitability, Hatschek established a small company in Austria, entered into an agreement with Russian asbestos mines, under which he agreed to purchase the entire production of asbestos in exchange for the Russians refraining from selling it to competitors that were not licensed to use the Eternit patent, and licensed the product to other businessmen interested in manufacturing it in other countries without becoming himself a shareholder of those companies.

By the time of Hatschek's death in 1914, the product was quickly becoming a sensation. Business men in several European countries jumped on the cement-asbestos bandwagon. The licensees were a handful of handpicked businessmen who set up independent companies in various parts of Europe and beyond, all of which included Eternit as part of their trade name. Among them, members of two families dominated the Eternit cartel over the years: the Emsens family, which established Eternit Belgium, which was later acquired by the Etex Group, and the Schmidheiny family, which established Eternit Switzerland, which was later acquired by the cement group Holcim. Founded in 1905 by the Emsens, an exceptionally wealthy and well-connected family belonging to the "old nobility,"[21] Eternit Belgium operated plants in Belgium, controlled Eternit France and its operations, and contributed to establishing Eternit-Brazil. In 1969, it established a company in Luxembourg, TEAM, by joining forces with two other major asbestos firms, Johns-Manville and Turner & Newall. TEAM went on to develop Eternit businesses in Pakistan, Indonesia, Japan, China, Nigeria, and Senegal.[22] By 1989, Eternit Belgium held 86 percent of TEAM's shares. Acquired in 1920 by the Schmidheiny family, Eternit Switzerland operated plants in Switzerland, bought shares of a crocidolite mine in South Africa, and owned significant shares of Eternit Belgium until 1989, when Stephan Schmidheiny sold his shares to Belgian shareholders.[23] In South Africa, the Schmidheinys owned and operated the third largest mine after Cape's and Gencor's through two subsidiaries, Kuruman Cape Blue Asbestos (KCB) and Danielskuil Cape Blue Asbestos (DCBA).[24] In 1985, Eternit Switzerland was the world's second largest seller of asbestos.[25] The Schmidheiny brothers are or have been major shareholders and board members in other key Swiss companies such as Swissair, Nestlé, Swatch, UBS Asea Brown Boveri, and Holcim. Stephan is the fifth richest Swiss businessman, a resident of Costa Rica, a philanthropist (in 2009, Forbes profiled him as "the Bill Gates of Switzerland")[26] and a recently convicted defendant

---

21   Krols and Teugels, "The dirty legacy of asbestos."

22   Robert F. Ruers, "The International Asbestos Cartel," World Asbestos Report, http://worldasbestosreport.org/conferences/gac/gac2004/ws_G_4_e.php.

23   Ibid.

24   Laurie Kazan-Allen. "Jail Time for Eternit Executives." Published electronically June 28, 2005. http://ibasecretariat.org/lka_jail_for_eternit_exec.php.

25   Laurie Kazan-Allen. "Eternit Pre-Trial Manoeuvre in Italy." Published electronically March 11, 2009. http://ibasecretariat.org/lka_eternit_pre_tria_manouevre_120309.php.

26   Tatiana Serafin, "The Bill Gates Of Switzerland," *Forbes* 2009, 58.

in a criminal trial in Torino, Italy, concerning almost three thousand asbestos deaths among Italians. Thomas is currently a director of Holcim.

Throughout the twentieth century, these Belgian and Swiss companies led a very successful business relationship that involved sharing licenses to the Eternit patent, engaging in anticompetitive cartelization, joining investments in new manufacturing facilities, handpicking shareholders among a restricted number of powerful and well-connected families (the Emsens, the Schmidheinys, the Hatscheks, and the Cuveliers), and appointing interlocking directorates. Krols and Teugels describe Eternit-Belgium as a "feudal" company in which "[t]op management had far more direct contact with leading political officials than with ordinary workers."[27] An investigative report commissioned by the Dutch Socialist Party concluded that four families owned shares in Eternit companies since the early twentieth century and exercised influence over, and in many cases controlled, the Eternit business world-wide.[28] Members of the four prominent families have rotated for three generations on boards of the various Eternit companies around the world.[29] Shareholders of one Eternit company would sit on the board of a different Eternit company so that each company could easily collaborate with and keep an eye on other Eternit businesses. Even today, an Emsens sits on the board of Etex, a Schmidheiny sits on the board of Holcim, and two of the Hatscheks sit on the board of Eternit Austria, which is currently led by a Swedish manager who was employed by Eternit-Germany and Eternit Switzerland before landing in Austria.

Business coordination was facilitated by a cartel that was formalized in 1929, years in which the various Eternit companies agreed to share technology, purchase raw asbestos together, and divide up the market to reduce competition. This agreement, a cartel, was named SAIAC. Ernst Schmidheiny, the majority shareholder of Eternit Switzerland was appointed secretary and meetings were often held in Zurich. SAIAC was intended as a tool to divide the market horizontally among asbestos "competitors." As the 1929 Annual Report of Turner & Newall reveals, SAIAC divided the world market into a "miniature League of Nations."[30] Furthermore, through SAIAC, Eternit companies coordinated a strategy of deception, influence, and—as was customary in the asbestos industry—of deception. It is not a coincidence that SAICA was established in 1929, the year in which "independent researchers identified the symptoms and causes of asbestosis."[31] Membership in SAIAC of various Eternit businesses was certainly instrumental to protecting their interests through coordinated lobbying efforts.

27  Krols and Teugels, "'A Licence to Kill': the Dirty Legacy of Asbestos."

28  Robert F. Ruers and Nico Schouten, *The tragedy of asbestos. Eternit and the consequences of a hundred years of asbestos cement* (Socialistische Partij, 2006), http://international.sp.nl/publications/tragedyofasbestos.pdf.

29  Krols and Teugels, "The dirty legacy of asbestos."

30  Ruers, "The International Asbestos Cartel".

31  McCulloch and Tweedale, *Defending the indefensible: The global asbestos industry and its fight for survival*, 79.

SAIAC members met regularly to decide a response to attacks by scientists, trade unions, the press and governments. Meetings organized at European level by Eternit's Belgian and Swiss officials were always on the theme of "asbestos and health." During a review of the situation in Paris in 1979, company representatives decided that "[s]ubstantial investment will be necessary at various European levels to maintain the asbestos lobby against workers, unions, clients, and politicians. In the long term, it will be in the industry's interest to find substitute products, but it is essential that no company abandons asbestos."[32]

One of the few "outsiders" that entered the business circle created by the Emsens and the Schmidheinys was Adolfo Mazza, an Italian engineer who, as an Eternit licensee, set up the asbestos firm Eternit Pietra Artificiale (renamed Eternit Spa in 1942) and later invented and patented the first machine manufacturing cement-asbestos pipes. Mazza's venture prospered over the years and Mazza gained his place in Eternit's circle. To strengthen its business, in 1952 Mazza solicited capital contributions from the Emsens and the Schmidheinys, who accepted and became shareholders and directors of Eternit Spa. After investing in Eternit Italia, the Emsens and the Schmidheinys slowly took control of the company. By 1966, the Belgians were responsible for mast managerial decisions. In 1972, the year in which the Mazza family sold its shares to the other shareholders, the managerial torch was then passed to the Swiss family, which by the end had took the lead in investing the Italian business, which was nonetheless losing money (see Figure 6.8).

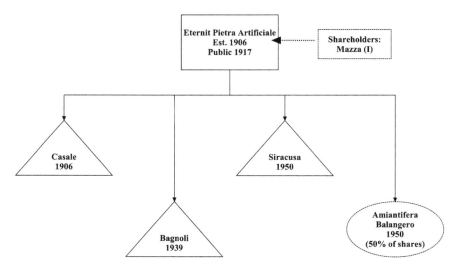

**Figure 6.8      Eternit (1906-1952)**

---

32   Krols and Teugels, "The dirty legacy of asbestos."

The legacy of the Emsens's and Schmidheinys' involvement with Eternit Italia brought legal problems to both families. While in all other countries, companies of the Eternit group have substantially avoided accountability for their asbestos businesses, Eternit has experienced tough times in Italian courts where a belligerent group of asbestos victims often collaborating with a fierce criminal prosecutor pursued compensation in ways unparalleled in other jurisdictions in which the Eternit business had flourished.[33] Even in Italy though, where victim mobilization put substantially more pressure than in other jurisdictions, the Eternit corporate approach, blending, cartelization, lobbying and connection among the boards of the various companies participating in the cartel, contained the liability for many years. For the most part, victims' efforts to secure tort compensation could only target a single company, that is, the company owning and running the specific Eternit plant that had employed the victim. The absence of a parent company limited the victims' ability to target the decision-making center and allowed for assets to be transferred from country to country, thus subtracting them from post-judgment attachment. With regard to the Italian case, as a result of increasing risk of adverse judgment, the Swiss and Belgian shareholders implemented a restructuring of the Italian business to diminish the risk of liabilities (see Figure 6.9).

Between 1980 and 1986, the single operating parent company, which had owned and operated four asbestos-cement plants (one of them was formally owned by a wholly owned subsidiary but effectively "rented" and operated by the Italian parent company), sold its plants to four newly established subsidiaries and became a non-operating parent company with no assets. (The building hosting the production was not part of these assets, as it was given to a third party which cleaned up the site in exchange for the symbolic amount of one Euro.) By the time the first round of verdicts against Eternit Spa were enforceable, the holding company had been deprived of all of its assets, which in turn were since then owned by the various companies established in 1981. The only step the law could take with Eternit Spa was to declare its bankruptcy and liquidate it in 1986 (see Figure 6.10).

Since the bankruptcy created a substantial obstacle to further civil litigation, victims turned to the criminal justice system. A criminal trial eventually took place in Casale in 1993. The trial led to the conviction of the managers of the local company but did not involve the Belgians or the Swiss, who had been the real decision-makers and certainly the true deep pockets in the event of a conviction. At that point, some EUR 3m was put together and divided among 1,700 victims, all of whom were creditors of the bankrupt holding company. The bankruptcy proceedings lasted a few more years as claimants tried to attach the personal assets of Stephan Schmidheiny, the majority shareholder of both the Swiss company

---

33   Gianpiero Rossi, "L'impiego dell'amianto in Italia in contesto civile e professionale—i casi di cronaca," in *Amianto: responsabilità civile e penale e risarcimento danni*, ed. Filippo Martini (Santarcangelo di Romagna: Maggioli Editore, 2012), 18-22.

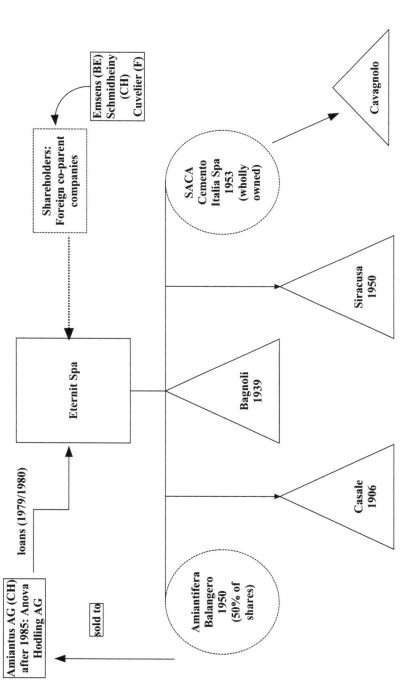

Figure 6.9    Eternit (1972–1980)

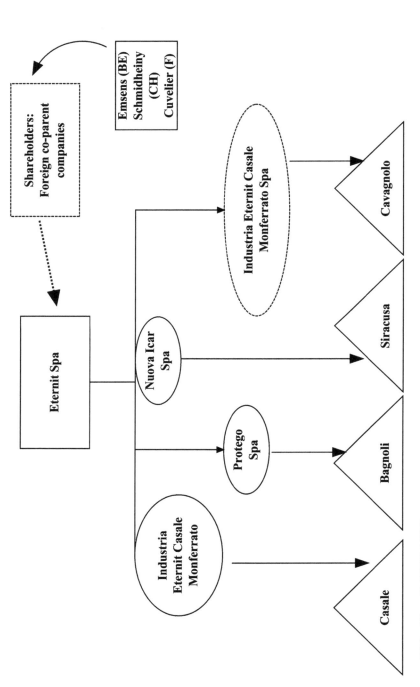

Figure 6.10   Eternit (1980-1986)

and its Italian branch. The bankruptcy court refused to disregard the corporate entity and hold any shareholder personally liable. Approximately EUR 5.5m, most of which was made available by Stephan's brother, Thomas, was distributed to 500 claimants who had filed claims after the first round of payments in 1993. Victims who received payments signed releases of liability. It took nine more years for members of the Emsens and the Schmidheiny families to be found responsible for asbestos causalities caused by the operations of the Italian Eternit companies. Accountability stems from the conviction at the trial level, upheld on appeals, of Stephan Schmidheiny, along with Belgian baron Louis de Cartier de Marchienne, who became involved with asbestos after marrying an Emsens in the 1950s. In 1998, the two businessmen had been charged with harsh accusations originating from a criminal investigation of three thousand asbestos deaths among Italians: 2,600 Eternit employees and 300 residents of communities located close to one of the four Italian Eternit plants.[34] The trial, which started in 2009, ended on February 13, 2012. Both defendants were found guilty of criminal negligence and sentenced to 16 years imprisonment.[35] On June 3, 2013, the Court of Appeals upheld the conviction and increased the sentence for Stephan Schmidheiny to 18 years.[36] The defendants were ordered to pay damages to the over 6,000 civil claimants who had joined the criminal trial as victims seeking civil damages. For each death, damages awarded range between EUR 30,000 and EUR 35,000, for a total amount of EUR 95 million. In addition, defendants were ordered to pay damages to the municipalities of Casale Monferrato and Cavagnolo, to the Piemonte Region, and various labor unions and nonprofit organizations, as well as indemnify the worker's compensation board to payments made to claimants throughout the years. In addition, the Court found four of the foreign co-parent companies (Etex, Anova, Amindus, and Becon), which had held shares of Eternit Spa, jointly and severally liable for all damages caused by the criminal conduct of Schmidheiny and de Cartier de Marchienne. These entities' liability is in addition to the personal liability of the two co-defendants.[37] This trial, which was quickly labeled the "Great Asbestos Trial,"[38] brought key decision-makers behind the Eternit cartel and foreign parent companies to justice for the first time since the production of Eternit materials began. It is important

---

34   *Richiesta di Rinvio a Giudizio [Indictment], Case 24265/04*, Schmidheiny and De Cartier De Marchienne, (Procura della Repubblica [Office of the Prosecutor], Torino, October 10, 2008) (Italy).

35   *Sentenza [Judgment] n. 5219/09*, Schmidheiny and De Cartier De Marchienne, (Tribunale [Trial Court], Torino, February 13, 2012) (Italy).

36   *Sentenza [Judgment] n. 5621/12*, Schmidheiny and De Cartier De Marchienne, (Corte d'Appello [Court of Appeals], Torino, June 3, 2013) (Italy). Louis de Cartier de Marchienne died on May 21, 2013 at the age of 92, a few days shy from the appeal sentence of the Turin trial.

37   However, because of Louis de Cartier de Marchienne's death, plaintiffs must file a tort claim in Belgium to recover damages against Etex.

38   David Allen and Laurie Kazan-Allen, eds, *Eternit and the Great Asbestos Trial* (London: The International Ban Asbestos Secretariat, 2012).

to stress though that the theory of law that was deployed to achieve this result was not tort theory along with the "piercing the corporate veil" doctrine. Rather the case was grounded on individual criminal liability of mangers/directors/ shareholders of asbestos firms. Civil law alone was insufficient to deliver justice to Eternit victims. Furthermore, in the aftermath of the judgment, defendants have refused to pay compensation to the victims, who are currently exploring strategies to attach defendants' assets and but also to find the financial resources to fight the enforcement battle.[39]

A grim picture emerges from these three stories. James Hardie, Cape, and Eternit were able to avoid accountability for decades: at least one generation of workers was exposed to asbestos after the companies had become aware of the risk associated with the "magical fiber." Reluctantly, these companies paid some compensation to the victims over the years often trying to escape liability by using corporate screens and other strategies intended to prevent key assets from being subjected to attachment as victims tried to enforce judgments. To some extent, corporate and procedural laws trumped tort law: theories of separate entity and limited liability as well as jurisdictional barriers enabled corporate actors' strategies aiming at hiding assets from tort creditors by relocating them in safe jurisdictions or transferring them to newly established separate legal entities. This is an important piece of the story of asbestos compensation as a set of cultural responses to the asbestos epidemic. The next and concluding chapter will pull together the different pieces of this story.

---

39   AFEVA, "Lettera al Ministro della Salute Prof. Renato Balduzzi [Letter to Prof. Renato Balduzzi, Head of the Health Ministry]," http://ibasecretariat.org/italian_lettera_al_ministro_jun_2012.pdf.

# Chapter 7
# Asbestos compensation as a set of cultural responses to the dark side of industrialization

Since the early days of its modern use, asbestos has killed thousands of victims. To address the rise of the asbestos epidemic, countries have developed various responses, which range from banning use to compensating victims of asbestos. This book has presented a comparative inquiry of how victims' compensation has been used in Belgium, England, Italy, and the United States as a set of cultural responses to the asbestos epidemic. This perspective allows readers to appreciate how capitalist societies have deployed legal tools—assignments of responsibility, compensation, and obligation related to injury—to address the risks generated by industrialization. Ultimately the book aims to assess how the tension between profits and equity, which is inherent to capitalism, has been confronted in the context of the asbestos epidemic. Overall, the evidence presented shows that asbestos compensation emerged as a response to the rise of the asbestos epidemic in all four countries. These responses were all organized and structured by reference to collective cultural schemas, some of which were shared among countries. A particularly influential perceptual frame that all four countries shared is the moral economy schema, which emerged from collective constructions and as a particular pattern of meaning of the welfare state. To justify the existence of the welfare state in capitalist democracies, this perceptual frame "assumed capital and state reciprocities with labor and citizens and an ethical obligation to minimal social reproduction."[1] Its influence on the rise of asbestos compensation is clear: the asbestos epidemic became in fact slowly perceived as injurious to the extent to which it was a breach of the prevailing norms of the moral economy. This cultural process translated into victims understanding the link between asbestos exposure and their injuries, triggering expectations of redress, and producing mobilization to secure compensation. It is Friedman's total justice becoming reality.

Asbestos compensation was thus born. The initial response to the perceived injuriousness of the asbestos epidemic of all four countries was to extend workers' compensation coverage to victims of occupational exposure to asbestos. It reproduced the cultural imperatives of the moral economy. While a source of satisfaction for many victims, the initial structuration of asbestos compensation confined institutional responses to the asbestos epidemic to workers' compensation thus excluding from compensation many victims (self-employed victims, spouses, victims of environmental exposure, victims of diseases not recognized under

1 Robinson, *Latin America and global capitalism: a critical globalization perspective*, 14.

workers' compensation). This phase led to a hegemonic normalization of asbestos disease within the confines of the welfare state. This model was however challenged over time when victims triggered counter-hegemonic processes aimed at expanding compensation to new categories of victims and new types of diseases. These reactions diverged cross-nationally and led to routinized processes, rules, and outcomes of asbestos compensation that currently differ greatly across nations.[2] These comparative differences are the product of unique macro- and micro-level structural conditions and nation-specific cultural experiences, which both contributed to structuration processes that pushed asbestos compensation in different directions.

The result is that victims now receive compensation from a mix of sources (torts damages as well as payments from workers' compensation, social security *ad hoc* compensation schemes, settlements, and bankruptcy trusts) that differ across nations. In the United States, victims' primary path to compensation is personal injury litigation against manufacturers of products containing asbestos. Asbestos litigation has been a particularly controversial and highly debated phenomenon in American law because of its massive size, inefficiency and high transaction costs, failure to deliver individual treatment of claims, and impact on industries that had very little to do with the firms that caused the asbestos epidemic. In England, asbestos compensation is constituted by a mix of payments coming from workers' compensation, settlements and judicial awards, and *ad hoc* compensation funds. The English experience's unique traits include the unique role of workers' compensation claims as gatekeepers and funding sources of personal injury litigation, the consistent involvement of insurance companies in settlement negotiations, and the development of contested doctrines that apply only to asbestos cases. In Italy, asbestos compensation is also the result of a combination of workers' compensation payments and judicial awards for personal injuries. However, the former source is much more prominent than the latter, because of the key role that unions have played in the transformation of asbestos compensation in Italy, the contested nature of employers' immunity, and the peculiar use of criminal investigation to which personal injury claims are joined. In Belgium, the bulk of asbestos compensation comes from workers' compensation payments and, more recently, an *ad hoc* mesothelioma compensation fund that compensates victims of any exposure to asbestos, occupational or not. Asbestos disease became compensable much later than in other countries, and the strict workers' compensation rules that establish employer's immunity victims have compressed victims' mobilization in courts to a handful of personal injury cases, all unsuccessful with the exception of a 2011 case brought by a victim of secondhand exposure.

It is also important to recognize that cultural change replicated structural inequalities. Through gradual steps, the asbestos industry was able to influence compensation processes in its favor by delaying its emergence, avoid its consequence,

---

2  I use the term "routinization" to refer to a stage of maturity of claim emergence in which the response to asbestos epidemic can be described as a set of stable legal norms, policy outcomes, and practices.

and strategically involve the institutions of the welfare state to minimize the costs of the private sectors. No matter what the structural conditions and nation-specific cultural experiences were, asbestos companies dominated the emergence and transformation of asbestos compensation to the detriment of victims, whose only response was to engage in compensation wars against asbestos defendants. These wars were more successful in some countries than in others. Where they failed, they produced unsatisfactory remedies and limited opportunity for compensation.

## The breach of the prevailing norms of the moral economy

Compensation for injury involves a process that involves claiming a remedy and culminates with a payment. In their seminal paper on the emergence and transformation of disputes, Felstiner, Abel, and Sarat set the theoretical framework for reasoning about how harmful events lead to claiming. Disputes are social constructs that "reflect whatever definition the observer gives to the concept."[3] This theoretical insight led to a shift in the scholarly study of disputing from actual disputes to their antecedents in an effort to capture the full significance of disputes as social constructs. A critical antecedent of disputing entails victims' shift in perception of events as injurious. "In order for disputes to emerge and remedial action to be taken, an unperceived injurious experience … must be transformed into a perceived injurious experience."[4] A victim must thus reinterpret "trouble, problems, personal and social dislocation" that take place in everyday life as injurious for compensation opportunities to arise.[5] This reinterpretation occurs when victims attribute new meanings to everyday occurrences by draining from "the common repertoire of legal schemas and resources."[6]

The emergence of asbestos compensation perfectly fits this framework. After having failed to perceive asbestos disease as injurious for decades because of the lack of knowledge of asbestos toxicity and because of the widespread attitude that dying while or because of working was an acceptable fact of life—a sentiment captured by Merle Haggard in the *Workin' Man Blues*: "I ain't never been on welfare, that's one place I won't be/Cause I'll be working long as my two hands are fit to use"[7]— victims' legal consciousness awakened as a result of the progressive reinterpreting the personal and social displacement caused by disease. While this process took place at different times in the four countries researched in the book, the same cultural schema triggered the process of reinterpretation of asbestos victims in all four countries: the moral economy that justified the welfare state in capitalist democracies.

---

3 Felstiner, Abel, and Sarat, "The Emergence and Transformation of Disputes: Naming, Blaming, Claiming …": 631-632.

4 Ibid., 633.

5 Ibid.

6 Ewick and Silbey, *The common place of law: stories from everyday life*, 247.

7 Merle Haggard, *Workin' Man Blues* (lyrics) (1969).

Mau's definition of moral economy is "the ongoing logic of social support for, and acceptance of, the redistributive nature of welfare provision whereby a commitment to the fate of the less-well off, the disadvantaged and people at risk is recognized."[8] This schema became part of social actors' everyday life in industrialized societies as a consequence of the emergence of the welfare state. The welfare-regulatory state, from its appearance to its post-World War II apogee during the golden years of the Keynesian Welfare National State and Atlantic Fordism, assumed capital and state reciprocities with labor and citizens and an ethical obligation to minimal social reproduction.[9] These assumptions provided ethical justification for the existence of the welfare state and produced a culture of moral economy that contributed to social actors' repertoire of schemas to interpret the institutions and practices and the welfare state. The emergence of the welfare state was an intellectual statement signaling convergence in a *via media* between unfettered capitalism and socialism, which renounced possessive individualism and embraced "an ideal of solidarity to supplement the customary liberal commitment to personal freedom."[10]

After asbestos disease became perceived as injurious because it constituted a breach of the prevailing norms of a moral economy, asbestos compensation emerged as cultural response to this breach. As evidence of asbestos toxicity became known, asbestos workers began to realize that they were "victims" of exposure to a toxic substance, their disease was preventable, and would not have occurred if employers had made different decisions with regard to workplace safety. Asbestos disease was thus not one of those misfortunes that happen in life, one that needed to be tolerated and endured, but an "injurious" event perpetrated in breach of the principles supporting the ideas of a moral economy. Capital accumulation was no longer justified if pursued at the expenses of social reproduction. The breach of this shared understanding of the moral justification of capitalist economies produced expectation of redress whenever the minimum of social reproduction was lost. Citizens began to expect the welfare state to come to rescue of those in need and to redress the deficit of social reproduction. This expectation of redress translated progressively into an expectation of legal redress, which Lawrence Friedman labels total justice.[11] Karen Tani documented that in the United States "the rise of a vibrant language of rights within the federal social welfare bureaucracy" took place during the 1930s and 1940s, when the welfare state was expanded as a consequence of the Great Depression.[12] "As early as

---

8    Steffen Mau, *The moral economy of welfare states: Britain and Germany compared* (London; New York: Routledge, 2003), 31.

9    Jessop, *The future of the capitalist state.* 55-94; Robinson, *Latin America and global capitalism: a critical globalization perspective*, 14.

10    Kloppenberg, *Uncertain victory: social democracy and progressivism in European and American thought, 1870-1920*, 7.

11    Friedman, *Total Justice*.

12    Karen M. Tani, "Welfare and Rights Before the Movement: Rights as a Language of the State," *Yale Law Journal* 122, no. 2 (2012).

1935," Tani writes, "some Americans … deliberately and persistently employed rights language in communications about welfare benefits."[13]

The emergence of asbestos compensation is thus connected to the rise of the culture of total justice that pervaded the aftermath of the Second Industrial Revolution. Individuals came to see that many of the "troubles, problems, personal and social dislocation"[14] experienced in everyday life in industrial societies were man-made. These cultural transformations allowed asbestos victims to identify the injurious nature of diseases caused by exposure to the magical mineral, to "name" it in a legal sense, to transform it into a grievance.[15] In this light, the data presented in this book provide comparative support to Lawrence Friedman's thesis and show that legal culture's total justice turn is true not only in the United States but also in many other Western industrialized nations.

## Hegemonic reproduction of the moral economy

In all countries, the initial response to the perceived injuriousness of the asbestos epidemic that each nation took was to extend entitlement to workers' compensation payments to victims of disease caused by occupational exposure to asbestos. The structuration of asbestos compensation thus initially reproduced the moral economy. This schema not only infused meaning that enable victims to seek appropriate compensation; it also became the source of ideas on how to deal with the growing demands for compensation of asbestos victims and the measure of such compensation. It played a double role: it contributed to the emergence of asbestos compensation and it dictated its structural horizon by shaping ideas of what the *proper* institutional responses to asbestos claiming needed to be (see Figure 7.1).

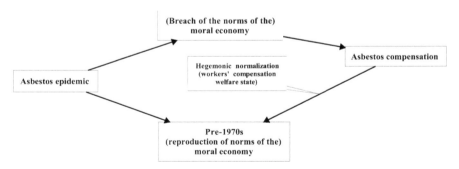

**Figure 7.1     Hegemonic normalization of the asbestos epidemic**

---

13    Ibid.
14    Felstiner, Abel, and Sarat, "The Emergence and Transformation of Disputes: Naming, Blaming, Claiming …", 633.
15    Ibid.

The moral economy schema is in fact both intrinsically and extrinsically an expression of hegemonic order. Intrinsically, the moral economy provides justification not only for capitalist accumulation but also for capitalist domination. If accumulation of wealth is justified by guaranteeing a minimum of social reproduction for all citizens through the institutions of the welfare state, the moral obligations of the capitalist class are discharged by making the expected contributions to the welfare state. The moral economy did not demand further duties. By identifying in workers' compensation and other institutional arms of the welfare state the compensation solution to the asbestos epidemic, asbestos companies were also able to further manipulate legal culture. Hegemonic interpretations merged into the narrative that the welfare state itself, rather than personal injury litigation, was the proper legal response to the emergence of asbestos disease.

The result was a hegemonic normalization of asbestos disease with institutional responses that limited the remedies available only to some victims (those injuries by occupational exposure) and some diseases. The values of the moral economy became a vehicle of institutional reproduction of existing power structures, of corporate power in particular.[16] In this regard, power is the product of coordination of cultural strategies involving the participation of different types of groups all contributing to the creation of a "hegemonic interpretation that is combined into a single narrative, with each element reinforcing rather than contradicting the others."[17] As Susan Silbey demonstrated, law is implicated in hegemony: mediating processes through which local practices areas aggregated and condensed into systemic institutionalized power are "at work in and through law."[18] The result of this processes are "situations where meanings are so embedded that representational and institutionalized power is invisible."[19] Hegemony is thus so deeply embedded in everyday life that it is invisible, subterranean. Therefore, "subjects do not question dominant structures and cannot make justice claims against the aspects of structure and power that are invisible."[20]

Working compensation as policy response to the rise of the asbestos epidemic constituted an institutional reproduction of capitalists' power in which the values that made the moral economy were hegemonically deployed to preserve concentration of power as it had been for half a century. Since its early days,

---

16   Patterson, "The mechanisms of cultural reproduction. Explaning the puzzle of persistance," 141-142.

17   Back et al., *Cultural sociology: an introduction*, 29, 113.

18   Silbey, "Making a Place for Cultural Analyses of Law"; Silbey, "Legal culture and cultures of legality."

19   Susan S. Silbey, "Ideology, Power, and Justice," in *Justice and power in sociolegal studies*, ed. Bryant G. Garth and Austin Sarat (Evanston: Northwestern University Press, 1998), 276.

20   Ibid.

workers' compensation was envisioned as a structural arrangement geared to support members of the working class who became unable (temporarily or permanently, partially or fully) to work as a consequence of serving capitalists' interests but also to crush class conflict. Workers' compensation systems had in fact in fact emerged in Europe and North American since the late nineteenth century as a response to the industrial-accident situation.[21] It was a creative and innovative response that brought new ideas and created new institutions in industrialized nations. It was a compromise between the working class's demands for redress in the event of accident and the industrialists' demands for protection of invested capital and efficient management of industrial risks. This is true in all four countries researched in this book, including the United States, a country that is often labeled as "exceptional" for its lack of a socialist workers' movement.[22] While it is true that the US welfare state grew more slowly and later than in Europe and developed less extensively,[23] it became nonetheless an important part of the class struggle between capitalists and workers. Although supplemented by private enterprise, which "has performed many social functions ... that long were dominated by government or corporatist bodies in Europe,"[24] the institutions of the welfare state were extensively involved in the structuration of asbestos compensation. Extending the long arms of workers' compensation to the asbestos disease epidemic was instrumental in addressing class conflict between asbestos firms and workers.

The reproduction of the moral economy in asbestos compensation had powerful ideological effects: it reinforced capitalists' hegemonic stands and minimized threats to the *paix sociale*; it addressed asbestos victims' concerns; at the same time, it contained demands for compensation to workers' compensation remedies. This strategy proved to be effective, to different degrees, in the United States, Italy, and Belgium, where workers' compensation is traditionally seen as

---

21  John Fabian Witt, *The accidental republic: crippled workingmen, destitute widows, and the remaking of American law* (Cambridge, MA: Harvard University Press, 2004), 22-29.

22  Seymour Martin Lipset, *American exceptionalism: a double-edged sword* (New York: W.W. Norton, 1996); Theda Skocpol, *Protecting soldiers and mothers: the political origins of social policy in the United States* (Cambridge, MA: Belknap Press of Harvard University Press, 1992); Theda Skocpol, *Social policy in the United States: future possibilities in historical perspective* (Princeton: Princeton University Press, 1995). This approach has been criticized for being a structuralist approach in which actors' preferences are assumed to be "endogenous to the institutional environment in which they operate" and for exaggerating historical differences between American and Western European models. Matthew Allen, "The varieties of capitalism paradigm: not enough variety?," *Socio-Economic Review* 2, no. 1 (2004); Manley, "Theorizing the unexceptional US welfare state."

23  Hacker, *The divided welfare state: the battle over public and private social benefits in the United States.*

24  Kagan, *Adversarial legalism: the American way of law*, 52.

the exclusive remedy for workers and personal injury claims for occupational diseases against the (former) employer are severely restricted. As the following figure demonstrates, in many countries in addition to the four included in this study workers' compensation was the policy response to the emergence of the asbestos epidemic (see Figure 7.2). The medical literature recognized asbestos exposure as a cause of asbestosis in the 1930, of mesothelioma in the 1950s, and or lung cancer in the 1960s. Asbestosis was the first disease to become compensable. Mesothelioma and lung cancer followed decades after. In recent years, pleural plaques and cancer of the larynx have been included in a handful of countries.

The inclusion of asbestos disease under workers' compensation is a measure of the success of the ideals, beliefs, and expectations connected to the moral economy to define what policy responses were appropriate to address asbestos victims' demands for total justice. The practices and processes that emerge from asbestos claiming reinforced the belief that rebalancing the harm to social reproduction would be sufficient remedy. The moral economy became the measure of proper legal redress. Compensation of asbestos victims was in fact measured, and found to be satisfactory, in relation to its ability to redress the imbalance between social reproduction and capitalist accumulation.

Asbestos compensation practices thus reproduced power imbalances and became the vehicle of hegemonic stands of the capitalists. These stands had been integral part of the welfare state since its birth and had contributed to the emergence of the moral economy schema. Moving classic liberalism away from individualism and the self-guiding market,[25] welfare states emerged from pragmatic reasons—capitalists' fear of uncontrolled class conflict. Although attempts to crush workers' mobilization were launched around the turn of the nineteenth century, class conflict proved to be more resilient than expected. Industrialists came to appreciate workers' compensation as a tool that, along with other structural components of the welfare, promised to contain and manage class conflict and workers' protests and demands for better working conditions. After initial resistance, capitalists eventually supported the constitution of workers' compensation and the welfare state as the lesser evil to address class conflict. Fulfilling the promise of the architect of the welfare state, Prussian Chancellor Otto von Bismarck, who envisioned a "moral economy" as the way to mitigate social unrest created the Employer's Liability Law of 1871, the welfare state became capitalists' ideological tool to curb workers' class struggle.

This is true also with regard to asbestos disease. Before embracing workers' compensation, the industry tried to crush victims' nascent claim consciousness by deploying several tactics along with an extensive cover-up of asbestos toxicity what has been extensively researched and documented by

---

25  Manley, "Theorizing the unexceptional US welfare state," 175.

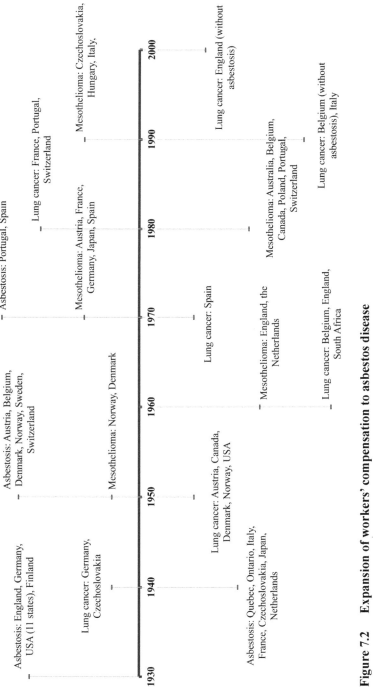

**Figure 7.2   Expansion of workers' compensation to asbestos disease**

business historians[26]—it is not a coincidence that the SAIAC Cartel, through which key asbestos European and US companies agreed to "exchange technical knowledge, centralize research activities, standardize product ranges and organize the export business" and "divided up global markets, pressurized national governments, fixed retail prices, and extracted favorable business terms from asbestos producers,"[27] was established in 1929, the year in which "independent researchers identified the symptoms and causes of asbestosis."[28]

The industry vehemently opposed the recognition of asbestosis as compensable disease as well as any form of workplace regulation. The industry also proposed confidential settlement to victims in the hope of dissipating victims' demands. Companies made *ex gratia* payments in exchange for workers agreeing to confidential settlements. In 1927 a Massachusetts asbestos textile worker filed a claim. "A group of Johns-Manville workers launched claims in 1929 and by the mid-1930s at least 69 more state compensation suits were brought against the company. During the 1930s, claims were filed against other leading manufacturers, such as Raybestos-Manhattan. The latter compensated about twenty cases in the 1930s."[29] Money however was also offered with the promise that payments would remain confidential. Johns-Manville went even further when in 1933 it settled 11 cases in exchange for their attorney's promise that he would never "directly or indirectly participate in the bringing of new actions against the Corporation."[30] Payments, which were not very generous, were kept secret by the parties involved. Workers rarely talked about them with fellow victims and as a result claim consciousness struggled to emerge. Turner

---

26    The literature on the asbestos industry cover up is vast. Some of the monographs that discuss firms implicated in the asbestos industry in Italy, Belgium, England, and the United States are Brodeur, *Outrageous misconduct: the asbestos industry on trial*; Castleman, *Asbestos: medical and legal aspects*; Odette Hardy-Hémery, *Eternit et l'amiante, 1922-2000: Aux sources du profit, une industrie du risque* [Eternit and asbestos, 1922-2000: At the origins of profits, an industry of risk] (Villeneuve d'Ascq: Presses Universitaires du Septentrion, 2005); Jock McCulloch, *Asbestos blues: labour, capital, physicians & the state in South Africa* (Oxford, Bloomington: James Currey, Indiana University Press, 2002); McCulloch and Tweedale, *Defending the indefensible: The global asbestos industry and its fight for survival*; Ruers and Schouten, The tragedy of asbestos. Eternit and the consequences of a hundred years of asbestos cement; Tweedale, *Magic mineral to killer dust: Turner & Newall and the asbestos hazard*.

27    Laurie Kazan-Allen, "Introduction," in *Eternit and the Great Asbestos Trial*, ed. David Allen and Laurie Kazan-Allen (London: The International Ban Asbestos Secretariat, 2012), 9.

28    McCulloch and Tweedale, *Defending the indefensible: The global asbestos industry and its fight for survival*, 79.

29    Ibid., 158.

30    Brodeur, *Outrageous misconduct: the asbestos industry on trial*.

& Newall did the same in England; Eternit with Italian and Belgian victims; James Hardie with Australian victims.[31]

Finally, companies set up private compensation funds quietly compensating victims without the need for them to file claims. Turner & Newall set up its self-funded Asbestosis Fund in the 1940s. The Fund was administered by an external insurance company, Commercial Union, so that the company did not have to confront its employees or former employees directly. Between 1931 and 1948, the Asbestosis Fund paid GBP 87,938 to 140 asbestosis victims.[32] These payments represent the first steps of asbestos compensation in England more so than workers' compensation since Turner & Newall's employees comprised the majority of early victims of asbestos exposure. The Fund was gradually wounded down after 1948 when the government took the lead in the administering of compensation for occupational diseases by abolishing the 1897 system of workers' compensation and creating the IIDB. Eternit set up its compensation fund in the 1980s for similar reasons. In its original form, the fund offered payments to workers below the age of 65 and affected by asbestosis resulting in a degree of disability exceeding 33 percent. They were offered payments equal to the difference between the workers' compensation benefit and their last salary. The fund was later expanded to include former employees who had developed mesothelioma in 2000, victims of secondhand exposure in 2001, and victims of environmental exposure in 2006. Overall at least two asbestosis victims and 70 mesothelioma victims were compensated, including 12 victims of household exposure and two of environmental exposure. Mirroring Turner & Newall's thinking Eternit wound up its plan in 2007 after the establishment of the 2007 Asbestos Fund, which pulled together public money to compensation asbestos and mesothelioma victims.

When the rise of victims' demands for compensation seemed inevitable the industry rapidly came to see the asbestos regulations as the lesser of two evils, as a more desirable outcome than litigation and realized that there was an opportunity to shape regulations so that the industry could secure immunity at a low cost. This position is clearly reflected in the words of Vandiver Brown, Johns-Manville's corporate attorney, who in 1950 told an audience of fellow asbestos executives: "eliminate the jury ... the shyster lawyer and the quack doctor ... provide a forum for evidence that might cast doubt on disability ... the worst Workmen's Compensation Commission is preferable to the best jury."[33] At that point, the industry began lobbying for narrow coverage of asbestos diseases,[34] which successfully framed opportunities for compensation very narrowly. For instance, the 1931 asbestos

---

31    McCulloch, "The Mine at Baryulgil: Work, Knowledge, and Asbestos Disease," 119, 122.

32    Wikeley, "Turner & Newall: Early Organizational Responses to Litigation Risk."

33    Brown comments, 6th Saranac Symposium (1950), cited in McCulloch and Tweedale, *Defending the indefensible: The global asbestos industry and its fight for survival*, 159.

34    Nicholas J. Wikeley, "The Asbestos Regulations 1931: A Licence to Kill?," *Journal of Law and Society* 19 (1992).

regulations in England "only applied to workers employed on or after 1 May 1931" and allowed compensation only of those workers who had been employed in "a restricted number of asbestos jobs," workers employed in certain "scheduled areas" of manufacturing plants, which exposure entitled victims to compensation.[35] Ultimately, the inclusion of asbestos disease to workers' compensation coverage looked reasonable to all of the parties involved. Victims would receive some compensation. The industry would avoid getting dragged in front of courts. Labor unions' role as representatives of workers would be reinforced, in the public eye and eyes of their members. The success of the reproduction of the moral economy schema in the structuration of responses to the asbestos epidemic corroborates Foucault's insight on workers' compensation in general. The French intellectual argued that workers' compensation is a form of *justice de classe*, conceived by the capitalist class to enforce inequality between social classes, industrialists and workers, with the latter carrying an unfair share of social and economic burdens.[36]

## Litigation as counter-hegemonic response

The hegemonic influence of the moral economy schema became contested over time. Hegemonic interpretations often trigger counter-hegemonic reactions. After power becomes institutionally structured, contestation becomes difficult. Yet, power is occasionally locally contested as is hegemonic interpretations.[37] This is the case of asbestos when victims began challenging these structural responses to the asbestos epidemic, and triggered counter-hegemonic process aimed at expanding compensation to new categories of victims and new types of diseases. This is a counter-hegemonic response to the subterranean cultural forces that pushed victims to accept workers' compensation as sufficient legal redress (see Figure 7.3). Litigation was the victims' process that successfully channeled counter-hegemonic stances. This strategy was deployed when victims began realizing that that asbestos compensation as a culture response was merely reproducing the welfare state thus limiting opportunities for total justice. Irving J. Selikoff, a scientist, doctor, and author of the 1964 celebrated study of asbestos insulation workers that established a link between asbestos and lung cancer, lamented in 1986 that workers' compensation as a fair social bargain had failed: "the quid has disappeared and the quo has remained."[38]

---

35    Geoffrey Tweedale and David J. Jeremy, "Compensating the Workers: Industrial Injury and Compensation in the British Asbestos Industry, 1930s-60s," *Business History* 41, no. 2 (1999): 103.

36    Foucault's analysis referred to the 1898 French law on industrial accidents. See Henry, *Amiante, un scandale improbable: sociologie d'un problème public*, 25.

37    Silbey, "Ideology, Power, and Justice," 276.

38    Selikoff to Hon. Jack B. Weinstein, Chief Judge, United States District Court, April 21, 1986, in McCulloch and Tweedale, *Defending the indefensible: The global asbestos industry and its fight for survival*, 161, fn. 121.

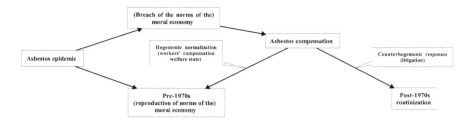

**Figure 7.3    Counter-hegemonic responses to the asbestos epidemic's normalization**

There are two strands of counter-hegemonic litigation. The first strand is personal injury litigation directed towards corporate entities to supplement workers' compensation payments. It developed from the premise that workers' compensation payments became seen as insufficient to provide satisfactory legal redress. Product liability in the United States, negligence in England, *danno morale* and, until 2000, *danno biologico* in Italy enabled victims to successfully achieve this goal. In the United States, product liability led to a dramatic shift of perspective: while claims have often been grounded on occupational exposure, the legal doctrine deployed in personal injury litigation successfully challenged the welfare state paradigm and positioned asbestos compensation in a different cultural environment—companies' liability for exposing consumers to a dangerous product. Counter-hegemonic goals were quickly achieved. Asbestos litigation generated ideas, precedents, and theories that entrepreneurial attorneys soon redeployed in the representation of other claimants. Asbestos litigation became the "mother" of many mass torts against tobacco, drug, and car companies. Counter-hegemonic goals were obtained with such degree of success that it triggered a counter-counter-hegemonic reaction—the argument that the United States were experiencing a litigation explosion and the birth of tort reform programs to curb the "excesses" of tort litigation.[39] In England, labor unions demanded that victims filed a workers' compensation claim before funding the personal injury claim. This was true in Italy too, where the welfare state provided a special retirement package on the top of workers' compensation payments. As a result, In England and Italy, workers' compensation preserved its centrality as a necessary step to seek further compensation.

The second strand was directed against workers' compensation administrations to challenge eligibility requirements. The goal was to expand compensation to a wider range of victims than those whose rights to compensation had been recognized under the wings of the welfare state. Since the welfare states emerged, in part, to curb the wave of class struggle that rose during the Second Industrial Revolution, protections and remedies afforded by its institutions primarily benefitted individuals injured while working, the workplace being the ideological

---

39    Haltom and McCann, *Distorting the law: politics, media, and the litigation crisis.*

battlefield of the welfare state. Consequently, victims of occupational exposure benefitted from more generous redress for the harms of asbestos exposure than victims of non-occupational exposure, who would find solace exclusively in disability payments and free health care. Workers' compensation eligibility further narrowed the need for victims to show that they were suffering from certain asbestos diseases (initially lung cancer was not compensated) and that their exposure to asbestos fibers had been of a certain length, amount, and associated with certain occupations. Litigation against workers' compensation administrations aimed to relax eligibility requirements. This strand of litigation was particularly active in Italy and England, where the litigation was successful in broadening entitlements. Mobilization was successful in expanding compensation to a broader number of victims of occupational exposure but less successful with regard to victims of secondhand and premises exposure. *Ad hoc* compensation funds also developed a reaction to litigation. These schemes represent a success for victims but the structures intended to reduce litigation by "normalizing" compensation for selected new cases. Belgium is the country in which litigation achieved the least amount of success. Powerful cultural forces and limited structural constraints suffocated litigation ambitions. To date, only one case, brought by a victim of premises exposure, was successful. However, the mobilization process that accompanied this case had the secondary effect of generating interest in asbestos among politicians and in society. As a consequence, asbestos has become a publicly debated issue. Litigation has thus achieved some counter-hegemonic results. In the United States, the shattering impact of personal injury litigation obfuscated workers' compensation as a desirable path to compensation for asbestos workers (which, for the record, has not been totally neglected by victims and plaintiff lawyers)[40] and the need to challenge workers' compensation eligibility. The result is that litigation against state workers' compensation administration has been of little impact.

Litigation against workers' compensation administrations and against corporate entities was a counter-hegemonic strategy aimed at moving beyond dominant interpretations of asbestos disease as an injurious event to be redressed within the confines of the welfare state. While social structures are for the most part taken for granted and not subject to conscious consideration and engagement, asbestos victims were able to challenge hegemonic paradigm and create a space for contestation. Contestation was certainly motivated by the desire to expand compensation to new victims and increase compensation for victims eligible under workers' compensation. Moral considerations also contributed to the rise of counter-hegemonic litigation. Victims rejected the principle of "no fault" compensation and demanded companies' accountability for their wrongdoings. No fault is a principle that lies at the hearth of the welfare states. Workers' compensation pays victims based on the assumption that nobody—neither the

---

40   Field and Victor, *Asbestos claims: the decision to use workers' compensation and tort*, 12.

employer nor the state—is to be blamed for the disease. As evidence that asbestos companies had hidden proofs of asbestos toxicity was being brought to light, victims grew progressively unsatisfied with a response premised on the principle of "no fault." Victims began using personal injury litigation as a path to the truth, to justice, to full compensation. In the United States, this has resulted in an excess of blaming as evidenced by the fact that litigation is now targeting many peripheral defendants that, while potentially liable under the rules of product liability, have very little to share with the leading asbestos firms that caused the asbestos epidemic. At the opposite spectrum of retribution, the Italian criminal justice system has delivered accountability in the form of criminal liability of some of the Eternit executives who, during the past half century, participated in key corporate decisions that contributed to the growth of disease among Italian victims.

**Divergent routinized practices**

Counter-hegemonic mobilization embodied the struggle over the constitution of the responses to the asbestos epidemic, created a space of contestation that the welfare state had closed off by structuring asbestos compensation as a reproduction of the moral economy, and transformed asbestos compensation and produced a novel path to claiming for victims of other epidemics. While counter-hegemonic efforts were launched in all four countries, ensuing processes diverged cross nationally and led to routinized rules and outcomes of asbestos compensation that differ greatly across nations.[41] These comparative differences are the product of two causes: country-specific cultural schemas that pushed the structuration of asbestos compensation in different directions and the different timing of victims' mobilization, which produced interactions between actors and macro- and micro-level structural conditions that are unique to each national experience (see Figure 7.4).

With regard to the contribution of country-specific schemas to the cultural repertoires that produced asbestos compensation, these include over time: consumerism, fear of concentrated power, individualism, self-reliance, and the faith in the markets in the United States; individualism, a culture of self-reliance and faith in the markets rooted in liberalism fused with Keynesianism (and the resulting expectation of welfare assistance and state intervention in the economy) and unionism in England; workerism, corporatism, interdependence in tension with the individualistic belief that a person's value exceeds her ability to generate income (embodied in the emergence of *danno biologico*) in Italy; in Belgium, the tension between pragmatic fatalism and political fragmentation on the one hand and the belief in interdependence and the reliance on compensation democracy on the other hand.

---

41 I use the term "routinization" to refer to a stage of maturity of claim emergence in which the response to asbestos epidemic can be described as a set of stable legal norms, policy outcomes, and practices.

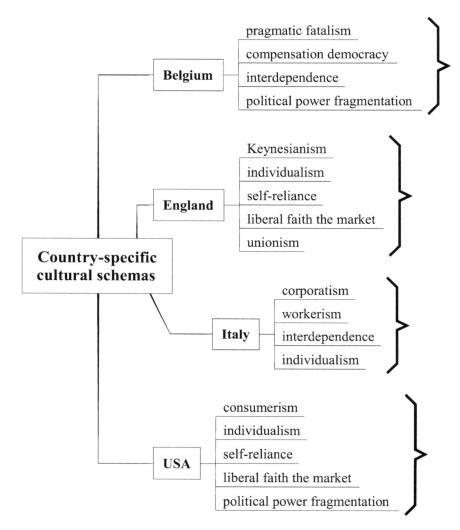

**Figure 7.4    Country-specific cultural schemas**

These changes were not sudden. They took place over the course of years and transformed asbestos compensation in slow and progressive stages. The stages are ordinarily tree: pre-emergence, emergence, and routinization.[42] The pre-emergence stage comprises the interval between the emergence of the asbestos epidemic and the victims' ability to secure some compensation. This stage may or may not include attempts to secure compensation. If attempts are present,

---

42   Felstiner, Abel, and Sarat, "The Emergence and Transformation of Disputes: Naming, Blaming, Claiming ..."; McGovern, "Resolving Mature Mass Tort Litigation."

they may have failed or may have had no impact on the appearance and rise of asbestos compensation. The emergence stage captures the moment when victims attempted, sometimes successfully, to secure compensation. At the third stage, asbestos compensation is routinized, that is, patterns of social actions are clearly routinized through cultural scripts and embedded in organizational, some of which are institutional, practices. The result is significant divergence of routinized practices of asbestos compensation.

In Belgium, asbestos compensation has been (almost) entirely routinized as workers' compensation (efforts to seek compensation in courts have eluded success in all but one case).[43] This unique outcome is a result of the fact that asbestos compensation has fully reproduced the moral economy paradigm—a paradigm with significant longevity since the retrenchment of the welfare state of the past three decades has been more modest than in other industrialized nations despite the adoption of neoliberal polices.[44] This is in great part due to additional cultural schemas that contributed to the preservation of the moral economy: compensation democracy and pragmatic fatalism. Compensation democracy is an expression that defines the cultural underpinning of Belgium's rigid and hierarchical regulation of labor relations, cadenced by top-down, bipartite agreements that dispensed substantial gains to workers and unions in exchange for giving up key demands. Pragmatic fatalism acted as a schema interpreting asbestos disease as a fact of life, to be kept private, and accepted as a fact of life. These cultural schemas contribute to a repertoire that prevented victims from unhinging employers' immunity in torts. Employers' immunity was one of the pillars of workers' compensation which, when asbestos victims began perceiving asbestos disease as injurious, had grown to occupy a central role in resolving disputes between labor and capitalism. Workers' compensation was the result of capitalists' successful campaign against workers' efforts to secure compensation and other rights through the mutuality companies that operated since the 1850s as small private funds providing insurance coverage to workers with no direct involvement of government or industrialists and by joining civil claims to criminal trials, a right that the Belgium Code of Criminal Procedure granted since 1878. It was a success because it guaranteed, and still does, employers' immunity in torts. Workers' compensation put an institutional lid on asbestos victims' mobilization and has not weakened since then. Efforts to sue the employers have rarely been successful, and the norms of the moral economy have persisted thanks to the support of compensation democracy and pragmatic fatalism. On the other hand, Belgium succeeded in establishing a victims' fund that is rather comprehensive if compared to other nations as it provides compensation to victims of non-

---

43   Only one personal injury case has been successful before this book manuscript was finalized. For an account of this case, which presents exceptional traits and may be overturned in appeal, see Chapter 2.

44   Vandaele, "From the seventies strike wave to the first cyber-strike in the twenty-first century. Strike activity and labour unrest in Belgium," 196.

occupational exposure. This is the result of victim groups' mobilization and their ability to instill into Belgian political consciousness the idea of interdependence with regard to asbestos harms. Rooted in the culture of compensatory democracy, interdependence allowed advocated first and institutions later to frame asbestos disease as a harm that needed to be "socialized,"[45] and it has been in the form of the 2007 Asbestos Victims Fund.

In England, counter-hegemonic litigation and routinization were guided by a culture of self-reliance and faith in the markets fused with expectation of welfare assistance in England. Workers' compensation was the primary remedy available to asbestos victims.[46] Its primacy was not the result of structural constraints embedded in the law because, in contrast to Italy, Belgium and the United States, English workers were never barred from suing their employer.[47] The success of administrative compensation is by contrast due to the Keynesian tradition of welfare intervention combined with individualistic values and faith in the markets. One of the effects of Keynesianism was the central role that unions played in the organization of the English economy. As a result, initial support to victims' claiming came from unions, which agreed to support victims but to fund only personal injury claims that had been recognized for compensation under the IIDB.[48] This stand partially reproduced the moral economy schema (and unions' allegiance to the welfare state) but also opened new ways for victims' total justice demands to be pursued. Unions' willingness to fund litigation in fact led to successful litigation against employers. The rise of personal injury litigation is thus an expression of cultural schemas that looked beyond the moral economy without trumping it. These cases rose under the auspices of individualism, self-reliance and faith in the markets. These beliefs justified victims' quest for tort compensation and produced union-driven mobilization of claims in the tort system. The result of unions' supporting asbestos litigation is threefold: claims were filed early (the first asbestos personal case was filed in 1950 against Cape); personal injury claims' growth was steady and settlements tailored to individual claims; administrative compensation never lost its appeal even after the growth of personal injury litigation and the establishment of various compensatory schemes because it is still seen as a source funding of personal injury cases. The routinization of litigation took place after the

---

45   *Problématique en lien avec l'amiante et les produits de substitution à l'amiante— Propositions de loi [Issues relating to asbestos and its substitutes—Bills]*, Avis 1.826 (Conseil National du Travail, November 27, 2012) (Belgium).

46   As noted earlier in the book, I refer to the Industrial Injuries Disability Benefit as "workers' compensation." The reference is technically improper because England chose not to have a workers' compensation system. However, as a matter of substance, the IIDB is a functional equivalent of workers' compensation.

47   Employers had not enjoyed immunity since 1948 when immunity established by Workmen's Compensation Act of 1897 was repealed.

48   The role of labor unions in mobilizing cases is thoroughly investigated in Durkin, "Constructing law: comparing legal action in the United States and United Kingdom", *passim*.

peak of union membership of 1979,[49] when England shifted to monetarism under the leadership of Margaret Thatcher and labor relations moved away from wage setting and employment security.[50] Moreover, the era of monetarism emphasized liberal values as well as the reliance on the markets. This produced an increase on personal injury litigation as the market-inspired solution to the asbestos epidemic in which victims would take responsibility for proving harm, causation, and fault, and compensation would only be awarded if a court was satisfied with the evidence presented. The three decades of asbestos compensation that followed have not changed the reality: although its mechanisms were partially contested, asbestos compensation currently involves a mix of payments from the IIDB, *ad hoc* schemes, and litigation.

In Italy, victims channeled their claims in the workers' compensation system for decades. The faith in workers' compensation was certainly the heritage of the cultural influence of corporatism. During the Fascist era, Mussolini imposed a system of labor relations in which the government occupied a controlling role mediating the interests of "corporatist" interests (labor and capital). Capital in particular found a strong ally in the state, which in turn recognized fascist unions as the only lawful representatives of workers in collective bargaining, which the Labor Charter of 1927 made a mandatory mechanism of negotiations between labor and capital. These cultural schemas became embedded in Italian labor relations and, when asbestos victims developed consciousness of the injuriousness of asbestos disease, victims expected unions to play a key role in mobilizing cases. Initially, this did not happen: labor unions showed no interest in mobilization asbestos cases, and victims, in particular residents of Casale, resorted to grassroots mobilization in the 1980s. Grassroots activism developed along cultural lines inscribed in Italian labor movement by workerism or *operaismo* in the 1970s. Workerism's mission was to affirm workers' right in autonomy from "the dictates of the labour movement and capital."[51] Grassroots activism is also the movement that demonstrated some interest in workplace safety in the wake of the political and cultural transformations triggered by the protests of 1968. Occupational health concerns became an integral part of labor relations only in the 1990s when the new epoch of world capitalism, dominated by transnational capital and neoliberal policies, brought a culture of job flexibility that demanded

49   Chris Wrigley, *British trade unions since 1933* (Cambridge, UK; New York: Cambridge University Press, 2002), 18.

50   Hall, "The movement from Keynesianism to monetarism: Institutional analysis and British economic policy in the 1970s," 91-92; Graeme Lockwood, "Trade union governance: The development of British conservative thought," *Journal of Political Ideologies* 10 (2005): 358.

51   Wright, *Storming heaven: class composition and struggle in Italian autonomist marxism*, 3.

a rethinking of unions' strategies to represent worker's interests.[52] After labor unions agreed to "an emergency industrial relations reform that abolished wage indexation and temporarily banned enterprise-level bargaining,"[53] labor relations were expanded. From a narrow focus on full employment and wages increase, they now incorporated workplace safety and other issues that, until then, had always been treated as secondary. The rethinking of labor relations eventually incorporated asbestos issues. Asbestos however became a political issue only in the late 1980s when the ban on asbestos use imposed by the European Union sanctioned the end of the asbestos industry, thus leaving workers of an entire industrial sector unemployed. As a result, since the 1990s, unions have supported asbestos claiming by mobilizing workers' compensation claims and personal injury litigation. Mobilization led to stable patterns of asbestos compensation that involve a mix of social security, administrative compensation, and, to a lesser extent, tort damages. Corporatist influences are reflected in the fact that victims and activists could not easily escape the paradigm of workers' compensation exclusivity, which the tripartite alliance between the state, labor unions, and capital had nurtured since then. It took years of persistent efforts from victims and activists to organize claim mobilization outside the boundaries of workers' compensation and achieve consistent results in personal injury cases. Victims however have experienced significant resistance on the part of government towards expanding compensation and have devised creative strategies. To complement workers' compensation payments, they deployed creative strategies to claim personal injury damages in court, and in particular joining civil claims for damages to criminal prosecutions. Personal injury cases were made possible by the rise of a new legal doctrine (loss of bodily integrity or *danno biologico*), which had been formally recognized by the Constitutional Court in 1986 and which was the way in which legal theory channeled cultural demands for total justice and individualistic belief that a person's value exceeds her ability to generate income.[54] In the meanwhile, legislative solutions have been partially successful in addressing asbestos compensation but have only helped victims of occupational exposure. Workerism is still influential as strands of grassroots activism still play an important role mobilizing victims (victims of non-occupational exposure in particular) that unions do not support.

---

52   Robinson, *A theory of global capitalism: production, class, and state in a transnational world*, 5.

53   Baccaro and Lim, "Social Pacts as Coalitions of the Weak and Moderate: Ireland, Italy and South Korea in Comparative Perspective," 29.

54   The loss of bodily integrity assumed that legal protection of a "person" ought to be construed beyond the redress of the loss of capacity to generate income. The person that emerged from the 1960s and 1970s deserved legal protection as an entity that pursued "self-fulfillment ... in the private and social life," and that was capable of personal and social development in affection and relationships. See Markesinis et al., *Compensation for personal injury in English, German and Italian law: a comparative outline*, 85-91.

In the United States, workers' compensation was for many years the only remedy available to victims as personal injury claims against the employer were, and still are, barred. However, victims progressively turned away from workers' compensation and focused on personal injury litigation against manufacturers of asbestos compensation products. This was possible when the demands of total justice encountered the wave of consumerism that had been pushing American law towards the recognition of compensation rights to Americans as consumers of defective products.[55] The 1973 opinion in *Borel v. Fibreboard Paper Products Corporation* embodies the formalization of these cultural instances. In this opinion, a court of appeals concluded that asbestos was an unreasonably dangerous product and that consumers exposed to it had a remedy under an emerging body of product liability law. This paradigm-shifting opinion was the result of decades of growth of product liability, which lessons had been condensed by the American Law Institute in 1965 in the *Second Restatement of the Law of Torts*, labor unions' support of epidemiological research and workers, claims for compensation, and the entrepreneurial spirit of Ward Stephenson and a handful of creative lawyers who transformed rather mundane workers' compensation claims in personal injury cases. Product liability theories emerged from the contested and imperfect nature of the American welfare state. In fact, there has always been tension between the welfare state and the deeply seeded cultural values of American society. America's faith in individualism, self-reliance, and freedom to contract as well as the lack of class consciousness and distrust towards centralized power built a welfare state that was more fragile, incomplete, and contested than European welfare states. Consequently, demands for redistribution were partially left unattended in the United States. Yet, the cruel reality of Fordism and increased reliance on man-made machines left many Americans harmed by no fault of themselves. Led by Cardozo's 1916 path-breaking opinion in *MacPherson v. Buick*, courts began supplementing the gaps in the need for social reproduction that European welfare states were guaranteeing, and developed new remedies to innocent users or bystanders injured by defective products. These remedies were created not to the benefit of the working class but to a new category of victims: consumers. The result of *Borel*, which put asbestos personal injury cases on product liability law's trajectory, was to transform asbestos victims, who up until then had been struggling with the limited protection of workers' compensation and the welfare state, into consumers harmed by an unreasonably dangerous product. *Borel* changed the paradigm of asbestos compensation wiping out asbestos firms' tort immunity, opening the door to litigation, and pushing dozens of asbestos defendants to seek protection under bankruptcy law. In the decades that followed, legislative efforts to resolve asbestos compensation failed. Reform of asbestos compensation was a matter of "common sense," as Barnes frames it, but a culture of adversarial legalism, rooted in institutional and political fragmentation, as well as the belief

---

55   Lizabeth Cohen, *A consumers' republic: the politics of mass consumption in postwar America*, 1st ed. (New York: Knopf; Random House, 2003).

in courts and litigation as proper venues to resolve policy issues, prevented the various constituencies from agreeing on which victims should be compensated and how the system would be funded.[56] The policy void was filled by bankruptcy trusts, which progressively emerged as an additional source of compensation for asbestos victims. Nonetheless, the initial framework that repositioned asbestos victims from workers to consumers has never been abandoned, and litigation still plays the lion's share of routinized compensation.

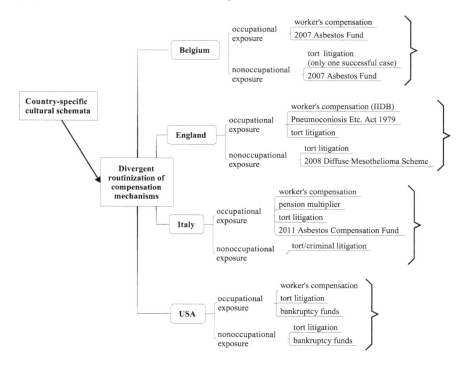

**Figure 7.5    Divergent routinization of compensation mechanisms**

The result of counter-hegemonic litigation was to redirect the focus of asbestos compensation mechanisms from workers' compensation and the welfare state to compensation and courts. Since the effects of counter-hegemonic responses poured into existing mechanisms slowly, at different times, and filtered by national-specific cultural schemas, routinized practices differ greatly from country to country. In 2013, the structure of asbestos compensation in the United States combines tort litigation, bankruptcy trust claims, and workers' compensation; in England, tort litigation, workers' compensation, and *ad hoc* compensation

---

56    Barnes, *Dust-up: asbestos litigation and the failure of common sense policy reform*; Kagan, *Adversarial legalism: the American way of law*.

funds; in Italy, tort and criminal litigation, workers' compensation, and *ad hoc* compensation funds; and in Belgium, only workers' compensation and *ad hoc* compensation funds. Differences in routinized practices of asbestos compensation should not however hide the overall convergence of all legal systems towards ensuring redress of demands for total justice. This convergence is not unique to asbestos: as Lawrence Friedman argues, it is a defining trait of the modern legal system.[57] Yet, whether converging or diverging, the most important aspect of legal change is the dominance of corporate interests throughout the structuration of asbestos compensation, from the emergence of the asbestos epidemic to the routinization of compensation mechanisms (see Figure 7.5). We will now turn to this issue.

## Legal change and structural inequalities

The centennial history of asbestos compensation shows that cultural frameworks change over time and how structural change is produced and reproduced by the transformation of cultural schemas. Asbestos compensation as a cultural response to the asbestos epidemic has been produced progressively as the structural outcome of ongoing struggle for political and policy dominance and power of the various actors involved in the issue (corporate entities, insurance companies, victims, lawyers, unions, judges, doctors, scientists, and policy-makers). Actors were the vehicle of cultural change, and the respective power of actors was central to deciding which factors would be deployed in asbestos compensation discourses revolving around and what weight these factors should have in reshaping compensation as a cultural response to the asbestos epidemic.

Resulting structuration processes are rather unstable because they are often contested at the micro level and are dependent upon structural and cultural changes at the macro-level. At the macro-level, the echo of capitalism transformations reverberated in asbestos compensation. "Epochal changes in the system of world capitalism have had transformative effects on the world as a whole and on each region integrated in or rearticulated, to the system," William Robinson argues.[58] The two important macro-level changes that have affected asbestos compensation are the transition to two different epochs of capitalism. Capitalism can be divided into epochs,[59] three of which overlap with the asbestos epidemic. Asbestos use began when capitalism was "monopolist" or "corporate."[60] During this epoch, characterized

57   Friedman, "Is There a Modern Legal Culture?"

58   William I. Robinson, "Global capitalism theory and the emergence of transnational elites," *Critical Sociology* 38, no. 3 (2012): 354.

59   Robinson, *A theory of global capitalism: production, class, and state in a transnational world*, 1-32.

60   Robinson, *Latin America and global capitalism: a critical globalization perspective*, 8-9.

by mass production, faith in the systematic application of science to industry, the rise of the chemical, steel, railroad, and other new capital-intensive lead industries, sees the "crystallization of national capitalist classes that took control of these markets, and the appearance of the oligopolistic structure of modern capitalism."[61] These structural conditions led to the growth of a monopolistic asbestos industry, tightly controlling scientific evidence of asbestos toxicity and hierarchically repressing class struggles with the help of the institutions of the nation state. Compromise with the working class, in relation to workplace regulation of asbestos, meant that compensation of asbestos workers became possible only when, in the aftermath of World War II, capitalism transitioned to an epoch of New Deal capitalism, welfare capitalism, or social capitalism, which common sense assumption of the moral economy combined capital accumulation with social reproduction and which, as we have seen, was an extremely influential cultural frame in the production of asbestos compensation. State intervention in the economy and a redistributive logic were transformed in the 1970s, when the oil crises and the abandonment of the gold standard, which had guaranteed to the US government convertibility of dollars into gold at a fixed rate inaugurated a new epoch of capitalism, once characterized by global capitalism. This epoch was defined by a constriction of private capital's capacity for accumulation and triggered a capitalist global counter-revolution that reversed the culture of moral economy. The 1970s produced deep transformations: Fordism's decline, deregulation, labor market flexibility, and economic globalization.[62] The state lost its centrality in the coordination of the economy, flexibility of capital and of labor became dominant perceptual frames to assign meaning to economic and class relations, and welfare states progressively retrenched. Asbestos compensation was also transformed as a result of transition of global capitalism. Labor was made flexible, capital/labor relations were progressively de-unionized, and asbestos victims' traditional reliance on the welfare state was betrayed. The "global legal and regulatory structure that was created to facilitate emerging globalized circuits of accumulation" enabled "free operation of capital within and across borders and the harmonization of accumulation conditions worldwide" but created barriers to compensation making it difficult for victims to enforce judgments and for nation states to seek contributions from companies, many of which were filing for bankruptcy or engaging in extensive restructuring that cut loose any links to liabilities generated under the auspices of Fordism in epochs of corporate and welfare capitalism.[63] Global neoliberalism, which was a "global counter-revolution" of "centers of power in the world system," caused retrenchment also in the welfare assistance to asbestos

---

61   Ibid., 8.

62   Hutton and Giddens, eds, *Global capitalism*; Edward Luttwak, *Turbo-capitalism: winners and losers in the global economy*, 1st U.S. ed. (New York: HarperCollinsPublishers, 1999); Robinson, *Latin America and global capitalism: a critical globalization perspective*, 19.

63   Robinson, *Latin America and global capitalism: a critical globalization perspective*, 16.

victims and triggered their pursuit of compensation by resorting to litigation. Promoting a culture of competitive individualism based on labor flexibility, markets and commodification, the neoliberal ideology was contrasted by asbestos victims' creative counter-hegemonic processes that entailed litigation against government, to contrast deregulation and preserve the role of the state as economic decision-maker and mediator of capital-labor relations, and litigation against corporate entities, to rebalance the retrenchment of the welfare state and cuts in social programs as well as making the private sector accountable for past tortious actions, even if some of the key companies that had caused the asbestos epidemic had disappeared from the judicial landscape because of bankruptcy or merged with other corporate entities.

One of the sources of weaknesses of asbestos compensation's mechanisms is the fact that they partially replicate structural inequalities. Through gradual steps, the asbestos industry was able to influence compensation processes in its favor by delaying its emergence, avoid its consequence, and strategically involve the institutions of the welfare state to minimize the costs of the private sectors. No matter what the national contours of asbestos compensation are, corporate interests have in fact dominated the emergence and transformation of asbestos compensation.[64] Asbestos companies exercised dominant influence on its emergence and transformation to the detriment of victims, who often needed to fight compensation wars against asbestos defendants left and that these wars ended with unsatisfactory remedies and limited opportunity for compensation. They contributed to the creation of and subsequent enjoyment of a favorable legal environment in which opportunities for delaying and avoiding liability abounded.

Corporate power and domination has been the result of the industry's exploitation of existing structural features of legal systems so that structural inequalities could be preserved, lobbying efforts pushing towards the enactment of policy reform and adoption of judicial opinions that shifted the balance of power towards asbestos companies, and manipulations of the cultural environment in which victim's mobilization took place. In contrast, victims struggled to secure compensation and every step of the process of emergence of asbestos compensation was contested: victims struggled in transforming the unperceived injurious experience of asbestos into a perceived experience; in identifying ways to claim and obtain redress in law; in establishing and expanding the requirements needed to recover in workers' compensation or in torts; in enforcing judgment against asbestos companies; in obtaining legal reform that would secure stable compensation for future victims.

With regard to exploiting existing structural features of the legal system, asbestos corporate entities made strategic use of procedural laws depriving victims of the fruits of their mobilization by compressing their opportunities for enforcing judgments in foreign jurisdictions and substantives laws recognizing the separateness of corporate entities and the limited liability of stakeholders. Corporate structures were in fact instruments of corporate dominance being corporate power importantly located in the exploitation of the principles of separate

---

64    I am indebted to Susan Silbey for this insight.

personality of corporate entities and shareholder limited liability. This point is clearly illustrated by the various instances in which victims, often unsuccessfully, struggled to enforce judgments against asbestos companies.[65] Cape's ability to avoid enforcement of judgments for its operation in the United States is a case that illustrates both structural barriers to enforcement. Litigation was brought by employees of Pittsburg Corning Corporation's Texas-based plant manufacturing asbestos pipe insulation materials. Raw asbestos originated from Cape's South African mines. Approximately 2,000-3,000 victims filed tort lawsuits in the span of a few years. Only the first group, comprised of 462 victims, was able to settle their claims and recover some money. The remaining victims litigated their clams after the settlements. However, by then victims were able to secure a judgment against Cape, the company had exhausted insurance coverage and enacted an exit strategy that involved abandoning the corporation with all the asbestos liabilities, moving the ownership of any business assets left to Liechtenstein, and running the business through new companies owned by trustworthy individuals who had no formal links with the conglomerate. The result was that, when victims tried to enforce their judgments in England, English courts denied enforcement on limited liability grounds. Not only the restructuring successfully separated the conglomerate from its US liabilities and removed its assets from the jurisdictional reach of US courts. It also allowed Cape to keep doing business in the United States through a network of formally independent companies whose liabilities remained distinct and separate from Cape. Cape's liabilities for its mining business in South Africa were also severely eased by South African victims' difficulty in claiming damages both in their home country and in England.[66] Earlier in this book, I also provided similar accounts for James Hardie—a conglomerate that was able to undergo corporate restructuring moving its profitable operations away from Australia, where the company was routinely named defendant in asbestos lawsuits, to a jurisdiction in which enforcement of Australian judgments was extremely difficult, leaving behind just empty corporate shells with no assets—and Eternit—a corporate group that coordinated a network of independent companies in various nations through a system of interlocking directorates, cartels, technology licenses, and informal meetings without any risk of liabilities flowing from one company to the other. Victims were able to obtain compensation from James Hardie only after political pressure and extensive consumer boycotts. In the case of Eternit, over 2,600 Eternit employees and more than 300 residents of communities located close to one of the four Italian Eternit plants secured a favorable verdict in 2012 at the end of what was labeled the "Great Asbestos Trial."[67] However, it is uncertain whether

---

65    Andrea Boggio, "Linking corporate power to corporate structures: An empirical analysis." *Social & Legal Studies* 22 (2013) 107-131. http://sls.sagepub.com/content/early/2012/09/24/0964663912458447.abstract.

66    Boggio, "The Global Enforcement of Human Rights: The Unintended Consequences of Transnational Litigation," 327-333.

67    Allen and Kazan-Allen, eds, *Eternit and the Great Asbestos Trial*.

and when victims will actually receive payments since the convicted defendants not only appealed the verdict but are also two wealthy foreign individuals whose assets are scattered around the world and buried in banks, trusts, and businesses.[68]

Asbestos companies were also able to limit their liability exposure by supporting the structuration of asbestos compensation under the auspices of the welfare state. Liability was contained by way of embedding tort immunity in asbestos compensation, treating victims of occupational and non-occupational exposure differently, and spreading a share of their liabilities through the institutions of the welfare state. First, companies were able to enjoy immunity from tort liabilities for decades (with the exception of England, the principle of employers' immunity for negligence was embedded in workers' compensation systems throughout welfare democracies). While this prohibition was at some point bypassed in Italy and, to a larger extent, in the United States, the requirement to show the employer's *faute intentionelle*, which *de facto* bars victims from suing their employer, has survived the test of time in Belgium, where, after a decade of legal and political challenges to this principle, asbestos victims are still kept out of the courtroom. Second, the deployment of the welfare state in structuring asbestos compensation has limited workers' compensation eligibility to victims of occupational exposure. Victims of non-occupational exposure have thus relied almost exclusively on litigation, which was very successful in the United States but relatively unsuccessful elsewhere. Third, a share of asbestos companies' liabilities were socialized through the institutions of the welfare state—workers' compensation, disability schemes, pensions, *ad hoc* compensation funds, and national health insurance. While some of these costs were eventually recouped by the state, indemnification has been partial and not timely. Furthermore, in an era of retrenchment of the welfare state, companies were able to limit their liability exposure by supporting the establishment of *ad hoc* compensation schemes aiming not only to guarantee long term, equitable and financially congruous compensation for all victims of asbestos but also to ensure protracted companies' immunity. In the United States, repeated efforts to legislate failed in part because of the inability of insurers and defendants to agree on allocation of liability and in part because of victims (or better their policy advocates) were split as to whether a legislative solution was a good outcome. Where legislative reform succeeded, the outcome is not the best possible for victims. In Italy, the 2011 Asbestos Fund is limited to victims of occupational exposure even if lobbying efforts had been made to extend eligibility of victims of non-occupational exposure. In Belgium, eligibility under the 2007 Asbestos Fund is extended to *all* victims of mesothelioma and asbestosis. However, in the best tradition of "compensation democracy," victims had to give up certain demands as part of the process that led to the establishment of the Fund: victims of lung and larynx cancers are excluded and eligible victims are barred from bringing personal injury claims against the companies that employed them. All mesothelioma cases, which are most feared by defendants, are removed from the court system, thus indirectly undermining

---

68  "Signori Ministri vi chiediamo formalmente aiuto."

further claim mobilization since asbestos litigation has developed in the other three countries' research in this book around mesothelioma cases.

Asbestos companies also enjoyed a significant competitive advantage in mobilization of advocacy resources. They outweighed victims in courtroom advocacy aiming to establish favorable legal doctrines and in lobbying efforts pushing towards the enactment of policy reform that shifted the balance of power towards asbestos companies. Skillful advocacy enabled companies to persuade courts to adopt highly beneficial doctrines. The industry keep pushing the so-called "chrysotile defence" in the policy arena as well as in courts, that is, the argument challenging "whether a pure chrysotile exposure at high levels can be causative, much less at minute levels,"[69] with the results that claims based on exposure to chrysotile fibers are hard to prove. Italian courts espoused the causation criteria for mesothelioma cases that, since mesothelioma can be caused by any exposure to asbestos, even to a single fiber, it is the plaintiff's (often impossible) burden to show that that incriminated fiber reached the victims exclusively because of the defendant's fault. Winning compensation in lung cancer cases in which the victim is a smoker or is asbestosis-free, are also problematic. Victims' limited access to expertise and financial resources delayed mobilization. In fact, establishing the requirements needed to recover in workers' compensation proved to be a rather sophisticated process, often requiring assistance of experts (lawyers, unions, activists, health care practitioners, scientists). To do so, victims had to identify ways to gather financial resources, mobilize expertise, build social networks to effectively claim benefits that should have been, at least theoretically, easy to grab given the moral foundations of the welfare state. Yet, their claims were often contested by governmental agencies with a non-trivial rate of failure to recover. Proof of exposure, causation, and negligence was novel and, even when routinized, extremely complex. Proof of exposure to asbestos in workers' compensation claims was particularly difficult for Italian and English victims as the law did not consider as "risky" many occupations that entailed exposure to asbestos. Italian victims in particular engaged in several waves of litigation to expand the narrow eligibility to recover from the workers' compensation administration.

Finally, the industry's extensive and successful efforts to conceal evidence of asbestos toxicity contributed to victims' tolerating asbestos disease in their everyday lives for decades. For years, victims failed to perceive the disease as injurious, a shift in perception that was possible only when evidence of asbestos toxicity became public. This step has been particularly problematic in Belgium where the lack of commitment of the medical profession to epidemiological studies delayed the process even more than in other countries. Moreover, even after evidence of asbestos toxicity had become public, companies resorted to various legal strategies to discourage mobilization of claims: confidential settlements, *ex gratia* payments, plaintiff attorneys' promises of not representing asbestos

---

69  Toohey and Matthews, "Liability For The Post-Sale Installation Of Asbestos-Containing Replacement Parts Or Insulation," 41.

victims in the future, private compensation funds. Again, this contributed to the "normalization" of asbestos disease as a fact of life for which no one was liable and thus compensation was not expected.

## Assessing the past, looking into the future

Interactions on the topic of asbestos compensation often leads scholars and practitioners to ask me the question which form of asbestos compensation is superior? Socio-legal scholars tend to avoid this question, and rightfully so since what they are offering to the audience is neither policy prescriptions nor normative views of how law and society should interact. They offer in-depth analyses of how societies deploy law to organize social life. While these analyses are certainly not value-free—a researcher's point of view matters in framing the study as well as collecting and interpreting data—they are not value-driven. Scholars are citizens and therefore ought to raise normative issues when they see them. In this spirit, I will close the book by highlighting some of the ethical issues that asbestos compensation raises. These are primarily issues of fairness among victims and availability of long-term commitment to compensation.

Questions of fairness are certainly implicated in the treatment of victims of non-occupational exposure. In Belgium, these victims receive administrative compensation only if they develop mesothelioma but not for other diseases caused by asbestos exposure. In Italy, they are at the mercy of courts in a context of fragmented litigation. The 2012 verdict in the Eternit trial offered new hopes of recovery as it established the principle of personal criminal and civil liability of asbestos entrepreneurs that created a threat for the public by disregarding asbestos regulations. The "public" comprises victims of occupational and non-occupational exposure. In England, the welfare state offers very little compensation to victims of non-occupational exposure and, although some cases have been successfully tried, courts seem reluctant to embrace these cases. In the United States, while the nature of the exposure is not important since the manufacturer of a dangerous product has the duty to protect consumers, including bystanders, establishing that exposure took place and proximate cause between exposure and disease is challenging. In addition, some courts refuse to extend defendants' liability to individuals living close to asbestos-contaminated facilities.

Questions of fairness are also implicated in the tension between compensating all victims and compensating the sickest first. Scholars of resource allocation often contrast the "sickest first" policies with first-come first-served policies.[70] This is an issue that surfaces in the context of asbestos compensation. Indeed it is a contested

---

70   For a discussion of resource allocation in the context of organ transplantation, see Randolph L. Schaffer et al., "The sickest first? Disparities with model for end-stage liver disease-based organ allocation: One region's experience," *Liver Transplantation* 9, no. 11 (2003).

one indeed. Sickest asbestos victims are certainly victims of mesothelioma and lung cancer. These diseases reduce dramatically victims' life expectancy and bring significant amounts of pain and suffering to patients and their close social circles. Legal systems have struggled with this issue especially with regard to victims of exposure who present pleural thickening and other signs of respiratory problems or victims who were exposed to significant doses of asbestos but are not sick. Some of these victims are "walking worries", as they are not sick but they worry about becoming sick, especially those who worked in asbestos plants and witnessed the death of most of their co-workers. The Unites States has struggled with this issue more than Europe. For years, some plaintiff lawyers bundled exposure-only cases with cancer cases with the intent of driving the settlement value of the bundle up. Defendants were under pressure to settle in case the opponents decided to try the malignancy case. Many settled their claims thus creating a problem of money going to non-sick victims, and defendants could be driven into bankruptcy thus compromising the value of claims of cancer victims not included in the bundle (bankruptcy trusts only pay a fraction of the value of the claim). Over time, bankruptcy trusts were able to set eligibility rules that create a substantial disincentive for plaintiff lawyers to keep representing unimpaired victims. In Europe the system dealt with the issue in a different way. Most of these cases never reached the litigation arena, recovery prospects being limited to eligibility under one of the welfare state programs. In Italy, walking worriers have received a pension supplement since the early 1990s. The more common approach has been to set by law a threshold of exposure and disability that victims needed to meet to qualify to receive benefits. Yet, these threshold levels have been generously set in Italy and Belgium, where the level of disability for all asbestos diseases are set respectively at 6 and 1 percent.[71] In England, the minimum level of disability for pleural plaques is fourteen percent.[72] In England the issue has spilled over into litigation, not surprisingly given the fact England is the European country in which personal injury litigation is used more extensively in asbestos compensation. Pleural plaques were viable claims for years. Their viability was contested, and eventually suppressed by the House of Lords in 2007.[73] In Scotland and Northern Ireland, the House of Lords ruling was overruled by law, not in England, where legislative efforts have failed.[74]

The conclusion is that not all victims were born equal: victims of mesothelioma caused by occupational exposure to asbestos face significantly higher chances

---

71  Boggio, "Comparative Notes On The Asbestos Trust Fund," 6.

72  Ibid.

73  *Johnston (Original Appellant and Cross-respondent) v. NEI International Combustion Limited (Original Respondents and Cross-appellants) Rothwell (Original Appellant and Cross-respondent) v. Chemical and Insulating Company Limited and others (Original Respondents and Cross-appellants) Etc.* [2007] UKHL 39 (England) on appeal from [2006] EWCA Civ 27 (England).

74  *The Damages (Asbestos-related Conditions) Act of 2009* (England).

of recovery than any other victims. The significantly reduced chances of compensation for victims of non-occupational exposure are rooted in the history of the structuration of asbestos compensation, which has rewarded occupational diseases over other kinds of exposures, in part because expansion of asbestos compensation was supported by the industry to reduce class struggle, and has resulted in a primacy of occupational exposure that is hardly defensible in terms of fairness to other victims. All systems are characterized by significant rigidity as the asbestos epidemic changes the faces and the biographies of victims: while the recursivity of social processes has affected the dominant perceptual frames and favored progressive expansion of asbestos compensation, legal change has occurred slowly.

An interesting result of marginalization of certain victims is the emergence of asbestos victims' advocacy groups. They emerge in all four countries, mostly by initiative of asbestos widows who could not recover damages caused by their husbands' death or who became sick themselves. In the United States, these victims are primarily those for which a record of exposure cannot be reconstructed. Durkin refers to the victims represented by these groups as "desperate" cases.[75] In England, the group is comprised mostly of non-unionized victims. To them, even if the victims had been exposed to asbestos in the workplace, finding an attorney was very hard when unions were acting as funders and gatekeepers of cases. SPADE, one of the first English groups was established by the widow of a mesothelioma victim who had worked for the postal service. He was not eligible to receive IIDB benefits because he had not worked in a qualifying occupation. In Belgium, the national asbestos victim association was established by the joint efforts of relatives of a victim who was entitled to payments under workers' compensation because he had worked in a non-qualifying occupation (an elevator maintenance company) and of an asbestos worker's widow and sons, all of whom developed mesothelioma because of environmental exposure. In Italy, the national asbestos victim association aimed to represent a broad range of victim, both occupational and non-occupational exposure cases. The twofold goal was, at the national level, to pursue a more radical agenda than the one pushed forward by unions and, at the local level, to allow the greatest number of victims to obtain compensation. In all countries, these groups developed mobilization tactics parallel to the main mobilizers (plaintiff attorneys in the United States and unions in Europe). In England and Italy, the presence transformed asbestos compensation because their views and strategies became incorporated in routinized practices. In England, the plaintiff bar became a claim mobilizer and embraced some of these "desperate" cases. In Italy, the Eternit trial, with a mix of occupational, environmental, and secondhand exposure victims, reflects the broader mobilization vision of the national asbestos victim association.

---

75   Durkin, "Constructing law: comparing legal action in the United States and United Kingdom", 89.

The analysis of equity issues must also take into account how compensation is funded and the future of funding. In European nations, where the welfare state tradition is stronger, the state substituted itself to tortfeasors and subsidized the costs of the asbestos epidemic. In the United States, plaintiff lawyers successfully chased new defendants. The chase was so successful that defendants are now so far removed from the dangerous days of asbestos use that the merits of accountability are questioned. Indeed, it was an expensive and inefficient chase that consumed 58 percent of the money transacted to compensate asbestos victims. In 2005, Carroll and colleagues estimated that, from its inception through the end of 2002, the total spending of asbestos litigation amounted to approximately USD 70 billion. As a result, claimants' net compensation equaled about USD 30 billion (42 percent of total spending).[76]

With regard to setting aside money for future victims, the issue seems, on its face, less problematic when compensation comes from the welfare state. Although they cannot be taken for granted by victims especially after the significant retrenchment of the past three decades, the institutions of the welfare state, including workers' compensation, are here to stay and built to deliver compensation and other benefits for the foreseeable future. In countries in which the welfare system is weaker and compensation money originates primarily from corporate defendants and insurance companies, the prospects are more uncertain. These entities may disappear as a matter of corporate law, and a successor's liability does not always guarantee compensation since purchasing companies often create new legal entities and use contract law to avoid acquiring toxic liabilities of previous businesses. In the United States, efforts to establish more stable compensation funds have all failed, and, given the competing interests and views of the various stakeholders, unlikely to succeed in the foreseeable future.[77] England, on the other hand, set up two *ad hoc* funds (the 1979 Pneumoconiosis Act and a scheme assuring recovery in the event no employer's insurance can be found), has been recently proposed.[78] These mechanisms intend to guarantee continuity in payments to victims, at least those who can claim an occupational exposure.

As the wave of asbestos is peaking in this decade, asbestos compensation is still very much contested. Routinized practices have led to stability in the way in which asbestos compensation is reproduced. Stability is likely to persist because the asbestos disease is about to decline in the four countries researched. However, these patterns seem to be overall inadequate to deal with the problem of future victims because they rely on processes and institutions that are themselves contested. The remains of the welfare state are indisputably a rather weak foundation to guarantee compensation for all future victims especially after its extensive retrenchment, its

---

76   Carroll et al., *Asbestos litigation*, 87-106.

77   Barnes, *Dust-up: asbestos litigation and the failure of common sense policy reform, passim.*

78   Department of Work and Pensions, "£300m support for future mesothelioma victims."

dependency upon political systems, and the overall vulnerability and economic uncertainty of the global economy. I wish to end this book on a more optimistic note. While "the arc of the moral universe is long" as Martin Luther King Jr. famously said, "but it bends toward justice," it is more appropriate to be cautious and imagine the future of asbestos compensation as more somber. While I would love "to wear rainbow every day and tell the world that everything's okay," I will side with Johnny Cash and I will be a "man in black."[79] The future trajectory of asbestos disease and compensation appears in fact to be contested and uncertain.

---

79   Johnny Cash, "Man in Black" (lyrics) (1971).

# Bibliography

AAP. "Boycotts hit James Hardie sales." Published electronically May 16, 2005. http://www.theage.com.au/news/Business/Boycotts-hit-James-Hardie-sales/2005/05/16/1116095891708.html.

———. "Hardie fund to get top-up." *The Sydney Morning Herald*. Published electronically March 27, 2012. http://www.smh.com.au/national/hardie-fund-to-get-topup-20120327-1vwle.html.

ABEVA. "Oui a un fonds d'indemnisation, non à l'immunité [Yes to a compensation fund, no to immunity]." *ABEVA News*, 2007.

———. "Un an de fonctionnement de l'AFA (Fonds amiante) [A year of operations of the AFA (Asbestos Fund)]." *ABEVA News*, 2008, 1.

AFEVA. "Lettera al Ministro della Salute Prof. Renato Balduzzi [Letter to Prof. Renato Balduzzi, Head of the Health Ministry]." http://ibasecretariat.org/italian_lettera_al_ministro_jun_2012.pdf.

Allen, David, and Laurie Kazan-Allen, eds. *Eternit and the Great Asbestos Trial*. London: The International Ban Asbestos Secretariat, 2012.

Allen, Matthew. "The varieties of capitalism paradigm: not enough variety?" *Socio-Economic Review* 2, no. 1 (2004): 87-108.

American Thoracic Society. "Diagnosis and Initial Management of Nonmalignant Diseases Related to Asbestos." *American Journal of Respiratory and Critical Care Medicine* 170, no. 6 (2004): 691-715.

"Amiante – L'Abeva réclame un élargissement des indemnisations et davantage de prevention [Asbestos – L'Abeva calls for expansion of compensation and more prevention]." *LeVif.be*. Published electronically May 15, 2013. http://www.levif.be/info/belga-generique/amiante-l-abeva-reclame-un-elargissement-des-indemnisations-et-davantage-de-prevention/article-4000303200565.htm.

"Amiante: le premier à se lever [Asbestos: the first to rise]." *Imagine demain le monde* 3, March, 2007.

"Amianto, condannati cinque dirigenti FS [Asbestos, five railroad executives found guilty]." *Corriere della Sera (Bologna)*. Published electronically March 13, 2009. http://corrieredibologna.corriere.it/bologna/notizie/cronaca/2009/13-marzo-2009/amianto-condannati-cinque-dirigenti-fs-1501085490317.shtml.

"Amianto, confermata in Appello l'assoluzione di Fanfani [Asbestos, Fanfani's acquittal upheld on appeal]." *Il Piccolo*. Published electronically July 23, 2011. http://ilpiccolo.gelocal.it/cronaca/2011/07/23/news/amianto-confermata-in-appello-l-assoluzione-di-fanfani-1.742699.

"Amianto, riparte il maxi-processo [Asbestos, the super-trial resumes]." *Il Messaggero Veneto*. Published electronically October 30, 2012. http://messagg

eroveneto.gelocal.it/cronaca/2012/10/30/news/amianto-riparte-il-maxi-pro cesso-1.5947880.

Amodio, Ennio, and Eugenio Selvaggi. "An Accusatorial System in a Civil Law Country: The 1988 Italian Code of Criminal Procedure." *Temple Law Review* 62 (1989): 1211-1224.

Anderson, Eugene R., Irene C. Warshauer, and Adrienne M. Coffin. "The Asbestos Health Hazards Compensation Act: A Legislative Solution to a Litigation Crisis." *Journal of Legislation* 10 (1983): 25.

Andress, Hans-Jürgen, and Henning Lohmann. *The working poor in Europe: employment, poverty and globalisation.* Cheltenham; Northampton, MA: Edward Elgar, 2008.

Asbestos Liability Risk Analysis Group. "Asbestos Claims and Litigation: Update and Review: 2010 New Case Filing: Summary and Analysis," 1-15. Published electronically November 1, 2011. http://www.alragroup.com/docu ments/asbestos%20paper%202011.pdf.

―――. "Asbestos Claims and Litigation: Update and Review: 2011 New Case Filing: Summary and Analysis." 1-11. Published electronically October 15, 2012. www.alragroup.com/documents/Asbestos_paper_2012.pdf.

Association of British Insurers. *Guidelines For Apportioning and Handling Employers Liability Mesothelioma Claims.* London, October 28, 2003.

Atiyah, P.S. "Tort Law and the Alternatives: Some Anglo-American Comparisons." *Duke Law Journal* 6 (1987): 1002-1044.

"Au moins 200 morts chaque année à cause de l'amiante [At least 200 deaths caused by asbestos every year]." *FMP News*, 14, January 21, 2011, 1.

Azagra-Malo, Albert. "Los fondos de compensación del amianto en Francia y en Bélgica [Asbestos Injuries Compensation Funds in France and Belgium]." *Indret: Revista para el Análisis del Derecho*, no. 3 (2007): 1-16.

Baccaro, Lucio, and Sang-Hoon Lim. "Social Pacts as Coalitions of the Weak and Moderate: Ireland, Italy and South Korea in Comparative Perspective." *European Journal of Industrial Relations* 13, no. 1 (2007): 27-46.

Back, Les, Andy Bennett, Laura Desfor Edles, Margaret Gibson, David Inglis, Ronald Jacobs, and Ian Wooward. *Cultural sociology: an introduction.* Chichester, West Sussex; Hoboken, NJ: Wiley-Blackwell, 2012.

Baele, Stephanie. "La Belgique: des crises aux opportunités [Belgium, from crises to opportunities]." *Émulations* 10 (2012): 7-12.

Bar, Christian von. *The common European law of torts.* Oxford; New York: Clarendon Press; Oxford University Press, 1998.

Barella, Guido, "Morti d'amianto, un pool d'indagine [Asbestos deaths, a team of prosecutors]." *Il Piccolo*, June 26, 2008.

Barnes, Jeb. *Dust-up: asbestos litigation and the failure of common sense policy reform.* Washington, DC: Georgetown University Press, 2011.

Barnes, Jeb, Thomas F. Burke, and Malcolm Feeley, eds. *The Politics of Legalism,* Law, Courts and Politics Series: Routledge, 2013.

Bartrip, Peter W.J. "History of asbestos related disease." *Postgraduate Medical Journal* 80, no. 940 (2004): 72-76.

BBC News. "Damages won after asbestos death." Published electronically December 13, 2006. http://news.bbc.co.uk/2/hi/uk_news/england/6176641.stm.

―――. "'No-win, no-fee' changes announced by Ken Clarke." Published electronically March 29, 2011. http://www.bbc.co.uk/news/uk-12890256.

―――. "Asbestos exemption to 'no-win, no-fee' changes." Published electronically April 24, 2012. http://www.bbc.co.uk/news/uk-politics-17833607.

Best, Richard. "Liability for Asbestos Related Disease in England and Germany." *German Law Journal* 4, no. 7 (2003): 661-683.

Betlem, Gerrit, and Michael Faure. "Environmental Toxic Torts in Europe: Some Trends in Recovery of Soil Clean-up Costs and Damages for Personal Injury in the Netherlands, Belgium, England and Germany." *Georgetown International Environmental Law Review* 10 (1998): 855-890.

Beveridge, William H.B.B. *Social insurance and allied services: utilisation of Approved Society Administration under the alternative scheme proposed by the National Conference of Friendly Societies, and other Approved Society organisations: detailed plan: report.* London: Twentieth Century Press, 1943.

Bianchi, Claudio, and Tommaso Bianchi. "Malignant mesothelioma: global incidence and relationship with asbestos." *Industrial Health* 45, no. 3 (2007): 379-387.

―――. "Malignant pleural mesothelioma in Italy." *Indian Journal of Occupational and Environmental Medicine* 13, no. 2 (2009): 80-83.

Biederman, Christine, Thomas Korosec, Julie Lyons, and Patrick Williams. "Toxic Justice." *Dallas Observer*, August 13, 1998.

Blamires, Cyprian, and Paul Jackson. *World fascism: a historical encyclopedia.* Vol. 1, Santa Barbara, CA: ABC-CLIO, 2006.

Blankenburg, Erhard R. "Civil Litigation Rates as Indicators for Legal Cultures." In *Comparing Legal Cultures*, edited by David Nelken. 41-68. Brookfield, VT: Dartmouth Press, 1997.

Bocken, Hubert. "Tort Law." In *Introduction to Belgian law*, edited by Hubert Bocken and Walter de Bondt. 244-273. Bruxelles; The Hague; Boston: Bruylant; Kluwer Law International, 2001.

Boggio, Andrea. "Comparative Notes On The Asbestos Trust Fund." *Mealey's Litigation Report, Asbestos*, 1, no. 6 (2003): 1-7.

―――. "The Global Enforcement of Human Rights: The Unintended Consequences of Transnational Litigation." *The International Journal of Human Rights* 10, no. 4 (2006): 325-340.

―――. "Linking corporate power to corporate structures: An empirical analysis." *Social & Legal Studies* 22 (2013) 107-131

Boschma, Ron A. "The rise of clusters of innovative industries in Belgium during the industrial epoch." *Research Policy* 28 (1999): 853-871.

Bourdieu, Pierre. *La domination masculine* [Masculine domination]. Paris: Seuil, 1998.

Brickman, Lester. "On the Theory Class's Theories of Asbestos Litigation: The Disconnect Between Scholarship and Reality." *Pepperdine Law Review* 31 (2004): 33-170.

———. "Ethical Issues in Asbestos Litigation." *Hofstra Law Review* 33 (2005): 833-912.

———. *Lawyer barons: what their contingency fees really cost America*. New York: Cambridge University Press, 2011.

———. "Written Statement Filed at the Hearing on How Fraud and Abuse in the Asbestos Compensation System Affect Victims, Jobs, the Economy and the Legal System Held Before The Subcommittee On The Constitution Of The U.S. House Of Representatives Committee On The Judiciary." 2011.

Brodeur, Paul. *Outrageous misconduct: the asbestos industry on trial*. 1st ed. New York: Pantheon Books, 1985.

Bronstad, Amanda. "Asbestos is rearing its head; Plaintiffs' firms are injecting life into a once-'sleepy' California docket." *The National Law Journal*, December 19, 2011.

Burke, Thomas Frederick. *Lawyers, lawsuits, and legal rights: the battle over litigation in American society*. Berkeley: University of California Press, 2002.

Cape plc. "Proposal for a Scheme of Arrangement under Section 425 between Cape plc and the other Scheme Companies and their respective Scheme Creditors." http://www.capeplc.com/cape/uploads/wysiwyg/documents/Schemeexplan atorystatement15March2006.pdf.

Carrington, Paul D. "Asbestos Lessons: The Unattended Consequences of Asbestos Litigation." *The Review of Litigation* 26, no. 3 (2007): 583-611.

Carroll, Stephen J., Deborah R. Hensler, Jennifer Gross, Elizabeth M. Sloss, Matthias Schonlau, Allan Abrahmse, and J. Scott Ashwood. *Asbestos litigation*. Santa Monica, CA: RAND Corporation, 2005.

Carroll, William K. *The making of a transnational capitalist class: corporate power in the twenty-first century*. London; New York: Zed, 2010.

Castleman, Barry I. *Asbestos: medical and legal aspects*. 5th ed. New York: Aspen Publishers, 2005.

Cazzola, Giuliano. "La miniera d'amianto [The asbestos mine]." *Il Sole-24 Ore*, November 17, 2003.

Chellini, Elisabetta, Alessandro Marinaccio, and Massimo Nesti. "La sorveglianza dei casi di mesotelioma maligno e la definizione delle esposizioni ad amianto: i dati ReNaM 1997 [Malignant mesothelioma monitoring and asbestos exposure requirements: ReNaM 1997 data]." *Epidemiologia e Prevenzione* 27, no. 3 (2003): 147-153.

Clerens, J. "Recherches sur l'asbestose pulmonaire en Belgique [Research on pulmonary asbestosis in Belgium]." *Archives Belges de Médecine Sociale* 9 (1950): 557-565.

Cless, Jacques, and Vincent Neuprez. "L'appréciation par la Cour d'arbitrage des exonérations de responsabilité civile dans le droit des accidents du travail [The Court d'arbitrage's treatement of immunity in the law of occupational accidents]." *Revue de Jurisprudence de Liège, Mons et Bruxelles* (2001): 780-785.

Cohen, Lizabeth. *A consumers' republic: the politics of mass consumption in postwar America*. 1st ed. New York: Knopf; Random House, 2003.

Conférence du Jeune Barreau de Charleroi. *La loi relative à la protection contre la violence et le harcèlement moral ou sexuel au travail: deux années d'application* [The law on sexual harrassment on the workplace: a two-year assessment]. Actes de l'après-midi d'étude organisé le 18 février 2005. Brussels: Kluwer, 2005.

Cooke, William E. "Fibrosis of the lungs due to the inhalation of asbestos dust." *British Medical Journal* 2, no. 3317 (1924): 147-140.2.

———. "Pulmonary asbestosis." *British Medical Journal* 2, no. 3491 (1927): 1024-1025.

Cousy, Herman, and Dimitri Doshout. "Compensation for Personal Injury in Belgium." In *Compensation for personal injury in a comparative perspective*, edited by Bernhard A. Koch and Helmut Koziol. Vienna; New York: Spinger, 2003.

Cutler, James. "Asbestos and the media." *British Medical Journal* 285, no. 6344 (1982): 814.

D'Amico, Franco. "Malattie da amianto: il bilancio di un dramma senza fine [Asbestos disease: numbers of a never ending tragedy]." Published electronically August 10, 2012. http://www.anmil.it/Chisiamo/ReteeServiziANMIL/Il PatronatoANMILpresentein79Sedi/Malattiedaamianto/tabid/2191/language/it-IT/Default.aspx.

D'Orta, Lino. "La matassa di leggi sul 'killer' amianto [The puzzle of regulation of 'killer' asbestos]." *IL—Bimestrale di informazione dell'INAIL* 6 (2003): 1-4.

De Beys, Bénédicte. "Belgique Le fatalisme tranquille? [Belgium: gentle fatalism?]." Published electronically June 13, 2007 http://www.eurosduvill age.eu/708-BELGIQUE-Le-fatalisme.html?lang=fr.

De Brucq, Danielle. "Une Vaste Enquête: 'Les Maladies Professionnelles en Europe.' Déclaration, Reconnaissance et Indemnisation [A broad inquiry: 'Occupational diseases in Europe.' Filing, Adjudication and Compensation]." *Revue Belge de Sécurité Sociale* 2 (2001): 372-385.

De Groot, Gerard-René, and Conrad J.P. Van Laer. "The Dubious Quality of Legal Dictionaries." *International Journal of Legal Information* 34 (2006): 65-86.

de Kezel, Evelien. "La Réparation du dommage corporel à la suite d'une exposition à l'amiante [Compensation for bodily injuries caused by exposure to asbestos]." *Revue Générale des Assurances et des Responsabilités* 8 (2001): 13426.

Deidda, Beniamino. "Il fondo per il risarcimento delle vittime dell'amianto: opportunità, necessità, prospettive [The Asbestos Victims Compensation Fund: opportunities, needs, perspectives]." Published electronically April 10, 2009. http://olympus.uniurb.it/index.php?option=com_content&view=article

&id=2807:2009-deidda-beniamino-fondo-per-le-vittime-da-amianto-in-italia&catid=29:approfondimenti-tematici&Itemid=40.

Del Duca, Louis F. "An Historic Convergence of Civil and Common Law Systems-Italy's New Adversarial Criminal Procedure System." *Dickinson Journal of International Law* 10 (1991): 73-85.

Department of Work and Pensions. "Prescribed diseases." http://www.dwp.gov.uk/publications/specialist-guides/technical-guidance/db1-a-guide-to-industrial-injuries/prescribed-diseases/.

————. "£300m support for future mesothelioma victims." *Newsroom.* Published electronically July 25, 2012 http://www.dwp.gov.uk/newsroom/press-releases/2012/jul-2012/dwp085-12.shtml.

Diandini, Rachmania, Ken Takahashi, Eun-Kee Park, Ying Jiang, Mehrnoosh Movahed, Giang Vinh Le, Lukas Jyuhn-Hsiarn Lee, Vanya Delgermaa, and Rokho Kim. "Potential years of life lost (PYLL) caused by asbestos-related diseases in the world." *American Journal of Industrial Medicine.* Published electronically June 12, 2013.

Dixon, Lloyd S., and Geoffrey McGovern. *Asbestos bankruptcy trusts and tort compensation.* Santa Monica, CA: RAND Corporation, 2011.

Dixon, Lloyd S., Geoffrey McGovern, and Amy Coombe. *Asbestos bankruptcy trusts: an overview of trust structure and activity with detailed reports on the largest trusts.* Santa Monica, CA: RAND Corporation, 2010.

Doll, Richard. "Mortality from lung cancer in asbestos workers." *British Journal of Industrial Medicine* 12, no. 2 (1955): 81.

Donna, A. "Considerazioni su un nuovo caso di associazione fra asbestosi e neoplasia polmonare [Considerations on a new case of asbestosis associated with lung cancer]." *Medicina del Lavoro* 58, no. 10 (1967): 561-572.

Durkin, Thomas E. "Constructing law: comparing legal action in the United States and United Kingdom." University of Chicago, 1994.

Edelman, Lauren B., Gwendolyn Leachman, and Doug McAdam. "On Law, Organizations, and Social Movements." *Annual Review of Law and Social Science* 6, no. 1 (2010): 653-685.

Editorial. "Hardie's fund hits trouble." *Newcastle Herald*, April 24, 2009.

Engel, David M. "The Oven Bird's Song: Insiders, Outsiders, and Personal Injuries in an American Community." *Law & Society Review* 18, no. 4 (1984): 551-582.

Engel, David M., and Michael W. McCann, eds. *Fault lines: tort law as cultural practice.* Stanford: Stanford Law Books, 2009.

Esping-Andersen, Gosta. *The three worlds of welfare capitalism.* Princeton: Princeton University Press, 1990.

————. *Social foundations of postindustrial economies.* Oxford: Oxford University Press, 1999.

"Eternit condamné à dédommager les victimes de l'amiante [Eternit will pay damages to the victims of asbestos]." *Lalibre.be.* Published electronically

November 28, 2011. http://www.lalibre.be/actu/belgique/article/703028/eter nit-condamne-a-dedommager-les-victimes-de-l-amiante.html.

"Eternit condamnée: 'C'est un jour historique' [Eternit found liable: 'An historical day']." *Lavenir.net*. Published electronically November 28, 2011. http://www. lavenir.net/article/detail.aspx?articleid=DMF20111128_036.

"Eternit fera probablement appel [Eternit will likely appeal]." *Le Soir*. Published electronically November 28, 2011. http://www.lesoir.be/actualite/ belgique/2011-11-28/la-justice-a-ose-resister-au-lobby-belge-de-l-amiante-879930.php.

Eurogip. *La branche 'accidents du travail—maladies professionnelles' dans les pays de l'UE-15. Gestion, organisation, missions* ['Occupational injury and diseases' in the EU-15 zone. Management, organization, goals]. Paris: Eurogip, 2005.

―――. *Asbestos-related occupational diseases in Europe. Recognition, Figures, Specific systems*. Paris: Eurogip, April, 2006.

―――. *Les maladies professionnelles liées à l'amiante en Europe. Une enquête dans 13 pays* [Occupational diseases caused by asbestos in Europe. A 13-country inquiry]. Paris: Eurogip, 2006.

―――. *Compensation of permanent impairment resulting from occupational injuries in Europe*. Paris: Eurogip, 2010.

Ewick, Patricia, and Susan S. Silbey. *The common place of law: stories from everyday life*. Chicago: University of Chicago Press, 1998.

Factories and Workshops. *Annual Report of the Chief Inspector of Factories and Workshops for the Year 1898*. Vol. London: 1898.

Fagnart, Jean-Luc. *La responsabilité civile: chronique de jurisprudence 1985-1995* [Tort liability: Case law chronicle of 1985-1995]. Bruxelles: Éditions Larcier, 1997.

Farnsworth, Kevin, and Chris Holden. "The Business-Social Policy Nexus: Corporate Power and Corporate Inputs into Social Policy." *Journal of Social Policy* 35, no. 3 (2006): 473-494.

Feder, Barnaby J. "Paying asbestos damages." *The New York Times*, September 18, 1982.

Federici, Antonio. *Il danno biologico nel sistema previdenziale* [Social security and "danno biologico"]. Milan: Giuffrè, 2009.

Feldman, Eric A. "Blood Justice: Courts, Conflict, and Compensation in Japan, France, and the United States." *Law and Society Review* 34, no. 3 (2000): 651-701

Felstiner, William L.F., Richard L. Abel, and Austin Sarat. "The Emergence and Transformation of Disputes: Naming, Blaming, Claiming ..." *Law and Society Review* 15 (1981): 631-654.

Felstiner, William L.F., and Robert Dingwall. *Asbestos Litigation in the United Kingdom: An Interim Report*. Chicago: American Bar Foundation, 1988.

Ferrante, Daniela, Marinella Bertolotti, Annalisa Todesco, Dario Mirabelli, Benedetto Terracini, and Corrado Magnani. "Cancer Mortality and Incidence of

Mesothelioma in a Cohort of Wives of Asbestos Workers in Casale Monferrato, Italy." *Environmental Health Perspectives* 115, no. 10 (2007): 1401-1405.

Field, Robert I., and Richard B. Victor. *Asbestos claims: the decision to use workers' compensation and tort*. Cambridge, MA: Workers Compensation Research Institute, 1988.

Fonds des Maladies Professionnelles. "Qu'est-ce qu'une maladie professionnelle? [What is an occupational disease?]." http://www.fmp-fbz.fgov.be/web/content. php?lang=fr&target=citizen#/about-occupational-diseases.

———. "Maladies professionnelles provoquées par l'amiante. Critères de reconnaissance et d'indemnisation [Occupational diseases caused by asbestos. Criteria for assessment and compensation]." Published electronically 2007. http://www.fmp-fbz.fgov.be/afa/pdf/afabrochuref.pdf.

———. "Liste belge des maladies professionnelles [List of occupational diseases in Belgium]." Published electronically February 12, 2013. http://www.fmp-fbz.fgov.be/web/pdfdocs/Lijsten/FR/Liste%20belge%20des%20maladies%20 professionnelles.pdf.

Franchimont, Benoit. "L'amiante a tué 171 fois autour de Harmignies! [Asbestos has killed 171 times around Harmignies!]." *Soirmag.lesoir.be*. Published electronically May 14, 2013. http://soirmag.lesoir.be/l%E2%80%99amiante-tu%C3%A9-171-fois-autour-harmignies-2013-05-14-29758.

Franchimont, Michel, Ann Jacobs, and Adrien Masset. *Manuel de procédure pénale* [Textbook of Criminal Procedure]. 4th ed. Brussels: Editions Larcier, 2012.

Freccero, Stephen P. "An Introduction to the New Italian Criminal Procedure." *American Journal of Criminal Law* 21 (1993): 345-383.

Friedman, Lawrence M. *Total Justice*. New York: Russell Sage Foundation, 1985.
———. *The Republic of Choice: Law, Authority, and Culture*. Cambridge, MA: Harvard University Press, 1990.
———. "Is There a Modern Legal Culture?" *Ratio Juris* 7, no. 2 (1994): 117-131.

Gaakeer, Jeanne. "Iudex translator: the reign of finitude." In *Methods of Comparative Law*, edited by Pier Giuseppe Monateri. Research Handbooks in Comparative Law, 252-269. Cheltenham; Northampton, MA: Edward Elgar, 2012.

Geeroms, Sofie M.F. "Comparative Law and Legal Translation: Why the Terms Cassation, Revision and Appeal Should Not Be Translated ..." *The American Journal of Comparative Law* 50, no. 1 (2002): 201-228.

General Insurance Practice Executive Committee and UK Asbestos Working Party. *Pleural Plaques*. Consultation Paper. London: Ministry of Justice, 2008.

Genn, Hazel. *Personal Injury Compensation: How Much is Enough?* Report n. 225. London: Law Commission, 1994.

Gerd-Rainer Horn. "The Belgian Contribution to Global 1968." *Belgisch Tijdschrift voor Nieuwste Geschiedenis—Revue belge d'histoire contemporaine* 35, no. 4 (2005): 597–635.

Gibbs, Stephen. "Mines and Communities: Boycott call on Hardie gathers pace." *MAC: Mines and Communities*. Published electronically August 4, 2004. http://www.minesandcommunities.org/article.php?a=5544&l=1.

Giddens, Anthony. *Central problems in social theory: action, structure, and contradiction in social analysis*. Berkeley: University of California Press, 1979.

———. *The constitution of society: outline of the theory of structuration*. Berkeley: University of California Press, 1984.

Gottschall, E. Brigitte. "Taking a retrospective look at asbestos-related thoracic disease produces interesting results." *Radiology* 255, no. 3 (2010): 681-682.

Gramsci, Antonio. *Letters from prison*. 1st ed. New York: Harper & Row, 1973.

Grégoire, Denis. "Former asbestos cement workers search for justice." *HESA Newsletter* 29 (2006): 36.

Greillier, Laurent, and Philippe Astoul. "Mesothelioma and Asbestos-Related Pleural Diseases." *Respiration* 76, no. 1 (2008): 1-15.

Guariniello, Raffaele. *Se il lavoro uccide: riflessioni di un magistrato* [If working kills: reflections of a prosecutor]. Nuovo politecnico. Torino: G. Einaudi, 1985.

———. "Dai tumori professionali ai tumori extraprofessionali da amianto [From occupational to non-occupational asbestos cancers]." *Foro Italiano* 126, no. 5 (2001): 278.

Gutierrez, Ricardo. "La Justice a osé résister au lobby belge de l'amiante [A court dared to oppose the asbestos lobby]." *Parti du Travail de Belgique*. Published electronically November 28, 2011. http://www.lesoir.be/actualite/belgique/2011-11-28/la-justice-a-ose-resister-au-lobby-belge-de-l-amiante-879930.php.

Hacker, Jacob S. *The divided welfare state: the battle over public and private social benefits in the United States*. New York: Cambridge University Press, 2002.

Hall, Peter A. "The movement from Keynesianism to monetarism: Institutional analysis and British economic policy in the 1970s." In *Structuring Politics. Historical Institutionalism in Comparative Analysis*, edited by Sven Steinmo, Kathleen Thelen, and Frank Longstreth. 90-113. Cambridge, MA: Cambridge University Press, 1992.

Hall, Peter A., and David W. Soskice. *Varieties of capitalism: the institutional foundations of comparative advantage*. Oxford; New York: Oxford University Press, 2001.

Haltom, William, and Michael W. McCann. *Distorting the law: politics, media, and the litigation crisis*. Chicago: University of Chicago Press, 2004.

Hanlon, Patrick M., and Anne Smetak. "Asbestos Changes." *N.Y.U. Annual Survey of American Law* 62 (2007): 525-606.

Harding, Anne-Helen. *The Great Britain Asbestos Survey 1971-2005. Mortality of workers listed on the Great Britain Asbestosis or Mesothelioma Registers*. London: Health and Safety Executive, 2010.

Hardy-Hémery, Odette. *Eternit et l'amiante, 1922-2000: Aux sources du profit, une industrie du risque* [Eternit and asbestos, 1922-2000: At the origins of profits, an industry of risk]. Villeneuve d'Ascq: Presses Universitaires du Septentrion, 2005.

Harr, Jonathan. *A civil action*. 1st ed. New York: Vintage Books, 1996.

Heirbaut, Dirk. "The Belgian Legal Tradition: Does it Exist?". In *Introduction to Belgian law*, edited by Hubert Bocken and Walter de Bondt. 8-12. Bruxelles; The Hague; Boston: Bruylant; Kluwer Law International, 2001.

Hemerijck, Anton, and Ive Marx. "Continental Welfare at a Crossroads: The Choice between Activation and Minimum Income Protection in Belgium and the Netherlands." In *A long goodbye to Bismarck? The politics of welfare reforms in continental Europe*, edited by Bruno Palier. 129-156. Amsterdam: Amsterdam University Press, 2010.

Hennebert, Paul. "Maladies professionnelles. Le point de vue du médecin [Occupational diseases. The doctor's viewpoint]." *Travail et Droit* 2 (1935): 13-15.

Henry, Emmanuel. *Amiante, un scandale improbable: sociologie d'un problème public* [Asbestos, an improbable scandal: sociology of a public issue]. Rennes: Presses Universitaires de Rennes, 2007.

Hensler, Deborah R. "A brief history of asbestos litigation in the United States." In *Asbestos. Anatomy of a mass tort*, edited by Munich Re. 26-32. München: Münchener Rückversicherungs-Gesellschaft, 2009.

Hensler, Deborah R., William L.F. Felstiner, Molly Selvin, and Patricia A. Ebener. *Asbestos in the Courts. The Challenge of Mass Toxic Torts*. Santa Monica, CA: The Institute for Civil Justice, 1985.

Hills, Ben. "The James Hardie story: asbestos victims' claims evaded by manufacturer." *International Journal of Occupational and Environmental Health* 11, no. 2 (2005): 212-214.

Hodges, Christopher J.S. "Introduction." In *Multi-party actions*, edited by Christopher J.S. Hodges. 3-8. Oxford; New York: Oxford University Press, 2001.

Hodgson, J.T., D.M. McElvenny, A.J. Darnton, M.J. Price, and J. Peto. "The expected burden of mesothelioma mortality in Great Britain from 2002 to 2050." *British Journal of Cancer* 92, no. 3 (2005): 587-593.

Holden, Chris, and Kelley Lee. "Corporate Power and Social Policy." *Global Social Policy* 9, no. 3 (2009): 328-354.

Hollevoet, Kevin, Kristiaan Nackaerts, Joël Thimpont, Paul Germonpre, Lionel Bosquee, Paul De Vuyst, Catherine Legrand, et al. "Diagnostic performance of soluble mesothelin and megakaryocyte potentiating factor in mesothelioma." *American Journal of Respiratory and Critical Care Medicine* 181, no. 6 (2010): 620-625.

Hollevoet, Kevin, Joris Van Cleemput, Joël Thimpont, Paul De Vuyst, Lionel Bosquée, Kristiaan Nackaerts, Paul Germonpré, et al. "Serial measurements of mesothelioma serum biomarkers in asbestos-exposed individuals: a prospective longitudinal cohort study." *Journal of Thoracic Oncology* 6, no. 5 (2011): 889-895.

Hughes, Janet M., and Hans Weill. "Asbestosis as a precursor of asbestos related lung cancer: results of a prospective mortality study." *British Journal of Industrial Medicine* 48 (1991): 229-233.

Hutton, Will, and Anthony Giddens, eds. *Global capitalism*. New York: The New Press, 2000.

INAIL. "Dati previdenziali per lavoratori esposti all'amianto ex ¶ 132, comma 8, legge n. 257/93 e successive modifiche [Coverage data for workers exposed to asbestos under ¶ 132, section 8, law n. 257/93 and following amendements]." Published electronically 2009. http://www.amiantomaipiu.it/files/amiantomaipiu_page_6_resource_file3_orig.pdf.

———. *Rapporto Annuale 2010 con analisi dell'andamento infortunistico* [2010 Annual Report with accident trend analysis]. Vol. Rome: INAIL, July 5, 2011.

———. *Rapporto Annuale 2011: Parte quarta/statistiche Infortuni e malattie professionali* [2011 Annual Report: Section Four/occupational accident and disease statistics ]. Vol. Rome: INAIL, July 5, 2012.

INPS. "Comunicazione [Communication]." n. 39781. Rome: INPS, 2004.

Jackson, David F. *Report of the Special Commission of Inquiry into the Medical Research and Compensation Foundation*. Sydney: The Cabinet Office: New South Wales Government, 2004.

James Hardie Industries. "Amended and Restated Final Funding Agreement (Amended FFA), Copy conformed to include all amendments to 31 March 2009." http://www.ir.jameshardie.com.au/public/download.jsp?id=3776.

Jasanoff, Sheila, and Dogan Perese. "Welfare State or Welfare Court: Asbestos Litigation in Comparative Perspective." *Journal of Law and Policy* XII, no. 2 (2004): 619-639.

Jégo, Marie. "Dans l'Oural, la mine d'amiante à ciel ouvert pollue toujours la ville d'Asbest [In the Ural, an asbestos mine pullutes the city of Asbestos daily]." *Le Monde*, November 10, 2009.

Jessop, Bob. *State theory: putting the capitalist state in its place*. Cambridge, UK: Polity Press, 1990.

———. *The future of the capitalist state*. Cambridge, UK; Malden, MA: Polity; Blackwell, 2002.

"Johns-Manville: from a Basement to a Multi-Billion Dollar Business." *The Telegraph*, Febraury 4, 1978.

"Johns-Manville To Sell Facility In Belgium." *Toledo Blade*, February 4, 1983.

Jonckheere, Eric. "Actions and achievements of Belgium asbestos victims and their families." In *2007 International Asbestos Conference for fair and equal compensation for all asbestos victims and their families*. Yokohama, Japan 2007.

Judicial Conference of the United States. Ad Hoc Committee on Asbestos Litigation. *Report of the Judicial Conference Ad Hoc Committee on Asbestos Litigation*. 1991.

Judicial Studies Board. *Guidelines for the assessment of general damages in personal injury cases*. 10th ed. Oxford; New York: Oxford University Press, 2010.

Kagan, Robert A. *Adversarial legalism: the American way of law*. Cambridge, MA: Harvard University Press, 2001.

Kaiser Aluminum and Chemical Corporation. "Third Amended Asbestos Trust Distribution Procedures, November 20, 2007." http://www.kaiserasbestostrust. com/Files/Third%20Amended%20Trust%20Distribution%20Procedures%20 00013238.pdf.

Kakalik, James S., Michael G. Shanley, William L. F. Felstiner, and Patricia A. Ebener. *Costs of Asbestos Litigation*. Santa Monica, CA: RAND Institute for Civil Justice, 1983.

Kalanik, Lynn M., Mary McNulty, and Christina M. Stansell. "Johns Manville Corporation." In *International Directory of Company Histories*, edited by Tina Grant and Miranda H. Ferrara. Vol. 64, 209-214. Detroit: St. James Press, 2005.

Kazan-Allen, Laurie. "T&N plc: News." *British Asbestos Newsletter* no. 27. Published electronically Spring 1997. http://www.britishasbestosnewsletter. org/ban27.htm.

———. "Mesothelioma: A European Epidemic." *British Asbestos Newsletter* no. 34. Published electronically Spring 1999. http://www.britishasbestosnewsletter. org/ban34.htm.

———. "Asbestos Compensation in Europe." Published electronically July 7, 2000. http://ibasecretariat.org/lka_eu_comp.php.

———. "London Asbestos Meetings, April 2002." Published electronically May 3, 2002. http://ibasecretariat.org/lka_london_meetings_rep_0402.php.

———. "Jail Time for Eternit Executives." Published electronically June 28, 2005. http://ibasecretariat.org/lka_jail_for_eternit_exec.php.

———. *Asbestos: the Human Cost of Corporate Greed*. Brussels: European United Left/Nordic Green Left, 2006.

———. "One Step Forward, Two Steps Back." *British Asbestos Newsletter* no. 65. Published electronically Winter 2006-2007. http://www.british asbestosnewsletter.org/ban65.htm.

———. "Update on T&N Ltd." *British Asbestos Newsletter* no. 68. Published electronically Autumn 2007. http://www.britishasbestosnewsletter.org/ban68. htm.

———. "Eternit Pre-Trial Manoeuvre in Italy." Published electronically March 11, 2009. http://ibasecretariat.org/lka_eternit_pre_tria_manouevre_120 309.php.

———. "Introduction." In *Eternit and the Great Asbestos Trial*, edited by David Allen and Laurie Kazan-Allen, 8-14. London: The International Ban Asbestos Secretariat, 2012.

———. "Belgium's Asbestos Killing Fields." Published electronically May 23, 2013. http://www.ibasecretariat.org/lka-belgium-asbestos-killing-fields.php.

Kemp, David. A. "Damages for Future Pecuniary Loss." In *Damages for personal injury and death*, edited by David A. Kemp. London: Sweet & Maxwell, 1998.

Kempf, Hervé. "Asbestos, la ville maudite de l'amiante [Asbestos, the damned asbestos city]." *Le Monde*, December 28, 2005, 146.

Keynes, John Maynard. *Laissez-faire and communism*. New York: New Republic, 1926.

Kloppenberg, James T. *Uncertain victory: social democracy and progressivism in European and American thought, 1870-1920*. New York: Oxford University Press, 1986.

Knight, Elizabeth. "Looking for the joke in logic of James Hardie moving to Ireland." *The Sydney Morning Herald*. Published electronically June 17, 2009. http://www.smh.com.au/business/looking-for-the-joke-in-logic-of-james-hardie-moving-to-ireland-20090616-cgjb.html.

Koch, Bernhard A., and Helmut Koziol. *Compensation for personal injury in a comparative perspective*. Vienna; New York: Springer, 2003.

Kostiner, Idit. "Evaluating Legality: Toward a Cultural Approach to the Study of Law and Social Change." *Law & Society Review* 37, no. 2 (2003): 323-368.

Krols, Nico, and Marleen Teugels. "'Licence to Kill': the Dirty Legacy of Asbestos." *Le Monde Diplomatique*, January 18, 2007.

———. "The dirty legacy of asbestos." *Le Monde Diplomatique*, January 22, 2007.

Lacquet, L. M., L. van der Linden, and J. Lepoutre. "Roentgenographic lung changes, asbestosis and mortality in a Belgian asbestos-cement factory." *IARC Scientific Publications*, no. 30 (1980): 783-793.

LaDou, Joseph. "The asbestos cancer epidemic." *Environmental Health Perspectives* 112, no. 3 (2004): 285-290.

LaDou, Joseph, Barry Castleman, Arthur Frank, Michael Gochfeld, Morris Greenberg, James Huff, Tushar Kant Joshi, et al. "The Case for a Global Ban on Asbestos." *Environmental Health Perspectives* 118, no. 7 (2010).

Laenens, Jean, and George Van Mellaert. "The Judicial System and Procedure." In *Introduction to Belgian Law* edited by Hubert Bocken and Walter De Bondt. 85-86. Bruxelles; The Hague; Boston: Bruylant; Kluwer Law International, 2001.

Lahaye, Marie-Christine. "Le combat d'un homme. Luc Vandenbroucke [The fight of a man. Luc Vandenbroucke]." *Inter-Environnement Wallonie* 43 (1998): 16.

Lahnstein, Christian. "Asbestos and Other Emerging Liability Risks—Including Some Critical Remarks on Risk Debates and Perceptions." In *European Tort Law 2002*, edited by Helmut Koziol and Barbara C. Steininger. 530-540. Vienna: Springer, 2003.

"La parole à ... Xavier Jonckeere, président de l'Abeva (Association belge des victimes de l'amiante) [The microphone to ... Xavier Jonckeere, president of Abeva (Belgian Asbestos Victims Association)]." *Le Bulletin de l'Andeva* 22. Published electronically March 31, 2007. http://andeva.fr/?La-parole-a-Xavier-Jonckeere.

"La testimonianza di Romana Blasotti Pavesi: 'Un solo malato di mesotelioma non vale un conto in banca spropositato' [Romana Blasotti Pavesi's testimony: 'a single mesothelioma victim is not worth a huge bank account']." *Casalenews*. Published electronically June 28, 2010. http://www.casalenews.it/notizia/cronaca/2010/06/28/la-testimonianza-di-romana-blasotti-pavesi-un-solo-malato-di-mesotelioma-non-vale-un-conto-in-banca-spropositato/amianto-eternit/f02d2208965df21b1577b1930ef2926d.

Law Commission. *Personal Injury Compensation: How Much is Enough.* Vol. 225, London: Law Commission, 1994.

———. *Damages for Personal Injury: Medical, Nursing and Other Expenses.* Consultation Paper. Vol. 144, London: Law Commission, 1996.

———. *Damages for Personal Injury: Medical, Nursing and Other Expenses; Collateral Expenses.* Vol. 262. London: Law Commission, 1999.

Law, Jonathan, and Elizabeth A. Martin. *A dictionary of law.* 7th ed. Oxford; New York: Oxford University Press, 2009.

Lefèvre, Jonathan. "Eternit: 'Maintenant c'est aux politiques d'agir' [Eternit: Now is up to the politicians to act]." *Parti du Travail de Belgique.* Published electronically November 29, 2011. http://www.ptb.be/nieuws/artikel/eternit-maintenant-cest-aux-politiques-dagir/print.html.

Levin, JeVrey L., Jerry W. McLarty, George A. Hurst, Angela N. Smith, and Arthur L. Frank. "Tyler asbestos workers: mortality experience in a cohort exposed to amosite." *Occupational and Environmental Medicine* 55, no. 3 (1998): 155-160.

Lin, Ro-Ting, Ken Takahashi, Antti Karjalainen, Tsutomu Hoshuyama, Donald Wilson, Takashi Kameda, Chang-Chuan Chan, et al. "Ecological association between asbestos-related diseases and historical asbestos consumption: an international analysis." *The Lancet* 369, no. 9564 (2007): 844-849.

Lipset, Seymour Martin. *The first new nation: the United States in historical and comparative perspective.* New York: Basic Books, 1963.

———. *American exceptionalism: a double-edged sword.* New York: W.W. Norton, 1996.

Lockwood, Graeme. "Trade union governance: The development of British conservative thought." *Journal of Political Ideologies* 10 (2005): 355-371.

Lord Denning M.R., Edmund Davies L.J., and Stamp L.J. "Sales v. Dicks Asbestos and Insulating Co. Ltd." *Managerial Law* 11, no. 4 (1972): 239-259.

Lotito, Franco. "Considerazioni introductive [Introductoty remarks]." Paper presented at the conference "A che punto è la notte", Turin, April 28, 2011.

Lukes, Steven. *Power: a radical view.* 2nd ed. New York: Palgrave Macmillan, 2005.

Luttwak, Edward. *Turbo-capitalism: winners and losers in the global economy.* 1st U.S. ed. New York: HarperCollinsPublishers, 1999.

McCann, Michael W. *Rights at work: pay equity reform and the politics of legal mobilization.* Chicago: University of Chicago Press, 1994.

————. "Law and Social Movements: Contemporary Perspectives." *Annual Review of Law and Social Science* 2, no. 1 (2006): 17-38.

McCulloch, Jock. *Asbestos blues: labour, capital, physicians & the state in South Africa*. Oxford, Bloomington: James Currey, Indiana University Press, 2002.

————. "The Mine at Baryulgil: Work, Knowledge, and Asbestos Disease." *Labour History* 92 (2007): 113-128.

McCulloch, Jock, and Geoffrey Tweedale. *Defending the indefensible: The global asbestos industry and its fight for survival*. Oxford: Oxford University Press, 2008.

McGovern, Francis E. "Resolving Mature Mass Tort Litigation." *Boston University Law Review* 69 (1989): 659-694.

————. "The Tragedy of the Asbestos Commons." *Virginia Law Review* 88, no. 8 (2002): 1721-1756.

————. "Asbestos Legislation II: Section 524(g) Without Bankruptcy." *Pepperdine Law Review* 31 (2004): 233-260.

————. "The Evolution of Asbestos Bankruptcy Trust Distribution Plans." *N.Y.U. Annual Survey of American Law* 62 (2006): 163-185.

Maher, Ann. "Judge eliminates advance asbestos trial setting in Madison County." Published electronically March 30, 2012. http://www.legalnewsline.com/news/235666-judge-eliminates-advance-asbestos-trial-setting-in-madison-county.

Manley, John F. "Theorizing the unexceptional US welfare state." In *Class, power and the state in capitalist society: essays on Ralph Miliband*, edited by Paul Wetherly, Clyde W. Barrow and Peter Burnham. 170-205. Basingstoke; New York: Palgrave Macmillan, 2008.

Mantle, Peter. "Pre-Trial Considerations." In *Damages for personal injury and death*, edited by David A. Kemp. 50-66. London: Sweet & Maxwell, 1998.

Marinaccio, Alessandro, Alessandra Binazzi, Davide Di Marzio, Alberto Scarselli, Marina Verardo, Dario Mirabelli, Valerio Gennaro, et al. "Pleural malignant mesothelioma epidemic: incidence, modalities of asbestos exposure and occupations involved from the Italian National Register." *International Journal of Cancer. Journal International du Cancer* 130, no. 9 (2012): 2146-2154.

Marinaccio, Alessandro, Fabio Montanaro, Marina Mastrantonio, Raffaella Uccelli, Pierluigi Altavista, Massimo Nesti, Adele Seniori Costantini, and Giuseppe Gorini. "Predictions of mortality from pleural mesothelioma in Italy: a model based on asbestos consumption figures supports results from age-period-cohort models." *International Journal of Cancer. Journal International du Cancer* 115, no. 1 (2005): 142-147.

Markesinis, Basil, Michael Coester, and Guido Alpa, eds. *Compensation for personal injury in English, German and Italian law: a comparative outline*, Cambridge studies in international and comparative law. Cambridge; New York: Cambridge University Press, 2005.

Marx, Ive, and Gerlinde Verbist. "When Famialism Fails: The Nature and Causes of In-Work Poverty in Belgium." In *The working poor in Europe: employment, poverty and globalisation*, edited by Hans-Jürgen Andress and Henning Lohmann. 77-95. Cheltenham; Northampton, MA: Edward Elgar, 2008.

Marx, Karl. *Misère de la philosophie (réponse à "La Philosophie de la Misère" of M. Proudhon)* [The poverty of philosophy (a reply to "La philosophie de la misère" of M. Proudhon)]. Paris: V. Giard & E. Brière, 1896.

Masera, Luca. "Danni da amianto e diritto penale [Asbestos damages and criminal law]." *Diritto Penale Contemporaneo*. Published electronically October 29, 2010. http://www.penalecontemporaneo.it/materia/2-/23-/-/134-danni_da_ami anto_e_diritto_penale/.

Mau, Steffen. *The moral economy of welfare states: Britain and Germany compared*. London; New York: Routledge, 2003.

Mazza, Mimmo. "Taranto, 30 indagati per i morti all'ILVA [Taranto, 30 people under investigations for deaths at ILVA]." *La Gazzetta del Mezzogiorno*. Published electronically May 25, 2011. http://www.lagazzettadelmezzogiorno. it/notizia.php?IDNotizia=429364.

Merler, Enzo, Vittoria Bressan, and Anna Somigliana. "Mesoteliomi negli edili: frequenza, stima del rischio, carico polmonare di fibre di amianto, domande e riconoscimenti per malattia professionale nel Registro regionale veneto dei casi di mesotelioma [Mesothelioma in construction workers: risk estimate, lung content of asbestos fibres, claims for compensation for occupational disease in the Veneto Region mesothelioma register]." *Medicina del Lavoro* 100, no. 2 (2009): 120-132.

Merry, Sally, and Susan S. Silbey. "What Do Plaintiffs Want? Reexamining the Concept of Dispute." *Justice System Journal* 9, no. 2 (1984): 151-178.

Merryman, John Henry. *The civil law tradition: an introduction to the legal systems of Western Europe and Latin America*. 2nd ed. Stanford: Stanford University Press, 1985.

Modave, J. L., M. Melange, J. Macq, A. Leblanc, and A. Minette. "Réflexions à propos de 19 cas d'asbestose fortuitement découverts dans la population d'une collectivité industrielle de la Basse-Sambre [Reflections on 19 cases of asbestosis discovered by chance in the population of an industrial region in the Basse-Sambre]." *Revue de l'Institut d'hygiène des mines* 30, no. 3 (1975): 111-131.

Molitor, Marc. "Négociations et tensions autour de la création du Fonds amiante [Negotiations and conflicts surrounding the establishment of the Asbestos Fund]." *Courrier hebdomadaire du CRISP* 3, no. 2048-2049 (2010): 5-61.

"Morte da amianto, solo due colpevoli [An asbestos death, only two defendants guilty]." Published electronically June 10, 2009. http://www.cartiglianonews. it/rassegna-stampa/morte-da-amianto-solo-due-colpevoli.

"Morti d'amianto, la Fincantieri congela i risarcimenti [Asbestos deaths, Fincantieri freezes payments]." *Il Piccolo*. Published electronically January 25, 2011. http://ilpiccolo.gelocal.it/cronaca/2011/01/25/news/morti-d-amianto-la-fincantieri-congela-i-risarcimenti-1.20597.

Mukherjee, Siddhartha. *The emperor of all maladies: a biography of cancer.* 1st ed. New York: Scribner, 2010.

Munich Re, ed. *Asbestos. Anatomy of a Mass Tort.* München: Münchener Rückversicherungs-Gesellschaft, 2009.

Muratorio, Alessia. "La declinazione della probabilità causale qualificata nell'esposizione all'amianto [Qualified probability as standard of proof for harm caused by asbestos exposure]." *Argomenti di diritto del lavoro* 1, no. 2 (2010): 239-246.

Nawrot, Tim S., Greta Van Kersschaever, Elisabeth Van Eycken, and Benoit Nemery. "Belgium: historical champion in asbestos consumption." *The Lancet* 369, no. 9574 (2007): 1692.

Nay, Salvator Y. *Mortel amiante [Deadly asbestos].* Bruxelles: EVO-Société, 1997.

———. "Asbestos in Belgium: use and abuse." *International Journal of Occupational and Environmental Health* 9, no. 3 (2003): 287-293.

Nelken, David. "Comparing legal cultures." In *The Blackwell companion to law and society*, edited by Austin Sarat. 113-127. Malden, MA: Blackwell Publishing, 2004.

———. "Law, Liability, and Culture." In *Fault Lines*, edited by David M. Engel and Michael W. McCann. 21-44. Stanford: Stanford Law Books, 2009.

Nigro, Luciano. "Un processo che non s'è arenato, la sentenza è un monito per tutti [A trial that did not stop is a warning for everybody]." *La Repubblica (Bologna).* Published electronically November 23, 2004. http://ricerca.repubblica.it/repubblica/archivio/repubblica/2004/11/23/un-processo-che-non-arenato-la-sentenza.html.

Nishikawa, Kunihito, Ken Takahashi, Antti Karjalainen, C. P. Wen, S. Furuya, T. Hoshuyama, M. Todoroki, et al. "Recent mortality from pleural mesothelioma, historical patterns of asbestos use, and adoption of bans: a global assessment." *Environmental Health Perspectives* 116, no. 12 (2008): 1675-1680.

Observatoire des Données de l'Environnement. *Chapter 24. Mesotheliome* [Chapter 24. Mesothelioma]. Interface Santé et Environnement. Vol. Bruxelles: IBGE, October, 2008.

Oliver, Suzanne L., and Leslie Spencer. "Who Will the Monster Devour Next?" *Forbes Magazine*, February 18, 1991, 75.

Oliver-Jones, Stephen. "Payments into Court." In *Personal injury handbook*, edited by Daniel Brennan, Patrick Curran, and Matthias Kelly. London: Sweet & Maxwell, 1997.

Oorschot, Wim van, Michael Opielka, and Birgit Pfau-Effinger. *Culture and welfare state: values and social policy in comparative perspective.* Cheltenham, UK; Northampton, MA: Edward Elgar, 2008.

Oxford University Press. *Oxford English Dictionary.* Oxford; New York: Oxford University Press, 2000.

Park, Eun-Kee, Ken Takahashi, Tsutomu Hoshuyama, Tsun-Jen Cheng, Vanya Delgermaa, Giang Vinh Le, and Tom Sorahan. "Global Magnitude of Reported and Unreported Mesothelioma." *Environmental Health Perspectives* 119, no. 4 (2011): 514-518.

Pasture, Patrick. "Histoire et représentation d'une utopie: l'idée autogestionnaire en Belgique [History and representation of a utopia: the concept of self-management in Belgium]." In *Autogestion, la dernière utopie*, edited by Frank Georgi. 143-156. Paris: Publications de la Sorbonne, 2003.

Patterson, Orlando. "The mechanisms of cultural reproduction. Explaning the puzzle of persistance." In *Handbook of cultural sociology*, edited by John R. Hall, Laura Grindstaff and Ming-Cheng Lo. 139-151. London; New York: Routledge, 2010.

Paxton, Robert O., and Julie Hessler. *Europe in the twentieth century*. 5th ed. Boston, MA: Wadsworth/Cengage Learning, 2012.

Pellerano, Fernando. "Avviato il censimento dei morti per l'amianto killer [Asbestos victims' census is under way]." *La Repubblica (Bologna)*, March 13, 2001.

Pelliccia, Luigi. *Le nuove pensioni* [The New Pensions]. 2 ed. Santarcangelo di Romagna: Maggioli Editore, 2011.

Perrodet, Antionette. "The public prosecutor." In *European criminal procedures*, edited by Mireille Delmas-Marty and John R. Spencer. 415-458. Cambridge; New York: Cambridge University Press, 2002.

Pétré, Marianne, and Enrico De Simone. "L'indemnisation en droit civil et la question de l'immunité de l'employeur [Tort liability and employer's immunity]." Published electronically September 25, 2011. http://www.progresslaw.net/docs/20110502113417WHFV.pdf.

Peysner, John. "A Revolution By Degrees: From Costs to Financing and the End of the Indemnity Principle." *Web Journal of Current Legal Issues* 1. Published electronically February 23, 2001. http://webjcli.ncl.ac.uk/2001/issue1/peysner 1.html.

Philipsen, Niels J. "Industrial Accidents and Occupational Diseases: Some Empirical Findings for The Netherlands, Belgium, Germany and Great Britain." *Tort and Insurance Law Yearbook* 20 (2007): 159-196.

Pizzi, William T., and Luca Marafioti. "The New Italian Code of Criminal Procedure: The Difficulties of Building an Adversarial Trial System on a Civil Law Foundation." *Yale Journal of International Law* 17 (1992): 1.

Plevin, Mark D., Leslie A. Davis, and Tacie Yoon, H. "Where Are They Now, Part Six: An Update On Developments In Asbestos-Related Bankruptcy Cases." *Mealey's Asbestos Bankruptcy Report* 11, no. 7 (2012): 1-55.

Plevin, Mark D., Robert T. Ebert, and Leslie A. Epley. "Pre-Packaged Asbestos Bankruptcies: A Flawed Solution." *South Texas Law Review* 44 (2003): 883-921.

"Pour les victimes de l'amiante [To asbestos victims]." *Le Soir*, May 14, 2007.

"Precisazione di Laudisio: 'Amianto, il grosso dei processi è rimasto a Gorizia' [Laudisio's remarks: 'Asbestos, the bulk of the trials remained in Gorizia']." *Il Messaggero Veneto*. Published electronically August 7, 2008. http://morire dicantiere.wordpress.com/2008/08/07/precisazione-di-laudisio/.

Preisser, A.M., D. Wilken, and X. Baur. "Changes in Lung Function Due to Asbestosis and Asbestos-Related Pleural Plaques." *American Journal of Respiratory and Critical Care Medicine* 179, no. 1 (Meeting Abstracts) (April 1, 2009): A5895-.

Products Research, LLC. "Welcome to Asbestos Catalogs. At a glance: manufacturers with asbestos based products." http://www.asbestoscatalogs.com/.

"Publication du rapport des 5 ans du Fonds amiante [Publications of the five report on the Asbestos Fund]." *FMP News*, 21, March 28, 2012, 1.

Redazione di Reality. "Casale Monferrato: Una Chernobyl italiana [Casale Monferrato: An Italian Chernobyl]." La7, http://www.la7.it/approfondimento/dettaglio.asp?prop=reality&video=5478.

Redding, Bryan. "Los Angeles Jury Awards $200 Million in Punitive Damages for Secondhand Asbestos Exposure." *Litigation Blog*. Published electronically April 30, 2010. http://www.lexisnexis.com/community/litigationresourcecenter/blogs/litigationblog/archive/2010/04/30/los-angeles-jury-awards-200-million-in-punitive-damages-for-secondhand-asbestos-exposure.aspx.

Rickard, Lisa A. "Never-ending asbestos quagmire." *The National Law Journal*, November 7, 2011.

Riverso, Roberto. "La difficile giustizia per i lavoratori esposti all'amianto [Tough justice for asbestos workers]." *Questione Giustizia* 1 (2009): 1-20.

Robinson, Bruce W.S., and Richard A. Lake. "Advances in Malignant Mesothelioma." *New England Journal of Medicine* 353, no. 15 (2005): 1591-1603.

Robinson, William I. *A theory of global capitalism: production, class, and state in a transnational world*. Baltimore: Johns Hopkins University Press, 2004.

———. *Latin America and global capitalism: a critical globalization perspective*. Baltimore: Johns Hopkins University Press, 2008.

———. "Global capitalism theory and the emergence of transnational elites." *Critical Sociology* 38, no. 3 (2012): 349-363.

Robreno, Eduardo C. "Asbestos Personal Injury Litigation in the Federal Courts: MDL-875." http://www.paed.uscourts.gov/documents/MDL/MDL875/MDL%20875%20Overview.pdf.

Rogers, W.V.H., John A. Jolowicz, and Percy H. Winfield. *Winfield and Jolowicz on tort*. 15th ed. London: Sweet & Maxwell, 1998.

Rombola, G. "Asbestosi e carcinoma polmonare in una filatrice di amianto (spunti sul problema oncogeno dell'asbesto) [Asbestos and pulmonary carcinoma in an asbestos worker (problems of carcinogenic action of asbestos)]." *Medicina del Lavoro* 46, no. 4 (1955): 242-250.

Roselli, Maria. *Amiante & Eternit: Fortunes et forfaitures* [Asbestos & Eternit. Fortunes and Forfaitures]. Translated by Marianne Enckell from German. Lausanne: Editions d'en bas, 2008.

Ross, Malcolm, and Robert P. Nolan. *History of asbestos discovery and use and asbestos-related disease in context with the occurrence of asbestos within ophiolite complexes*. Geological Society of America Special Paper. Vol. 373, Geological Society of America, 2003.

Rossi, Gianpiero. "L'impiego dell'amianto in Italia in contesto civile e professionale—i casi di cronaca [Asbestos use in Italy in the public and private sectors—chronicled cases]." In *Amianto: responsabilità civile e penale e risarcimento danni*, edited by Filippo Martini. 15-49. Santarcangelo di Romagna: Maggioli Editore, 2012.

Roth, William. *The assault on social policy*. New York: Columbia University Press, 2002.

Rubino, G.F., G. Scansetti, A. Donna, and G. Palestro. "Epidemiology of pleural mesothelioma in North-western Italy (Piedmont)." *British Journal of Industrial Medicine* 29, no. 4 (1972): 436-442.

Ruers, Robert F. "The International Asbestos Cartel." World Asbestos Report, http://worldasbestosreport.org/conferences/gac/gac2004/ws_G_4_e.php.

Ruers, Robert F., and Nico Schouten. *The tragedy of asbestos. Eternit and the consequences of a hundred years of asbestos cement*. Socialistische Partij, 2006. http://international.sp.nl/publications/tragedyofasbestos.pdf.

Rughi, Diego. "Benefici amianto: una tutela in evoluzione [Asbestos benefits: evolving regulations]." *Dati INAIL* 7 (2003): 1-27.

Salas, Denis, and Alejandro Alzarez. "The public prosecutor." In *European Criminal Procedures*, edited by Mireille Delmas-Marty and John R. Spencer. 488-541. Cambridge, UK; New York: Cambridge University Press, 2002.

Salvatori, Laura, Alessandro Santoni, and Darren Michaels. "Asbestos: The current situation in Europe." Paper presented at the ASTIN Colloquium, Berlin, August 24-27, 2003.

Schaffer, Randolph L., Sanjay Kulkarni, Ann Harper, J. Michael Millis, and David C. Cronin. "The sickest first? Disparities with model for end-stage liver disease-based organ allocation: One region's experience." *Liver Transplantation* 9, no. 11 (2003): 1211-1215.

Schepers, Gerrit W.H. "Chronology of asbestos cancer discoveries: Experimental studies of the saranac laboratory." *American Journal of Industrial Medicine* 27, no. 4 (1995): 593-606.

Schmidt, Sanford J. "Supreme Court ruling crucial in 'take-home' asbestos cases." *The Telegraph*, March 25, 2012.

Schuck, Peter H. "Mass Torts: An Institutional Evolutionist Perspective." *Cornell Law Review* 80 (1995): 941-989.

Scola, Paola. "All'Acna stessi benefici di chi lavorò l'amianto [ACNA workers will receive the same benefits of those who worked with asbestos]." *La Stampa (Nord-ovest)*, December 6, 2003.

Searcey, Dionne. "For One Asbestos Victim, Justice is a Moving Target." *Wall Street Journal*, June 17, 2013, A1.

Selikoff, Irving J., Jacob Churg, and E. Cuyler Hammond. "Asbestos Exposure and Neoplasia." *JAMA—Journal of the American Medical Association* 188, no. 1 (1964): 22-26.

———. "The occurrence of asbestosis among insulation workers in the United States." *Annals of the New York Academy of Sciences* 132, no. 1 (1965): 139-155.

Serafin, Tatiana. "The Bill Gates Of Switzerland." *Forbes*, 184, 2009, 58-59.

"Signori Ministri vi chiediamo formalmente aiuto [Gentlemen, we formally ask you for help]." *Alessandrianews.it*. Published electronically November 4, 2012. http://www.alessandrianews.it/politica/signori-ministri-vi-chiediamo-fo rmalmente-aiuto-15457.html.

Silbey, Susan S. "Making a Place for Cultural Analyses of Law." *Law & Social Inquiry* 17, no. 1 (1992): 39-48.

———. "Ideology, Power, and Justice." In *Justice and power in sociolegal studies*, edited by Bryant G. Garth and Austin Sarat. 272-308. Evanston: Northwestern University Press, 1998.

———. "Legal culture and cultures of legality." In *Handbook of Cultural Sociology*, edited by John R. Hall, Laura Grindstaff, and Ming-Cheng Lo. 470-479. London; New York: Routledge, 2010.

Skocpol, Theda. *Protecting soldiers and mothers: the political origins of social policy in the United States*. Cambridge, MA: Belknap Press of Harvard University Press, 1992.

———. *Social policy in the United States: future possibilities in historical perspective*. Princeton: Princeton University Press, 1995.

Slapper, Gary, and David Kelly. *The English legal system*. 11th ed. Abingdon, UK; New York: Routledge, 2010.

Solomon, Albert. "Radiological features of asbestos-related visceral pleural changes." *American Journal of Industrial Medicine* 19, no. 3 (1991): 339-355.

Sprague, Christopher. "Damages for Personal Injury and Loss of Life: The English Approach." *Tulane Law Review* 72 (1997): 975-1021.

Stapleton, Jane. *Disease and the compensation debate*. Oxford; New York: Clarendon Press; Oxford University Press, 1986.

Stearns, Peter N. *The industrial revolution in world history*. 3rd ed. Boulder, CO: Westview Press, 2007.

Steele, Jenny, and Nick Wikely. "Dust on the Streets and Liability for Environmental Cancers." *The Modern Law Review* 60, no. 2 (1997): 265-275.

Stella, Federico. *Giustizia e modernità: la protezione dell'innocente e la tutela delle vittime* [Justice and modernity: protecting the innocent and compensating the victim]. 2 ed. Milano: Giuffrè, 2002.

Strang, Carter E., and Karen E. Ross. "'Take-Home' Premises Liability Asbestos Exposure Claims—2009 Update." *Mealey's Litigation Report* 24, no. 22 (2009): 1-8.

Sypnowich, Christine. "Law and Ideology." In *The Stanford Encyclopedia of Philosophy*, edited by Edward N. Zalta. Stanford: The Metaphysics Research Lab, 2010.

Takamura, Gakuto. "The French Indemnification Fund for Asbestos Victims: Features and Formative Historical Factors: Preliminary Observations for a Comparative Analysis of Asbestos Relief Frameworks." In *Asbestos Disaster:*

*Lessons from Japan's Experience*, edited by Kenichi Miyamoto, Kenji Morinaga, and Hiroyuki Mori, 303-314. Tokyo: Springer, 2011.

Tani, Karen M. "Welfare and Rights Before the Movement: Rights as a Language of the State." *Yale Law Journal* 122, no. 2 (2012): 101-170.

Taylor, A.J. Newman. *Asbestos-related Diseases: Report by the Industrial Injuries Advisory Council in Accordance with Section 171 of the Social Security Administration Act 1992 Reviewing the Prescription of the Asbestos-related Diseases*. Vol. 6553, The Stationery Office, 2005.

*The Government's plans for reforming legal services and the courts*. Vol. 4155, Lord Chancellor's Department, 1998.

Thompsons Solicitors. "Five figure compensation for lagger's asbestos disease." Published electronically March 16, 2009. http://www.thompsons.law.co.uk/ntext/lagger-pleural-plaques-pleural-thickening.htm.

———. "Insurers challenge asbestosis compensation." Published electronically March 20, 2009. http://www.thompsons.law.co.uk/ntext/insurers-challenge-asbestosis-compensation.htm.

———. "BPD 650,000 damages for mesothelioma widow." Published electronically April 29, 2009. http://www.thompsons.law.co.uk/ntext/damages-for-mesothelioma-widow.htm.

———. "Successful fight for asbestos compensation." Published electronically May 8, 2009. http://www.thompsons.law.co.uk/ntext/successful-fight-asbestos-compensation.htm.

———. "MOD settle Devonport asbestos claim." Published electronically May 26, 2009. http://www.thompsons.law.co.uk/ntext/mod-settle-devonport-asbestos-claim.htm.

Toohey, James K., and Rebecca L. Matthews. "Liability For The Post-Sale Installation Of Asbestos-Containing Replacement Parts Or Insulation." *Mealey's Litigation Report* 25, no. 21 (2010): 40-54.

Tweedale, Geoffrey. "Management strategies for health: J.W. Roberts and the Armley Asbestos Tragedy, 1920-1958." *Journal of Industrial History* 2 (1999): 72-95.

———. *Magic mineral to killer dust: Turner & Newall and the asbestos hazard*. Oxford: Oxford University Press, 2000.

———. "Science or public relations? The inside story of the Asbestosis Research Council, 1957-1990." *American Journal of Industrial Medicine* 38, no. 6 (2000): 723-734.

———. "Sources in the History of Occupational Health: The Turner & Newall Archive." *Social History of Medicine* 13, no. 3 (2000): 515-533.

———. "Asbestos and its lethal legacy." *Nature Reviews Cancer* 2, no. 4 (2002): 311-314.

Tweedale, Geoffrey, and Laurie Flynn. "Piercing the Corporate Veil: Cape Industries and Multinational Corporate Liability for a Toxic Hazard, 1950-2004." *Enterprise and Society* 8, no. 2 (2007): 268-296.

Tweedale, Geoffrey, and David J. Jeremy. "Compensating the Workers: Industrial Injury and Compensation in the British Asbestos Industry, 1930s-60s." *Business History* 41, no. 2 (1999): 102-120.

United States Congress. "Congressional Record, Fairness in Asbestos Injury Resolution Act of 2003." S4078. Statement by Senator Orin Hatch, 2004.

Université catholique de Louvain. "Émotions des Belges face à la crise: respect et fatalisme [Belgians' emotions towards the crisis: respect and fatalism]." http://www.uclouvain.be/cps/ucl/doc/ir-ipsy/documents/Communique_dePresse_FR.pdf.

Van de Voorde, H., E. Meulepas, A. Gyselen, and O. Koppen. "Doodsoorzaken bij de bevolking woonachtig rond en bij de arbeiders werkzaam in een asbestverwerkende nijverheid in het noorden van Brabant [Mortality in the population living close to, and in employees working in, an asbestos industry in the North of Brabant]." *Acta tuberculosea et pneumologica Belgica* 58, no. 6 (1967): 924-942.

Van de Weyer, R. "Bilan de l'indemnisation de l'asbestose [An assessment of asbestosis compensation]." *Acta Tuberculosea et Pneumologica Belgica* 64, no. 3 (1973): 304-351.

van Meerbeeck, Jan P., Arnaud Scherpereel, Veerle F. Surmont, and Paul Baas. "Malignant pleural mesothelioma: the standard of care and challenges for future management." *Critical Reviews in Oncology/Hematology* 78, no. 2 (2011): 92-111.

Vandaele, Kurt. "From the seventies strike wave to the first cyber-strike in the twenty-first century. Strike activity and labour unrest in Belgium." In *Strikes around the world, 1968-2005: case-studies of 15 countries*, edited by Jacobus Hermanus Antonius van der Velden, Heiner Dribbush, Dave Lyddon and Kurt Vandaele. 196-221. Amsterdam; Edison, NJ: Aksant, 2007.

Vandemeulebroucke, Martine. "Amiante: un condamné va en justice [Asbestos: the victim of a deadly disease seeks justice]." *Le Soir*, December 18, 1996, 16.

———. "Le tribunal déboute le technicien rendu gravement malade par l'amiante. Exposition à l'amiante sans faute intentionnelle [The court dismisses the technician who asbestos made severally sick. Exposure to asbestos without 'faute intentionnelle']." *Le Soir*, October 2, 1997, 17.

———. "Prends ton indemnité et tais-toi: l'Inspection ignorait la présence d'amiante sur les lieux [Take your benefits and shut up: the inspector ignored the presence of asbestos in the workplace]." *Le Soir*, October 2, 1997, 17.

Vanderhaege, Thierry. "Coverit compte ses morts [Coverit counts those that are dead]." *Le Soir Magazine*, November 9, 2005, 10-12.

Verrender, Ian. "The shameful legacy of James Hardie." *The Sydney Morning Herald*. Published electronically May 5, 2012. http://www.smh.com.au/business/the-shameful-legacy-of-james-hardie-20120504-1y3vx.html.

Vilrokx, Jacques, and Jim Van Leemput. "Belgium: the great transformation." In *Changing industrial relations in Europe*, edited by Anthony Ferner and Richard Hyman. 315-347. Malden, MA: Blackwell Publishers, 1998.

Volpedo, Mirco, and Davide Leporati. *Morire d'amianto: l'Eternit di Casale Monferrato: dall'emergenza alla bonifica* [Dying of asbestos: The Eternit at Casale Monferrato: from emergency to clean-up]. Genova: La clessidra, 1997.

Voorhees, Theodore Jr., and Eric Hellerman. "Peripheral Defendants As Litigation Targets: Defense Strategies For The Next Wave." Paper presented at the Fourth National Forum: Asbestos Litigation, San Francisco, February 28, 2003.

Wagner, J.C., C.A. Sleggs, and P. Marchand. "Diffuse pleural mesothelioma and asbestos exposure in the North Western Cape Province." *British Journal of Industrial Medicine* 17 (1960): 260-271.

Wikeley, Nicholas J. "The Asbestos Regulations 1931: A Licence to Kill?" *Journal of Law and Society* 19 (1992): 365-378.

———. *Compensation for industrial disease*. Aldershot, Hants; Brookfield, VT: Dartmouth, 1993.

———. "Social Security Appeals in Great Britain." *Administrative Law Review* 46 (1994): 183-212.

———. "Turner & Newall: Early Organizational Responses to Litigation Risk." *Journal of Law and Society* 24, no. 2 (1997): 252-275.

———. "The First Common Law Claim for Asbestosis: Kelly v. Turner & Newall Ltd (1950)." *Journal of Personal Injury Litigation* (1998): 197-210.

———. "Nancy Tait. Tenacious campaigner for the victims of asbestos diseases." *The Guardian*, February 22, 2009.

———. "The New Mesothelioma Compensation Scheme." *Journal of Social Security Law* 16, no. 1 (2009): 30-49.

Williams, Tim, Pippa Slade, and Jack Raeburn. "Lump sum compensation for asbestos related lung disease." *Thorax* 53, no. 7 (1998): 535.

Witt, John Fabian. *The accidental republic: crippled workingmen, destitute widows, and the remaking of American law*. Cambridge, MA: Harvard University Press, 2004.

———. "US asbestos and silica litigation in the 1930s." In *Asbestos. Anatomy of a Mass Tort*, edited by Munich Re. 32-33. München: Münchener Rückversicherungs-Gesellschaft, 2009.

Wright, Steve. *Storming heaven: class composition and struggle in Italian autonomist marxism*. London; Sterling, VA: Pluto Press, 2002.

Wrigley, Chris. *British trade unions since 1933*. Cambridge, UK; New York: Cambridge University Press, 2002.

# Index

Bold page numbers indicate figures, *italic* numbers indicate tables.

For Product Safety Concerns and Information please contact our EU
representative GPSR@taylorandfrancis.com
Taylor & Francis Verlag GmbH, Kaufingerstraße 24, 80331 München, Germany